On Comics and Legal Aesthetics

What are the implications of comics for law? Tackling this question, *On Comics and Legal Aesthetics* explores the epistemological dimensions of comics and the way this once-maligned medium can help us think about – and reshape – the form of law. Traversing comics, critical, and cultural legal studies, it seeks to enrich the theorisation of comics with a critical aesthetics that expands its value and significance for law, as well as knowledge more generally. It argues that comics' multimodality – its hybrid structure, which represents a meeting point of text, image, reason, and aesthetics – opens understanding of the limits of law's rational texts by shifting between multiple frames and modes of presentation. Comics thereby exposes the way all forms of knowledge are shaped out of an unstructured universe, becoming a mask over this chaotic 'beyond'. This mask of knowing remains haunted – by that which it can never fully capture or represent. Comics thus models knowledge as an infinity of nested frames haunted by the chaos without structure. In such a model, the multiple aspects of law become one region of a vast and bottomless cascade of perspectives – an infinite multiframe that extends far beyond the traditional confines of the comics page, rendering law boundless.

Thomas Giddens is senior lecturer in law at St Mary's University, Twickenham. He researches critical, comics, and cultural legal studies. He founded the Graphic Justice Research Alliance in 2013 and edited the collection *Graphic Justice: Intersections of Comics and Law* (Routledge 2015). He also edits the on-going 'Graphic Justice' special collection at *The Comics Grid: Journal of Comics Scholarship* and is a founding Co-Director of St Mary's Centre for Law and Culture.

Discourses of Law

Series editors: Peter Goodrich, Michel Rosenfeld and Arthur Jacobson
Benjamin N. Cardozo School of Law

This successful and exciting series seeks to publish the most innovative scholarship at the intersection of law, philosophy and social theory. The books published in the series are distinctive by virtue of exploring the boundaries of legal thought. The work that this series seeks to promote is marked most strongly by the drive to open up new perspectives on the relation between law and other disciplines. The series has also been unique in its commitment to international and comparative perspectives upon an increasingly global legal order. Of particular interest in a contemporary context, the series has concentrated upon the introduction and translation of continental traditions of theory and law.

The original impetus for the series came from the paradoxical merger and confrontation of East and West. Globalization and the internationalization of the rule of law has had many dramatic and often unforeseen and ironic consequences. An understanding of differing legal cultures, particularly different patterns of legal thought, can contribute, often strongly and starkly, to an appreciation if not always a resolution of international legal disputes. The rule of law is tied to social and philosophical underpinnings that the series has sought to excoriate and illuminate.

www.routledge.com/Discourses-of-Law/book-series/SE1036

Titles in the series:

On Comics and Legal Aesthetics: Multimodality and the Haunted Mask of Knowing
Thomas Giddens

Liberalizing Contracts: Nineteenth Century Promises Through Literature, Law and History
Anat Rosenberg

A Mosaic of Indigenous Legal Thought: Legendary Tales and Other Writings
C.F. Black

Masculinity and the Trials of Modern Fiction
Marco Wan

The publisher gratefully acknowledges the support of the Jacob Burns Institute for Advanced Legal Studies of the Benjamin N. Cardozo School of Law to the series Discourses of Law.

On Comics and Legal Aesthetics

Multimodality and the Haunted Mask of Knowing

Thomas Giddens

Routledge
Taylor & Francis Group
LONDON AND NEW YORK

First published 2018
by Routledge

2 Park Square, Milton Park, Abingdon, Oxfordshire OX14 4RN
52 Vanderbilt Avenue, New York, NY 10017

Routledge is an imprint of the Taylor & Francis Group, an informa business

First issued in paperback 2019

British Library Cataloguing in Publication Data
A catalogue record for this book is available from the British Library

Library of Congress Cataloging in Publication Data
Names: Giddens, Thomas, author.
Title: On comics and legal aesthetics : multimodality and the haunted mask of knowing / Thomas Giddens.
Description: Abingdon, Oxon ; New York, NY : Routledge, 2018. | Series: Discourses of law | "a Glasshouse book" | Includes bibliographical references and index.
Identifiers: LCCN 2017052832 | ISBN 9781138224032 (hardback)
Subjects: LCSH: Comic books, strips, etc.--History and criticism. | Law and literature.
Classification: LCC PN6714 .G49 2018 | DDC 741.5/9--dc23
LC record available at https://lccn.loc.gov/2017052832

ISBN: 978-1-138-22403-2 (hbk)
ISBN: 978-0-367-40447-5 (pbk)

Typeset in Galliard
by Taylor & Francis Books

'Adrift in the cosmos …
we must build in empty space …
the greatest good that we can muster.'

—Melanie Williams (2002) *Empty Justice: One Hundred Years of Law, Literature and Philosophy*, Routledge-Cavendish, p 218.

Contents

Figures

Cover image: from *Adamtine* by Hannah Berry. Published by Jonathan Cape. Reprinted by permission of The Random House Group Limited. © 2012.

Acknowledgments

For their generosity of both time and thought in reading previous drafts of the chapters that make up this book, I would like to thank the following scholars (in alphabetical order, to avoid any argument[1]): Christine Battersby, Paul Fisher Davies, David Gurnham, Chris Lloyd, Desmond Manderson, Les Moran, Justine Poon, Stephen Skinner, Kieran Tranter, Mitch Travis, Nayeli Urquiza Haas, Melanie Williams, and David Yuratich. Despite the alphabetisation, Stephen Skinner deserves particular mention. Much of the groundwork for this book was done during my time as a PhD student of his, and his detailed and methodical (dare I say relentless?) shepherding of my doctoral thesis has no doubt had untold influence across my work within and beyond the present volume. A special and separate thanks to Timothy D Peters, who had enough of a masochistic tendency to submit to reading and commenting upon a full draft of the manuscript for this book. The above notwithstanding, all the inadequacies of the following work are resoundingly my own.

I wish also to extend a deeper and far less professional gratitude to Helen Giddens, without whom my existence, and no doubt this book, would be much diminished.

Two institutions are worthy of note in their support of my work, predominantly through the making of time for me to undertake research and writing. Firstly, St Mary's University, Twickenham, London, UK. St Mary's provided me with a sabbatical in 2015, removing the overwhelming pleasures of teaching and administration from my daily life – an act that greatly contributed towards the completion of this work. Secondly, the Law Futures Centre at Griffith Law School, Gold Coast, Queensland, Australia. I was lucky enough to take up residence as a Visiting Research Fellow at Griffith from July to August 2016, during which I was given space to pursue work on this book within a critically supportive cultural legal environment.

More formalities: parts of this book have been previously published. Significant elements of Chapter 2, relating to the analysis of *The Ghost in the Shell*, appeared as Thomas Giddens (2015) 'Law and the Machine: Fluid and Mechanical Selfhood

1 Except perhaps linguistic ones.

in *The Ghost in the Shell*' in T Giddens (ed) *Graphic Justice: Intersections of Comics and Law*, Routledge. The bulk of Chapter 3 appeared as Thomas Giddens (2015) 'Navigating the Looking Glass: Severing the Lawyer's Head in *Arkham Asylum*' 24 *Griffith Law Review* 395. Significant elements of Chapter 3 also appeared as Thomas Giddens (2017) 'Graphic Justice and Criminological Aesthetics: Visual Criminology on the Streets of Gotham' in E Carrabine and M Brown (eds) *The Routledge International Handbook of Visual Criminology*, Routledge. Chapter 3 integrates and adapts these earlier versions into the monograph narrative, with some of the introductory elements of the 'Navigating' article also being transferred and integrated into Chapter 1. These elements have been reproduced here with permission of the publisher (in all cases, Taylor and Francis). In addition, all the visual excerpts from comics that have been reproduced across this book have been done so with the permissions of the various copyright holders; these permissions have been suitably acknowledged in the figure captions.

Preface

Keith Aoki was a practitioner of 'art during law school', and produced numerous legal comics during his time as a student at Harvard.[2] Later, Aoki penned a journal article entitled 'PIERRE and the Agents of REASON' that engaged with the work of Pierre Schlag in comics form – complete with secret headquarters and metalevel debates between the journal's editors over whether it was appropriate for a comics work to appear in a law review.[3] Aoki later went on to create, alongside James Boyle and Jennifer Jenkins, the comics work *Bound by Law? Tales from the Public Domain*, a critical guide to navigating the complex realms of intellectual property.[4] Amidst other publications, he also produced his own comics law review article on the history of copyright[5] that outlined much of the premise for a further 'tale from the public domain' on the history of copyright in music.[6] This book is not about Keith Aoki, nor the substance of his immensely wide body of work of which I have not even scratched the surface.[7] Rather, it seeks an understanding of a question raised by the simple existence of his legal comics creations. Namely, what does it mean to put comics and law together? As one rather close-minded law review editor announces in Aoki's piece on Schlag: 'This piece infuriates me on the level of representation'.[8] But what is actually at stake in the representational and formal shift implied by the copresence of law and comics? What does it say about the typically rational and textual form of mainstream legal knowledge? What about the wider structures of human knowing? It is with this formal level of the meeting of law and comics and its epistemological ramifications

2 For an overview, see Kennedy (2012).
3 Aoki (2003).
4 Aoki et al (2008).
5 Aoki (2010).
6 Boyle and Jenkins (2017). This project was only recently published, as *Theft! A History of Music*. Due to his untimely death in 2011, Keith Aoki was unable to see the completion of this project.
7 On Keith's legacy more generally, see the special issue on 'Super Aoki' that forms volume 45, issue 5, of the *UC Davis Law Review* from June 2012.
8 Aoki (2003), p 10.

that I engage in this book, seeking to elaborate the ways comics – as a hybrid or 'multimodal' form – can help us think about the limits of law's rational texts.

In order to unpack the implications of comics' and law's coexistence, perhaps the first step should be a lawyerly one: to seek a definition. Not of law,[9] but of comics.[10] And lest the thought of comics' representational forms infuriate too many of this text's more legally oriented readers, let us throw in some Latin for good measure. To wit: the term 'comics' derives from the Latin *comicus*, relating to comedy and humour.[11] Now, whilst there are many comics that do rely on humour (hence the term 'funny pages'), the medium hosts such a wide variety of narratives and genres that 'comedy' can in no way be considered a defining feature. But despite attempts to shift the dominant definitional term to 'graphic fiction' – arguably out of a desire to shake off some of the medium's cultural baggage[12] – the label 'comics' persists. Indeed, it has become the accepted term in academic study,[13] going as far as defining the field that most closely examines the medium: 'comics studies'. A *juris comicus*, then, would be a jurisprudence of humour, of comedy – my own previous use of the term *lex comica* would also suffer from this same error.[14] As a term, *comicus* is both too small and too broad for the purposes of understanding comics in general, or its relationships with law specifically: there are many comics that are not comedies, and many comedies that are not comics.

So much for the Latin stylings. Let us trace further: the root of *comicus* derives from the Greek *komos*,[15] a term linked not exclusively with comedy but with more general merriment, festival, and revelry.[16] The carnivalesque nature of the *komos* can be seen in its role in classical Greek drama, notably the way it has been seen to operate as a counterpoint to order and refinement. Time to cite some authority. As Morgan outlines, by using the *komos*:

> the poet can emphasise his own story's particularity and all the virtues that go with his professional persona, such as discipline in the choice of subject matter and stringent adherence to the rules of the genre.[17]

9 A can of worms, indeed!
10 Another can of worms, as we'll see in Chapter 1.
11 Chambers Etymological Dictionary.
12 On comics' history of censorship and cultural denigration, see Barker (1984); Nyberg (1998). And, for a concise summary of the 'naming' issues in comics, see Sousanis (2015), p 60.
13 In comics studies the term 'comics' is generally used when referring to the medium, and is treated as a singular object: 'As for any medium, such as film, it is now standard to treat *comics* as singular': Chute and DeKoven (2012), p 175. For clarity: comics *is* a medium; comics *are* examples of that medium.
14 See Giddens (2015c). Note also the Twitter handle of the Graphic Justice Research Alliance, a research network that explores intersections of comics, law, and justice: @LexComica.
15 Chambers Etymological Dictionary.
16 Chambers Etymological Dictionary.
17 Morgan (1993), p 5.

One can clearly see in its characteristics of merriment and mockery the seeds of what would develop into satire and modern notions of *comicus* and humour. In its lack of discipline, meanwhile, perhaps we also begin to glimpse the infuriating nature of comics for those committed to the neatly ordered texts of law – they just don't look right. Against generic and formal order, the *komos* is full of 'spontaneity and festivity',[18] and in bringing 'all its threat of undiscipline and rout'[19] it is clearly a force in tension with the legalistic order of precision, particularity, and generic adherence – that is, with the ordered, normative universe of law.

The *komos* is valuable in understanding the formal order of law. For without the *komos* – as Greek poets knew of their own artistry – the wonderfully ordered classifications of law have no meaning, no context within the disorder of life.

> The *komos* was a swarming band of drunken men who engaged in dancing, laughter, obscenity, and mocking language, and who generally dispensed with social conventions and inhibitions. The *komos* represented a more accessible and less severe form of Dionysian self-abandonment ... and a more public 'dismemberment' of human norms and hierarchies.[20]

The link with the Dionysian is important. It solidifies the tensions between *komos* and wider social and communal structures, placing the *komos* in a mediating position between the public and social order of the *nomos* and the complete abandonment of that order signalled by the Dionysian. The *komos* is thus the revelry on the boundary of the regulated order of society, the carnival at the limit of the rule; it is the chaos subdued by the *nomos*. It enables a public engagement with disorder, without losing grip of the ordered world. It mediates between the *nomos* and the unstructured universe.

So, do comics retain this quality of the *komos*? My argument in this book sits firmly in the positive, and it is by thinking a comics-as-*komos* that the profound implications of comics for law can be elaborated. It is the broad hypothesis of this book not only that the expansive multimodal nature of comics means it retains the mediating quality of the *komos*, but that comics can thereby help us think about the limits of legal knowledge against the chaos of an unstructured universe. And to encounter comics-as-*komos*, we need to look in detail at the mechanics and operation of the comics form, as well as its thematic resonances, in relation to the regulated order of law. As will be seen across the following chapters, the comics form exists at a meeting point between different orders of knowing and fluidly engages its multiple formal aspects – text, image, logical rules, layout, materiality, aesthetic affect, sequence, *inter alia* – in navigating its epistemological positioning. And this multimodal complexity, like the *komos*, avails insight into the constructed and fluctuating nature of the present conditions of the world, and thereby

18 Morgan (1993), p 5.
19 Morgan (1993), p 12.
20 Hatab (2005), p 157.

'dissolves a fixation on forms', opening up to a vast sea of alternatives.[21] In short, comics augur the reformation of law.

References

Keith Aoki (2003) 'PIERE and the Agents of REASON' 27 *University of Miami Law Review* 1.

Keith Aoki (2010) 'Pictures within Pictures' 36 *Ohio North University Law Review* 1.

Keith Aoki et al (2008) *Bound by Law? Tales from the Public Domain*, Duke University Press.

Martin Barker (1984) *A Haunt of Fears: The Strange History of the British Horror Comics Campaign*, Pluto.

James Boyle and Jennifer Jenkins (2017) *Theft! A History of Music*, Duke University Press.

Hillary Chute and Marianne DeKoven (2012) 'Comic Books and Graphic Novels' in D Glover and S McCracken (eds) *The Cambridge Companion to Popular Fiction*, Cambridge University Press.

Thomas Giddens (2015c) 'Lex Comica: On Comics and Legal Theory' in T Giddens (ed) *Graphic Justice: Intersections of Comics and Law*, Routledge.

Lawrence J Hatab (2005) *Nietzsche's Life Sentence: Coming to Terms with Eternal Recurrence*, Routledge.

Duncan Kennedy (2012) 'Remembering Keith Aoki's Casual Legal Studies: Art During Law School' 45 *UC Davis Law Review* 1817.

Kathryn A Morgan (1993) 'Pindar the Professional and the Rhetoric of the Κωμοσ' 88 *Classical Philology* 1.

Amy Nyberg (1998) *Seal of Approval: The History of the Comics Code*, University Press of Mississippi.

Nick Sousanis (2015) *Unflattening*, Harvard University Press.

21 Hatab (2005), p 157.

Chapter 1

On comics and other ways of knowing

> Once one starts looking around, comics appear everywhere …[1]

To begin our journey, comics needs to be introduced – not as a juvenile phenomenon of disposable culture, nor as a sophisticated narrative medium of increasing cultural capital, but as a way of knowing. As a medium, comics is multimodal, in that it employs, exploits, or presents a variety of different modes of communicating – visual, textual, graphic, linguistic, spatial, narrational, and so forth – in a complex layering of multiple frames. This 'multiframe' has sophisticated aesthetic and formal rules that can be enforced, played with, or rejected to different ends. Because of this, as a way of knowing comics encounters complex boundaries and intersections between different forms of knowledge. And this epistemological mediation makes comics a deeply relevant form through which to think about the limits of law's textual-rational order. This chapter argues that, through the lens of legal aesthetics, law can be seen to have a conscious/unconscious structure, with a conscious legality that is grounded in reason and textual discourse underpinned by a legal unconscious of visuality, embodied experience, emotion, and aesthetic engagement. Moreover, that comics' multimodal form, and its wider complexity as a multiframe, can navigate these conscious/unconscious legalities, a navigation that the remainder of the book will pursue as it works towards a reimagining of law as a multimodal phenomenon integrated into an infinite multiframe of knowing.

This opening chapter introduces comics on a theoretical level in the context of legal aesthetics, indicating the epistemological significance of placing comics alongside law. The first main section introduces the frame of cultural legal aesthetics occupied by the book and sets up the idea of a conscious legality of rational text, the unconscious of which is populated with the repressed visual, sensory, and aesthetic dimensions of the legal institution. The second main section then focuses directly on the connections between comics and law, encountering the sustained attempts to theorise the comics form within the discipline of comics studies and highlighting its systemic formal qualities, before moving to more aesthetic

1 Priego (2014), np.

ground to explore the idea of the multiframe and how comics may circulate beyond the page, including in the structures of law. Overall, it is the multimodality of comics (as *komos*[2]) that enables it to navigate complex boundaries and interactions between conscious and unconscious legality, as well as other ways of knowing more generally.

Drawing the frame

Cultural legal aesthetics

The manifold ways in which legality and culture intertwine can directly inform our understandings of law and its status in contemporary life.[3] A leading contemporary movement in this regard is that of cultural legal studies, which is about exploring this world outside traditional law and doctrine: moving beyond the rational text and frolicking in the rich diversity of the worlds of human culture.[4] Indeed, it is asserted that it is only by crossing the threshold at law's traditional limits that these important cultural dimensions can be encountered, reflected upon, and interrogated. But this is no simple interdisciplinarity; cultural legal studies does not just involve taking aspects or insights from other disciplines and applying them to law.[5] Rather, it is my contention that in crossing law's cultural threshold we are challenging the very existence of that threshold.

When we reject the limits of traditional legal texts, we not only challenge law's limits but also the forms in which law can appear – and thus cultural legal studies can be wrought as a breed of aesthetics. As aesthetics, the focus shifts to the consideration of the form and presentation of knowledge – be it visual, verbal, multimodal, or otherwise. In this expanded world – this world of cultural legal aesthetics – we find multiple forms of law beyond the dry texts of statutes, judgments, and policy documents: a jurisprudential world of popular imagination and visual codes, diverse in its cultural dynamism, burgeoning with the traces and hallmarks of legality.[6] But this 'other world' is also one of rich humanity and aesthetic experience,[7] of the complex human realities that dwell beyond the limits of law's rational order.[8] In moving toward a cultural legal aesthetics, we are

2 See the Preface.
3 See, for example, Goodrich (1990); MacNeil (2007); Manderson (2000); Sherwin (2000).
4 See, for example, Sharp and Leiboff (eds) (2015).
5 On interdisciplinarity generally see Nissani (1997), and in law Vick (2004).
6 See, for example, Gisler et al (eds) (2012); MacNeil (2007); Manderson (ed) (2018); Sharp and Leiboff (eds) (2015); Sherwin (2000); Tranter (2012).
7 Manderson (2000).
8 See Wender (2008), who examines the processes by which the phenomenal experiences of criminality on the streets are translated into bureaucratic categories of criminal law, becoming 'problems' amenable to judicial 'solution'.

discovering that law is bigger than we had thought – and bigger than traditional legal study was able to think.

There is a strong connection between the traditional boundaries of law and the limits of rationality; the black letter orthodoxy of yesteryear may have receded significantly in certain scholarly circles,[9] but the priorities of mainstream study and practice remain those allied with a particular rational order,[10] arguably in tension with the fluidity of the aesthetic. In his musical analysis of legal aesthetics, Desmond Manderson notes that as 'a discipline traditionally based on the paramountcy of reason, philosophy has tried not to explain the power of the aesthetic but to tame it'.[11] The belief that truth was 'out there' to be discovered underlay most classical quests for knowledge; the world and the universe beyond was something ultimately knowable, and true knowledge could only be obtained through reason and rationality. Although some thinkers tried to render the observation of beauty an objective experience, they were constantly undermined by the inherent contingency of aesthetic production and perception; the woolly subjectivity of the aesthetic could at best only mimic or implicate a more rationally objective truth.[12] As Richard Sherwin notes – acknowledging law's need to have an authoritative source of truth if it is to achieve justice – in modernity it is scientific rationalism that provides law's 'authorising function'.[13] But law is more than this:

> Analytic rationality and the culture of argument must join with emotional knowledge and the interpretive methods of narrative and visual expression as co-equal sources of truth, knowledge, and value.[14]

That is, they must join as ways of knowing, found beyond reason and logic in the realm of the aesthetic. Aesthetics, though, is not necessarily so easily divided from rationality. The aesthetic can be understood to infuse our broad understanding of the world.[15] Aesthetics is not simply the analysis of art, but an episteme. It is something that permeates the very process of knowing: with aesthetics, what is communicated by art is not as important as how it is communicated.[16] We

9 Note seminal works such as Goodrich (1990); MacNeil (2007); Sherwin (2000); Twining (1991); Weisberg (1984); White (1985); Williams (2002).
10 See, for example, Douzinas and Nead (1999), p 3; Ellsworth (2012); Gearey (2001), pp 1–23; Manderson (2000), pp 96–98. And cultural legal studies itself can be seen to be, if not silenced, then at least marginalised outside mainstream law: MacNeil (2007), p 1.
11 Manderson (2000), pp 5–6.
12 Manderson (2000), pp 4–9.
13 See Sherwin (2011), p 21. This can be evidenced through the popularity of the law and economics movement, founded as it is upon ideals of rational logic and quantification.
14 Sherwin (2011), p 22.
15 See Barron (2000), pp 302–303. See also Giddens (2012), pp 95–96.
16 See Manderson (2000), p 10.

experience art, as we do everything else, through the physical perception of our senses. Thus:

> the aesthetic realm suffuses our engagement with everything about us … It is part of what it means to be a human being, part of our relationship with the world … Nothing remains untouched by the aesthetic temperament.[17]

Neither law nor comics can escape the aesthetic; they are bound inexorably by their shared character as human objects. Life, the world, our experiences, our emotions, our understandings: whether encoded into legal rules or comics panels, they are all filtered through the aesthetic perception of our senses. Aesthetics speaks to our sensations and emotions; it is a way of knowing that is beyond purely rational understanding[18] and is embedded in our contexts of culture and experience.[19]

This book is about comics and its form, about comics' relationship with legality and jurisprudence, and about the implications of comics and law existing together as two examples of, in some sense, the same thing – as ways of knowing. In this regard, it is not about 'popular culture' *per se*, but is more accurately a work of cultural legal aesthetics. William MacNeil's method of 'reading jurisprudentially', deftly demonstrated in his seminal work *Lex Populi*,[20] captures much of what I do in the following pages – taking comics as a form of legal discourse, unpacking their legal meanings and juristic insights, and thereby encountering, as a dimension of popular culture, a form of *lex populi* or law 'by and for the people'.[21] Indeed, despite its cultural baggage as a denigrated and dismissed art-form, the comics medium has taken over huge regions of the popular imaginary[22] and extended its tendrils into all manner of human artefacts. Film, television, merchandise, clothing, political protest,[23] violent crime[24] – all have been informed in some way by comics. As a global medium with increasing cultural impact, comics certainly plays into the broader cultural or communal understandings within a *lex populi*.

17 Manderson (2000), pp 23–24.
18 Manderson (2000), pp 10–11.
19 Manderson (2000), p 18.
20 See MacNeil (2007).
21 See MacNeil (2007), pp 155–157.
22 Just scratching the surface of the wealth of academic literature on comics that has emerged in recent years, but clearly demonstrating comics' increasing cultural and academic capital, see, for example, Bramlett (ed) (2012); Carrier (2000); Hague (2014); Hatfield (2005); McCloud (1993); McLaughlin (2005); Miller (2007); Nyberg (1998); Phillips and Strobl (2013); Sabin (2010).
23 Comics inspired political protests include the 'Occupy' mask, and the use of superhero costumes by Fathers 4 Justice: see, respectively, Griffin, 'A History of the Anonymous Mask', www.dazeddigital.com/artsandculture/article/16360/1/a-history-of-the-anonymous-mask, 7 July 2016 and Groombridge (2015).
24 James Holmes is the obvious example: see Sanchez et al, 'Batman Cinema Shooting: James Holmes "Told Police He Was the Joker"', www.telegraph.co.uk/news/worldnews/northamerica/usa/9416529/Batman-cinema-shooting-James-Holmes-told-police-he-was-The-Joker.html, 7 July 2016.

My broader aim, however, is to push beyond MacNeil's notion of an intertextual jurisprudence. The real significance of comics for the exploration of, and beyond, law's cultural threshold lies not only in its global capital or impact – its potential status as a *lex populi* – but in something much more profound: in its implications for the very nature of knowledge and law's relation to the wider ecosystem of knowing. This is what makes this book a work specifically of cultural legal *aesthetics*. MacNeil's vision of an intertextual jurisprudence works expressly against the limited study of law in the doctrinal tradition: for MacNeil, culture, literature, and jurisprudence can be read together in a joyful transgression of boundaries.[25] But, thanks in large part to the work of people like MacNeil alongside other leading cultural legal studies scholars such as Alison Young, Desmond Manderson, and Adam Gearey, this need to orient against an established order has been mitigated. The 'joy' of jurisprudence[26] has been unleashed, and cultural legal studies has gained a deal of traction in recent years, particularly following something of a visual turn in jurisprudence.[27] But the discipline remains largely an intertext that, despite all its value and insight, is necessarily 'inter': to bring together requires a pre-existing separation, a separation that works like *Lex Populi* needed to expressly transgress, but which now – building on the work of MacNeil and others – I am in a privileged position of being able to deny.

My project in this volume is to move cultural legal studies, through engagement with comics and legal aesthetics, to a space where we can acknowledge that such boundaries no longer exist. This is a work of legal reform – that is, a cultural legal aesthetics that opens a space where we may be free to engage, imagine, and create law in different forms – to 're-form' law. Not to get too far ahead of myself (as this is much of the work of particularly the latter stages of this book[28]), whilst the themes and substance of comics narratives may give insights for juristic understanding through jurisprudential reading, I contend that it is ultimately the comics form that is of real value to critical understanding, both in law and more generally, and that will enable us to work toward a cultural legal aesthetics of openness and radical (re)creation. By expanding the multiframe beyond the comics page, and situating the multimodality of law as part of an infinite multiframe of knowing, as this book aims to do, the boundaries of traditional legal study, as well as between differing interdisciplinary approaches to law and other forms of knowledge, break down. Each frame becomes just one element in a complex ecosystem of knowing, integrated as much as separated, bounded as well as boundless. Within such a multiplicity, we can abolish law's cultural threshold and understand law as part of a rich and universal tradition of encountering or creating the world from infinite

25 See MacNeil (2007), pp 1–10. For a sustained analysis of the enjoyment of law, see Hourigan (2015).
26 See MacNeil (2007), pp 9–10.
27 Note, for example, Douzinas and Nead (eds) (1999); Goodrich (2013); Manderson (ed) (2018); Sharp and Leiboff (eds) (2015); Sherwin (2012); Young (2005).
28 See notably Chapters 5 and 6.

possible perspectives. In such a project, we are not crossing boundaries but denying their existence. Law is more than a single frame – always more.

Comics and conscious legality

The aesthetics of law paints a complex picture, but one that is generally couched in concerns of epistemology and knowing. In line with my general intention to do away with boundaries in terms of law's relationship with culture, understanding law on an aesthetic level results in a legality that is both limited and richly fluid – depending on your perspective. In order to conceptualise this dual legality as encountered in legal aesthetics, the current work turns to psychoanalysis, an area of understanding that involves exploration of the unconscious order that flows beneath or outside conscious forms, informing, rupturing, challenging, and shaping them; a latent world, always inherent within consciousness.[29] Through an aesthetic lens, a conscious legality can be seen operating in a sphere of practical outcomes and rational discourse – a law limited in its adherence to the rational text. This consciousness exists in a complex tension with its own repressed unconscious. These repressed aspects of law are those that are outside or challenge the stability of rational text: the fluid, open, embodied, or pluralistic understandings of legality and justice.

In psychoanalysis, the unconscious is generally understood to be made up of repressed memories, things hidden in the past that return in the present. This 'return' can occur in various ways.[30] Freud, for example, argued that many expressions of disgust or dislike are actually the return of repressed desires in a reversed form; thus, widespread condemnation of salacious crimes can be read as a way for members of society to enjoy a 'morally safe' release from their repression of taboo desires.[31] But the idea of the legal unconscious can tell us much more than this notion of condemnation-as-repressed-desire. It can tell us about the limits of rational legality. Thus, a central concept in my construction of law's conscious/unconscious is that of reification, which is instrumental in much of the repression that produces the legal unconscious and worth outlining in a little detail. The work of Manderson is useful in elaborating this concept, as it is in its sustained engagement with legal aesthetics more broadly. Reification is a central feature of the rational thought of modernism,[32] paradigmatic of which is the denial of what Manderson calls the 'fifth' (or human) dimension:

> One of [modernism's] effects has been the effacement of its own fifth-dimensionality – the human and subjective nature of its symbolism – and the presentation of its shadow [in four dimensions] as something unavoidable and

29 See, for example, Freud (1997).
30 Gurnham (2014), pp 15–23.
31 Gurnham (2014), pp 20–21.
32 Manderson (2000), p 160.

> objective. The reification of time and space is thus both an aspect and a technique of modernism: an aspect of how it orders the world and a technique for the totalization of that order.[33]

Thus the physical world and the shadows of five-dimensional objects – such as monuments, ideas, legal structures – are seen as stable, natural, and external, something to be uncovered and explored. But the recognition of this fifth or 'human' dimension, the recognition of the role of human creativity in the constitution of seemingly stable objects, renders these things interpretive, indeterminate, and contested.[34] Modern law, then, becomes a reified structure, divorced from its ontological or cultural conditions of production. This reification can be seen, for example, in the emergence of the 'black letter' tradition in English law during the late Victorian period.[35] But looking back further, the reified tradition can be unpacked through the historical tracing of the way rational modern law emerged via a repression of its other. Peter Goodrich's detailed analysis in *Oedipus Lex* describes an oppositional structure of law – between its conscious and unconscious dimensions – that, on an epistemological level, closely resembles the legal aesthetics I am outlining here.[36] Goodrich observes the institutional unconscious – the aesthetic adornments and theatre of the legal process,[37] the artistry of judicial interpretation[38] – and through historical analysis of the war on images in the Reformation comes to the conclusion that the conscious text masks an unconscious order.

> The [legal] text is only ever a sign of apparent juridical community, of a mixture of visual and epistemic control, of the combination of image and word. It is the visible surface or icon of a more complex source and belief, order and unity.[39]

As the conscious texts of law are produced, so too an 'other scene' of law emerges of all that the conscious order represses,[40] and neither conscious nor unconscious law can be fully understood without also encountering the other – an encounter that psychoanalysis facilitates.[41]

33 Manderson (2000), p 161. Manderson is here using the metaphor of shadows; just as a three-dimensional object casts a two-dimensional shadow, a five-dimensional object would cast a four-dimensional shadow.
34 Manderson's specific focus here is on the contested and indeterminate nature of law that recognition of the fifth dimension entails.
35 See Sugarman (1991).
36 See Goodrich (1995).
37 Goodrich (1995), pp 12–13.
38 Goodrich (1995), pp 30–32.
39 Goodrich (1995), pp 220–221.
40 Goodrich (1995), p 221.
41 Goodrich (1995), pp 243–247.

To be clear: my claim is not one of a dyadic tension between 'law' and 'aesthetics', although the unconscious dimensions of law are those that tend to be more 'aesthetic' than rational. Rather, it is a complex interplay of a certain limited kind of law (doctrinal, rational) and a more expansive vision that legal aesthetics allows us to perceive and conceptualise. Indeed, when configured epistemologically, psychoanalysis helps model the division between reason and unreason, bringing insight into the conscious legal project that grounds itself in rational textual discourse, but that always remains infused with and part of its irrational 'beyond'.[42] In denying law's boundaries, and at the same time thus engaging with a greatly expanded discursive universe within the wider multiframe of knowing, we are not only moving beyond orthodox legality, but also outside reason. We are expanding law's remit and nature to include not only the frames of modern rational thought – which we can conceptualise as law's consciousness – but also the multiple frames of the cultural, artistic, emotional, and irrational that law represses into its unconscious[43] – its 'other frames'. It is the work of Chapter 2 to set up this conscious/unconscious structure of modern law more fully, through engagement with comics, before Chapter 3 navigates its threshold in an encounter with madness, Chapter 4 considers the infinite context of the cosmic abyss, and Chapter 5 expounds the haunted nature of law's conscious frame that renders it precarious. This journey of expansion must be undertaken before the connotations of multimodality, and the infinite multiframe, can be fully worked through in Chapter 6. The remainder of this section, meanwhile, outlines some of the aesthetic dimensions of law in terms of this structure, and indicates how the multimodal quality of comics plays into it.

Through aesthetics, comics and law can be understood as different ways of knowing and communicating the world. It may seem that the overtly 'artistic' form of comics means it – or its reading – may engage more readily with the processes of its own creation and meaning-making. But this is the project of legal aesthetics, too: engaging law's unspoken processes and dimensions, its styles and presentations, its formats and contexts, its embodiment and symbolism and sociocultural circulation – its unconscious. For example, law may be predominantly text-based in its doctrinal practice and education[44] – at least, on a conscious level – but this textuality imposes certain limits on law's ability to represent and encounter meanings and practicalities of complex human life,[45] shaping the contours of legal knowing. The textuality of law is also entangled with its traditional reliance on rationality, with legal education downplaying – repressing – the role played by the imagination in processes of interpretation, instead training lawyers to interpret through the exercise of reason within textual limits,

42 See, for example, Aristodemou (2014); Goodrich (1995); Gurnham (2014). We will expand on this more fully in Chapter 3.
43 See Goodrich (1995).
44 Baríkowski et al (2013), pp 1–2; Stewart (1991), p 3.
45 Baríkowski et al (2013), pp 3–4.

emphasising boundaries over imagination.[46] Although taking place within a particular high-stakes practical and governmental context,[47] legal interpretation, 'like all interpretation, is *bounded creativity* – a combination of reason and imagination'.[48] Recognising the unconscious creative play that interpretation in legal theory and practice involves arguably brings with it the anxiety of contingency, exposing troubling tensions between 'an inarticulate yet replete universe of sensation and a fully articulated, fully categorizable, and consequently empty universe of the purely symbolic'.[49] But this contingency, which may be seen to threaten the legal order, can easily be seen as enabling the opening of spaces of cultural legal aesthetics wherein law's possible forms and meanings can be explored.[50]

As jurisprudes, 'injustice' may be something that we feel – it is emotional, passionate, and experiential, rather than rational and theoretical; without this 'feeling' of the 'wrongness' of things, attempts to produce theories and models for achieving justice would be useless intellectual exercises.[51] Indeed, reason is but one amongst many ways of knowing that are all grounded in sensory experience and human living. The creative play of interpretation is part of this broader cultural legal aesthetics, this unconscious realm of legality beyond textual order and rational coherence. But engagement with the aesthetic dimensions of law is not an abandonment to meaningless relativism or incomprehensible chaos, but can give critical insight into the values that shape systems of law and judgment. The idea of balance, for instance, underlies concerns with proportionality and the social response to wrongdoing.[52] The scientific truth that Sherwin observes as founding the authority of modern law is also full of rhetorical preferences, such as those of formulaic elegance.[53] Similarly, the idea of chaos may be unwanted not necessarily due to any nihilism or meaninglessness it may suggest, but simply because it is not appropriately ordered – like comics, it looks wrong. For example, Elaine Scarry notes that the beauty of symmetry is important in the creation of just systems, not only in the sense of an analogy of balance but because it is something we can more readily perceive than the infinite complexities of an operational, concrete

46 Webster (2013), p 90.
47 As Cover famously put it, within a 'field of pain and death': see Cover (1986).
48 Webster (2013), p 90. Emphasis in original.
49 Stewart (1991), p 144.
50 Webster (2013), pp 91–93. Comics also highlight the contingency of visual images, with practices such as comics journalism questioning the truthfulness of photography: see Vanderbeke (2010).
51 Douzinas and Gearey (2005), pp 28–32.
52 Manderson (2000), p 196. This can also be seen in the classical natural law tradition: 'The idea of proportion is crucial; it brings justice close to the aesthetic beauty immanent in the harmony of the world': Douzinas and Gearey (2005), pp 84–85. See also, for an analysis of how *Batman Begins* ruptures the tendency towards a model of justice-as-balance, Peters (2007).
53 See Sherwin (2011), p 22. See also, on the cultural and institutional biases of scientific knowledge, Levins (1996); and, on the historical emergence of the mainstream bias toward quantitative knowing, Poovey (1998).

system.[54] Indeed, recognising that the chaos of life and legal systems can be 'beautiful' and represent a generative potential, and can thereby help move towards a positive and productive embrace of pluralism, can reorient approaches to law and legal theory and invigorate our sensitivity towards the local and the humanistic.[55]

Moreover, even aesthetic creations operate, not insignificantly, through concepts and rational understanding,[56] which rest upon an abstraction of perception.[57] Aesthetic creations, no differently from scientific or historical ones, involve rational concepts in their development, within a context of sensory perception:[58] 'What is it that enables us to *know* something … if not our ability to penetrate beyond the immediacy of brute matter …?'[59] And comics is no exception. Indeed, Alison Young claims that law and aesthetics meet in a relationship of coimplication, where law implies the presence of the aesthetic and the aesthetic implies the presence of law. Law, as a primarily textual and rational phenomenon, is able to exist and maintain its form of authority, judgment, and logic through its exercise and deployment of (unconscious) images. Indeed, the visual image has a strong tradition in law,[60] including in the visual presentation of text.[61] The institution thus presents itself via the layout of courtrooms, the wearing of wigs, gowns, and other uniforms, and the formats of case reports. In this way law implies the presence of its sensory dimensions – accessible via the aesthetic – even if such presence remains part of the institution's unconscious.

Similarly art, as a primarily emotional or sensual phenomenon, produces, interprets, and values its forms in relation to particular rules: of creative processes, of formats and display; in this way the aesthetic implies the presence of rules, of judgment – of law.[62] Such interplay is clear in the comics form: as we will see more fully in the next section, there are a great deal of technical 'rules' and systemic structures to navigate and play with when encountering the comics form. Comics has (albeit debated) formal rules and expectations that works manipulate and navigate, and are judged in relation to. But reason is not enough; structural engagement does not capture all that comics[63] or law are or can be. Aesthetic engagement enables us to perceive other layers (of atmosphere, of texture, of form, of visuality, and of aesthetic dimensions more generally) that, alongside formal rules, play into the meanings available in the encounter with an

54 Scarry (2000), pp 97–109.
55 See Manderson (2000), pp 177–183.
56 See Della Volpe (1978), pp 17–19, discussing, for example, poetry.
57 Della Volpe (1978), p 22.
58 Della Volpe (1978), pp 23–24.
59 Della Volpe (1978), p 20. Emphasis in original.
60 See Goodrich (2013).
61 As Goodrich states, 'the printed word is simply another figurate sign … [that lawyers] interpret and unpack': Goodrich (2013), p xxviii. We return to the visuality of text in detail in Chapter 6.
62 Young (2005), pp 8–10.
63 See the debate over language and structure in comics in Chapter 6.

object.[64] Thus, in the comics examples I read throughout this book I seek to encounter both structural and aesthetic dimensions; that is, I examine at various points general themes and content, as well as visual presentation and formal play.[65] Whilst I am arguing overall that it is the formal quality of comics – as a multimodal multiframe – that is of value in understanding law without boundaries, examining specific thematic dimensions is necessarily part of this project in terms of reading comics as a form of jurisprudence, as part of the expansive discourses of the *lex populi*. Accordingly, depending on the example, some readings tend more towards aesthetic content and visuality than structural form and vice versa. Thus, across the book as a whole, my goal is to encounter comics not simply as a vehicle for narrative and thematic engagement (although this is part of what they are), but also as a specific form of communication and presentation with its own aesthetic – that is, epistemological – implications for law.

This inclusive approach to analysis, encountering legalistic formal rules as well as the fluidity of perception, might be unsettling in its coimplication of law and aesthetics. Feeding on the classic association of the aesthetic with the non-rational and non-knowable, the coimplication of law and aesthetics has uncomfortable connotations for the legal tradition that would rather repress the presence of its visual and aesthetic dimensions:

> In the abject discomfort of a co-implicated relation between jurisprudence and aesthetics, we find that which the legal tradition would prefer not to be revealed – uncertainty, affectivity, contingency, difference, the peripatetic and nomadic, the marginal, the image.[66]

But, just as we noted with chaos and disorder, the aesthetic need not threaten law.[67] As Manderson claims, aesthetic judgment and ideals of justice share key characteristics, such as resisting settled interpretations through critical reflection, invoking empathy and consideration of the other, and building communal understandings.[68] Moreover, as with Young, the unconscious dimensions of law can be seen on a more practical level in the images it uses to maintain itself. Indeed, Adam Geary outlines this dimension when he describes 'the panoply of images that characterise legal practice' and that demonstrate the history, autonomy, and

64 See Armstrong (2003), who shows how aesthetic experience allows us to grasp an otherwise inaccessible moral significance in a particular painting.
65 The examples I have chosen are undoubtedly influenced not only by the comics works I have encountered, but also my own personal tastes (not least because this in many ways drives the set of comics I encounter). Appendix A includes brief overviews and limited publication details for each of the major examples I engage with.
66 Young (2005), p 12.
67 In Chapter 3, we will explore the 'irrational threat' that exploration of law's unconscious brings, through Batman's navigation of his encounters with madness.
68 See Manderson (2000), pp 197–199.

continuity of law:[69] courtroom architecture;[70] legal dress;[71] the formalities of official conduct. Gearey also observes the way that, through recognising the aesthetic aspects of law, we can gain insight into the processes that law employs to establish and maintain its own order and authority.[72]

Law also arguably has a significant narrative dimension.[73] As Jerome Bruner observes, stories involve a challenge to the status quo, an attack on the current order and the mediation of that attack, resulting in either a new order or the re-establishment of the existing order;[74] like law, they are a way of dealing and coming to terms with the vicissitudes of life[75] and thus share law's cultural function of mediating between what should happen and what does:[76]

> Story making is our medium for coming to terms with the surprises and oddities of the human condition and for coming to terms with our imperfect grasp of that condition ... once [deviant acts are] domesticated in narrative, [they] bear the stamp of the culture ... [and] become legitimized as interpretable transgressions or mishaps or lapses in human judgment ... they become the stock unexpected.[77]

In this way, law has a distinctly narrative function: it is storytelling that creates and sustains law, for law is storytelling, not just in the courtroom, but in the very processes of encoding and applying the rules that govern society and culture.[78] Law is thus an aesthetic resource, another way of making sense of the world.

What all this boils down to is that, despite its conscious associations with rational order, law is a deeply aesthetic pursuit. Indeed, law can be seen to operate 'by a language of symbolic meaning expressed in sensory form' – a rational structure encountered via the aesthetic.[79] This description, as the work of Ian Hague suggests, can be applied to comics as an embodied, sensory phenomenon:

69 Gearey (2001), p 29.
70 For an aesthetically enriched examination of the role of architectural ornament in courtroom architecture, see Haldar (1999). See also Mulcahy (2011).
71 On dress and law, see Watt (2013).
72 See Gearey (2001), pp 17–22.
73 On the application of psychoanalysis to legal narration, see Gurnham (2014), pp 30–45.
74 See Bruner (2002), pp 14–15.
75 Bruner (2002).
76 Bruner (2002), pp 92–93.
77 Bruner (2002), pp 90–91. And for these legal resources for event handling to be meaningful, they must match their meaning to the culture that they both govern and of which they are a part: Bruner (2002), pp 49–50.
78 Moreover, as Manderson tells us, stories do not 'lay down laws', but rather 'lay down ways of being' for us: Manderson (2003), p 90. They retell myths, producing codes of being that enable us to make sense of the uncertainties of existence, in turn shaping the emergence of civilisation. Children's stories are particularly important in this regard, tapping into the deep myths of civilisation and instilling them in each successive generation: see Manderson (2003).
79 Manderson (2000), p 196.

> [T]he power of comics lies not just in their [symbolic language] … but also in their tactile, olfactory and even auditory and gustatory qualities. Reading comics is not just a visual process, it is a multisensory *experience*.[80]

In an institutional sense, to do justice is not simply to achieve a particular outcome, but to achieve it through the correct formal pathways; it is not what justice *is* that matters, so much as its processes and mechanics – what it *does*. To engage the 'unconscious' of law is to explore its rich aesthetics, the dimensions of its institution that are repressed or unencountered in the 'conscious' operation of practical doctrine. Constructing this through psychoanalysis enables the latent meanings and dimensions of law's rational-textual consciousness to be unpacked and explored, and thus legality to be understood in a much wider sense. It allows law's boundaries to be broken down, and thus for law to be seen as larger than its conscious order, but without hiding that dominant order from critical view. From this perspective, the more aesthetic dimensions of law and justice can be encountered as part of its conscious operation, just as Freud unpacked dreams in a way that uncovered repressed aspects of his subjects' consciousness that were still part of their waking lives.[81] In this way, 'conscious' law becomes one frame amongst many 'other frames' to which it is connected within a larger multiframe of knowing. We can reframe law in multiple ways simultaneously, and it is a central contention of this book that the multimodal mediation of the comics form – as *komos* – can be situated solidly within this project, integrating law into the wider ecosystem of the multiframe and thereby removing its boundaries.

Taking the aesthetic seriously on a philosophical level necessarily involves recognising and accepting the epistemological challenges it raises: the limits of reason and rational understanding; the plurality, difference, and uncertainty present in the world beyond rationality; and, the subjectivity and local nature of aesthetic and sensory understanding. For the study of law, an object that has for large swathes of its recent history been built upon ideals of rationality, turning to the aesthetic encounters the same latent challenges. It exposes the culturally embedded and aesthetic underpinnings of legal structures, observing their origins in living human experience – in the messy contingency of life. Problems of plurality and abstraction appear, alongside understandings of how these structures emerge through the repression of alternative orders – of other frames – and come to operate as part of the broad human endeavour to understand the world and our place in it. The ways law knows, its constructions of reality, are shaped and formed not from objective or divine sources of truth and justice, but from human contexts and aesthetic preferences and practices. Law may be abstracted from human reality, but then so is art – and so are comics and other constructions of meaning and knowledge. 'The point is therefore not to try to imagine the possibility of its [abstraction's] absence but to acknowledge its

80 Hague (2014), p 25. Emphasis in original.
81 See Freud (1997).

incompleteness'.[82] The multimodal quality of comics, trembling on the meeting point of a range of different forms of knowledge and communication, exposes precisely this incompleteness and its inevitability. In the next section, we turn to encounter the theorisation of comics and to expound the concept of the multi-frame, before moving through the expansion of law in the subsequent chapters.

Komos and *nomos*

On the form of comics

The tradition of legal aesthetics works to articulate the visual, sensory, and embodied dimensions of law and justice processes; in part, its project is to expose the reading processes and visuality – the mechanics of meaning and authority – utilised by law and its institution. These aesthetic engagements not only bring about deeper questioning of how law produces and articulates its own meaning, how it presents itself in society and establishes and maintains its power, but also – I contend – opens up a fruitful connection with the reading of the comics form. It is through a concern with aesthetics that we are adverted to the processes of meaning-making in both comics and law – of how knowledge mediates sensory encounter, in the manner of the *komos* – and thus ultimately to the form and limits of knowing more generally. The multimodality of comics, as this book will show, has profound implications for our ability to encounter the limits of legal, and other, ways of knowing. If we are to begin to unpack the implications that the formal make-up of comics may have for legal knowledge and practice, analysis must include interrogations of the mechanics and formal operation of the medium. The focus of this section is thus on what comics do, rather than what they are, before moving in the next section to place comics more directly in relation to law and legal aesthetics.

Finding a settled definition of comics may be futile. As Thierry Groensteen has noted:

> any comic is necessarily (constitutionally) a sophisticated structure [and] only actualizes certain potentialities of the medium, to the detriment of others that are reduced or excluded. Consequently, searching for the essence of comics is to be assured of finding not a shortage but a profusion of responses.[83]

Accordingly, there have been a plurality of attempts to produce a general definition of comics in recent years. But whilst the present work is not concerned with the perhaps fruitless task of nailing down a solid answer to the question 'what is comics',[84] it is worthwhile thinking a little about how the form might be defined

82 Manderson (2000), p 48.
83 Groensteen (2007), p 12.
84 Indeed, such a project is likely impossible: see Groensteen (2007), pp 12–16.

in order to open up questions around the potential capacities and methods of reading comics, and thus its value to wider critical understanding – and thence to law.

The obvious and well-trodden starting point is Scott McCloud's famous definition of comics as 'juxtaposed pictorial and other images in deliberate sequence'.[85] David Carrier, on the other hand, grounds the uniqueness of comics in its word-image relationships rather than the need for a sequence. Although Carrier does accept a general sequentiality, it is the combination of words and images that he believes makes comics a unique art form.[86] Indeed, Ann Miller's semiotic approach identifies a range of types of text available for creative and narrative manipulation in the verbal dimension of comics, from external text on the cover, to dialogue, sound effects, and diegetic text in the narrative world,[87] with each capable of being manipulated in different ways (visual style, linkage with the diegesis, use of symbols, and so on), layering both meaning and complexity into the comics page.[88] Although fruitful in identifying some of the word/image interactions in comics, making word-image duality definitional on the one hand includes things like children's books and illustrated novels, whilst on the other excludes comics that may be termed 'silent' – those that avoid textual language as such, often relying on symbolic depictions in place of speech.[89] On this issue, theorists like Charles Hatfield elaborate McCloud's notion of 'pictorial and other images' more fully: like McCloud, Hatfield short-circuits the word/image distinction by understanding written words as another kind of image sequence (as 'other images'), accordingly arguing that there are multiple semiotic 'codes' operational in comics, some of which 'show' (depictions of the diegetic world and characters) and some of which 'tell' (symbols or traditional text as speech or narration, or iconic depictions such as 'speed lines').[90]

But there are problems with McCloud's formula. The requirement for 'juxtaposition', for example, would exclude situations where images complement each other. But it is perhaps McCloud's deep concern with sequentiality that is most troubling. Whilst the requirement of sequence blinds us to comics that use atemporal layouts or operate via a single panel,[91] McCloud famously uses his definition to include a whole host of historical and cultural artefacts within the bounds of comics, from the Bayeux Tapestry to ancient pictographic languages.[92] Such claims would put, for example, *The Amazing Spider-Man #96* alongside Egyptian

85 See McCloud (1993), pp 7–9.
86 See Carrier (2000).
87 Miller (2007), p 97.
88 See Miller (2007), pp 97–101.
89 See, for example, the analyses of various 'wordless novels' in Beronä (2001). See also, more generally, Groensteen (2007), pp 14–15.
90 See Hatfield (2005), pp 36–41. We will return to questions of the relationship between words and images and the visual dimensions of written text in detail in Chapter 6.
91 See Carrier (2000), pp 14–24, who argues that a single image can represent a narrative sequence through its implication of past and future events.
92 See McCloud (1993), pp 9–20.

hieroglyphs as being of the same cultural or aesthetic form. Whilst it may be possible to categorise things in this way, such conflation as a formal definition overlooks important conventional and aesthetic differences between the operation of a twentieth-century comics page and other pictorial sequences. Indeed, as Harvey points out, whilst comics may be a sub-set of 'sequential images', not all sequential images are comics.[93] Harvey defines comics in a less prescriptive manner: 'Comics consist[s] of pictorial narratives or expositions in which words … usually contribute to the meaning of the pictures and vice versa'.[94] Such a 'loose description' enables us to think about the things that whatever-it-is-that-comics-is[95] usually does (such as blend words and images, use sequential panel/page layouts, and so on), but without limiting what else they could do, such as not use words, avoid temporal sequence, or challenge layout or material conventions.

It has been contended that what comics does – its mechanics of sequence – highlights the subjective reading process. McCloud states that comics make use of the 'gutter', the blank space between comics panels over which our gaze must pass as we 'read' from one panel to the next. Theorising this idea, and in doing so dealing with the many situations where a delineated blank 'gutter' is not used (such as comics that use a simple line, a lack of borders, or an interpenetration of images), Groensteen observes that comics have a 'separative function':[96]

> the principle of the separation of images can never be truly denied … one could not connect the visual utterances if they were not distinct. The separative function is always in the work, even if the frame, which is ordinarily its privileged instrument, finds itself deliberately dismissed.[97]

Thus, for Groensteen, physical separation may not be needed so long as the images are 'cognitively isolatable, of the sort that they can be read separately', with delineations between images, like textual punctuation, dividing up the continuity to facilitate comprehension.[98]

McCloud asserts that the movement between separate images, if we are to understand what we are perceiving, requires us to piece them together into some sort of coherent whole – into the continuous narrative experience from which the creator arguably removed them.[99] McCloud claims that this 'closure' process, as

93 Harvey (2005), pp 18–19. For Harvey, illustrated manuscripts, the works of Hogarth, Mayan pictograms, and illustrated children's books, for instance, are not comics – although, like comics, they may all be pictorial sequences.

94 Harvey (2005), p 20.

95 This is the term used by Priego (2014) to maintain an openness on the question of definition.

96 See Groensteen (2007), pp 43–45

97 Groensteen (2007), p 45.

98 Groensteen (2007), p 43.

99 On the processes of 'breakdown' and 'gridding' in the creative processes of comics narratives, whereby creators translate the narrative they wish to capture into the panels and pages of the comics form, see Groensteen (2007), pp 117–121, 142–145. See also

we sequentially cross the gutter, demonstrates the inherently participatory nature of reading comics: the reader fills in the blank space of the gutter and thereby translates the fragmented images into a flowing narrative, and this is 'the magic and mystery that are at the very heart of comics'.[100] Carleton concurs, citing McCloud and concluding that 'comics are necessarily partial texts that require readers to bridge the gaps, or gutters, between panels by using their own imaginations'.[101] Similarly Miller argues that comics' narrative process is grounded in:

> the gap in the signifying chain through which temporal and spatial transitions are managed. The temporal and spatial hiatus implied by the inter-frame space is indeterminate, and allows for considerable variations in the rhythm at which a story is narrated.[102]

But although such processes advert us to the constitutive meaning-making project of the reader, such a subjective project is not unique to comics. Deciphering the shapes and marks of literature or the words of a statute, too, is a subjective encounter between reader and read, whereby meaning is constituted via the particular interactions between a text and its audience.[103] Indeed, this is part of what aesthetics is about, and part of what links comics with law: the reading processes, the styles of presentation, making meaning out of sensory input, mediating embodied reality and concept, rendering 'truth' in order to make a judgment or frame a regulation.

Despite the importance of needing to navigate interpanel relations, the potential for comics pages to be organised without linear or temporal sequence challenges an essentialist understanding of comics-as-sequence. But this does not mean denying that reading multiple images together is part of the interpretive process. Charles Hatfield, for example, demonstrates that a complex network of tensions exists between comics' different levels, beyond simple linearity. The multiple semiotic 'codes' (that 'show' and 'tell', as already mentioned), the individual image, the image sequence, the page layout, the narrative experience, the comics object we hold – all these elements interact, and it is the reader's navigations of this complex interplay that constitutes the interpretive project.[104] In Hatfield's model, the sequence/layout tension can be seen as 'a tension between … narrative time and perceived space',[105] with the layouts of comics pages capable of

McCloud (1993). Despite McCloud's blunt claims that this continuity is simply transferred via the comics medium, with creator deconstructing and reader reconstructing it, there is, of course, no necessary connection or relation between the two, since a reader can always arguably encounter different meanings from those intended by a creator.

100 McCloud (1993), p 66.

101 Carleton (2014), p 162.

102 Miller (2007), pp 88–89.

103 See, for example, Fish (1989).

104 See Hatfield (2005), pp 36–67.

105 Hatfield (2005), p 52.

manipulation to encourage particular reading experiences (varying durations and dramatic significance, rupturing the linear reading experience, and so on).[106] Similarly, Ann Miller shows that comics involve spatiovisual organisation that can be exploited for aesthetic ends, for example using the bottom-right panel to build suspense whilst the reader is forced to turn the page, or varying size and shape of panels.[107] Seeing comics as simply 'sequential' overlooks such complexities.[108]

Focused on comics' atemporal complexity, Groensteen describes comics as a 'spatio-topical' system that is made up of multiple interacting functions.[109] Comics, for Groensteen, is grounded as a spatial system rather than a linguistic one: comics is first and foremost visual, and the panels that make up comics necessarily occupy a graphic space, and also a place within the wider network of panels.[110] In understanding this system of panels, he focuses on the effects and functions of framing, describing its multiple functions: from structuring the layout of the page, to separating the content of different panels, to partaking in the expression of an image and the rhythm of a work, to highlighting that which is to be read.[111] In understanding the comics form as a system of frames (a 'multi-frame'), Groensteen opens up avenues of meaning and interpretation that a linear or narrative model based on sequentiality is unable to encounter.

Thus, Groensteen concludes, as a system, comics is able to develop layers of meaning through the potentially complex interrelation or correlation of panels and images across a work – a process he calls 'braiding'. On top of, within, or intersecting the linear sequence of panels that constitute the dominant narrative, series or sets of panels – connected through, for example, shared visual, formal, or thematic elements – can be delineated, derived from the inherent potential for relationality between all panels that are always copresent in a work.[112] And

106 Hatfield (2005), pp 48–58.

107 Miller (2007), pp 83–86. See also Giddens (2012), pp 97–98; Groensteen (2007), pp 35–39; Versaci (2007), pp 15–16.

108 Indeed, Rocco Versaci has argued that comics, due to its complexity, is a highly suitable medium for exploring the depths of the human condition, with its own particular abilities distinct from other media such as literature. See Versaci (2007). Paul Crutcher (2011), meanwhile, has demonstrated the complexity at work in comics through examination of examples from *Batman*: multiple layered voices, each distinct in its visual presentation, can be seen in the intricately constructed *Dark Knight Returns*: Crutcher (2011), pp 59–60; juxtapositions between textual style and character depiction can be seen in Batman's depiction as demonic, but retaining reasonable speech: Crutcher (2011), p 61; complexities in the artists' control of the narrative and temporal pacing of a page can be seen in Alan Moore's deliberate manipulations in *The Killing Joke*: Crutcher (2011), p 59; and further complexity can be found in the use of visual atmosphere and texture to augment narrative themes in Dave McKean's artwork in *Arkham Asylum*: Crutcher (2011), p 62 (*Arkham Asylum* is the focus of Chapter 3).

109 See, generally, Groensteen (2007), pp 24–102.

110 Groensteen (2007), p 21.

111 See Groensteen (2007), pp 39–57.

112 Groensteen (2007), pp 145–147.

whereas the linear sequence is always oriented towards the vector of narrative progression, at the level of braiding this is not necessarily so:

> The network that they [braided panels] form is certainly an oriented network, since it is crossed by the instance of the story, but it also exists in a dechronologized mode, that of the collection, of the panoptical spread and of coexistence, considering the possibility of translinear relations and plurivectoral courses.[113]

Miller similarly highlights the ability of comics to visually cross-reference within themselves, linking particular narrative elements through shared formal, symbolic, or semantic depiction, which can add rich layers of narrative significance to a particular representation.[114] This systemic level of braiding opens up relations, connections, and meanings, unavailable within the purely linear sequence but often exploited by creators.[115]

Thierry Groensteen's work is widely influential in comics studies, with the understanding of the multiframe – the system of integrated units and connections – being applied by other writers. As Bukatman examines in Mike Mignola's *Hellboy* series, for example, atemporal panels can be used to build mood and challenge the presumption that comics are always simply sequential.[116] Invoking Groensteen, Bukatman argues that comics present something more like a 'database aesthetics',[117] whereby it becomes both object and network: 'a thing to hold and a complex space for the reader to activate and inhabit'.[118] Hatfield's interplay of tensions also highlights the deep complexity of the comics page in the way its multiple elements can interact in the project of creating meaning. Developing further the idea of the multiframe, Hannah Miodrag argues that comics are made up of infinitely nested units – pages, panels, images, words, texts, and so on – that all contribute to meaning-making but that cannot be reduced to a single integrated system of meaning.[119]

With such understandings, we can see that there is an atemporal concern with hybridity and multimodality in the comics form, with the copresence of multiple elements and modes of communication interacting in a complex multiframe to enable the production of meaning. Indeed, comics have been argued to function in the realm of 'hyperreading', with the complexities and multimodal dimensions of the page operating on multiple levels at once.[120] Text, image, page design and

113 Groensteen (2007), p 147.
114 Miller (2007), pp 95–97.
115 See Groensteen (2007), pp 149–155 for discussion of examples. We also explore some braided elements in *Watchmen* in Chapter 5.
116 Bukatman (2014).
117 Bukatman (2014), p 116.
118 Bukatman (2014), p 117.
119 See Miodrag (2013). Her work is discussed in more detail in Chapter 6.
120 Orbán (2014), pp 169–172. Ironically, Orbán highlights, despite hyperreading being initially a phenomenon of the digital age, comics still retain this phenomenon within their primary status as printed books.

quality, printing formats and materials – all potentially feed into the meanings and interpretations available in the comics reading process. From the materiality of Spiegleman,[121] to the aesthetic quality of panel constructions, colour, and artistry in *Hellboy*,[122] the comics form is a complex layering of multiple visual, tactile, and narrative resources.[123] Moreover, as Gómez Romero and Dahlman suggest, it may be that the 'hybrid nature of comics constitutes a poignant communication capable of producing alternative awareness'.[124] And, as Sousanis emphatically argues, alternative perspectives are vital in the quest for understanding, with comics being aptly suited to the task of opening our awareness up to multiple viewpoints and thus 'unflattening' knowledge.[125] Put differently, beyond sequential elaboration of narratives, the multimodality of comics might help challenge existing modes of understanding.

When we start to think more about how comics work, rather than trying to sharply delineate what they are, we start to ask meaningful questions about the reading process and the mechanics of the form – that is, about how comics articulate meaning. And it is with such questions – of how words and images interrelate, of how images and sequences play off each other, of how design and layout feed into reading processes, of how multiple modes of communication interact – that comics and the idea of the multiframe begin to display something of their deep significance for law as part of a cultural legal aesthetics that seeks to 're-form' law, as well as for wider critical discourse and understanding. Indeed, it is in the mediation between different orders – precisely in the medium's hybridity, in the necessary movement between modes and frames that its reading requires – that the critical value of comics-as-*komos* can most clearly be seen. It is 'inbetweenness' that makes comics both unique and uniquely useful. As is the broad claim of this book, it is via the complex multimodality of its form that the comics medium enables navigation of the multifaceted boundaries at the limits of rational language, that it is able to mediate as *komos* between the order of knowable forms and the chaos of an unstructured universe – at the limits of law's conscious institution of life.

Law and the multiframe

Hybridity is not unique to comics; theatre and cinema, to take obvious examples, also use multiple elements in their construction of meaning (narrative, image, music, dress, and so forth). But the particular blending of elements that the comics form is capable of is arguably more unique to the potentialities of comics than to any other medium. Again, we are talking about what comics can do rather

121 See Orbán (2014).
122 See Bukatman (2014).
123 See also Hatfield (2005), pp 32–67 for detailed exploration of the various tensions at work in one's encounter with the comics page.
124 Gómez Romero and Dahlman (2012), pp 22–23.
125 See Sousanis (2015), pp 49–68.

than strictly delineating what they are. And as we have seen, when examining the broad formal dimensions of comics, even without rendering any particular aspect 'definitional', this medium – once relegated to the pile of disposable, juvenile trash[126] – can be seen to encounter and exploit numerous intricacies and complexities in its construction and reading. It is the numerous elements and aspects variably present in the comics form that interact to produce this complexity, as a richly multimodal form. It is important to reiterate that this multimodality should not be reduced to simply 'word' and 'image' (even if 'words' may be framed, as Hatfield notes, as a kind of image-based semiotic code). As Ian Hague contends, comics are deeply multisensory, engaging all five of the classic senses:

> there is more to the medium than words and pictures … Readers do not interact with comics through their eyes alone; their whole bodies are involved in the *performance* of the work.[127]

Comics is thus 'a multisensory *experience*';[128] it is 'inbetween' a variety of forms, neither completely one thing nor another. Like Haraway's cyborg,[129] it is an intrinsically hybrid, unresolved medium: fragmented, capable of multiple (re) interpretations in the navigation of its complex constitution. Accordingly, as already indicated, the multimodality of comics can be seen as continuing the traditional function of mediating between different orders as found in the *komos*. The fact that theorisation of the form is preoccupied with questions of interacting elements and the mechanics of using such interaction to construct meaning goes some way to demonstrate the veracity this suggestion. But the function of the *komos* was not a general mediation – but specifically of mediating between social order and chaotic disorder.[130] It was a public function, and thus can be understood as operating in relation to law's *nomos*. Accordingly, as a work of cultural legal aesthetics, the examples encountered across this book aim to show that comics represent a contemporary juristic *komos*, a mediation of order and disorder – form and chaos, closure and potential – in legal knowing, as well as knowing more generally.

Ian Hague, in discussing attempts to define comics, shows that whatever definition of comics is used profoundly shapes the possible analyses of comics that can be undertaken; one's definition of comics thus always limits the scope of analysis (and ultimately of comics studies in general).[131] Works like those of Groensteen,

126 See Nyberg (1998).
127 Hague (2014), p 7. Emphasis in original. For Hague, as artefacts that are read as physically embodied objects, comics' materiality is the quintessential location where its meanings are negotiated: Hague (2014), p 28.
128 Hague (2014), p 25. Emphasis in original.
129 See Haraway (2000). See also Chapter 2, where Haraway's work is discussed in more detail.
130 See Hatab (2005), p 157.
131 See Hague (2014), pp 17–20.

Hatfield, McCloud, and others tend to assume that comics remain limited by their physical form – typically the printed volume – even if elements such as material quality and embodied reading form part of the analysis. However, when walking through the everyday world, it is possible to spot emanations of comics in marketing practices and other high-profile visual displays – albeit typically a particular kind of visualisation that seeks to replicate the view of comics popularised by Lichtenstein.[132] Although such examples arguably seek to resemble a particular vision of the printed comics page, they raise the possibility that 'whatever-it-is-that-comics-is' is not bounded by the graphic page (be it printed or electronic). Retaining such an openness in thinking about what comics might be, as Hague indicates, results in discourse and analysis also remaining open, meaning we can pay attention to materialities and dimensions of the medium beyond the bounds of page-based definitions. Thus, comics theorists may see the multiframic gridding typical of a comics page in the (literal) framing of windows, in the tiles of toilet walls,[133] and in countless other everyday, phenomenal objects. Indeed, as Ernesto Priego wonders: 'What if comics today are also elsewhere, beyond the book shop and the library, even beyond our Web browsers?'[134]

If there are indeed comics everywhere in this way, the relevance of the medium to wider critical discourse is multiplied as we open up to considerations as to how the variable mechanics outlined above might play out in wider social contexts, beyond the traditional boundaries of the page, but wherever multiple forms and modes of presentation interact. The multimodality of the form might thus be said to run through the everyday world, the multimodal realm of living society, the world made up of fragments and division, of multiple modes of being and appearing. As Priego notes:

> To the comics reader, the city is permeated by the ubiquitous imagery of comics. The commuter gets lost in the public transport grid like a reader gets lost in the layout of the comics page.[135]

On this level, it becomes clear that we can speak of the fragmentation of urban space as produced by legal regulation:[136] the regulatory frames of property cast over the urban geography produces something akin to a multiframe, a network of conceptual images to be read by owners, pedestrians, property developers, politicians, and corporations alike. And this fragmenting regulation, although perhaps

132 See Priego (2014).

133 Herd (2014).

134 Priego (2014), np. See also Wright (2014), who argues that many of the aesthetic principles of comics shape our contemporary digital environments – also influencing wider everyday social, cultural, and economic practices.

135 Priego (2014), np.

136 Young (2014), pp 42–43. Young's legislated city is discussed more fully in Chapter 3. More generally, law itself might be thought of as resting on a 'geography of mental spaces': Goodrich (1995), pp 9–10.

not always so intricate, extends across the whole territory of law, taking its ultimate form in the delineations of sovereign boundaries.[137] More generally, the multiple layered framings of legal regulations can be understood as an example of this expansive understanding of comics: the intricate, nested categories and concepts that constitute statutes and doctrine. Law thus becomes a multiframe containing multiple interrelating panels and sites of meaning to be explored as a complex network of braided relations that opens up avenues of meaning and connection beyond linear association. As a constitutive order, law's multiframe is the complex conceptual order that the legal subject, in Bukatman's words, activates and inhabits. Moreover, as is set out in Chapter 6, the multiframe can be expanded into the endless complexities and modalities of knowledge in general, representing an infinite ecosystem of knowing of which law is an integrated aspect.

Part of the justification for examining comics alongside law as an institution that regulates public life is to examine the role comics might play in relation to the regulation of social and political life – that is, the exercise of state power through law. The instant suggestion might be to turn to politically oriented comics, to those that engage with critical questions of politics and activism.[138] But my concern is less with the politics articulated in comics[139] than with the challenges and insights raised by the comics form itself. Beyond substantive or thematic analyses of morally, politically, or legally expressive works, the formal capacities and multimodalities of comics opens up to epistemological questions of great significance for legal knowledge, and knowledge more generally. Not all comics have political themes, but (definitional uncertainty notwithstanding) all comics are examples of comics form, and thus are all linked with multimodality, epistemological complexity, and the mediating function of the *komos*. My task in this book is not so much to engage the legal and political discourse within comics (although jurisprudentially themed works will be engaged with), but rather to unpack the challenges to the form of juristic knowing that the inbetween aesthetics of comics raises.

Like comics, law divides the world into a set of frames to be read and inhabited by its audience. Law's complex and pluralistic construction of categories and regulations, of nested clauses and conceptual objects, is the multiframe within which the legal subject is constituted. And like comics, law operates as a form of mediation. But where law's mediation is substantive, navigating competing interests and the exercise of state power through judicial processes without questioning its own institution, comics' mediation is formal, navigating tensions between multiple modes of (re)presentation. Indeed, comics' multimodality exposes the interactive boundaries between different orders of knowing, most superficially between those of the textual and the visual, but also the rational and the aesthetic. As *komos*,

137 The relationships between mapping, knowledge, and law are discussed in Chapter 6.
138 For brief analysis of such comics, see Carleton (2014).
139 For a thoroughgoing analysis of the question of sovereignty in superhero comics, see Curtis (2016).

comics thus enables a deeper and more profound mediation than that of law, exposing conscious rational and textual orders to unconscious aesthetics and visuality: exposing the rational-textual form of modern law to its repressed other, and celebrating our cultural legal exploration of this other. It is to examples of this mediation – working towards a multimodal and unbounded encounter with law – that the subsequent chapters now turn.

References

Maria Aristodemou (2014) *Law, Psychoanalysis, Society: Taking the Unconscious Seriously*, Routledge.

John Armstrong (2003) 'Moral Depth and Pictorial Art' in JL Bermúez and S Gardner (eds) *Art and Morality*, Routledge.

Zenon Baríkowski et al (2013) 'Introduction' in Z Baríkowski et al (eds) *The Arts and the Legal Academy: Beyond Text in Legal Education*, Ashgate.

Anne Barron (2000) 'Spectacular Jurisprudence' 20 *Oxford Journal of Legal Studies* 301.

David A Beronä (2001) 'Pictures Speak in Comics without Words: Pictorial Principles in the Work of Milt Gross, Hendrik Dorgathen, Eric Drooker, and Peter Kuper' in R Varnum and CT Gibbons (eds) *The Language of Comics: Word and Image*, University Press of Mississippi.

Frank Bramlett (ed) (2012) *Linguistics and the Study of Comics*, Palgrave.

Jerome Bruner (2002) *Making Stories: Law, Literature, Life*, Harvard University Press.

Scott Bukatman (2014) 'Sculpture, Stasis, the Comics, and Hellboy' 40 *Critical Inquiry* 104.

Sean Carleton (2014) 'Drawn to Change: Comics and Critical Consciousness' 73 *Le Travail* 151.

David Carrier (2000) *The Aesthetics of Comics*, Pennsylvania State University Press.

Robert M Cover (1986) 'Violence and the Word' 95 *Yale Law Journal* 1601.

Paul A Crutcher (2011) 'Complexity in the Comic and Graphic Novel Medium: Inquiry through Bestselling Batman Stories' 44 *The Journal of Popular Culture* 53.

Neal Curtis (2016) *Sovereignty and Superheroes*, Manchester University Press.

Galvano Della Volpe (1978) *Critique of Taste*, New Left Books.

Costas Douzinas and Adam Gearey (2005) *Critical Jurisprudence: The Political Philosophy of Justice*, Hart.

Costas Douzinas and Lynda Nead (1999) 'Introduction' in C Douzinas and L Nead (eds) *Law and the Image: The Authority of Art and the Aesthetics of Law*, University of Chicago Press.

Costas Douzinas and Lynda Nead (eds) (1999) *Law and the Image: The Authority of Art and the Aesthetics of Law*, University of Chicago Press.

Phoebe C Ellsworth (2012) 'Legal Reasoning and Scientific Reasoning' 64 *Alabama Law Review* 895.

Stanley E Fish (1989) *Doing What Comes Naturally: Change, Rhetoric, and Practice of Theory in Literary and Legal Studies*, Duke University Press.

Sigmund Freud (1997) *The Interpretation of Dreams*, Wordsworth.

Adam Gearey (2001) *Law and Aesthetics*, Hart.

Thomas Giddens (2012) 'Comics, Law, and Aesthetics: Towards the Use of Graphic Fiction in Legal Studies' 6 *Law and Humanities* 85.

Priska Gisler et al (eds) (2012) *Intersections of Law and Culture*, Palgrave Macmillan.
Luis Gómez Romero and Ian Dahlman (2012) 'Introduction – Justice Framed: Law in Comics and Graphic Novels' 16 *Law Text Culture* 3.
Peter Goodrich (1990) *Languages of Law: From Logics of Memory to Nomadic Masks*, Weidenfeld and Nicolson.
Peter Goodrich (1995) *Oedipus Lex: Psychoanalysis, History, Law*, University of California Press.
Peter Goodrich (2013) *Legal Emblems and the Art of Law: Obiter Depicta as the Vision of Governance*, Cambridge University Press.
Thierry Groensteen (2007) *The System of Comics*, University Press of Mississippi.
Nic Groombridge (2015) 'Stepping Off the Page: "British Batman" as Legal Superhero' in T Giddens (ed) *Graphic Justice: Intersections of Comics and Law*, Routledge.
David Gurnham (2014) *Crime, Desire and Law's Unconscious: Law, Literature and Culture*, Routledge.
Ian Hague (2014) *Comics and the Senses: A Multisensory Approach to Comics and Graphic Novels*, Routledge.
Piyel Haldar (1999) 'The Function of the Ornament in Quintilian, Alberti, and Court Architecture' in C Douzinas and L Nead (eds) *Law and the Image: The Authority of Art and the Aesthetics of Law*, University of Chicago Press.
Donna Haraway (2000) 'A Cyborg Manifesto: Science, Technology and Socialist-Feminism in the Late Twentieth Century' in D Bell and BM Kennedy (eds) *The Cybercultures Reader*, Routledge.
Robert C Harvey (2005) 'Describing and Discarding "Comics" as an Impotent Act of Philosophical Rigor' in J McLaughlin (ed) *Comics as Philosophy*, University Press of Mississippi.
Lawrence J Hatab (2005) *Nietzsche's Life Sentence: Coming to Terms with Eternal Recurrence*, Routledge.
Charles Hatfield (2005) *Alternative Comics: An Emerging Literature*, University Press of Mississippi.
Damon Herd (2014) 'It's All Comics: How Comics Scholars View the World' in E Priego and DN Wright (eds) *The Multimodality of Comics in Everyday Life*, MediaCommons.
Daniel Hourigan (2015) *Law and Enjoyment: Power, Pleasure, and Psychoanalysis*, Routledge.
Richard Levins (1996) 'Ten Propositions on Science and Antiscience' 46/47 *Social Text* 102.
William P MacNeil (2007) *Lex Populi: The Jurisprudence of Popular Culture*, Stanford University Press.
Desmond Manderson (2000) *Songs without Music: Aesthetic Dimensions of Law and Justice*, University of California Press.
Desmond Manderson (2003) 'From Hunger to Love: Myths of the Source, Interpretation, and Constitution of Law in Children's Literature' 15 *Law and Literature* 87.
Desmond Manderson (ed) (2018) *Law and the Visual: Representations, Technologies, and Critique*, Toronto University Press.
Scott McCloud (1993) *Understanding Comics: The Invisible Art*, HarperCollins.
Jeff McLaughlin (ed) (2005) *Comics as Philosophy*, University Press of Mississippi.
Ann Miller (2007) *Reading Bande Dessinée: Critical Approaches to French-Language Comic Strip*, Intellect.

Hannah Miodrag (2013) *Comics and Language: Reimagining Critical Discourse on the Form*, University Press of Mississippi.

Linda Mulcahy (2011) *Legal Architecture: Justice, Due Process and the Place of Law*, Routledge.

Moti Nissani (1997) 'Ten Cheers for Interdisciplinarity: The Case for Interdisciplinary Knowledge and Research' 34 *The Social Science Journal* 201.

Amy Nyberg (1998) *Seal of Approval: The History of the Comics Code*, University Press of Mississippi.

Katalin Orbán (2014) 'A Language of Scratches and Stitches: The Graphic Novel between Hyperreading and Print' 40 *Critical Inquiry* 3.

Timothy D Peters (2007) 'Unbalancing Justice: Overcoming the Limits of the Law in Batman Begins' 16 *Griffith Law Review* 247.

Nickie D Phillips and Staci Strobl (2013) *Comic Book Crime: Truth, Justice and the American Way*, New York University Press.

Mary Poovey (1998) *A History of the Modern Fact: Problems of Knowledge in the Sciences of Wealth and Society*, University of Chicago Press.

Ernesto Priego (2014) 'Popping Up: Cities and Comics as Common Place' in E Priego and DN Wright (eds) *The Multimodality of Comics in Everyday Life*, MediaCommons.

Roger Sabin (2010) *Adult Comics*, Routledge.

Elaine Scarry (2000) *On Beauty and Being Just*, Duckworth.

Cassandra Sharp and Marett Leiboff (eds) (2015) *Cultural Legal Studies: Law's Popular Cultures and the Metamorphosis of Law*, Routledge.

Richard K Sherwin (2000) *When Law Goes Pop: The Vanishing Line between Law and Popular Culture*, University of Chicago Press.

Richard K Sherwin (2011) *Visualizing Law in the Age of the Digital Baroque: Arabesques and Entanglements*, Routledge.

Richard K Sherwin (2012) 'Visual Jurisprudence' 57 *New York Law School Law Review* 11.

Nick Sousanis (2015) *Unflattening*, Harvard University Press.

Susan Stewart (1991) *Crimes of Writing: Problems in the Containment of Representation*, Oxford University Press.

David Sugarman (1991) '"A Hatred of Disorder": Legal Science, Liberalism and Imperialism' in P Fitzpatrick (ed) *Dangerous Supplements: Resistance and Renewal in Jurisprudence*, Pluto.

Kieran Tranter (2012) '"Come a Day There Won't Be Room for Naughty Men Like Us to Slip About at All": The Multi-Media Outlaws of *Serenity* and the Possibilities of Post-Literate Justice' 16 *Law Text Culture* 277.

William Twining (1991) 'Reflections on Law in Context' in P Cane and J Stapleton (eds) *Essays for Patrick Atiyah*, Clarendon.

Dirk Vanderbeke (2010) 'In the Art of the Beholder: Comics as Political Journalism' in M Berninger et al (eds) *Comics as a Nexus of Cultures: Essays on the Interplay of Media, Disciplines and International Perspectives*, McFarland.

Rocco Versaci (2007) *This Book Contains Graphic Language: Comics as Literature*, Continuum.

Douglas W Vick (2004) 'Interdisciplinarity and the Discipline of Law' 31 *Journal of Law and Society* 163.

Gary Watt (2013) *Dress, Law and Naked Truth: A Cultural Study of Fashion and Form*, Bloomsbury.

Elaine Webster (2013) 'From Interpretive Imagination to Contingency in Law: An Argument for Moving Beyond Text' in Z Baríkowski et al (eds) *The Arts and the Legal Academy: Beyond Text in Legal Education*, Ashgate.
Richard H Weisberg (1984) *The Failure of the Word: The Protagonist as Lawyer in Modern Fiction*, Yale University Press.
Jonathan M Wender (2008) *Policing and the Poetics of Everyday Life*, University of Illinois Press.
James Boyd White (1985) *The Legal Imagination: Abridged Edition*, University of Chicago Press.
Melanie Williams (2002) *Empty Justice: One Hundred Years of Law, Literature, and Philosophy*, Routledge-Cavendish.
David N Wright (2014) 'Comics Are the New Everyday Aesthetic and Socio-Cultural Paradigm' in E Priego and DN Wright (eds) *The Multimodality of Comics in Everyday Life*, MediaCommons.
Alison Young (2005) *Judging the Image: Art, Value, Law*, Routledge.
Alison Young (2014) *Street Art, Public City*, Routledge.

Chapter 2

A ghostless machine

> In order to understand anything it is necessary to kill it, to lay it out rigid in the mind.[1]

A cultural legal aesthetics focuses attention on the form of law and legal knowledge. It constructs law in relation to conscious and unconscious dimensions, with the order of reason and text roughly mapping onto conscious legality and the fluid, visual, sensory, and aesthetic onto law's unconscious. As we saw in the previous chapter, the multimodal quality of comics can help in navigating the boundaries and relations between such orders of legal knowing. As a first step, and taking the question of personhood as its focus, this chapter elaborates the idea of a rational-textual conscious legality, and its denial and repression of anything beyond its limits. The picture described is one of a 'ghostless machine' – a rational structure that, in its stasis as rational, is unable to perceive, capture, represent, or fully encode the meaningful human world or the vast complexity of the universe. This is not an unfamiliar idea, but we need to set out this ground, conceptualised as a legal consciousness, in order to explore the movement beyond its limits, into its unconscious. This is the movement that the following chapters undertake, and that comics critically enables.

The chapter proceeds in two main sections. The first focuses most directly on the legal person, through engagement with the problem of human–machine integration and its implications for legal understandings of personhood, while the second explores the epistemological connotations of a discipline that frames the human in purely rational terms. The first half of the chapter sets out the technologisation of our contemporary world that challenges the boundaries of the living human – a challenge quintessentially depicted in the classic manga work *The Ghost in the Shell* – which raises problems for the legal person that may be derived from it, before moving to consider the way *The Ghost in the Shell* brings forth the notion of an *anima* that constitutes the boundaries of life from an epistemological unconscious beyond understanding. The second half of the chapter then opens by introducing the character of Dr Manhattan from *Watchmen* in order to explore a

1 Unamuno (1954), p 90.

hyperbolic rational framing of knowledge that represses the uncertainty of the self, imagining the universe as a purely rational system in order to maintain a solid and knowable boundary around the legal subject. The chapter's final section then draws from Dr Manhattan the concept of a 'rational surface' of knowledge that represses other ways of knowing, ultimately highlighting the way in which a rational frame gives rise to a legal order that is problematically unable to encounter anything beyond that frame. Having elaborated this deliberately limited vision of law as a 'ghostless machine', the work of cultural legal aesthetics will then proceed as subsequent chapters become free to navigate and deny its boundaries, facilitated by the mulitmodality of comics.

Cyborg aesthetics

Human/technology

To begin the navigation of un/conscious legality, this chapter takes law's conscious reliance on the primacy of rational text to its logical extremes. It accordingly meditates on law as something shaped and limited by rational text, to the exclusion or repression of other (embodied, sensory, emotional, aesthetic) ways of knowing. In order to gain purchase on this idea, the concept of the person will be taken as a central example in law's structures of knowing – and one indicative of the high stakes involved in legal epistemology. Law conceptualises the individual through the idea of the legal person, but this is not a complete or unproblematic image. As we will see, due to the disciplinary focus or epistemological frame of conscious legality, only particular dimensions of the living universe become available to the structures of law – that is, become knowable. It is specifically to the problems faced in our contemporary world of increasing technologisation that my analysis is directed, in terms of delineating between person and property, between human and non-human. This is because the limits of the rational framing of legal knowledge – of law's rational surface – come into sharp relief as we navigate these uncertain boundaries.

Donna Haraway famously painted an intimate picture of the way developing science and technology and its suffusion throughout culture and society was breaking down traditional boundaries, including those between human and machine.[2] Since then technology and its use have become increasingly widespread, giving structure and articulation to late modern life.[3] Our already heightened 'sense of connection to our tools'[4] has become even more intimate. Mobile phones, for example, enable the expansion of our individual selves through the storage of personal data and augment our capacity for communication and integration with other similarly connected humans, and our interactions are

2 See Haraway (2000), notably pp 300–304, 313.

3 For more on the legal issues involved in the general increase in the technological nature of human life, see, for example, Goldsmith (2013); Moses (2007); Moses (2011).

4 Haraway (2000), p 313.

increasingly mediated through technological devices on a general level. Whereas, historically, simple mechanical devices such as pens enabled alternative means of human engagement, today our interactions are layered in a multifaceted range of communications protocols, from face-to-face interaction, telephone conversations, and video-conferencing, to texting, email, and instant messaging.[5] This has led in one respect to the sophisticated development and maintenance of virtual presentations of self in the form of visually and verbally captured experiences and information, collected in multimedia formats and made accessible and interactive via a multitude of social networking gateways – Facebook, Tumblr, Instagram, Twitter, to name but a few. Added to which is the increase in medical technologies, such as implants, prostheses, and hearing aids, that also embed our 'tools' more intimately into ourselves. The navigation of contemporary life, for many, thus involves not just the traditional sociocorporeal interactions of biologically limited human beings, but is blended with electronic data transfer and somatically integrated technology, and augmented by increasingly complex and sophisticated digital experiences.

This integration of the human and technological raises complex questions when it comes to delimiting the human and drawing the line between person and property.[6] The significance of this difficulty goes beyond our personal identities, and stems into what is arguably one of the most fundamental structures of legal knowledge. To a highly significant degree, law is a product of human activity and is applied by humans to other humans: if we are to develop and apply rules at all, we need to know who or what is the subject of those rules. What types of entity are included under law's protection and restraint? What entities should be included, and how should they be understood? And, of course, what is this 'we' that is able to develop all these rules in the first place?

Concerned with precisely these questions, Ngaire Naffine tackles legal personhood directly, invigorating our concern with the often unasked question: 'who is law for?'[7] She observes the tendency for strict legalists to dismiss the issue of personhood as 'a pure abstraction, a technical device within the great apparatus or machinery of law'.[8] Although the person may appear fluid within its various discursive, institutional, and material contexts,[9] the technical legal person is consciously delimited as the bearer of rights and duties, constituted purely by law for

5 For some thoughts on the shift from hard and quintessentially 'modern' technologies, such as the motor car, to the softer 'digital' technologies represented by mobile phones, see Tranter (2013).

6 To complicate the boundary further, there are also debates over whether one can have property in one's own (traditionally biological) body – that is, 'property in the person', or owning (parts of) oneself. See, for example, Quigley (2012); Richardson (2010). See also, for a general and critical genealogy of posthumanism, Herbrechter (2013), pp 31–73.

7 Naffine (2009).

8 Naffine (2009), pp 31–32.

9 See Travis (2015), pp 4–5

legal purposes.[10] This approach not only (deliberately[11]) overlooks broader philosophical, scientific, and religious debates on personhood, but ignores the real role that such 'extralegal' understandings play in legal determinations of what counts as a 'person' in law.[12] This denial is, of course, part of the way law produces its pragmatic certainty on this issue and thus enables the conscious 'machinery' of law to function; in the wider context of debates on personhood and the complexities of phenomenal life, law's person is a quintessential legal fiction: a *persona ficta*. But overlooking or denying the complex and multidisciplinary question of personhood more broadly that arguably underlies the *persona ficta* does not solve this crucial issue for law. Instead, it represses the question of personhood, and the humanity it arguably seeks to represent, as something outside the conscious legal order, outside the strictly legal person.

This division between the technical person of law – the *persona ficta* – and wider debates on personhood is encountered in biopolitical discourse. As Roberto Esposito notes:

> The concept of person functions as the crucial passage through which a biological material lacking in meaning becomes something intangible. Only a life that has crossed beforehand through the symbolic door of the person is believed to be sacred or is to be valued in terms of its qualities since only life is able to produce the proper credentials of a person.[13]

Esposito is talking here not just about a specifically legal person, but of a broader notion of personhood that covers membership of social and political life; what Kapica delineates as the 'natural' person that exists outside strictly legal categories,[14] but which is distinct from those beings or items that, as Esposito states, are just material lacking in meaning. And this notion of personhood is an example of a *dispositif* or apparatus – a concept derived from the work of Foucault that can be seen to correspond, as Agamben frames it, 'to a set of practices, bodies of knowledge, measures, and institutions that aim to manage, govern, control, and orient … the behaviors, gestures, and thoughts of human beings'.[15] As an apparatus, the category of 'person' comes to delineate the duality of the human between biological material and political appearance,[16] enabling the subject to be governed. Accordingly, as something that turns individuals into subjects, an

10 See generally Naffine (2009), Ch 3.
11 'The possession of any of these [physical, spiritual, or metaphysical] attributes would be extra-legal and so necessarily extraneous to any definition of law's person', Naffine (2009), p 34.
12 See Naffine (2009), Ch 4.
13 Esposito (2012), p 8.
14 See Kapica (2014), pp 615–617.
15 Agamben (2009), p 12.
16 See Esposito (2012), pp 20–22.

apparatus is 'a machine of governance'.[17] Indeed, whilst 'person' on one hand delineates membership of the human species, in a broad juristic sense it determines the position a being can take within the *nomos*.[18] Moreover, this entry into the normative order, as the connections between persona and theatrical masks indicate, is one of appearance – of a making visible of the human to public life.[19] The apparatus of the person is an optical one: 'To govern and to be governed is to be seen, to appear on stage, in the atrium or the forum, in public or private, as part of the political or economic scene'.[20] The tensions present in the way the category of person is delimited thus feed into the broader membership of the *nomos*, as well as the category of technical legal persons.[21]

In our contemporary technological contexts, this membership question rears up at the boundary between the biological and the technological that challenge understandings of the humanity that underlies questions of personhood. For Agamben, the apparatus is a disconcertingly broad category of technologies that subjectivate individuals to the forces of governance, made up of 'literally anything that has in some way the capacity to capture, orient, determine, intercept, model, control, or secure the gestures, behaviors, opinions, or discourses of living beings'.[22] His examples span not just state institutions but mobile phones, judicial measures, philosophy, and even language itself.[23] But if elements of our identities and experiences are becoming stored within or mediated through digital environments, if medical technologies are substituting our organs with engineered replacements, at what point could these technologies – which are all examples of subjectivating apparatuses for Agamben – start to become part of our human selves, and thus feed into understandings of the beings able to take their place in the normative or legal order? When does our connection to our tools, which Agamben says are most often tools of subjectivation, become so profound that they cease to be tools as such? That is, when does an apparatus, for instance a computer programme or robotic entity, become a being capable of subjectivation by some other apparatus as an individual?

This issue can be symbolised, as Donna Haraway argued, by the idea of the cyborg: a deeply unresolved being, the cyborg models complexity in a way that disrupts the attainment of monolithic, unitary understandings of personhood.

> The machine is not an *it* to be animated, worshipped and dominated. The machine is us, our processes, an aspect of our embodiment … There is no

17 Agamben (2009), p 20.
18 See Esposito (2012), pp 22–23.
19 See Goodrich (2012), notably pp 50–58.
20 Goodrich (2012), pp 56–57.
21 The question of the 'living human' and its relationship with the 'mask of persona' is encountered more directly in Chapter 5.
22 Agamben (2009), p 14.
23 See Agamben (2009), p 14.

> drive in cyborgs to produce total theory, but there is an intimate experience of boundaries, their construction and deconstruction.[24]

Wholeness is resisted by the cyborg; it is partial, fractured, divided. Haraway's analysis of our developing relationship with technology suggests that we lack unity and cohesion, and are made up of multiple, pluralistic dimensions; our various elements are still us, and machines are important parts of our embodiment and experience. Globally, human experience is now in large part shaped and mediated by code, binary number systems, and nexuses of algorithms; by operating systems, visual display units, and haptic feedback, not to mention the biomedical integration of artificial and bioengineered organs and prostheses into somatic humans. Amidst this complex and multiplying technological environment, this increasingly embedded development of technological apparatuses, classic understandings of our selves are threatened. We are emerging – 'becoming' – as a species in symbiosis with technology. The pluralistic challenges that the concept of the cyborg feeds into our streams of discourse are symbolic of this wider complexity. Accordingly, the cyborg models many of the issues in delineating the person in the face of a proliferation and integration of technologies. The complexity of the cyborg challenges the person as a unitary concept, opening up pluralistic understandings of life and identity.[25] Despite law's conscious assertions of certainty on such matters in terms of the technical legal person, the cyborg challenges our ability to distinguish between the broader 'human' person and mechanical beings traditionally devoid of such personhood. On a juridical level, this resolves to a blurring of person and meaningless matter – that is, more legalistically, of person and property, of what 'owns' and what can be 'owned'.

Science fiction is a significant discourse in the face of these posthuman challenges, being a vehicle for communicating, representing, and critiquing technoscientific advances,[26] and this remains true of science fiction comics.[27] Critically deploying the cyborg, a key example can be found in Shirow Masamune's *The Ghost in the Shell*[28] (hereafter, *Ghost*), which depicts complex challenges to the traditionally sealed idea of personhood in the context of advancing technology. An arguably foundational text in contemporary science fiction, its multiframe is populated with beings whose 'humanity' is unclear. The main protagonists are nearly all 'cyborgs', beings that, within *Ghost*'s diegesis, have been created from highly sophisticated technology but with a biohuman core – that is, a human brain

24 Haraway (2000), pp 315–316. Emphasis in original.
25 See Haraway (2000), notably pp 310–316.
26 Herbrechter (2013), pp 107–134. In a legal context, see Tranter (2011).
27 Harmon (2015).
28 Shirow (1995). Note that I will not be discussing any of the cinematic re-imaginings of Shirow's work, nor the sequel manga series that followed from *Ghost*'s popularity. My analysis focuses only on his original self-contained work. See Appendix A for an overview and details of this work.

and brainstem housed in a 'prosthetic body'.[29] It is worth noting, also, that these protagonists are law enforcement officers; in Shirow's future, legality has shifted alongside technology such that cyborgs are both agents and subjects of law.

The bodily self of Major Motoko Kusanagi, the main protagonist of *Ghost*, is predominantly depicted as human and she is graphically a being of flesh.[30] Although the engineering that creates Kusanagi's prosthetic body is so intricate and mimetic that her body appears organic, at times this 'humanity' is visually disrupted; for example, when Kusanagi's mechanical entrails are exposed (either through injury,[31] or somatic interfacing[32]) her robotic nature literally ruptures the seemingly human skin. Yet it is clear from the world of *Ghost* that Major Kusanagi and her cohort are alive: they are not mere 'lifeless' contraptions with no agency, such as a calculator or the AI 'bots common across *Ghost*'s diegesis. The physical bodies of these cyborgs are almost entirely mechanical, constructed from electronic devices and engineered materials. Yet it is these bodies that interact with the inhabited world – at least partly: these cyborgs are also able to directly interface with mechanical devices, communicate through networks, and infiltrate computer programmes as well as the minds/brains of others. They can patch into others' consciousnesses and 'brain dive' into other minds.[33] Whilst our current levels of integration may not be so sophisticated, like us the characters in *Ghost* inhabit a virtual as well as a physical world. In such an existence, the boundaries and limits of the person as a traditional biologically bounded human become profoundly unclear, on both a bodily and a conceptual level.

Yet such blurring of the biological human is not unique to technology: it can be seen in the phenomenon of procreation. Like *Ghost*, Christine Battersby's *The Phenomenal Woman*[34] deeply problematises the traditional boundaries of the living individual as simply coinciding with those of the physical body. Battersby observes that it is 'normal' to be a woman, and therefore normal (although far from essential) to give birth: to grow 'others' within oneself and birth those beings

29 Shirow (1995), pp 101–106. And, as all criminal lawyers know, a living brainstem is the quintessential sign of a living person in law: see *R v Malcherek and Steel* [1981] 1 WLR 960.

30 Although beyond the scope of this chapter, the gendered aspects of *Ghost* are significant. For instance, Kusanagi is often highly sexualised, and on occasion takes part in graphic sexual activity. Beyond questions of sexual objectification, such depiction gives a sensual dimension to her mechanical body, further problematising where her humanity ends and her mechanics begin (this chapter also puts aside the boundary between humans and animals: but see Naffine (2009), pp 119–142). For more on the sexualised treatment of Kusanagi's body across the *Ghost in the Shell* transmedia canon (that is, beyond the original *Ghost* itself, and beyond just Shirow's work), see the ten-part blog series on 'The Major's Body' starting with Napier (2014).

31 For example, Shirow (1995), p 224.

32 For example, Shirow (1995), p 278.

33 See, for example, Shirow (1995), p 18.

34 Battersby (1998).

as 'separate' individuals. Despite this, classic philosophies like those of Kant[35] hold that the phenomenal world is a product of our capacity to order sensory experience under concepts, and exists in dynamic tension with our selves that emerge as sharply delineated from the world we inhabit.[36] And concomitant with this self/other divide is Kant's distinction between our ability to experience ourselves via an 'inner sense', and the external world via an 'outer sense'. Our outer sense relies on the imposition of a spatial framework over sensory data, whilst inner sense is purely introspective and has no such spatial dimensions. The spatial limits of our bodies thus become the limits of our phenomenal selves and the body becomes a simple somatic container, housing the self.[37] Thus, Battersby argues, Kantian metaphysics is unable to conceive of internal bodily spaces – notably, the potential existence of another being within the womb.[38]

From this classical perspective, machines are not living humans: they are outside the body, and hence are not able to fall into the category of 'self'. But this Kantian perspective means that we are unable to think about internal bodily spaces – which may or may not be populated with technologies – let alone understand their metaphysical relationship with our selves or how they play into the notion of personhood, beyond assuming they are simply part of the human that personhood seeks to capture. Similarly, if aspects of ourselves are located outside the body – housed in or mediated through a virtual environment, for example – in Kant's metaphysics we also remain unable to 'think' these as part of the living human. Against the idea of the somatic container, and through her analysis of 'alternative' philosophies,[39] Battersby puts forward a model of the human self in a dynamic state of restless stability, patterned through a symbiotic flux with an interpenetrating otherness and in a constant state of becoming:[40]

> That which is the self's 'essence' or identity emerges through patterns of flow … Neither fully autonomous nor completely determined, the self is

35 Naffine also addresses Kant, in relation to the autonomous moral actor, such as that imagined as the person in dominant criminal responsibility discourse: see Naffine (2009), pp 59–79. On the tensions between this autonomous model and its lack of engagement with the living context of human conduct, see Giddens (2015a).

36 See Kant (1959); Kant (2000). See also Battersby (1998), pp 61–63. The Kantian concept of autonomy rests on this division, requiring us to be the source of our behaviour as rational beings rather than succumbing to the influences of the phenomenal world of the not-self: see Korsgaard (1998), notably pp xxviii–xxix.

37 See also Naffine (2009), pp 146–147

38 See Battersby (1998), pp 70–71, and, for her extended discussion on Kantian metaphysics when faced with the existence of women, Ch 4.

39 Notable amidst Battersby's 'alternatives' are Nietzsche's *Beyond Good and Evil* and *Thus Spoke Zarathustra*, where the self emerges as a collection of flowing energies – see Battersby (1998), pp 54–57 – and Kierkegaard's *Stages on Life's Way*, where the self is seen as emerging from interplay between past and present, self and other – see Battersby (1998), Chapter 8.

40 For Battersby's extended development of this model, see particularly Battersby (1998), Chs 9–10.

> produced relationally: in the resonance between self and other; in a 'present' that is a generative caesura between future and past.[41]

Although focused on the 'human' otherness represented by the foetus, such an analysis is useful for thinking about the problems of integrative technologies and AI, allowing us insight into the complex and shifting threshold between human and technology.

As Haraway asks, 'Why should our bodies end at the skin, or include at best other beings encapsulated by skin?'[42] Under Battersby's metaphysics of becoming, our bodies are not integrally or coincidentally our selves, nor are we static, unchanging beings. We are not only in a constant state of flux, but this flux is in a dynamic symbiosis with the external world. Like the engineered corporeal self of Major Kusanagi, humanity can be reconfigured through experience and interplay with the world 'outside'. Incorporating some machine or other into one's physical body, or developing aspects of oneself outside the body in a virtual environment, does not, in Battersby's model, necessarily undermine our selfhood or our ability to understand selfhood. Indeed, posthumanity can be seen 'as a process, as a "becoming human" in connection with an environment and non-human actors'.[43] Our new configuration can be patterned into our phenomenal experience of ourselves; the human self can (repeatedly) shift and adapt to new arrangements over time.

> On such a model, 'self' grows out of 'otherness', and 'sameness' is gradually patterned out of 'difference' … 'identities' are fluid and might be transformed – or dispersed or metamorphosed into new structures and propensities – as the configurations are subject to further historical change.[44]

It has been argued that the material a being is made from is irrelevant to whether that being is 'alive' or not.[45] Moreover, it may be the case that we need to abandon notions of humanisim altogether if we are to imagine a truly posthuman concept of personhood that does not re-embed the inequalities of patriarchy and anthropocentrism that would bias understandings in favour of the biologically human male.[46] As we have seen, Battersby's model gives an open and inclusive approach to posthuman selfhood, permitting multiple (re)configurations of

41 Battersby (1998), p 184.
42 Haraway (2000), p 314.
43 Herbrechter (2013), p 206.
44 Battersby (1998), p 209.
45 Susan Stuart, for example, argues that a phenomenal experience or 'sense' of an agent's embodied situation 'in the world' is necessary for true consciousness, due to the need for sensory data to be meaningfully differentiated for the mechanism to function as a decision-making agent, regardless of the material physically constituting that agent: see Stuart (2010).
46 See Kapica (2014).

humanity over time beyond traditional flesh. In this way, the limits of the biologically limited person can be accepted as changing and uncertain, and the human/technology threshold as permeable.

Ghosts and shells

Entry into personhood arguably renders material immaterial, thereby mediating spirit and flesh.[47] There is thus more to the human/technology threshold than the physical aspects of the body. Whilst on one level it is the incorporation of key biologically human parts (that is, brain and brainstem[48]) that maintains Kusanagi's humanity, more significantly this humanity is grounded by the eponymous phenomenon known as the 'ghost'. On one level, the ghost is a clear metaphor for the human soul: the ineffable 'something' that brings life. The permeability of human and machine, indicated in the previous section, arguably makes defining the 'human' in any concrete way impossible without relying on such a 'something'.

The concept of the ghost is distinct from the self's essence in Battersby's metaphysics of becoming: while Battersby's metaphysics involves a constantly shifting 'essence', something that is patterned over time through our complex, living interaction with the world of otherness, the 'ghost' represents a stable human core sealed off from the outside. The ghost is encoded into the mind of the cyborg, existing within the mechanical shell of the engineered body, animating it as a living entity. It is what separates a mere tool from a living being, a robot from a cyborg – apparatus from subjectivated individual – in the world of *Ghost*. Again connecting with the idea of the soul, in this instance as the source of the will, the ghost is seen as the seat of criminal responsibility.[49] And, as one character states whilst observing the lack of humanity of merely AI machines – machines with no 'soul' – there is '[s]omething sad about these ghostless 'bots ...'.[50] This 'ghost' is housed within software and hardware architecture, sealed away and protected by layers of security protocols. The ghost is not coincidental with the body or 'shell' in the manner of the somatic container; rather, it is portrayed as the essence of the living human, a metaphor for the soul that maintains a being's lifehood – even in the face of radical physiological reconfiguration and the

47 In Esposito's understanding, at least: see Esposito (2012), p 18; Goodrich (2012), p 58. For Agamben, the person signals a site of relentless struggle between the human and the subjectivating forces of an apparatus: see Agamben (2009), p 14; Goodrich (2012), p 58.

48 The importance of the brainstem in identifying humanity is also implied in law's definition of the end of life, which occurs with the death of the brainstem: see, in a zombie context, Travis (2015), p 6.

49 Whilst reporting on a cyborg's criminal activity, a newscaster states that 'an investigation will ... determine whether this crime was committed by his [the suspect's] ghost, or ... was a mechanical malfunction': Shirow (1995), p 146.

50 Shirow (1995), p 36.

complex interfacing of consciousness with other beings and devices. It is not a shifting essence, as Battersby's metaphysics would have it, but a static core within a shifting architecture of being.

A key character in *Ghost* is the Puppeteer. He is a being that was 'spontaneously created from the sea of information',[51] thereby becoming 'a self-aware life-form – a ghost'[52] with life beyond its original AI programming. When the Puppeteer appears, demonstrating the existence of a disembodied ghost with no somatic or biological referent, *Ghost*'s narrative delves into the question of what animates the ghost. It is this movement – to query the nature of the soul, and thereby raise ongoing philosophical difficulties in what makes something alive – that stands *Ghost* out as a critical work in posthuman science fiction. It moves beyond and without the physical or embodied contexts of the ghost as if, perhaps, 'life' and 'body' are Cartesian in their separability.[53] However, the ultimate blending of the Puppeteer and the Major makes it clear that such essential dualisms do not hold, and that the ghost – the soul or *anima* – remains ineffable.

The interaction between Major Kusanagi and the Puppeteer, and their eventual blending, takes place in a virtual environment that is articulated through visualisations of their selves and the networks that constitute them (accompanied by verbal narration and speech).[54] The true nature of life is described by the Puppeteer as he transcends his physical form: 'And in me, a giant network that includes me… / …is now connected to me'; he continues: '[w]e are part of it… / …our collective totality'.[55] *Ghost* thus imagines our place in the universe as part of a vast and immanent network. Our selves are complex networks of systems into which we are integrated; brain, heart, memories, thoughts, lungs; these are all parts of our individual networks – integrated and layered articulations of our mechanical selves. But 'we' are also elements in the Puppeteer's universal network. Our 'selves' are connected into this vast nexus, both separate and integrated; we are more than our connected parts, but our connected parts are all (interconnected and integrated) elements of our selves. Our bodies, memories, thoughts, hopes – each is merely one dimension of our complex selves, a self of becoming that can be reconfigured and, in Battersby's less immediate terms, patterned over time. As the Puppeteer's speech explains, we are integrated as a 'collective totality' into a universal network much larger than ourselves, a network of otherness that produces us. The comics form helps to elaborate the epistemological implications of this complex integrated network. The Puppeteer's limited

51 Shirow (1995), p 249.

52 Shirow (1995), p 248.

53 And also, perhaps, gendered: the Puppeteer, despite having no prior physical form, and at times inhabiting corporeally female robots, is still overtly referred to as 'male'.

54 See generally Shirow (1995), pp 266–277.

55 Shirow (1995), pp 276–277. A note on quotations from comics. It is common practice for text in comics to be split or to continue between multiple text boxes or speech bubbles. In order to reflect something of this arrangement, I will use a '/' across this book to denote where a quotation involves such a transition.

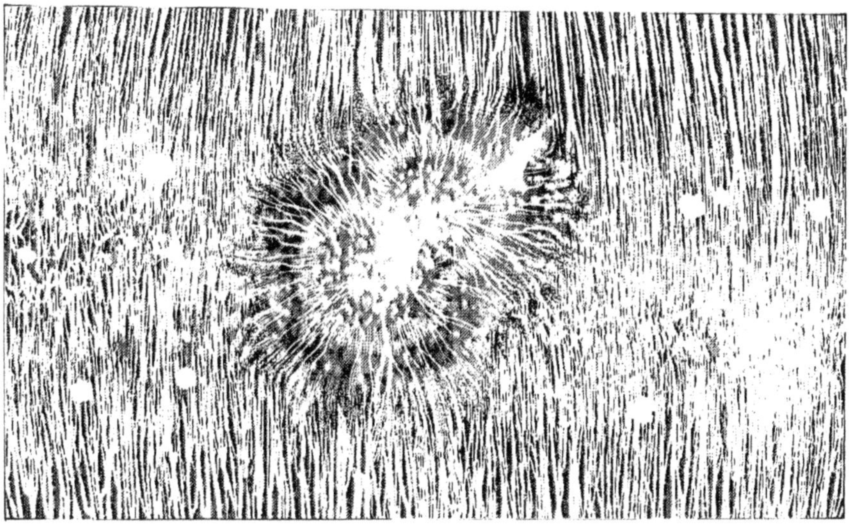

Figure 2.1 Shirow (1991), p 344 © 1991 Shirow Masamune/KODANSHA LTD. Reproduced with permission.

linguistic descriptions sit next to the multiple intricate visual elaborations, thereby highlighting the challenges inherent in conceptualising the complexity of the universe in text alone. The visual-verbal is also indicative of the lack of unity in the cyborg, thus indicating that the universe is fragmented and connected, like the separate-yet-integrated elements of the multiframe discussed in Chapter 1. The relationship between the elements of text, symbol, image, panel, sequence, and page in the multiframe of *Ghost* itself, thus come to represent the wider universal system that makes up existence for Shirow. As part of this larger system, what we think of as living beings become 'fruit' on the bifurcating branches of an infinitely complex and interconnected universal structure[56] (part of this universal network is represented in Figure 2.1).

Ghost's integrated systems model has overt similarities to Battersby's metaphysics of becoming, tracing the connections between the 'static' core of the living human and the wider complexity of the universal system, but in the action of *Ghost*'s fast-paced interactions it destabilises the boundaries between them more radically than Battersby's gentle patterning. The unsettling connotation of this intricate and immanently accessible universal connectivity is represented in *Ghost*'s dénouement, the crux of which can be found in Figure 2.2. Here we see Kusanagi and the Puppeteer merging, their ghosts combining into a single being (the same event, as it happens, seen in Figure 2.1 from the perspective of the universal network). The one element of Shirow's cyborgs that approached the status of essence (whether static or not) is violated, ruptured, challenged. The new combined being

56 See Shirow (1995), pp 337–338.

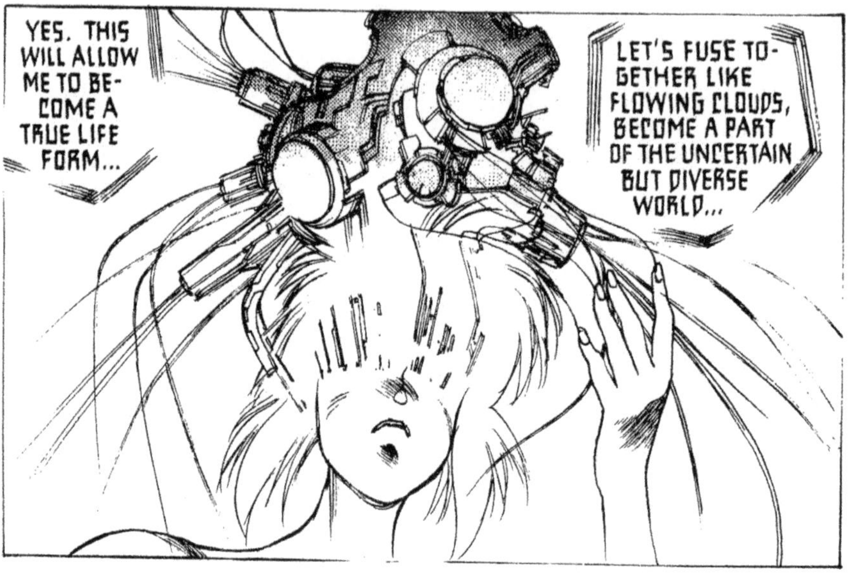

Figure 2.2 Shirow (1991), p 344 © 1991 Shirow Masamune/KODANSHA LTD. Reproduced with permission.

that emerges is not a hybrid, not a multiple personality, but a single being. It is Kusanagi's and the Puppeteer's life forces, their ghosts, that merge – not their multiple and complex personal systems. The result is a 'new' cyborg of somewhat uncertain identity, neither Kusanagi nor Puppeteer nor a simple combination of the two. The fact this new being has to be integrated into a new prosthetic body highlights the change; the fact the gender of this new body is unclear serves to foreground the uncertainty of the new being's identity in relation to traditional categories of being.[57]

The visual depiction in Figure 2.2 highlights the seemingly obvious difference between the mechanical and the organic, with the Puppeteer's form being mostly constituted by angled, technical, and mechanical lines, and Kusanagi by flowing, organic ones. The Puppeteer's claim that fusing with the 'human' Kusanagi will enable him to become a 'true life-form' initially seems to confirm this opposition (that organic means life, whilst mechanical does not). Yet this is at odds with the generally expansive understanding of lifehood throughout *Ghost*. This claim derives from the Puppeteer's loss of significant aspects of himself earlier in the narrative. When Kusanagi first interacts with the Puppeteer, large swathes of his personal network (or self) are lost. As he notes during that experience, 'The totality of my "self" is being radically simplified, but for some reason my true self

57 See Shirow (1995), p 346. Compare to n 53: Kusanagi is presented as female; the Puppeteer as male.

is not changing'.[58] This event undermines the Puppeteer's capacity to sustain his existence as a stable being, removing any 'slack' or 'play' in his system that would give him 'protection against catastrophe',[59] but without destroying his ghostly lifehood. It is by merging with Motoko Kusanagi, a fully complex and diverse being, that the Puppeteer hopes to overcome this problem – and thus become a 'true life-form'. His aim is to break out of his limited unitary mode of being, and to connect into the universal network. True life, on this reading, is not organic so much as wildly complex and adaptable, changeable. As the Puppeteer summarises, 'humans are always changing, and I want to be able to change too'.[60]

Although, as already noted, there is some debate over the necessity for a living being to be in some way 'organic',[61] *Ghost* demonstrates an inclusive concept of human life that goes beyond any requirement of biology – a ghost is more important than what houses it when it comes to lifehood. As Kusanagi muses, 'Sometimes I wonder if … what I think of as "me" isn't really just an artificial personality comprised of a prosthetic body and a cyberbrain'.[62] On the same page, it is expressly suggested that if a machine were made that was so close to human as to be indistinguishable, it would cease to be a 'robot' but would be 'human', and thus worthy of treatment as a human; even the phrase 'don't discriminate against robots' is used.[63] There is also an undertone throughout *Ghost* of 'cyborg rights' and the ethics of how to treat cyborg beings as opposed to mere robots, protecting their rights in a similar way to how human rights are protected today.[64] Here we see a clear shift into the order of legal and political personhood – cyborgs are persons in *Ghost*.

As already seen, it is the existence of the ghost that makes something human, which on one level seems to represent a simple 'essentialist' argument about human nature[65] that resonates strongly with the notion of the human soul – that there is something deep within us that truly delineates the ultimate boundaries of the human and at the same time transcends the physical.[66] Putting aside theological questions around its existence, we can approach the soul as an aesthetic category or concept: that is, the soul can be understood as that which animates life

58 Shirow (1995), p 271.
59 Shirow (1995), p 341.
60 Shirow (1995), p 343.
61 See, for an example of organic essentialism, Kohler (2010), pp 44–49; cf the more capacity-focused view of Stuart (2010).
62 Shirow (1995), p 106. A cyberbrain is a mechanically engineered brain, as opposed to the biological ones typically used to create cyborgs.
63 See Shirow (1995), p 106.
64 See, for example, Shirow (1995), pp 94, 104, 140.
65 cf Naffine (2009), pp 99–118.
66 Indeed, there are strong the spiritual overtones in the concept of the ghost: see Shirow (1995), p 277. And for discussion of religious approaches to personhood and the sanctity of life in general, see Naffine (2009), pp 99–198.

from beyond – as an *anima*.[67] It is the source of movement, 'an agent, or almost an artisan, in the sense that it acts through instruments by means of its own power'.[68] As Peter Goodrich notes of Cormenius's visual representation of the human soul – or *anima hominus* – it is something before and beyond the texts of law, an image that cannot be reduced to text.[69] For Goodrich, the apparatus of the person is also 'a visuality that precedes and exceeds language',[70] instituting the living being into the theatrical order of legality. Indeed, in its connections with 'the beyond', this visuality mediates the divine and the material in the institution of the person, playing into the 'impossible unity' of the person that anchors the 'something' of the *anima* to the physical embodiment of an individual.[71]

The notion of the *anima* – especially in its associations with the soul – may seem to perpetuate an essentialist understanding of lifehood, albeit one that is supposedly unknowable. But this unknowability should not be downplayed: the *anima*, the 'something' of life, can be read as an aesthetics precisely because it signifies the limits of knowledge. It implies an inaccessible beyond or absolute otherness that thus gives shape to the forms of knowing we create and inhabit – a kind of epistemological unconscious. Indeed, encounters with material events can be seen to repress the ineffability of the beyond we cannot know, such that the influences behind conscious awareness that are not acknowledged and – in the specific context of brain science – the distance between computational processes and the experience of living subjectivity potentially vanish.[72] As Žižek states of cognitive models of human thinking modelled on computer programming: 'the very gap between understanding (the experience of meaning, of the openness of a world) and the "mute" functioning of a machine potentially disappears'.[73] Countering this lifeless materialism, the *anima* is the ineffable beyond that breathes life into the individual, that indefinable *something* that differentiates the living being from the world of supposedly 'mute' or 'dead' matter. Written down, *anima* becomes shorthand for something that is not an essentialism or a foundation, but a symbol of that which is outside the frame of language, of knowing, that is often sought or desired in the quest for the 'truth' – of the person, of life, of the world.

The 'ghost' of Shirow's work thus represents the instinctual desire to distinguish humans from machines without collapsing the two together, a collapse that would either rob our existence of meaning and value, or extend 'humanity' to

67 On the way 'life' specifically has behaved as something of a limit to philosophical attempts to define and conceptualise it, from Aristotle's *De Anima* onwards, see Thacker (2010).

68 Casini (2010), p 503.

69 Goodrich (2013), p 46.

70 Goodrich (2012), p 55.

71 Goodrich (2012), p 58. This is Goodrich's summary of Esposito's understanding of personhood that mediates between spirit and flesh, divine and biological. See Esposito (2012), pp 19–22.

72 See Žižek (2006), pp 146–199.

73 Žižek (2006), p 165.

problematically non-animate devices and objects. The instinct for this 'something' is brought into focus when the mechanical nature of the traditional human is exposed – its meaningless material made visible. The relationship between 'soul' as animating principle and 'body' as physical human self may appear to be complicated by the cyborg, which is not the simple biological body considered in traditional discourses on the soul.[74] But the body, even in its purely organic state, can be considered as a mechanical system: the fleshly human can be reduced to a large extent to its physical functions, its electrochemical processes – a complex of valves and pressures and articulation points, of forces and flows and circuitry, of the physical, biochemical encoding of sensory data. And if it is to be more than mere machine, mere property, the human body must be articulated and 'brought to life' by something – by the *anima* that remains irreducible to knowledge, the ghost that might inhabit[75] the biomechanical shell of both human and cyborg alike.

But the visual distinction between organic and mechanical in Figure 2.2 highlights the radical uncertainty and fluidity of *Ghost*'s engagement with selfhood. Indeed, it is precisely this 'certain' distinction that the work profoundly undermines, and by juxtaposing the visual depiction of a clear difference between human and technology with an event where that difference is completely broken down, Figure 2.2 foregrounds the blurring of the human/technology threshold. Through *Ghost* we see a fluid self, a concept of life that is deeply unsure, with no certain boundary or essence, that ruptures any settled concept of personhood or technical legal personality derived from it. The work moves from a seemingly solid concept of the ghost – protected and sealed off, a static essence of humanity – to an expansive breaking down of life's boundaries as the unconscious uncertainty of the universe breaks through. Traversing this narrative, a concept of life emerges that is able to be deeply reconfigured, that is an intricate and restless blend of organic and technological. Although 'ghosts' may delineate lifehood as an ineffable soul of humanity, ultimately they retain an intractable and unconscious instability, making it wholly unclear where our own systems end and 'other' systems begin. The ghost is not a shifting essence, but an acceptance that life itself cannot be codified – that there is no 'essence', no sacred core, not even an unstable one, that can be obtained or described. Even ghosts can be taken apart and manipulated, reorganised and reconfigured, the same as a biological or mechanical body, with any essence remaining elusive. By diving into the ghost in

74 See, for example, Casini (2010).

75 The nature of this 'inhabiting' may be one of coincidence or of separateness, and is an issue that traditional discourses on the soul and its relationship with the body have examined at length: see Casini (2010). In our present context, if the ghost is separate from the shell (as Shirow's conception seems to suggest) the physical object that carries or is animated by that ghost becomes irrelevant when delimiting human lifehood – it is the ghost that is human, not the somatic container. But if the various parts of the human system are all necessarily 'enghosted', the question of humanity in the face of the cyborg becomes one of which elements in the integrated universal system are enghosted and which are not.

order to explore its nature and conceptualise its truth, we do not find answers – but mysteries. The *anima* slips away beyond grasp as the ghost dissipates back along the bifurcated pathways of the universal network that constitutes it: an uncertainty, a flowing cloud in the diverse system of the universe.

Disciplinary aesthetics

Regulating the ghost

The limits and capacities of the 'normal' human, as Nikolas Rose has argued, come to be defined in relation to available technology.[76] Indeed, technology can be seen to shape the very contours between life and death.[77] The sophisticated hybrid beings integrated into the multiframe of *Ghost* may not yet exist in our contemporary reality, but this speculative concept is symbolic of many of the complex interactions of human and technology that are taking place today. The unresolved meeting of human and machine in the concept of the cyborg symbolises our developing reliance upon technology in many contexts, and the concomitant shifting of the human/technology threshold. *Ghost*'s intricate navigation of this threshold suggests, like Rose, that as new forms of technology and new disciplinary techniques develop, so the apparatus of personhood will also develop as it responds to shifts in the categories of human and technology. *Ghost* highlights that this development will move beyond any traditionally stable categories of being: the ghost may signify the 'something' of the *anima*, but if this core can merge and reconfigure as thoroughly as bodies, this does not give us any stable understanding of when something is a living being. Rather, it affirms the fact that such neat concepts are not available – that the *anima* signals the unknowable, an epistemological unconscious. *Ghost* thus suggests that as science and technology develop increasingly sophisticated ways of mimicking and mediating life, of repairing or augmenting human capacities, as the boundaries of knowledge are pushed back and more of the secrets of somatic life are revealed to us – the more difficult defining that life will become.

The other side, of course, is that as knowledge of the human/machine increases, it becomes increasingly subjectivated by the disciplinary gaze of the apparatus. In *Discipline and Punish*, Michel Foucault described the processes by which the self becomes a subject of a certain regime of knowing. Indeed, such a concern is a large part of Foucault's thinking, which examines the processes by which particular

76 He argues that the technologies surrounding our somatic biology (medicine, genetics, biotechnology, psychiatry) have become increasingly 'molecular' and detailed – drugs, microscopes, x-rays, brain mapping, genes. These technologies have a normalising force, intervening and manipulating the self towards an ideal 'healthy' sate, such that what is 'normal' becomes shaped in terms of the technologies available and we are judged somatically good or bad – broken or healthy – in relation to what technology can do to us. See Rose (2001).

77 See Cooper (2002), p 88.

disciplines of human understanding are able to construct or create knowledge about the individual. As part of his general concern with examining how the individual becomes a subject (of knowledge, of categories, of themselves),[78] *Discipline and Punish* examines the processes and mechanisms of power that subject individuals to socioscientific penal knowledges (criminology, psychology, penology),[79] focusing on the development of detailed techniques of power that enable the knowledges of the self to be applied to the normalisation or 'discipline' of the individual who does not conform.[80] This is essentially the operation of the apparatus, whereby bodies of knowledge come to control human beings.[81] Foucault explores the shifts from the eighteenth century onwards, showing how certain public institutions arose[82] – not simply in terms of identifying specific causes, but by unpacking the sociocultural settings and epistemological underpinnings of which modern institutional forms are symptomatic.[83] Although not Foucault's direct concern, the disciplinary constitution of the legal subject can be understood through a Foucaultian frame. Indeed, Goodrich notes how Foucault's analysis traces the shifts in the theatrical appearance of the person:

> The apparatus is the mechanism or device by which the theatrical appears in the person of the player. In an older language, the apparatus is the scaffold; the public staging of the spectacle of judgment, of execution, whose visibility, now as then, is the most charged of the dimensions of law's application. But the scaffold is simply the extreme and modernity learned, as Foucault so well elaborated in terms of the disciplinary, that internal images and self-governance, the apparatus of the person *tout court* were likely to be far more effective – functional – mechanisms of governance than more direct expressions of repressive power.[84]

Following this shift, power no longer exists in modern society as something to be attained and wielded; Foucault argues that we have shifted from a top-down model of sovereignty to a power that is exercised via a net-like organisation of interrelationships, through which individuals flow as targets and elements of its

78 See Foucault (1982), pp 777–778.
79 *Discipline and Punish*, as Foucault tells us, is focused on our subjectivation to knowledge and the associated processes and practices of normalisation, while his later work tackles more directly the question of the ethical relation to the self: see Foucault (1997).
80 For Foucault, disciplinary techniques of power involve a focus upon the body and the organisation of its movements – a political technology of the body – that renders that body 'docile', enabling it to be 'subjected, used, transformed and improved': Foucault (1977), p 136.
81 Note, for example, Agamben (2009), p 12.
82 Foucault (1977).
83 Hunt and Wickham (1994), p 6.
84 Goodrich (2012), p 56.

articulation.[85] Indeed, the increasing integration of human and technology – being and apparatus – arguably helps to indicate the continuation of this movement. Individuals become hybrids, cyborg beings of living individuals and the machines of subjectivation. Historically, over the eighteenth and nineteenth centuries Foucault observed a general permeation of modern society with the disciplinary ethos of subjectivation and normalisation,[86] with institutions from the factory, to the school, to the hospital, employing the increasingly detailed techniques of power (grades, shift-work, regulation of class length, medical files) to subjectivate the individual.[87] Within this broader structure, the legal institution can be seen as part of the disciplinisation of human life, with law taking a privileged position in society in relation to the knowledge it produces:

> Not only do the procedures of law (trial, cross-examination, etc.) provide authorised means by which the truth is discovered, but once enunciated law provides the guarantee of this truth ... Indeed in modernity law, along with science, provides the privileged source of truth.[88]

This connection between law and science – as providers of an authorised version of the world – is important in terms of unpacking conscious law's rational reification of the subject.

In order to expand more on the rational apparatus of law, and its implications for understandings of life and the human, another classic comics work will be encountered; namely, Alan Moore and Dave Gibbons's *Watchmen*.[89] The reasons for analysing this work alongside *Ghost* are not immediately apparent. My focus in the second half of this chapter is on the rational apparatus, on the way the universe is reified into rational-textual forms and the problems this entails in relation to legal knowledge. A key example of such rational reification and its perils can clearly be read through the character of Dr Manhattan, and this is why *Watchmen* is now introduced into the analysis. *Watchmen* imagines an alternative 1980s US where 'masked vigilantes' (that is, people dressing in costume to fight crime, but who are not 'superpowered') are a real phenomenon that has become the source of much social tension. It is a dark and psychologically rich narrative, highly critical of the concept of the hero and widely discussed in both comics studies and

85 Foucault (1980), pp 97–98; Foucault (1982), p 788.
86 Foucault asks by what means power is exercised – see Foucault (1982), pp 785–786 – arguing that we should not start from the centre of power and try to discover its extremities, but rather we should begin with those extremities – the molecular, infinitesimal, everyday capillaries of power – and 'ascend' to see how power comes to be 'invested, colonised, utilised, involuted, transformed, displaced, extended etc., by ever more general mechanisms': Foucault (1980), p 99. Foucault thus analyses the micro operations of power across multiple disciplines, demonstrating the commonalities they share in the way disciplinary knowledge is constituted.
87 See, generally, Foucault (1977), pp 135–169. Note also Richardson (2009), p 36.
88 Hunt and Wickham (1994), pp 41–42.
89 Moore and Gibbons (1986). See Appendix A for an overview and details of this work.

wider popular culture.[90] But for my current purposes, as already noted, the focus will be on Dr Manhattan.[91] In particular, what is of interest is his vision of the universe as being, like the universe in *Ghost*, a complex system.

In *Watchmen*, Dr Manhattan is the only character who actually possesses superpowers. A victim of a scientific accident, physicist Jon Osterman is disintegrated but manages to piece himself back together. Through this process, he gains the ability to see all of time and space, predict the future,[92] and interact with the world on a subatomic level, manipulating particles and synthesising matter: he becomes Dr Manhattan.[93] Dr Manhattan's perspective is a radically materialist one, a hyperbolic scientification of the universe with troubling implications for personhood under the gaze of rational knowledge. For Dr Manhattan's knowledge is constituted only by the molecules, atoms, particles, forces, and trajectories found in scientific models, and thereby radically represses the fluid complexity of an unstructured universe. Dr Manhattan's rational universe, knowable in its completeness from his 'super' perspective, becomes a reified system of scientific laws akin to that of classical physics.[94] This universal machine is depicted symbolically in *Watchmen* as a system of giant cogs, a watch-like structure predictable in its progress.[95]

As an exercise in disciplinary constitution, the universal system of Dr Manhattan can be seen as a product of his specific perspectives. It has no outside; the universe

90 There are many dimensions to be explored within the intricate complexities that make up *Watchmen*, far from all of which will be encountered in this volume (although I do return to discuss Rorschach in Chapter 5). See *inter alia*, for examples of other analyses of *Watchmen*, Di Liddo (2009), pp 54–61 (on its intertextuality); Thomson (2005) (on its deconstruction of superhero tropes); Petty (2015) (on the way it implicates the reader in violence).

91 Alongside Dr Manhattan (Jon Osterman), the main characters of *Watchmen* are Rorschach (Walter Kovacs), Nite Owl (Dan Drieberg), Silk Spectre (Laurie Juspeczyk), The Comedian (Edward Blake), and Ozymandias (Adrian Veidt), and are supported by a host of minor masked hero characters. Working in the context of justice, but variably outside the official system, all of these characters encounter issues of sovereignty and state monopolies on violence. These are important issues in the legal study of superheroes, and have been discussed elsewhere. See, for example, Bainbridge (2015); Curtis (2016); Giddens (2015b); Sharp (2012); Spanakos (2014).

92 For more on how *Watchmen* engages with this issue in relation to debates around free will and determinism, see Ward (2009).

93 Dr Manhattan is so named for the obvious connotations it has for US enemies in relation to the Manhattan project. Indeed, Dr Manhattan spends much of his narrative – despite his awesome powers – being generally manipulated by government agents to perpetuate and protect state interests: he is deployed in warzones and used in weapons demonstrations, for example.

94 On the deterministic universe of classical physics, see Hodgson (2002), p 85.

95 See, for example, Moore and Gibbons (1986), Ch 9 p 5. Note that *Watchmen* was originally published in 12 instalments, which were collected as a single 'graphic novel' in the 1986 edition. Each chapter is paginated independently, hence my use of the form 'Ch 9 p 5' for pinpoint citations, which refers to page 5 of Chapter (or issue) 9 of the work.

is not a system in and open to an environment, as might be seen in systems theory[96] – the world human systems operate within is part of the universal system, integrated, connected, as in *Ghost*'s transcendental network. But Dr Manhattan's universe is a colder, deader place than Shirow's, being constituted in purely scientific terms as objectively knowable and predetermined. As already noted, law borrows heavily from science in its reification of the world into an objective reality to be known in completeness.[97] And conscious legal knowledges, due to law's status as a source of moral and regulatory answers, play an important role in constituting the subject – in subjectivating the individual to this rational-scientific apparatus.

In doing so, they present their picture of the subject as complete, even when the human self can be seen to be much more than what the frame of the legal subject, or even personhood, might contain – but these excesses are repressed, forming an unconscious. For example, in criminal law understandings of the legal person are produced through a particular theoretical and epistemological lens – a particular disciplinary gaze – that presumes a certain kind of rational capacity for choice and autonomy, despite such concepts not necessarily reflecting the complexity of human conduct.[98] Moreover, as Goodrich notes, the legal subject only gains life in law (i.e. legal personhood) through its codification in legal texts; one cannot come before the law as pure ego, but must be *named*.[99] And this encoding of the human into the symbolic order of law enacts a simulation: the legal order is read as if it is real, a universal totality like that of Dr Manhattan. And within law's virtual world, the fictional legal person speaks and is heard as if they are a full, living human.[100] This disciplinary subject is a fiction – a *persona ficta* – but the texts of law institute life '*as if* it were the universal and inextinguishable order of existence'.[101] Conscious law is, within itself, a universal system – complete and total. And with such a totalisation the apparatus becomes secured, thereby dehumanising the subject: 'once the mask is made safe, it doesn't matter what happens to the face on which it rests'.[102] Like the ideal world of conscious law, then, Dr Manhattan's is a totalised universe of measured order and logic; a product of a specific disciplinary power and perspective, constituting itself within its own limits.

This constitution of an ordered universe by law can be found in *Ghost*, the diegetic world of which is not without regulation – it has its own disciplinary legal

96 See Herbrechter (2013), p 201.

97 See also, for example, Farmer (2010); and also note the authority law derives from its adherence to scientific rationalism: Sherwin (2011), pp 21–22.

98 See Giddens (2015a); Naffine (2009), pp 59–79.

99 Goodrich (1990), pp 281–282. 'The entry of the individual into the symbolic, the transition from zero to one, from lack to identity, is the condition of institutional existence, the capture of the subject by law': Goodrich (1990), p 282.

100 Goodrich (1990), pp 283–285.

101 Goodrich (1990), p 284.

102 Esposito (2012), p 30.

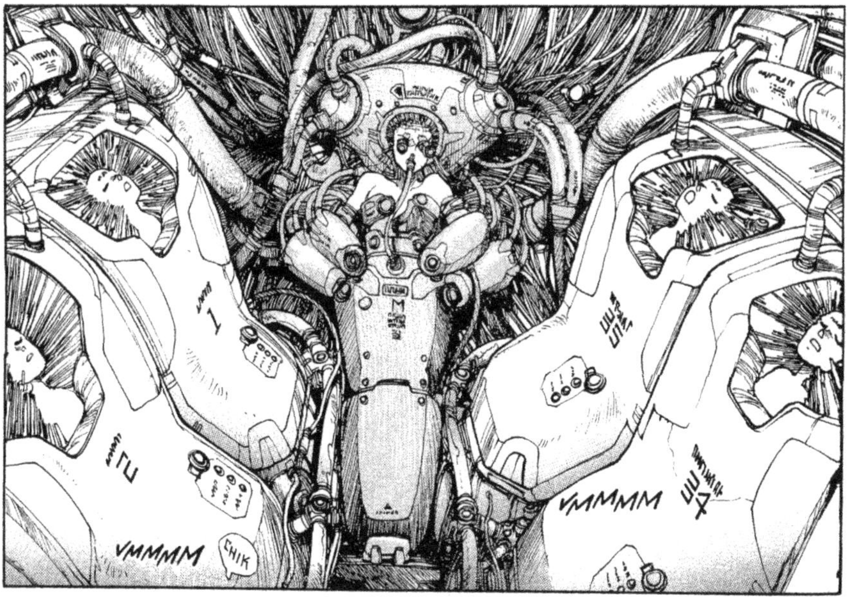

Figure 2.3 Shirow (1991), p 138 © 1991 Shirow Masamune/KODANSHA LTD. Reproduced with permission.

subject. There are references throughout *Ghost* to various rules and regulations pertaining to ghosts and cybernetic technology, including, as already mentioned, 'cyberbrain ethics' – but also the need for 'ghost keys' and heavy security to protect people's core identities from infiltration and injury. One major example is the prohibition on 'ghost dubbing'. Like most of *Ghost*'s diegetic regulation, this is only referred to in passing. Ghost dubbing involves making copies of a cybernetic individual, and can be seen taking place in Figure 2.3. The ghost dubbing process explicitly demonstrates both the replicability and mechanical permeability of the self in the world of *Ghost*. All the beings present in Figure 2.3 are radically integrated into their mechanical surroundings, the central 'original' particularly so. But the point is not just that the bodies of these beings are integrated into mechanical devices and circuitry – their systems are fully interlinked: the memories and capacities of the one are being transferred and imprinted into the other; the ghost, the defining life-force of the one being duplicated, mapped, and 'dubbed' into the replicant software and hardware architecture of the other. The one literally becoming the other.

Just like the merging of two living ('ghostly') beings into a new, single being (as highlighted by Figure 2.1 and Figure 2.2), ghost dubbing challenges not only the stability of self, but also the uniqueness of individuals. Indeed, the ghost dubbing system, in all its intricacies and complexes, its subroutines and automations, represents the core problematics of cyborg life in the context of retaining or understanding traditional notions of humanity in the face of advancing technology. Such activities clearly undermine the very notion of an individual, of a unique being or self. WJT Mitchell notes how the idea of biocybernetic reproduction or copying results in the loss of the 'aura' or 'breath' of the original[103] – the 'something' of its lifehood. Humans thus become replicable, able to be formatted, wiped, copied, reprogrammed – like a machine. The posthuman problem is not just that machines may take on human life and by extension, via the *persona ficta*, legal rights and duties, but that humans could also at the same time be said to be machines. Despite disciplinary technologies potentially enabling different visions of what 'the human' might be, if we develop machines so complex that they become defined as human, they may also still remain machines since they were developed as such – being products of particular scientific and engineering knowledges. Accordingly, those factors that were traditionally 'human' become simply products of mechanical systems, and perhaps worthy of only the same respect and value as those systems: as property.[104] Of similar concern, humans may also become apparatuses in themselves, subsumed into the mechanisms of governance for its own sake.[105]

Thus, beyond its complicating of the human/technology threshold and its expansive view of lifehood, perhaps the key jurisprudential lesson from *Ghost* is this: that legal regulation seeks to police the uncertainties of life that advancing technology exacerbates. Ghost dubbing may imagine the thick end of the wedge, but symbolically we can see in it the wider issues of our relationship(s) with technology, and the suggestion of a terrible fear at the heart of human–machine integration: that humans may be nothing more than machines, meaningless matter outside the juridical order. In one sense, *Ghost*'s diegetic regulation arguably shies away from the difficult end of the human question – that the work as a whole raises – in order to preserve a certain line between the living and the mechanical, between self and other, and thus also between subject and apparatus. The prohibition on ghost dubbing in *Ghost* thus tries to stop the blurring of living being and apparatus, and uses law to bring some degree of certainty to the boundaries of life. It thus also seeks to secure the mask of the person as safely as possible, maintaining the subjectivation of life under the apparatus of personhood – keeping us where it can see us.

103 See Mitchell (2005), pp 319–320.

104 Contemporarily, such concerns can be raised in relation to such biotechnologies as transplants, stem cells, and artificial organs. Transplants radically challenge any stable identification of self with body: see Lock (2002). Stem cells suggest the ability of technology to manipulate the physical body and create (organic) mechanisms that can be patched into existing personal systems: see Pearlman (2013). Whilst implanting mechanical parts into the human body effectively gives rise to a nascent biomechanical cyborg. In a different register, the notion of person-as-property also raises the question of slavery, which is beyond the scope of the current work.

105 Note Agamben (2009), p 11: an apparatus is 'a pure activity of governance devoid of any foundation in being'.

Following the strings

Through its speculation on the existence of cyborgs and concomitant confrontation of the posthuman question of human–machine integration, *The Ghost in the Shell* radically challenges the apparatus of the person. *Ghost* elaborates a deep unconscious fluidity to the human that concepts of the person, and the strictly legal person in particular, work to repress. In order to begin to unpack the conscious world-view of law, and thus contextualise the free movement of a cultural legal aesthetics, a direct consideration of the rational confines of legal knowledge – and the movement past them – is required.

On the level of the individual or self, as read above with Battersby and Haraway, the vision in *Ghost* is one of a fluidity that challenges the stasis or predictability that Dr Manhattan's universal system implies. With its movement to the ineffability of the *anima* – symbolised by the elusive, eponymous ghost – Shirow's manga opens up to an aesthetics of lifehood characterised by change, reconfiguration, and interaction. A shifting undercurrent over which disciplinary negotiations take place and produce the known or authorised world of the person. Such a vision of the self, particularly in its aesthetic dimension, brings us back to the work of Foucault. As Battersby explains:

> Delineating a self that is neither totally free, nor totally determined, the Foucaultian self … emerges together with its 'others' from intersecting force-fields of power. Foucault is thus useful for thinking the … self that gains its specificity as it remains in a continuous dynamic play of power with other bodies and other forces.[106]

For Foucault, the individual 'is not a fixed reality … but a historical, cultural and linguistic construction (or fiction)';[107] not a person but a subject: constituted through the complex interrelation of knowledge and power, and through our ethical relation to ourselves. But in his work on ethics, Foucault describes a conception of identity that focuses upon the 'aesthetics of existence', or the 'art of oneself'.[108] For Foucault, the human self is not stable and predetermined; it is a work of art:

> What strikes me is the fact that, in our society, art has become something that is related only to objects and not to individuals or to life. That art is something which is specialized, or done by experts who are artists. But couldn't everyone's life become a work of art? Why should the lamp or the house be an art object but not our life?[109]

106 Battersby (1998), p 206.
107 Huijer (1999), p 62.
108 Foucault (1997a), p 207.
109 Foucault (1997a), p 261.

Foucault himself delineates four interrelated ethical elements: the part of the self requiring attention; the way the self constructs itself in relation to some moral code; the ethical work or self-forming activity to be done; and the *telos* of development towards a particular (ethical) goal.[110] Foucault's ethics thus asks how the self understands itself, with the work done upon the self seen as part of an ongoing project of development. As Marli Huijer tells us:

> In Foucault's perspective, ethics is conceived of neither as a coherent set of moral prescriptions nor as a study of moral behaviours. Instead, he viewed ethics as an ethical attitude aimed at transforming the relationship with oneself into a work of art.[111]

This is a powerful, life-shaping force for Foucault: 'a very strong structure of existence, without any relation with the juridical power per se, with an authoritarian system, with a disciplinary structure'.[112] Like the radical fluidity that challenges clear notions of self in *Ghost*, Foucault's ethics thus forms a field of influence upon the self that is outside the apparatus, beyond processes of disciplinary subjectivation. Foucault's aesthetics of the self gives a fuller picture of the individual, with the self's ethical dimension allowing it to 'break free' from the deterministic view associated with disciplinary power/knowledge.

Although in tension with an individual's ability to shape themselves through self-work, Foucault's vision remains one whereby it is disciplinary power – framed in particular epistemic contexts – that gives rise to particular visions of the world. The aesthetics of the self shows a way in which the conscious rational framing of personhood might be challenged. But the more general point I am working at here is the idea that a rationally framed discipline will produce – indeed, can only see – a rational world; or will work towards such a world as an ideal, as it reduces and represses elements and dimensions that do not fit its frame. *Ghost* indicates quite clearly that things may be otherwise, that there may be 'something' outside the order of a rational apparatus, as signalled by the *anima*. With Dr Manhattan, meanwhile, Moore and Gibbons warn of reducing the universe to a knowable, rational system – a system that can only see through such a lens will not see human life as anything other than another quantifiable part of the universal system: a shell without an *anima*, a machine without a ghost.

Accordingly, what is at work in *Watchmen* and *Ghost* runs deeper than the conceptual limits of the human, to the nature of conceptualisation itself. At the same time, read as an aesthetics it also queries the form of knowledge, indicating a movement without the boundaries of the rational frame. Dr Manhattan claims that he is 'a puppet who can see the strings',[113] an assertion that has

110 Foucault (1997a), pp 263–265.
111 Huijer (1999), p 61. See also Golder and Fitzpatrick (2009), p 113.
112 Foucault (1997a), p 260.
113 Moore and Gibbons (1986), Ch 9 p 5.

epistemological significance beyond his ability to predict the future, and this epistemic quality links strongly with the Puppeteer in *Ghost* and back to the 'something' of the *anima*. A puppet, it can be said, is dead matter: an object devoid of life or any kind of human 'spark'. To be a puppet is not to be human, not just because a puppet lacks autonomy but because it has no *soul*. It is a dead machine, articulated but static, without an *anima* of its own – it is non-animate. As Scott Bukatman argues, to be alive is not simply to move but to be driven by one's own impetus.[114] As his analysis of synthetic life narratives indicates – from Frankenstein's monster, to Walter McCay's disobedient *Gertie the Dinosaur* (one of the earliest examples of animation), to Pinocchio's assertion of independence, to the runaway androids in *Blade Runner* – it is creations that misbehave that take on lifehood:[115] 'disobedience makes creations into something more than mere machines'.[116] It is the puppeteer, via connective strings, that breathes movement into the puppet and brings it to the illusion of life – but, as Bukatman claims, something is only itself alive once the strings have been cut. On one level this signals a shift to autonomy,[117] but we can also frame the soul, the ghost, as a kind of puppeteer that animates the machine of the human – one far more mysterious than the visible strings on the puppet. And so the severing of strings does not bring to life, so much as shift the source of animation to something unknowable – to other strings. Hence Dr Manhattan's claim to 'see the strings', not to remove them. Indeed, as Sousanis suggests, and as Manderson stated in relation to reification in Chapter 1, the task is not to remove or avoid the strings, but to recognise their inevitability.[118]

Framed in the context of a law grounded in rational text, as Jules Luis Vives recognised in the sixteenth century, it is not the dead matter of pen and ink that creates writing – but something else:

> That the soul is the principal agent means that although the instruments of the soul – the heat, humours and spirits – act on the body, they do not work by means of their own power but only through the power that they receive from the soul. The ink forms different letters and the pen writes them, but all this depends finally not on these instruments but on the writer.[119]

The Puppeteer in *Ghost* was created spontaneously from the deep complexity of the universal network, independent from any kind of physical birth or creation or the integration of biologically human elements. True to Bukatman's thesis, he disobeyed his AI programming in order to become a ghost – he became pure life,

114 See Bukatman (2012), pp 135–163.
115 Bukatman (2012), pp 136–137.
116 Bukatman (2012), p 146.
117 See Bukatman (2012), p 146.
118 See Sousanis (2015), p 135.
119 Casini (2010), p 503, expounding the work of Juan Luis Vives on the nature of the soul.

exceeding any disciplinary subjectivation. The animation of the Puppeteer can thus be read as a symbol of lifehood itself: pure ghost, unmediated by mechabiology, beyond any apparatus. He is the quintessential puppeteer – with a capital 'P'. He is that which brings life to the mechanical body, the 'divine' aspect of the 'impossible unity' of the person. To 'see the strings' is not only to recognise the inanimate nature of the puppet, but also to see beyond that inanimation to the vitality that brings it to life – to see past the boundaries of the ghostless machine to the Puppeteer, the unconscious order of the *anima*, that lies beyond.

In this way, Dr Manhattan's claim exposes a deep critique of rational knowledge that can be seen to permeate his whole vision of the universe just as it does conscious law. Articulated through *Watchmen*'s comics form, Dr Manhattan signifies the problematics of a rational surface of knowledge that fails to go beyond its own limits – that fails to follow where the strings lead and thus penetrate to the exterior of the rational apparatus, of the ghostless machine of reason and law. Dr Manhattan's radically positivist (and, admittedly, hyperbolic) view of the world denies the value in human life; it is a rationalisation of humanity that reifies it to shifting particles obeying predictable paths through time and space. He can only see one limited set of strings, and knows them in totality. But, as Žižek makes clear, material reality is in itself not everything because it cannot account for consciousness – there is always something more,[120] and this excess is repressed by the rational order of knowing. Dr Manhattan's is thus a universe where individuals have no *anima* to bring the predictable materiality of their molecular bodies to life; a universe of dead puppets. It is populated only by predictable systems of physical matter, and the molecular patterns of human life are too 'brief and mundane' within the vast and intricate mechanism of the universe to be of any value.[121]

Dr Manhattan expresses his rationalisations of the vast physical world in textual form. He describes a vast canyon on the surface of Mars, as he and fellow hero Laurie Juspeczyk are depicted floating above it in a vessel Dr Manhattan has synthesised from the sands of a Martian desert:

> It stretches more than three thousand miles, so that one end knows day while the other endures night. / Temperature differences breed shrieking winds that herd oceans of fog along a canyon four miles deep. / Does the human heart know chasms so abysmal?[122]

120 See Žižek (2006), p 168.
121 Moore and Gibbons (1986), Ch 9 pp 17–19.
122 Moore and Gibbons (1986), Ch 9 p 19. Sadly I was unable to secure permissions to reproduce the visual appearance of this example (or any example from *Watchmen*). I hope my textual descriptions will suffice for the purposes of articulating my argument, even though my argument is in part that such textualisations can never capture the excess of the visual.

Dr Manhattan's vision of the infinite beauty of the material universe explicitly rejects the capacity for the human to encounter or contain anything approaching the depth and variation of even just the Martian landscape. Presented as text embedded within an aesthetic field of analogue and irreducible visuality, the irony of his claims comes into focus. For his rational-textual frame not only cannot encounter the living experiences of humanity, but the vast chasm of the universe also only appears to him within a closed systemic encounter. The isolation of his view from the excess of the universe is emphasised in the stylisation of his speech bubbles, which contain his spoken text within double lines rather than the standard single line typical of most comics, emphatically sealing his text away from the uncertainty of the visual. This is further emphasised in the shrouded nature of the Martian landscape, which is only hinted at beneath flowing clouds that fill the canyon over which Laurie and Manhattan are flying.[123]

Despite his omniscient rationalism, there is one thing that Dr Manhattan finds fascinating within the mechanics of the universe: 'events with odds against so astronomical they're effectively *impossible*, like *oxygen* spontaneously becoming *gold*', what he calls '*thermodynamic miracles*'.[124] Like the behaviour of a human being, oxygen turning into gold is merely a shifting arrangement of particles, but it is such an incredibly rare pattern within the universal system that it becomes a scientific 'miracle' that even the radically rational Dr Manhattan yearns to witness. It is this longing for rare and unique events that forms the basis of Dr Manhattan's (re)consideration of inherent human value, as he explains to Juspeczyk in their discussion on the surface of Mars, considering the value of humanity's continued existence:[125]

> I long to observe such a thing [as a thermodynamic miracle]. And yet in each human coupling a thousand million sperm vie for a single egg. Multiply *those* odds by countless *generations* against the odds of your ancestors being *alive; meeting*; siring *this* precise son; *that* exact daughter... / ...Until your mother loves a man she has every reason to *hate*,[126] and of that union, of the thousand million children competing for fertilization, it was *you*, *only* you, that emerged. / To distil so *specific* a form from that chaos of *improbability*, like turning *air* into *gold*... / *That* is the crowning *unlikelihood*. / The thermodynamic *miracle*.[127]

123 Comparisons can of course be made here to Nietzsche's famous opening passage to 'On Truth and Lies in an Extra-Moral Sense', where the persistence of the universe beyond the (arrogant) knowledge of 'clever animals' is highlighted. See Nietzsche (1990). We encounter the infinite context of the cosmos directly in Chapter 4.

124 Moore and Gibbons (1986), Ch 9 p 26. Emphases in original.

125 See Moore and Gibbons (1986), Ch 9 pp 26–28.

126 This man her mother had every reason to hate was Edward Blake (alias, 'The Comedian'), who attempted to rape her: see Moore and Gibbons (1986), Ch 2 pp 5–8. Importantly, note that Juspeczyk was the fruit not of that unsolicited union, but a subsequent consensual one.

127 Moore and Gibbons (1986), Ch 9 pp 26–27. Emphases in original. Allusions to Richard Dawkins's 'blind watchmaker' thesis can clearly be seen (indeed, it is the title of the chapter of *Watchmen* from which this example is taken). For Dawkins, it is

We can see that for Juspeczyk to be born in her particular form and specific time was so improbable as to be 'the crowning unlikelihood', as rare as a thermodynamic miracle and just as valuable. Dr Manhattan subsequently extends this rarity and concomitant value to each and every person on earth. Although one's existence and actions may be wholly predictable, the ephemerality and radical uniqueness of each individual human life-pattern makes it valuable even against the vast and desolate beauty of the enduring universe.[128] However, this conclusion that human life does have value simply as life remains an understanding that is unable to comprehend meaningful human existence. Dr Manhattan's model of human value is based upon the unlikelihood of our radically unique and individual existence, and as such remains rational (being derived from bioscientific understandings and statistical probabilities[129]) and symptomatic of a 'rational surface' of knowledge that represses other ways of knowing.

Again, Dr Manhattan expresses himself in text. This textual theorising of his rarity-based concept of human value is depicted (visualised) as taking place on the surface of Mars, a surface upon which can be seen a smiley face that is made up of the chance formation of the Martian landscape.[130] The image of the smiley face – two dots for eyes, and a simple curved line for the mouth, as one would find today in an emoticon – is a recurring image throughout *Watchmen*, from the first panel to the last. In its particular occurrence on Mars, it is deployed in a way suggestive of a rational surface that is one perspective to be taken when encountering the complex 'surface' of reality. Elsewhere Dr Manhattan refers to the geography of Mars as 'chaotic terrain',[131] and in Nietzsche's metaphysics the surface of reality is indeed chaotic: complex and irreducible, unable to be captured it in its entirety, with human (and particularly rational) knowledge only ever seeing from a limited perspective.[132] Dr Manhattan's basic thesis is that out of the complex and

through the generational filtering of otherwise chaotic forms that biological order 'evolves' without the imposition of design: see Dawkins (1986).

128 One point that comes from Dr Manhattan's argument is that if each and every human life is unique and valuable due to its rarity and unlikelihood, then the same could be said of all other reproducing life forms. See Moore and Gibbons (1986), Ch 12 p 18. This extension may have its own connotations for jurisprudence, but it is not considered here, but ultimately it is clear that Dr Manhattan's answer to the 'value' of human life does not help us delineate whatever-it-is-that-human-is.

129 For a tracing of the emergence of numbers and statistics as a pre-eminent mode of representing 'truth', see Poovey (1998).

130 See Moore and Gibbons (1986), Ch 9 p 27. It might be interesting to note that there actually *is* a smiley face on Mars, as Dave Gibbons notes in his account of the creation of *Watchmen*: see Gibbons et al (2008), pp 204–205.

131 Moore and Gibbons (1986), Ch 9 p 14. We turn to issues of cartography in Chapter 6.

132 For example:

> the creative spirit who is pushed out of any position 'outside' or 'beyond' … whose solitude will be misunderstood by the people as though it were a flight *from* reality – : whereas it is just his way of being absorbed, buried and immersed in reality.
>
> Nietzsche (1997b), p 66

seemingly 'chaotic' system of the universe, radically unique events arise in the form of human lives and their rarity gives human existence value. The smiley-face-surface of Mars that Dr Manhattan is visually depicted as theorising human value upon, as an abstract image of the face made up of simplified dots and lines, signifies the abstraction of Dr Manhattan's disciplinary rationalisations of the universe, connecting text with image in the comics form. This 'rational surface' is an abstracted and comparatively linear area of the Martian landscape, beyond which lurks the chaotic terrain of unmediated reality. It is a surface upon which the complex living human becomes the abstract simplicity of the smiley face. This deployment of the smiley face thus sets up a rational surface in *Watchmen*'s graphic dimension: an area of the complex surface of reality that is accessed through the abstraction of rational knowledge, and that is taken to be complete, knowable, and certain, its 'happy' stability reflecting a degree of complacency with regard to its reified foundations. Thus Dr Manhattan's valuation of human life remains purely statistical and logical, on the 'stable' surface of knowledge – the complacent rational surface of which the smiley face is symbolic.[133]

Dr Manhattan reduces the universe to mere machine – inanimate, ghostless – and the human being to an empty shell – just a sad, ghostless 'bot. Our existence may have *value* (due to our radical individuality), but it does not have *life* – his strings do not escape the rational surface. In contrast, Shirow's pondering of lifehood in *Ghost* suggests that although the universe may be a system, that system is so vast that it produces mystery rather than answers. This conflict can be seen in *Watchmen* in the visual-textual tensions between Dr Manhattan's textualisations of the physical world and the visualised 'flowing clouds' of the Martian canyon he describes to Juspeczyk, suggestive of the 'uncertain and diverse universe' in *Ghost* (see Figure 2.2). For Shirow, the universal network is infinitely complex and from its vastly interconnected pathways life spontaneously blossoms as something more than a mere machine, more than a product of statistics and logic. Against the lifeless materiality of Dr Manhattan, the strings of the universe are traced back in *Ghost* to reveal a Puppeteer in the form of ghostly lifehood – that ineffable

and 'body am I through and through, and nothing besides; and soul is just a word for something on the body': Nietzsche (2006), p 23. For extended discussion of Nietzsche's reconfiguration of surface and depth, see Battersby (2007). This is also discussed more fully in Chapter 5.

133 Indeed, we can see from Moore's own thoughts about rationality that he is expressly critical of reason's attenuation of human meaning and value:

> While it is arguable that Reason brought many great benefits and was a very necessary stage of our development, unfortunately this lead to materialism, where the physical material world was seen as the be-all and end-all of existence; where inevitably we were seen as creatures that have no spiritual dimensions, that have no soul, living in a soulless universe of dead matter.
>
> *The Mindscape of Alan Moore* (2003)

In this documentary Moore also accuses science of attributing human consciousness to mere biological processes.

something of the *anima* that avoids capture, reduction, or explanation, and as such remains emblematic of the beyond, of that outside knowing – the strings ultimately go *somewhere else*. Dr Manhattan demonstrates that to bring this *anima* inside the surface necessarily destroys and reduces it to abstract reification; the *anima* is the answer to the human question that remains quintessentially beyond the rational surface, masked by its reductions and simplifications and rational framings, and thus also remains outside the rational system of conscious law. As Thacker indicates, discourses on life tend to oscillate between reductive materialism and the sublimation of mysticism[134] – hence the 'impossible unity' of the person in Esposito. Between Dr Manhattan and *Ghost*, this split can clearly be seen. But, taking the *anima* as an aesthetics – as symbolic of an unconscious to knowledge – enables us to think about moving outside the rational frame of conscious legality, towards other ways of knowing as mediated by the comics-as-*komos*.

Disciplines only 'see' the world (and thus constitute their subject) via their particular nexus of power/knowledge – through their particular apparatuses. This necessarily involves effacing or repressing things beyond or outside of what can be seen through those lenses. The apparatus of legal personhood thus necessarily represses elements beyond its epistemological framing, with the world only perceived and understood in terms visible to the conscious apparatus of law. Taken to extremes, it is reduced to a rational-linguistic structure, and the human is reduced to a bundle of legal principles, to rights and agency. This is the mode of the technical legal person, but the broader human person who appears in the *nomos* suffers similar limitations insofar as they are constructed via a rational frame. That which remains outside the 'rational surface' of disciplinary encounter – the fluidity at the boundaries of the human, the 'chaotic terrain' of phenomenal lifehood, the indeterminacy of the image – is not part of conscious legal knowledge. As *anima*, it exceeds the rational framings of personhood. The conscious machinery of legal knowing, of reasoned comprehension and 'plain text', represses these uncertainties, enabling the reified and 'happy' disciplinary surface of law to prevail.

In this sense, the conscious world of law is a ghostless machine, a technical regime devoid – cleaned – of the rich uncertainties of human life, a product of rational text alone, of its epistemic grounding. Its vision of human life is limited, its disciplinary knowledge trapped within the perspective of the rational surface, contained only in words. This is a deliberately hyperbolic characterisation of legality, but one designed to highlight the limitations of rational text, and thus that law is always more than this. As I outlined in the opening chapter, part of the critical value of exploring legal aesthetics through the medium of comics is the ability of the comics medium to navigate and expose many of the complexities and relationships at the limits of rational text. In its nature as an aesthetic form, the comics medium already challenges any discipline that understands the world through reason alone; as an overtly visual form, it also challenges the primacy of words as the carriers of truth. This chapter has already shown how key examples of

134 See Thacker (2010).

the comics form can expose and challenge the dominant form of legal knowing, particularly in terms of its disciplinary adherence to a scientific rationalism. Indeed, the speech bubble itself, with its delineated boundary, can also be seen as symbolic of the rational surface. And if we are to follow the 'strings' of this ghostless machine into the world beyond its boundaries, if we are to venture into the realm outside law's textual bubble, following the movement of cultural legal aesthetics, it is apt not only that we have begun our journey through engagement with the multimodal comics that, as *komos*, can mediate between conscious knowing and its beyond – its *anima* – but also that subsequent chapters will continue this movement with that same companion.

References

Giorgio Agamben (2009) 'What Is an Apparatus?' in *What Is an Apparatus? And Other Essays*, Stanford University Press.

Jason Bainbridge (2015) '"The Call to Do Justice": Superheroes, Sovereigns and the State During Wartime' 28 *International Journal for the Semiotics of Law* 745.

Christine Battersby (1998) *The Phenomenal Woman: Feminist Metaphysics and the Patterns of Identity*, Polity Press.

Christine Battersby (2007) *The Sublime, Terror, and Human Difference*, Routledge.

Scott Bukatman (2012) *The Poetics of Slumberland: Animated Spirits and the Animating Spirit*, California University Press.

Lorenzo Casini (2010) '"Quid Sit Anima": Juan Luis Vives on the Soul and Its Relation to the Body' 24 *Renaissance Studies* 496.

Melinda Cooper (2002) 'The Living and the Dead: Variations on De Anima' 7 *Angelaki: Journal for the Theoretical Humanities* 81.

Neal Curtis (2016) *Sovereignty and Superheroes*, Manchester University Press.

Richard Dawkins (1986) *The Blind Watchmaker*, Norton.

Annalisa Di Liddo (2009) *Alan Moore: Comics as Performance, Fiction as Scalpel*, University Press of Mississippi.

Roberto Esposito (2012) 'The *Dispositif* of the Person' 8 *Law, Culture and the Humanities* 17.

Lindsay Farmer (2010) 'Time and Space in Criminal Law' 13 *New Criminal Law Journal* 333.

Michel Foucault (1977) *Discipline and Punish: The Birth of the Prison*, Penguin.

Michel Foucault (1980) 'Body/Power' in C Gordon (ed) *Power/Knowledge: Selected Interviews and Other Writings 1972–1977 by Michel Foucault*, Longman-Pearson.

Michel Foucault (1982) 'The Subject and Power' 8 *Critical Inquiry* 777.

Michel Foucault (1997a) 'On the Genealogy of Ethics: An Overview of Work in Progress' in P Rabinow (ed) *Ethics: Subjectivity and Truth (Essential Works of Foucault 1954–1984, Vol 1)*, Penguin.

Michel Foucault (1997b) 'Preface to the History of Sexuality, Volume Two' in P Rabinow (ed) *Ethics: Subjectivity and Truth (Essential Works of Foucault 1954–1984, Vol 1)*, Penguin.

Michel Foucault (1997c) 'Self Writing' in P Rabinow (ed) *Ethics: Subjectivity and Truth (Essential Works of Foucault 1954–1984, Vol 1)*, Penguin.

Dave Gibbons et al (2008) *Watching the Watchmen*, Titan Books.

Thomas Giddens (2015a) 'Criminal Responsibility and the Living Self' 9 *Criminal Law and Philosophy* 189.

Thomas Giddens (2015b) 'Natural Law and Vengeance: Jurisprudence on the Streets of Gotham' 28 *International Journal for the Semiotics of Law* 765.

Ben Golder and Peter Fitzpatrick (2009) *Foucault's Law*, Routledge.

J Goldsmith (2013) 'How Cyber Changes the Laws of War' 24 *European Journal of International Law* 129.

Peter Goodrich (1990) *Languages of Law: From Logics of Memory to Nomadic Masks*, Weidenfeld and Nicolson.

Peter Goodrich (2012) 'The Theatre of Emblems: On the Optical Apparatus and the Investiture of Persons' 8 *Law, Culture and the Humanities* 47.

Peter Goodrich (2013) *Legal Emblems and the Art of Law: Obiter Depicta as the Vision of Governance*, Cambridge University Press.

Donna Haraway (2000) 'A Cyborg Manifesto: Science, Technology and Socialist-Feminism in the Late Twentieth Century' in D Bell and BM Kennedy (eds) *The Cybercultures Reader*, Routledge.

Shawn Harmon (2015) 'Not Foresighting, Not Answering: Using Graphic Ficiton to Interrogate Social and Regulatroy Issues in Biomedicine' in T Giddens (ed) *Graphic Justice: Intersections of Comics and Law*, Routledge.

Stefan Herbrechter (2013) *Posthumanism: A Critical Analysis*, Bloomsbury.

David Hodgson (2002) 'Quantum Phsyics, Consciousness, and Free Will' in R Kane (ed) *The Oxford Handbook of Free Will*, Oxford University Press.

Marli Huijer (1999) 'The Aesthetics of Existence in the Work of Michel Foucault' 25 *Philosophy and Social Criticism* 61.

Alan Hunt and Gary Wickham (1994) *Foucault and Law: Towards a Sociology of Law as Governance*, Pluto.

Immanuel Kant (1959) 'Foundations of the Metaphysics of Morals' in *Foundations of the Metaphysics of Morals and What Is Enlightenment?*, Bobbs-Menil.

Immanuel Kant (2000) *Critique of the Power of Judgment*, Cambridge University Press.

Steven S Kapica (2014) '"I Don't Feel Like a Copy": Posthuman Legal Personhood and *Caprica*' 23 *Griffith Law Review* 612.

Alaric Kohler (2010) 'To Think Human out of the Machine Paradigm: Homo Ex Machina' 44 *Integrative Psychological and Behavioural Science* 39.

Christine M Korsgaard (1998) 'Introduction' in M Gregor (ed) *Groundwork of the Metaphysics of Morals*, Cambridge University Press.

Margaret M Lock (2002) *Twice Dead: Organ Transplants and the Reinvention of Death*, University of California Press.

WJT Mitchell (2005) 'The Work of Art in the Age of Biocybernetic Reproduction' in *What Do Pictures Want? The Lives and Loves of Images*, Chicago University Press.

Alan Moore and Dave Gibbons (1986) *Watchmen*, Titan Books.

LB Moses (2007) 'The Legal Landscape Following Technological Change: Paths to Adaptation' 27 *Bulletin of Science, Technology and Society* 408.

LB Moses (2011) 'Agents of Change: How the Law "Copes" with Technological Change' 20 *Griffith Law Review* 763.

Ngaire Naffine (2009) *Law's Meaning of Life: Philosophy, Religion, Darwin and the Legal Person*, Hart.

Claire Napier (2014) 'The Ghost in the Shell: The Major's Body (1)' http://womenwriteaboutcomics.com/2014/07/22/ghost-in-the-shell-the-majors-body-1/

Friedrich Nietzsche (1990) 'On Truth and Lies in a Nonmoral Sense' in P Bizzell and B Herzberg (eds) *The Rhetorical Tradition: Readings from Classical Times to the Present*, Bedford Books.

Friedrich Nietzsche (1997b) *Daybreak: Thoughts on the Prejudices of Morality*, Cambridge University Press.

Friedrich Nietzsche (2006) *Thus Spoke Zarathustra*, Cambridge University Press.

Jonathan Pearlman (2013) 'Kidney Grown from Stem Cells by Australian Scientists' www.telegraph.co.uk/news/worldnews/australiaandthepacific/australia/10520058/Kidney-grown-from-stem-cells-by-Australian-scientists.html

James Petty (2015) 'Violent Lives, Ending Violently? Justice, Ideology and Spectatorship in *Watchmen*' in T Giddens (ed) *Graphic Justice: Intersections of Comics and Law*, Routledge.

Mary Poovey (1998) *A History of the Modern Fact: Problems of Knowledge in the Sciences of Wealth and Society*, University of Chicago Press.

Muireann Quigley (2012) 'Property in Human Biomaterials: Separating Persons and Things?' 32 *Oxford Journal of Legal Studies* 659.

Janice Richardson (2009) *The Classical Social Contractarians: Critical Perspectives from Contemporary Feminist Philosophy and Law*, Ashgate.

Janice Richardson (2010) 'Feminism, Property in the Person and Concepts of Self' 12 *The British Journal of Politics and International Relations* 56.

Nikolas Rose (2001) 'The Politics of Life Itself' 18 *Theory, Culture and Society* 1.

Cassandra Sharp (2012) '"Riddle Me This…?" Would the World Need Superheroes If the Law Could Actually Deliver "Justice"?' 16 *Law Text Culture* 353.

Richard K Sherwin (2011) *Visualizing Law in the Age of the Digital Baroque: Arabesques and Entanglements*, Routledge.

Masamune Shirow (1995) *The Ghost in the Shell*, Dark Horse Comics.

Nick Sousanis (2015) *Unflattening*, Harvard University Press.

Anthony Peter Spanakos (2014) 'Hell's Kitchen's Prolonged Crisis and Would-Be Sovereigns: Daredevil, Hobbes, and Schmitt' 47 *PS: Political Science and Politics* 94.

Susan AJ Stuart (2010) 'Conscious Machines: Memory, Melody and Muscular Imagination' 9 *Phenomenology and the Cognitive Sciences* 37.

Eugene Thacker (2010) *After Life*, University of Chicago Press.

Iain Thomson (2005) 'Deconstructing the Hero' in J McLaughlin (ed) *Comics as Philosophy*, University Press of Mississippi.

Kieran Tranter (2011) 'The Speculative Jurisdiction: The Science Fictionality of Law and Technology' 20 *Griffith Law Review* 817.

Kieran Tranter (2013) 'Materiality and Memory: Motor Cars and Mobile Phones' 22 *Griffith Law Review* 532.

Mitchell Travis (2015) 'We're All Infected: Legal Personhood, Bare Life And *The Walking Dead*' 28 *International Journal for the Semiotics of Law* 787.

Miguel de Unamuno (1954) *Tragic Sense of Life*, Dover.

The Mindscape of Alan Moore (2003) directed by Dez Vylenz, Shadowsnake Films.

Arthur Ward (2009) 'Free Will and Foreknowledge: Does Jon Really Know What Laurie Will Do Next, and Can She Do Otherwise?' in MD White (ed) *Watchmen and Philosophy: A Rorschach Test*, John Wiley.

Slavoj Žižek (2006) *The Parallax View*, Massachusetts Institute of Technology Press.

Chapter 3

The irrational threat

... the great uncertainty that surrounds all things.[1]

Irrationality is a threat to law's ghostless machine; an uncertainty that surrounds rational legal forms. As we saw in the previous chapter, conscious law reduces the universe to a rational structure of textually articulated principles and categories; it is sombre, lifeless in the sense that it cannot capture true life. The *anima* – the 'something' of the human – always exceeds its logical structures. Subsequently, the aim of this chapter is to begin proper the movement without the rational texts of law – to begin our descent into the madness of cultural legal aesthetics. Into the brimming world outside the boundaries of consciously doctrinal legality, suffused with MacNeilean *joie de juridique*. Indeed, it is only by crossing this boundary, by venturing into the irrational and seemingly threatening beyond, that we can come to realise the removal of this boundary, for what lies beyond is not threat but the generative chaos of the unconscious. In order to cross this boundary, and also to invoke the mediating power of the *komos*, our comics companion in this chapter must be suitably liminal. To which end, our graphic source is one that navigates a jurisprudential and alchemical mediation of reason and unreason: Grant Morrison and Dave McKean's insanely brooding *Arkham Asylum*.[2]

To tell the jurisprudential story of reason meeting unreason in *Arkham Asylum*, this chapter has two broad sections. The first main section introduces Batman as an avatar of justice and gives an overview of his 'dark night of the soul' in the Asylum, whilst the second articulates the threat irrationality poses for conscious law, reconfiguring this as something to be embraced in the opening up of cultural legal aesthetics. More specifically, the chapter first introduces the broad juristics of Batman through the distinctly aesthetic criminologies of Alison Young and Jonathan Wender, highlighting the way Batman exceeds rational and legalistic structures, before examining the processes of repression that can be seen in both law and Batman's encounters with the Asylum's inmates. The chapter then examines

1 Foucault (2006), p 11.
2 Morrison and McKean (2004). See Appendix A for an overview and details of this work.

in more detail the threat posed to the rational legal order by that which is outside it, configuring the threat of the legal unconscious as the lawyer's severed head inside the house of law. Ultimately, Batman's journey through *Arkham Asylum* reminds law of the aesthetic and irrational contexts that it works to repress and from which it seeks to defend itself; it recalls the unreason outside law's logic, the chaos outside its order, the madness outside its reason. The chapter thus concludes with the lesson of Batman's encounters in the Asylum: that we should remember the 'madness' outside the legal order and thus see that law is always already more than its conscious 'sanity'.

Madness and aesthetics

Street bat, phenomenal city

From the outset, it is important to note that *Arkham Asylum* is not a typical Batman comic. Originally published in 1989, in the wake of Tim Burton's *Batman* film, it represents part of a wave of darker and 'more mature' superhero comics being published around that time.[3] Although an exception within the wider Batman canon, it remains one of the bestselling graphic novels in comics history and is thus a very popular iteration of the Batman character – a significant dimension of his contribution to the *lex populi*. The Batman we witness in *Arkham Asylum* is not the strong, capable hero of other stories, but a man struggling with his own demons. It is a disturbingly rich tale of Batman's dark night of the soul; it represents the ultimate testing of his rationality in the face of his repressed madness within Gotham's infamous madhouse. It is, in many ways, a counterpoint to the dominant versions of the heroic Batman, exposing the weakness and madness that fuels his wider fight for justice. As such, *Arkham Asylum* tells of the meeting of reason and unreason in a juridical context – of conscious law and the supposed threat of the unconscious that underpins it.

This is the reading I pursue here, although I admit that Batman, as a non-state crime fighter, can be seen to encounter a wide variety of other jurisprudential questions and concerns, from sovereignty,[4] states of exception,[5] and notions of juristic balance,[6] to questions of natural law[7] and violence.[8] But *Arkham Asylum*'s themes do not directly tackle such issues – it is expressly a tale of madness. Of the return of the repressed; of the unwanted insecurity of fluidity bubbling up from what were supposedly solid foundations. It thus seeks to undo or transcend the rational reification of the universe witnessed in the previous chapter. Already we

3 Common examples include Miller et al (2002); Moore and Bolland (1988); Moore and Gibbons (1986).
4 Sharp (2012).
5 Comerford (2015).
6 Peters (2007).
7 Giddens (2015b); Peters (2015).
8 Curtis (2016), pp 58–81.

see echoes of the repressive movement that Foucault identifies in the renaissance, compressing the cosmic madness of human tragedy into a quintessentially rational form – as the inaccuracy that is the counterpoint to the truth of reason, madness becomes reason's dyadic other.[9] As a man out for justice, Batman's encounter with this other-to-reason overtly examines the irrationality that troubles juridical structures of knowing. As madness, this irrationality becomes symbolic of the madness of law and justice: of that which conscious legality represses in the pursuit and maintenance of its 'ghostless' order. As unconscious, it becomes the *anima*, the puppeteer, the behind-the-scenes that shapes and moulds and animates the dead surface of conscious legality. Indeed, as an avatar for justice, Batman's liminal encounters with madness suggest that the unstructured chaos of which unreason is symbolic remains part of the rational order of justice that law's texts seek to codify – madness is its repressed 'other scene'.

But before I get to my analysis of *Arkham Asylum*, it is necessary to introduce Batman himself – not just as an extra-legal crime fighter nor as an exercise in popular sovereignty, but as a juridico-urban aesthetic that exceeds all logical structures – including those of the comics multiframe. Batman is a divided and conflicted character. One significant divide he embodies is that between his implicit claim to be an objective source of idealised, extralegal justice, and the deeply subjective and personal pain that fuels his fight for that justice. On the one hand, Batman is transcendent: a symbol or avatar of justice; outside the system, outside bureaucracy; outside limited resources and corruption. On the other hand, he is an embodied living being, trying to resolve the inner pain and trauma of his past.[10] There is a public/private tension that stems from Batman's more general divide in his institution of justice in both idealised and living contexts: he protects the innocent, attempting to prevent the trauma he has suffered being inflicted on others; he takes his deeply private pain and configures it as a public ideal as he turns his human body into the symbol of the Dark Knight.[11] And this tension, between ideal and phenomenal justice, represents overt tensions in un/conscious law: the rational-textual ideal of conscious law in tension with the broader unconscious fluidity of life, culture, aesthetics, sensation, image; between structure and what exceeds it.

In navigating Gotham's living morass, Batman can be seen to take up an aesthetic mantle similar to street artists – a connection that warrants some explanation. For Alison Young, law is a living force within the city, shaping its boundaries in multiple intricate ways[12] and creating 'legal territories in time and space'.[13] Ownership, curfews, noise regulations, and so forth, all build up a 'legislated city', made up of 'legible spaces and objects with singular owners, licensing some

9 See Foucault (2006), pp 3–43.
10 See Brody (1995).
11 Giddens (2015b).
12 Young (2014), pp 41–43.
13 Young (2014), p 42.

behaviours and criminalising others'.[14] As we saw in Chapter 1, this is part of the intricate structure of law's layered multiframe. Law is a conceptual structure, laid over the embodied spaces of the city, giving them everyday meaning and navigable structure, delineating the frames of socio-urban space to be inhabited and navigated by the subjects of law. This is a ghostless city, experienced in terms of restriction, seclusion, and division, with walls, fences, signs – everywhere separations of the urban environment, breaking it up into a multiframe of legally regulated spaces.[15] Importantly for Young, this is a structure that can always be challenged or ruptured by transgression: street art[16] transcends such boundaries, utilising space in illegitimate or unregulated ways.

As an emanation of the city's restless life, street art can be understood as counter-agency against the urban legal order: a street-level emergence, challenging preconceptions of singular ownership and the way public spaces should be used.[17] Accordingly, graffiti and street art are divorced from their creators who remain anonymous, hidden behind stylistic presentations of self through their visual notation upon the city; street art becomes authorless, part of a living dialogue within the restlessness of urban life[18] – as Young observes, 'the city is writing itself'.[19] The city may be written as an idealised multiframe in legislation, but an 'uncommissioned city', a phenomenal city, is also written – by the city itself.[20] In this sense, street art becomes a means by which the city can be transformed, shaped in tension with a simultaneous legal ordering; a counter-hegemonic aesthetic, an *anima* that exists as an alternative to the ghostless constructions of rational law and thus ruptures or exceeds the structures of the conscious legal multiframe.

Framed in such terms, there are many parallels between Young's urban aesthetics and the Dark Knight – particularly as a work of comics, as a creation of the multiframe. Like street art, Batman is 'uncommissioned' with respect to the dominant legal order: he has no official sanction, no regulatory oversight. He works outside the legal order, adhering to his own conception of legitimate conduct. Indeed, vigilantism, like street art and graffiti, is often seen to be simply 'criminal'[21] – a view that eschews many of the complexities involved in both practices. Moreover, like street art, Batman is working to transform the order of the city, to produce a new or alternative moral order that subverts a dominant one

14 Young (2014), pp 42–43.
15 Young (2014), pp 43–44.
16 Note the distinction between street art and graffiti, with street art taking on a wider variety of forms and aesthetics: see Young (2012), pp 298–299.
17 Young (2014), pp 52–53.
18 Young (2005), pp 50–74.
19 Young (2005), p 74.
20 Young (2014), p 53.
21 It is arguably law's commitment to a certain culture of property ownership, and the challenge represented by the existence of graffiti and street art to the normativity and authority of this culture, that results in graffiti's criminalisation: see Young (2012).

seen to be problematic or (in Batman's case) overtly corrupt. Young discusses the 'enchantment'[22] or aesthetic dissonance that the appearance of the unexpected in urban spaces can engender in observers; graffiti art can rupture the flow of people through the city's spaces as they are confronted by transgressive images.[23] Similarly, appearing as a giant swooping bat, cloaked in the trappings of cape and cowl, Batman enacts a type of aesthetic rupture. As a force emerging from a belief in an alternative legal order, a force to undermine the corruption that has infiltrated Gotham's public systems of justice,[24] this rupture takes on a significantly jurisprudential character. Batman's presence on the streets of Gotham enacts an 'enchantment' that jolts us from official legal worlds and alerts us to alternative possibilities and orders of justice. Batman, then, is quintessentially a work of cultural legal aesthetics, and we can already begin to see his engagement with the boundaries of conscious legality.

On a formal level, this jolting out of the official structures of law connects with the comics multiframe: it is not just Batman's thematic and narrative engagement with vigilantism that renders aesthetic dissonance and enchants us out of ghostless legality, but his formal presentation in the comics medium. To draw this out in preparation for our journey into *Arkham Asylum*, the connections with Young's aesthetics need to be furthered. Accordingly, street art's transgression of the legal architecture of the city can be seen as reminiscent of Batman's swooping navigation of the physical urban landscape: like the free-runners and space-hackers who clamber over the surfaces and into the bowels of the city, when Batman glides from rooftop to rooftop, sweeps down to street level, vaults walls and fences, clambers up fire escapes and drain pipes, enters buildings and basements, he transgresses the multiple boundaries of the juridico-urban landscape – he escapes the multiframe of the legislated city. Moreover, in his common depiction atop the spires and gargoyles of Gotham, Batman arguably becomes part of the cityscape itself, transcending further the bureaucratic intricacies of the legislated order.

> The illicit artists recast these intensely regulated city spaces as 'smooth' … in a performative demonstration that it is impossible to contain signification within strictly delimited boundaries.[25]

In the context of comics studies, such a 'rendering smooth' would break down the intricate layering of the multiframe of panels, images, texts, and pages that theorists such as Groensteen construct in relation to the formal dimensions of the medium. On a jurisprudential level, Batman exceeds the regulated structures of the city, but this excess is modelled in the formal dimension of the comics that gave birth to him. For, beyond the structures of the multiframe, there exists a field

22 Young (2014), pp 44–46.
23 Young (2014), pp 45–48.
24 Giddens (2015b).
25 Young (2012), pp 310–311.

of pure visuality or sensory encounter. It is over this aesthetic excess that the structures of the multiframe are built, breaking down any comics work into navigable elements. In this way, as we will begin to draw out in the analysis of *Arkham Asylum*, and as later chapters will make clear – notably Chapter 6 – comics also exceed their formal structure. Just as for Young there are two cities, one could indicate the existence of two dimensions in comics: the phenomenal comic is translated or compressed into the structured logic of the multiframe, just as the phenomenal city is reified into the rational forms of law to produce the legislated city. In both cases, what we can identify is a process of epistemological mediation – of *komos* – that represses the excessive living dimensions into a legal unconscious to enable knowable conscious forms to emerge. But in the comics form, the uniquely multimodal quality of the comics multiframe – where text, image, reason, and aesthetics come together – enables us to think about this epistemological repression in the meeting of rational legality and fluid life in a way the purely rational multiframe of conscious law does not.

Putting aside its substantive content, and the reading of Batman's extra-legal justice as simply representing natural law,[26] there is a complex epistemological process taking place in the production of the legislated city that Batman encounters – namely, the processes by which the legal system encounters the complex reality of life and encodes it into its own rational order. Uncommissioned street artists – including Batman – challenge the process of law's epistemic translation or 'capture' by transgressing the boundaries of legislated space, demonstrating their excessive qualities that the dominant order cannot contain. In the specifically multimodal form of *Arkham Asylum*, as we will see, this engagement between structure and excess – between reason and madness – is overt, with the rich and uncertain visualisation of the diegetic world playing directly into the limits of bureaucratic juridical order.

For Foucault, madness was once a tragic aspect of our humanity, but the emergence of the asylum represents the repression of that tragic madness into an oppositional dimension of reason – to be disciplined and controlled.[27] With the birth of the asylum, madness came to be observed and judged, catalogued into a scientific technology that sought only to classify, without dialogue.[28] The truth of humanity traditionally signified by madness – that we are frail and limited in the face of cosmic powers – is lost, hidden within reason:[29] madness becomes a problem with reason, with its malfunctioning in the insane subject, rather than something troubling and other to all that is rational.[30] In *Arkham Asylum*, we witness something akin to the undoing of this repression – a remembering of the madness that is part of humanity, of the madness that makes us what we are. The

26 For discussion on how Batman can be strongly allied with natural law theory, see Giddens (2015b).
27 See Foucault (2006), pp 463–511.
28 Foucault (2006), pp 487–488.
29 See Foucault (2006), pp 3–43.
30 Foucault (2006), p 521.

story is one of traversing the limits of reason, and ultimately of remembering madness as something that threatens from outside reason and coming to terms with the horror of this uncertainty that lurks beneath the surface of our waking minds – and symbolically the conscious order of rational justice and legal knowledge. As such, in *Arkham Asylum* we are not simply in the realm of the reason-based madness of the modern asylum described by Foucault, but in a more figurative world, pulling at the edges of the rational fabric. Indeed, as Morrison says in his original script when describing the world inside the Asylum: 'There is no reason here. We have reached the frayed edge of the rational world'.[31]

Arkham Asylum's basic structure tells of Batman restoring order to the infamous 'Arkham Asylum for the Criminally Insane', which has been taken over by its troubled inmates. In this overarching narrative, Morrison and McKean ostensibly retell the traditional superhero story: evil disrupts the peaceful order, so the hero (Batman) steps in and defeats that evil (the inmates), restoring the world order.[32] This typical tale is reconfigured in *Arkham Asylum* to be framed in terms of Batman's confrontation with his own inner madness: for Batman, 'good defeats evil' becomes 'reason defeats the irrational'. *Arkham Asylum* thus becomes the story of Batman's communion with his own repressed demons, represented by the troubled beings that inhabit the Asylum in which he is trapped and through which he must travel. *Arkham Asylum* traces a profound test of Batman's soul, and his emergence from his inner turmoil as a stable, sane being. It is Batman's recall, and rational conquering, of the madness of unreason; his phenomenal journey into the unconscious of his own rational order of justice. As Grant Morrison states, explaining the depiction of the Moon Tarot card on the opening page:

31 Morrison (2004), p 15. I make reference at a number of points to Morrison's script, although I do not engage directly in the level or type of authority to be given to it in reading *Arkham Asylum*. However, some words may be needed on this point. Thus, to clarify, my approach in using Morrison's script is to seek some insight into the purposeful engagement with reason and unreason in the work, but I do not see his creative intentions as determinative of the possible readings available. Indeed, I leave open the question of interpretation and, as we shall see in Chapter 6, there is really no limit as to the ways in which something can be read or framed.

32 In this respect, it should not be forgotten that Batman's justice arguably reproduces the dominant order he appears to fight (in a way that illicit graffiti typically does not). Picture Bruce Wayne – rich, white, and male. Indeed, superhero narratives are for the most part conservative, simply perpetuating the dominant order of justice-as-retribution. See Phillips and Strobl (2006); Phillips and Strobl (2013). Adkinson calls this phenomenon the 'hegemonic paradox': see Adkinson (2008), pp 249–253. Bruner's conception of narrative as the rupture, and consequent restoration or alteration, of the world order can also be seen in this basic narrative movement: see Bruner (2002). Accordingly, the 'alternative' orders of justice Batman represents are not necessarily unproblematic, nor even different from dominant ideals in contemporary 'real world' capitalist society; although fighting corruption, Batman does not necessarily resolve critical issues such as conflict or inequality. But despite this substantive conservatism, the formal operation and aesthetics of the Dark Knight can still be useful for thinking about alternatives to the dominant forms of conscious legal knowledge.

> The Moon card basically represents the darkness through which we must pass to reach the dawn … [it] represents trial and initiation – the supreme testing of the soul, where we must face our deepest fears, confront them and survive or be broken. In this single image are encoded all the themes of our entire story.[33]

Morrison and McKean embed a premodern, cosmic dimension to the madness[34] that Batman encounters within the Asylum's intricate structure. We see this in the recourse to the mysticism of the Tarot, including McKean's specific depiction of the moon reflected in nocturnal waters – with water having traditional associations with madness[35] as 'the great uncertainty that surrounds all things'[36] – and Morrison's later invocation of the deific forces of good and evil in St Michael and Satan (discussed below). Such cosmic madness represents a seething threat to Batman's rationality and his capacities as a bringer of justice. This threat can be seen to permeate the bureaucratic structures of justice on the level of their encounter with the messiness of phenomenal or 'living' existence. Jonathan Wender argues that, where agents of state law come into contact with complex and traumatic human experiences, they are required to translate those experiences into amenable bureaucratic categories.[37] The processes by which the police navigate the complexities of the living streets, like Batman, thus navigate the divide between the excessive dimensions of living crime and the bureaucratic categories or conscious multiframe into which that 'reality' is placed so that it can be 'solved'. The structure(s) of legal consciousness, of state bureaucracy, thus affect what and how we are able to know in the context of criminal justice, and an aesthetics of policing, as the front line of negotiation between living human action and the bureaucratic categories of criminal law, can expose the way in which life is compressed or translated into the administrative categories of justice:

> How do we face the ineffable mystery of human presence and render it into 'facts and circumstances' demanded by various practical ends? … For the police officer … immensely complex human predicaments must be pared down to administratively treatable 'problems' or judicially remediable crimes or violations of law.[38]

This exposes the poetic processes involved in making official, legal knowledge about criminality; for our purposes, it shows the unconscious dimensions of criminal legal knowledge and practice that are repressed in order to allow a 'rational' or 'objective' conscious praxis to prevail. The opening up of those repressed or 'mad'

33 Morrison (2004), pp 1–2.
34 See Foucault (2006), pp 19–21.
35 Foucault (2006), pp 11–12.
36 Foucault (2006), p 11.
37 Wender (2008).
38 Wender (2008), pp 49–50.

dimensions in *Arkham Asylum* thus threatens to undo the intricate metaphorisation of lived reality into legally amenable categories, to undo the juristic multi-framing of the world.

It is not uncommon for the aesthetic to be viewed with suspicion, precisely due to this ability to destabilise rational understanding.[39] But Wender argues that only by opening ourselves up to the aesthetic dimensions of encounter can we step back and appreciate the origins of bureaucratic knowledge.[40] Through his analysis of his own experiences as a 'philosopher cop',[41] Wender exposes the artistic dimensions of police bureaucratisation of life, whereby practical law enforcement 'functions as a form of poetry':[42]

> The police officer creates abstract, formal meaning ('problems') out of the vicissitudes of human predicaments through the use of a complex metaphoric schema. This schema functions on the streets essentially as it functions in the composition of formal poetry: by transferring the name of one thing to another, which is ontologically separate from it.[43]

It is clear that the epistemological point Wender is making transcends his particular jurisdictional location: although the particular rules and practices may differ between countries, police encounters with citizens involve essentially this same process of translating 'life' into criminal legal categories or 'problems' to be solved, even in Gotham. Traversing similar epistemological ground, Batman exists in a liminal space at the boundaries of the bureaucratic administration of justice. And the epistemological stakes of this liminality in relation to law's unconscious are exposed in *Arkham Asylum*, which performs an alchemical recollection and mediation of a deep unreason in the context of the pursuit for justice.

Into the Asylum

Arkham Asylum's juridical mediation of unreason is quintessentially a work of *komos*, and key in my examination of the boundaries of law's rational texts with other epistemological orders through the comics medium. The work's antagonism between reason and irrationality is a retelling of the essential battle between Batman and his arch-nemesis Joker in a way that draws out its epistemological dimensions. The battle of Batman and Joker transcends *Arkham Asylum*, spilling across swathes of the transmedia Batman canon: in comics, television, cinema, and computer games, Batman's fight with the Joker is arguably his most significant.[44]

39 See, for example, Douzinas and Nead (1999); Manderson (2000).
40 Wender (2008), pp 47–60.
41 Wender (2008), pp 1–12.
42 Wender (2008), p 129.
43 Wender (2008), p 130.
44 Just a small number of examples: Batman (1989); Miller et al (2002); Moore and Bolland (1988).

The Dark Knight faces criminality as a highly rational being, a great detective of huge ratiocentric capacity,[45] and Joker, in his penchant for irrationality and disorder, disrupts this. Whilst it may seem more prudent to explore rationality through his battles of logic with Riddler, the boundaries between reason and the irrational are more deeply crystallised in Batman's confrontations with Joker: his dangerous other, symbolic of that which is outside reason, that which threatens the rational order. Joker is the embodiment of madness, as Batman is the embodiment of rationality; Joker is chaos, whilst Batman is order; Joker lawlessness, Batman law; Joker unreason, Batman knowledge. As he navigates the inmates of the Asylum, Batman endures a relentless and profound encounter with Joker and the unconscious threat of which he and the 'rogues gallery' of Asylum inmates are symbolic.

As already outlined in Chapter 1, the legal unconscious is made up of that which is outside doctrinal law and practice. The legal institution needs to have knowledge of the human subjects and conduct it seeks to regulate, and this 'legal knowledge' forms law's particular dominant approach to comprehending the complexities of life. In constructing this 'legal consciousness', as Wender's aesthetics of bureaucracy indicates, there are inevitably elements that are omitted or pushed aside, aspects of existence that are left outside or remain uncaptured by the 'net' of legal knowledge.[46] It is these 'leftovers', these excessive dimensions of life repressed outside law's consciousness, that form law's epistemological unconscious. It is law's *other side*: 'the ideologies, fantasies and unconscious desires that support legal discourse from underneath'.[47] Aristodemou highlights this in law's social context, framing the conscious 'reality' of law as being surrounded by the visible secrets in the unspoken blind spot of both society and the legal institution (the paedophile public figure hiding in plain sight, the open secrets of governmental abuses like Abu Ghraib).[48] Similarly, Peter Goodrich argues that the legal unconscious is that which animates law beyond mere 'dead text' and gives it meaning: there is a legal 'beyond', an 'other scene', an 'imaginary source' that judicial interpreters and legislators 'find behind, between, or beyond the *literae* or words of law', and in doing so uncover legal meaning.[49] But law's unconscious also contains those cultural and aesthetic

45 See Giddens (2015b), pp 7–11.

46 The existence of such incompleteness is not unique to legal knowledge, as Nietzsche explains:

> The habits of our senses have woven us into lies and deception of sensation: these again are the basis of all our judgments and 'knowledge' – there is absolutely no escape, no backway or bypath into the *real world*! We sit within our net, we spiders, and whatever we may catch in it, we can catch nothing at all except that which allows itself to be caught in precisely *our* net.
>
> Nietzsche (1997b), p 73 (emphases in original)

47 Aristodemou (2014), p 3. Emphasis in original.

48 See Aristodemou (2014), pp 1–6. Aristodemou has also highlighted on the linguistic nature of law's conscious forms – it is through language that we construct and make possible rational law and truth: see Aristodemou (2000), pp 1–28.

49 Goodrich (1995), p 31.

artefacts, rich with legality, with which cultural legal studies engages. This unconscious is a threat to law's rational order. And this threat can be understood in terms of law's capacity to know about, and thus regulate, the world:

> The threat of the repressed within the [legal] institution is in one significant sense the threat of the unknown or, more precisely, the intimation of that which has not yet been determined, which is not mapped in advance by law's *regula* or calculus.[50]

Law is built upon the denial of this otherness, through a demarcation of which forms are legitimate in conscious law (primarily the logic of text), and which are not (namely images, the aesthetic). Those things that are delimited as outside the conscious order thus become a 'negative image' of law: its other, an imaginary underside that is an inversion of law's rational consciousness.[51] Conscious law pushes aside that which it is not, and the nature of the irrational beyond can be seen as a threat, as 'what nature, reason, and law must be defended against'.[52]

Encountering this 'other scene' within Batman's fight for justice, the central narrative of *Arkham Asylum* can be read as a navigation between conscious and unconscious law, framed in terms of confronting the 'madness' of unreason within the self and the threat this poses to rational understanding. Within the walls of Arkham Asylum, and between the covers of *Arkham Asylum*, Batman navigates the complex uncertainties of that which is outside rational order. Read in the context of the justice[53] that Batman is forever seeking, this encounter with unreason symbolically encounters the boundaries between conscious and unconscious law – Batman's journey walks the path of *komos*. What Batman faces is that which is outside reason, the disorder represented by the Joker and the other inmates who are complex symbols of the harm and criminality he seeks to quell; but they are also, *qua* representations of 'madness', symbolic of the dynamic sensuality of unstructured experience that exceeds rational attempts at order. Like life, Joker and the irrational forces he commands cannot be contained in reasoned explanations and structures of logic. This is reflected in the form of *Arkham Asylum* – notably Joker's speech, which is not contained in text bubbles. Rather, as can be seen in Figure 3.1, his words are visually stylised, blended with the fluid environment of the Asylum that is stylised and suggestive in McKean's richly textural artwork. Joker is thus deeply connected with that which exceeds the textual structures of the rational surface. From this epistemological perspective, the madness of the Asylum becomes symbolic of that which is pushed aside in the construction of law's conscious order. Law seeks to repress the madness of life outside its bubble of text, just as Batman seeks to repress the Joker and the chaos he and

50 Goodrich (1995), p 13.
51 Goodrich (1995), p 49.
52 Goodrich (1995), p 54.
53 Although typically retributive, Batman's justice can also be seen to be one of protection: see Giddens (2015b), p 5.

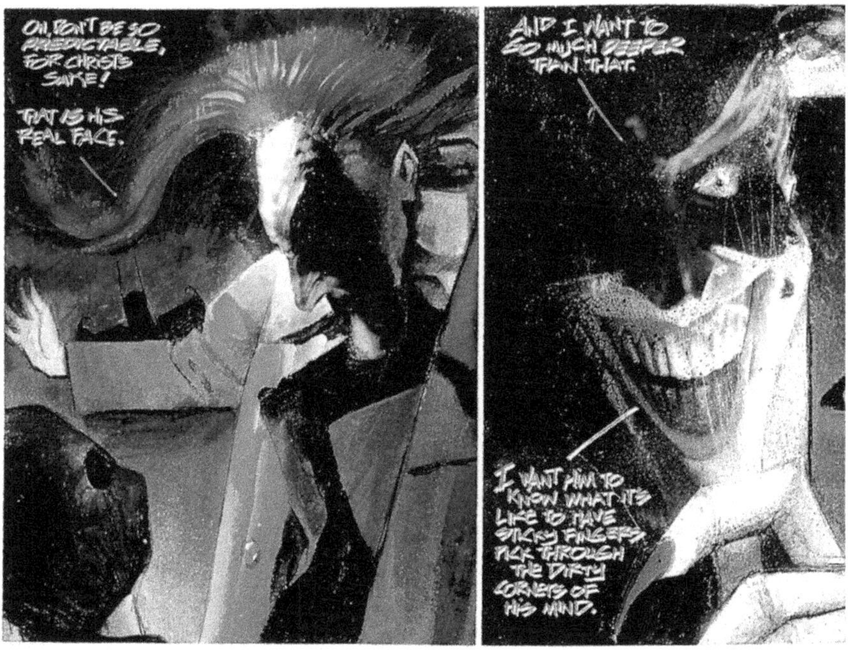

Figure 3.1 Morrison and McKean (2004), np. From *Batman: Arkham Asylum – A Serious House on Serious Earth* © DC Comics. Reproduced with permission.

his colleagues represent. In exploring the Asylum, the Dark Knight can be seen at the same time to explore the unconscious of law.

The narrative movement beyond the confines of conscious rationality can be seen from the very moment Batman enters the Asylum. As Morrison states: 'This is Alice-down-the-rabbit-hole territory. We are now outside logic. The recognisable Batman world of Gotham City and Commissioner Gordon and Bat Signals is behind us now'.[54] While navigating Arkham, Batman encounters the Asylum's inhabitants, each of whom threaten his rational order in different ways. Some of these encounters are more incidental than others, such as that with Tweedledee and Tweedledum,[55] who, beyond solidifying the idea of the Asylum as a Carroll-esque rabbit hole, suggest removing Batman's mask – a suggestion Joker dismisses as failing to go deep enough into the nasty corners of Batman's psyche.[56] Similarly, the bizarre merging of divinity, myth, and electricity in the god-like form of

54 Morrison (2004), p 13.

55 For a brief introduction to these 'minor' Batman villains, see www.comicvine.com/tweedledee/4005-13455/ and www.comicvine.com/tweedledum/4005-13454/ respectively.

56 As Joker admonishes, 'Oh, don't be so *predictable* for Christ's sake! / That *is* his real face'. See Figure 3.1. Emphases in original. We return to masking in Chapter 5.

Maxie Zeus,[57] who flings his own faeces at Batman in some kind of scatological fertility ritual, serves primarily to reinforce the madness and ritual horror of Batman's journey.

Clayface, meanwhile, poses a more visceral threat to Batman, and symbolically to the legal order, in his alliance with bodily disease.[58] Clayface is portrayed in *Arkham Asylum* as a wasting and sickly green creature, creeping in the shadows of Arkham, trying to pass his illness on to Batman: 'My skin is *sick*, Batman. / It's rotten and seeping. / Only you can help me'.[59] Clayface leers towards the reader as he reaches out to touch Batman, his ailing skin horrific in the shadows. 'I just want to *share* my disease', he says as he gets uncomfortably close.[60] Batman's response to this threat is one of horror and immediate panic. He screams for Clayface not to touch him, swiftly breaking the weak man's leg with a well-aimed kick.

What we see in this encounter is an example of Batman's repression of that which threatens him as a force for justice: Clayface represents the pain and trauma of sickness and disease that threatens the healthy body of Batman, and thus his physical capacity to fight criminality; Clayface is 'an avatar of filth and corruption, the personification of pestilence and infection'.[61] Read in a Foucaultian light, disease can be understood as the human body operating in a way that deviates from the 'normal' functioning prescribed by the structures of biology and medicine; illness resists the normalising power of disciplinary knowledge. Knowledge and control of the body is deeply political: across the twentieth century, medical technologies, for example, became more precise as life itself moved into the political sphere, with the health of the individual (rather than the wider population) justifying a new form of eugenics.[62] Beyond concerns of public health, illness thus becomes a political issue – a threat to the normal operation of a body that can fuel society through labour and consumption (disease thus needs not only to be cured, but to be labelled, categorised, reduced into reason – made amenable to control). In this way, Clayface's ravaged body becomes a threat to the social order as much as a personal threat to Bruce Wayne's physical integrity. As an avatar of justice, then, Batman's response of terrified violence keeps that threat outside consciousness: Batman does not engage with Clayface, does not try to heal him or share or understand his disease, but as a force for law and order simply suppresses him and turns away to preserve his own strength.

Similarly, in order to maintain itself as a logical system of reason – in order to preserve its own strength – law represses its unconscious dimensions: those

57 Again, see www.comicvine.com/maxie-zeus/4005-11343/ for an outline of this character's major appearances.

58 Clayface is a name that has been attached to a variety of different villains in Batman history, but many are allied in some way with disease. For a brief overview of the different incarnations, see www.comicvine.com/clayface-karlo/4005-9589/

59 Morrison and McKean (2004), np. Emphasis in original.

60 Morrison and McKean (2004), np. Emphasis in original.

61 Morrison (2004), p 16.

62 Rose (2001).

aesthetic aspects of law that dress it up and make it spectacular[63] – its institutional adornments and presentation, its ornaments and aesthetic trappings – are pushed aside to allow an image of objective rationality and unbiased truth to prevail.[64] In this process of reification, it is law's human dimension that is denied as our deeply subjective constructs of justice become separated from us as creators and are raised up as idealised and objective, without origin or bias.[65] This movement of repression – of 'antirrhesis'[66] – can again be seen in Batman's brief encounter with Scarecrow.[67] Scarecrow is deeply associated with fear, his primary activities involving the use of his own fear gas to strike terror into the innocent citizens of Gotham.[68] Batman's response to this symbolic encounter with pure fear is one of avoidance and denial. Batman does not face fear at this point, but hides behind a door and waits as Scarecrow makes his way down the dark corridor and continues off through the bowels of the Asylum. In this we see the fear symbolised by Scarecrow avoided, pushed aside, hidden, not encountered. It remains in the unconscious, unchallenged and unfaced. Just as Batman defensively represses the diseased threat of Clayface, so he does the pure fear of Scarecrow. Batman's capacity to bring his particular justice is thus secured and preserved through a denial of the disorder and threat posed by that outside his fight for rational justice, just as law's apparent coherence and order is arranged against the disorder beyond its boundary.[69]

In these early encounters in *Arkham Asylum*, we see a Batman filled with this defensive attitude of repression, a repression that Batman shares with the conscious legal order. As Morrison describes him in his script, Batman is 'constantly on the defensive, constantly expecting attack from some quarter … [he] is a frightened, threatened boy who has made himself terrible at the cost of his own humanity'.[70] And law, by pushing aside the rich aesthetic dimensions of life in order to construct its dominant order, similarly pays the cost of humanity, constituting the legal subject via 'a cold and enduring reason, a science, which forbids all images and so denies the power of all other laws'[71] – including those worlds of law that populate the cultural dimensions of life.

Except for Joker, perhaps one of the most famous residents housed in Arkham Asylum is Harvey Dent, and beyond the duality of good and bad lawyering he may represent,[72] he raises a critical reflection of the reification of legal knowledge.

63 See Gearey (2001), p 17, and generally pp 1–23.
64 See Goodrich (1995), pp 12–13 and generally.
65 See Manderson (2000), pp 158–162.
66 See Goodrich (1995).
67 Morrison and McKean (2004), np.
68 See, for example, *Batman Begins* (2005). Indeed, he is known as the 'Master of Fear': see www.comicvine.com/scarecrow/4005-3726/ for a character overview.
69 See Goodrich (1995), pp 220–221.
70 Morrison (2004), p 5.
71 Goodrich (1995), p 67. See also Naffine (2009), pp 31–43, who describes the orthodox view of legal personhood as one of abstract, technical capacities that pushes aside disruptive philosophical and spiritual concerns.
72 Rendleman (2009).

Harvey Dent was the District Attorney of Gotham before he became the villain Two-Face: one side of his face horribly scarred, one side of his personality horribly evil, obsessed with duality and relying on a two-faced coin – one side of it horribly scarred – to decide whether his victims live or die. With his connections to the legal profession, and his penchant for passing judgments on his victims, Dent's significance as a critical vision of dominant law is overt. The judgments and decisions Dent makes, like those of law, are based on ostensibly objective criteria, for what could be more objective than the toss of a coin? The result of a coin toss is disconnected from any contextual or prejudicial factors; it is blind to age, sex, race, ethnicity, religion, biography, history, politics, consequences, facts, circumstances, evidence, opinion, regulation, morality, guilt, innocence. And in this radical objectivity there is embedded a deep parody of law's consciousness of unbiased rationality. For the coin toss, in being so blind, produces outcomes that do not take into account the moral 'reality' of human conduct. From this starting point of 'true' or 'complete' objectivity,[73] the journey towards the kind of objectivity enacted by legal processes becomes one of determining which factors, which elements of context, history, and biography and so on, should be taken into account and how. The objectivity of law is thus exposed to be a product of multiple choices or assumptions about what is and is not relevant when trying to achieve moral truth.[74]

But on the pages of *Arkham Asylum*, this critical parody is taken further. As part of Dent's 'treatment', the psychiatrist Adams explains, he has been weaned off the duality-obsessed coin and onto the more complex, yet similarly 'objective', six-sided die. This, Adams claims, has enabled Dent to increase the sophistication and complexity of his decisions. From the die he has then been weaned onto a 78-card Tarot deck, thus supposedly enabling even more sophisticated decisions.[75] But in the increasing quantity of options, their objective quality is not altered, nor is Dent's ability to make his own decisions without relying on this objective guide. His decisions remain disconnected from influential factors beyond that which can change the physical order of the cards, including Dent's own preferences, personality, moral beliefs, and conscience. Dent's decision-making process becomes a near-literal house of cards, built on a tentative connection with living reality, increasingly complex yet in no way increasingly meaningful.

73 Note, of course, that not even the coin toss is completely objective, being subject to the various physical effects that influence the movement of objects through space, such as temperature, humidity, the force of the flip, the weight of the coin, the force of gravity, and so on – not to mention how we conceptualise and measure such phenomena, or, for that matter, how we define a 'coin' or what we mean by 'toss'.

74 Similar things can be said of (social) scientific objectivity, where inductive statistical correlation is unable to give an explanation for a result without first assuming what is and is not relevant to that result: see Crewe (2013), pp 30–32.

75 See Morrison and McKean (2004), np. The use of the Tarot is not insignificant, as Morrison's deployment of references to cards such as The Moon throughout *Arkham Asylum* indicate: see above, and discussion below.

Similarly law, when framed as something objectively separate from human bias, is disconnected from the social and cultural values that feed and shape it.[76] But even taking notions of social construction into account, although 'real' law may not be abstractly 'out there', divorced from our perception of it, it can still be argued to adhere to a particular model of objectivity through its reliance on the assumed existence of shared understandings or communal norms,[77] to which we can refer as pre-existing 'objective' sources of moral value. Indeed, there is arguably a more general shift towards an authoritative role for positive scientific objectivity in determining value-free morality, with other forms of moral pronouncements being seen as mere subjective opinion.[78] In its satire, Dent's coin-toss cuts through such hopes of objectivity, exposing the particular and limited set of forces that law (consciously) accepts as being able to legitimately influence a decision. The idea of law and justice as some fully objective 'truth' is shown up as deeply problematic, falling foul of everything antirrhesis implies.

Adams can be seen starting to explain Dent's 'weaning' process in Figure 3.2. In Batman's visual representation as a flowing shadow with no clear boundaries or definite presence is seen the complex fluidity of the world outside reason.[79] As already noted, the world of the Asylum is depicted as similarly uncertain, with McKean's artwork across the volume indicative of the madness against which Batman operates. The specifically multimodal structure of Figure 3.2 also represents Adams's rationalisations (*qua* text) amidst the uncertain visual environment of the Asylum; and, in the reference to Dent's duality, law's problematic rational order is invoked, presented in a radically fluid context, symbolic of the fluidity of life. Although still wedded to an abstract objectivity, Adams's discourse on Dent's rehabilitation – his weaning from dual-sided coin to six-sided die to 78-sided Tarot deck – begins to map a journey beyond law's rational opposition to chaos,[80] presenting a movement towards judgment as being made up of infinite possibilities. As she states: 'Soon he'll have a completely functional judgmental facility that doesn't rely so much on black and white absolutes'.[81] But as Dent is given an increasing number of options he becomes unable to make even the simplest of decisions. The practical benefits of binary decision-making are lost when a more complex or sophisticated moral schema is introduced. As a force that needs to know who is 'good' and who is 'criminal', although using a rich aesthetics to gain and display his power (a description that sounds a lot like the legal institution), Batman himself relies on the same binary logic as Dent. But in Dent we see a condensation and hyperbolic critique of law's (and Batman's) adherence to

76 See, for example, Fagelson (2002).
77 See Fagelson (2002).
78 Davis (2013).
79 Despite his representation as fluid, the justice he fights for is still one of order. This has interesting connotations for the process of law's repression, as is discussed below.
80 On rational law's oppositional relationship with chaos, see Manderson (2003), pp 177–183.
81 Morrison and McKean (2004), np.

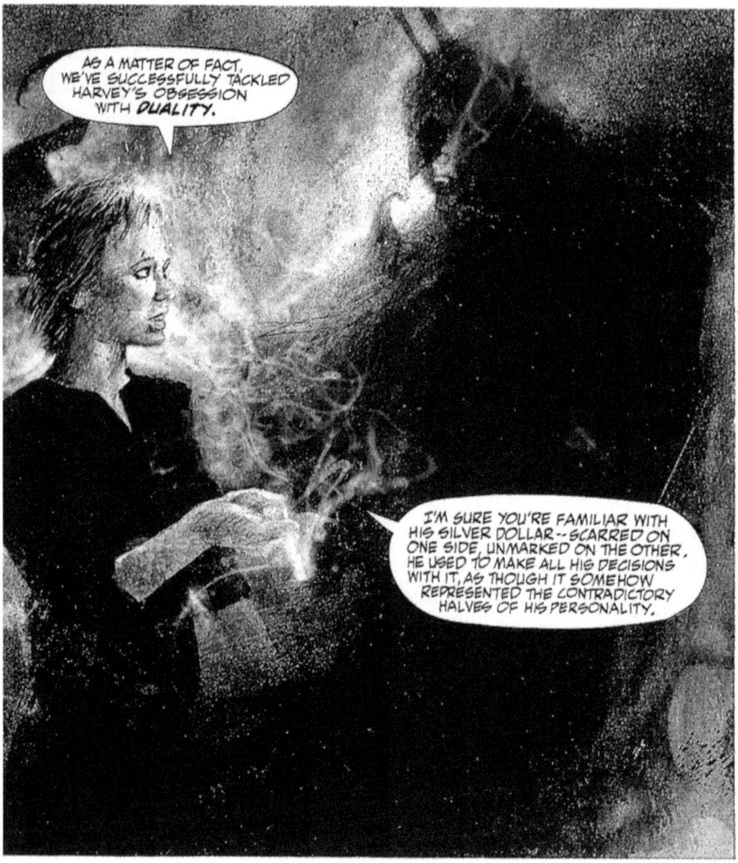

Figure 3.2 Morrison and McKean (2004), np. From *Batman: Arkham Asylum – A Serious House on Serious Earth* © DC Comics. Reproduced with permission.

objectivity. His reliance on a radically 'objective' coin-toss ridicules as it mimics law's quest for true objectivity in its decisions; but, to move into an arguably more sophisticated mode of moral determination, where things are not as simple as innocent/guilty or good/evil, undermines and potentially destroys law's practical capacity as a (moral) decision-maker.

Whilst Adams's attempts to cure Dent seek to enable a more sophisticated and capable engagement with moral life, his 'judgmental facility' remains trapped within a structure of radical objectivity, ghostless, abstracted from experience. This 'treatment' constructs a fragile house of cards that is unable to comprehend the rich complexity and ineffability of human life. Dent becomes lost in a maze of abstraction, unable to make the simplest of decisions. The fact Dent's cards are from the Tarot is not without significance: Tarot cards are rich with meaning beyond their rational or physical form – symbolic, metaphorical, mystical, emotional, cultural – and so are populated with unconscious dimensions beyond their logic as a system of objective choice. In this can be seen a metaphor for the ghostless structure of rational law and the threat of its repressed *anima*: the legal unconscious flows around the rational legal order, producing drafts of air that threaten to topple the objectivity of the lawyer's house of cards. Shying away from the move towards abstract chaos that the weaning onto the 78-sided deck signifies, and after having his coin returned to him in the final pages of *Arkham Asylum*, Dent realises the Tarot deck is just a pack of cards and knocks down the (literal) house of cards he has built, returning to the certain, simple objectivity of his coin. The denial of the Tarot deck as being anything more than just a pack of cards is again a repression of the aesthetic world of symbolic power and excessive life that law reifies itself from in order to maintain its objectivity.

Having introduced Batman's journey through *Arkham Asylum* as one that encounters law's unconscious, exposing its repression within dominant structures of rationality, the second half of this chapter now moves to draw out the work's central point or lesson: that madness makes the law what it is.

Headless lawyers

The maze that dreams

In his journey through the Asylum, on one level Batman can be read as walking a path of radical introspection: he enters not a building, populated with the otherness of civilisation (madness, criminality), but his own mind. As he explores the halls of Arkham, it becomes abundantly clear that it is the halls of his own unconscious that Batman travels. *Arkham Asylum* is not just a story about Batman quelling the disruption at the infamous psychiatric institution, but is a multifaceted metaphor, an alchemical ritual, for the mediation of chaos, for the quelling of the unreason in the human heart – and in the heart of law and justice. It is comics-as-*komos*. Batman's journey through the Asylum is a journey through the secrets of his own mind, his dark night of the soul. His various encounters with the inmates represent different qualities and dimensions of his own madness, his own animating traumas and desires. On the pages of *Arkham Asylum*, Batman is no longer the strong, swooping *deus ex justitia* of Gotham's streets, but (as we saw with his repressive attitude) becomes a neurotic mess struggling amidst all the things he strives to live against. Batman's journey is one into his own inner weakness and madness, the horrors and neuroses that live beneath the surface of his conscious mind and challenge his façade of stability and rational order – and symbolically, the order of law.

Morrison and McKean thus transfigure the world of Arkham into the inner world of Batman's psyche. The Asylum itself becomes Batman's mind. It is through Batman's encounter with Mad Hatter that this is made most explicit; as the Hatter explains:

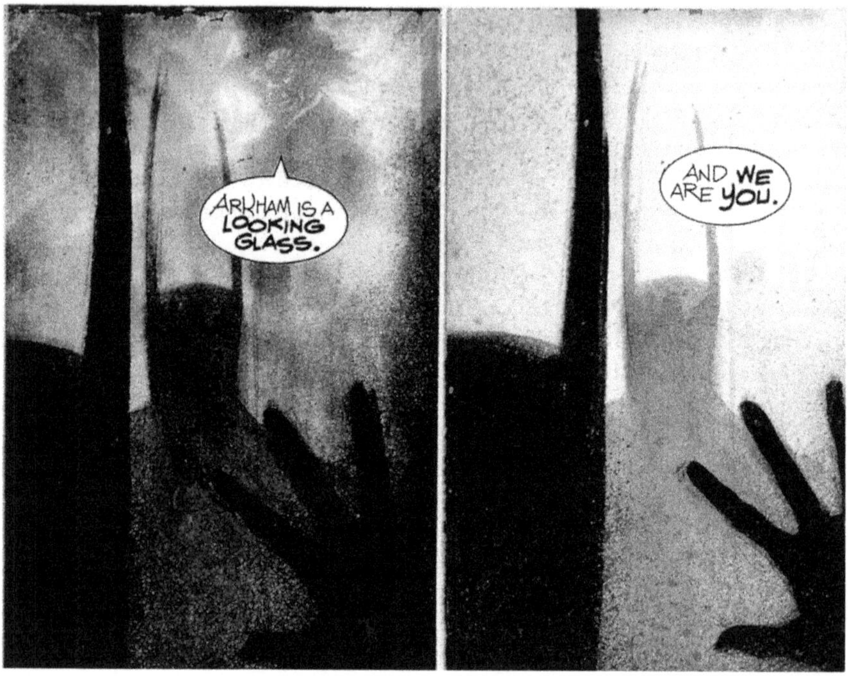

Figure 3.3 Morrison and McKean (2004), np. From *Batman: Arkham Asylum – A Serious House on Serious Earth* © DC Comics. Reproduced with permission.

> Sometimes I think the Asylum is a *head.* / We're inside a huge head that dreams us all into being. / Perhaps it's *your* head, Batman. / Arkham is a *looking glass.* / And *we* are *you.*[82]

In Figure 3.3 can be seen the visual representation of this idea: Batman looks towards the Mad Hatter, who is gradually replaced with a mirror image of Batman; the Hatter's otherness literally becoming Batman himself, a reflected image of the Dark Knight emerging from the swirling mess of the Hatter's room, a dream crystallising out of unconscious fluidity.[83] In the looking glass, quite literally, the Hatter is Batman – all the inhabitants of the Asylum are parts of Batman. The world of *Arkham Asylum* is a skewed and fluid reflection of Batman's waking mind, a 'negative image' of law's consciousness: a complex mess of repressed madness and irrationality, of unstructured sensuality and embodied, ineffable life.

The Hatter's notion of the Asylum as a living being dreaming its population into existence is echoed by Amadeus Arkham, the troubled founder of the institution. As he observes, Arkham Asylum 'is an organism, hungry for madness. / It

82 Morrison and McKean (2004), np. Emphases in original.
83 We discuss dreams in Chapter 6.

is the maze that dreams'.[84] With Amadeus's facing of trauma – an encounter that mirrors, and is mirrored by, Batman's – the connection between Asylum and legal unconscious is solidified. The trauma faced by Amadeus was, like Batman's, the murder of his family. Where Bruce Wayne witnessed his parents' death by a street thief, Amadeus came home to discover the bodies of Constance and Harriet Arkham, his wife and daughter, horribly dismembered and 'indescribably violated'.[85] The key feature of this trauma, which eventually leads to the fracturing of Amadeus's mind and his own communion with madness,[86] is the discovery that the person who had attacked his family had placed his daughter's dismembered head inside a dollhouse.

As can be seen in Figure 3.4, Harriet Arkham's face peers vacantly out through the dollhouse window. In this image are encoded many of the themes related to the transfiguring of Batman's narrative into an introspective journey through his own unconscious mind – and the configuring of Arkham itself as the unconscious of law. As Morrison reminds us, the dollhouse is symbolic of the Arkham house,[87] here containing the very core of Amadeus's trauma: the dismemberment of his beloved daughter. The dollhouse, then, contains Amadeus's own personal demons. But by specifically placing Harriet's *head* inside the house, that which fills the Asylum becomes more than just a symbol of Amadeus's trauma, but is also suggestive of that which dwells inside the head – dreams and madness. In Figure 3.4, the Asylum comes to be inhabited by the head in the house, thus setting up a complex layering: madness within trauma within Asylum/house. The madness enfolded in the trauma is contained and locked away, repressed and controlled – Arkham Asylum comes to house the unconscious itself. The unconscious nature of this trauma is reinforced in the comics form. The background to the panels in Figure 3.4 contain the excesses of blood that flowed from Harriet's and Constance's murder – the root of Amadeus's trauma. This blood acts as a background or sea upon which the conscious forms of Amadeus's experience (of the head in the house, of his linguistic speech) float and fracture into madness. The Asylum's contents are thus configured as madness and dreams – the unconscious symbolised by the head in the house – but the complexity is layered further when we recall, as Hatter announced above, that the Arkham house can be understood as a head dreaming its contents: the Asylum *is* the head in the house, dreaming itself.

Despite this symbolically complex butchering of his family, Amadeus still pursues his goal of establishing Arkham Asylum. Above the institution, Amadeus places a towering statue of St Michael who, as Amadeus tells us, is 'an image of

84 Morrison and McKean (2004), np.
85 Morrison and McKean (2004), np.
86 This event, as seen in Figure 3.4, is presented as the point at which Amadeus's mind starts its descent into insanity through the interjection of the 'cuckoo' clock, invoking that popular terminology for mental illness. The fracturing of Amadeus's mind is also seen in the fragmentation of the panels that become more disparate across the page.
87 Morrison (2004), p 35.

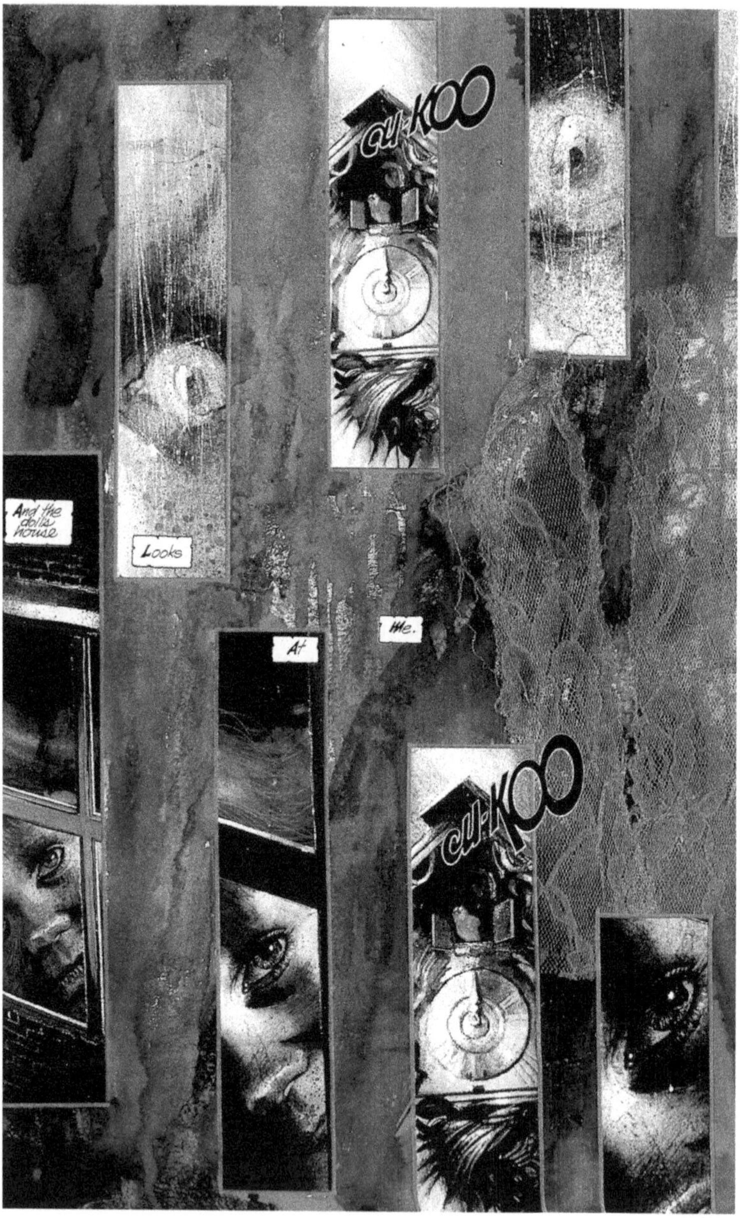

Figure 3.4 Morrison and McKean (2004), np. From *Batman: Arkham Asylum – A Serious House on Serious Earth* © DC Comics. Reproduced with permission.

the triumph of *reason* over the irrational'.[88] The Asylum is thus loaded with a borderline status, a site upon which (like the comics-as-*komos* that articulates it) reason and unreason meet and are mediated. After successfully setting up the Asylum, Amadeus eventually finds the fiend who murdered his family, takes him into his 'care', and on the anniversary of his family's death[89] uses the Asylum's electroconvulsive therapy machine to '*burn* the filthy bastard'.[90] After this cathartic retribution, Amadeus finds himself doomed to wander the Asylum, attempting to use routine and formalised order to stave off his encroaching madness:

> Routine is important, I think. A good routine diverts the mind from morbid imaginings. / … / My movements through the house have become as formalized as *ballet* and I feel that I have become an essential part of some incomprehensible biological process. / The house is an organism, hungry for madness. / It is the maze that dreams. / And I am *lost.*[91]

Amadeus's routines are not able to suppress the madness and disorder of life. He follows his 'ritual perambulations'[92] but does not gain meaning or solace by doing so, cannot secure his demons within their ordered structure, and ends up, like Dent above, becoming lost in the abstract maze of reason.

In a moment of dramatic (drug-fuelled) introspection, the narration of which is laid over the images of Batman fighting his own inner demons (the comics form thus making the profound connection between Amadeus's and Batman's stories), Amadeus comes to face the madness that rents his psyche and suffers a complete breakdown. He then dresses himself in his dead mother's wedding dress, and walks the halls of the Asylum, vowing to keep the world safe from the mad demons he has housed inside the skull that is Arkham's walls: 'I shall *contain* the presences that roam these rooms and narrow stairways / … / and pray they never break free'.[93] He is ultimately imprisoned within the Asylum he created, locked away with the madness he has sworn to contain. In his final moments, old and alone in the darkness of the institution, he uses his fingers to scratch into the floor his appreciation for being on the mad side of the veil, free from the shackles of rationality:

> I see now the virtue in madness, for this country knows no law nor any boundary. / I pity the poor shades confined to the Euclidean prison that is sanity. / All things are possible here, and I am what madness has made me. / Whole. / And complete. / And free at last. / … / I'm *Arkham.* / I'm *home.* / Where I belong.[94]

88 Morrison and McKean (2004), np. Emphasis in original.
89 True to the dark humour associated with the Joker, this anniversary falls on 1 April.
90 Morrison and McKean (2004), np. Emphasis in original.
91 Morrison and McKean (2004), np. Emphases in original.
92 Morrison and McKean (2004), np.
93 Morrison and McKean (2004), np. Emphasis in original.
94 Morrison and McKean (2004), np. Emphases in original.

This movement from imprisonment to freedom is a complex one, and one that feeds off the limits of rationality. The Asylum houses madness, it contains irrationality; although ostensibly a 'prison', it holds an infinite space. It is the space beyond rational order, outside of reason; a space of unstructured life, of phenomenal excess and infinite potential. It is the world beyond rational order, beyond textual signification and the limited concepts of reason and categories of law; an infinite, analogue variation of unstructured life outside the digital multiframe of reason.[95] This realm is not a void or an emptiness; its chaos does not imply nihilism and nothingness – nor even anarchy – but, as Manderson reminds us, is a realm of generative potential.[96] And, in the same way that the coastline has a fractal quality (becoming increasingly detailed and thus increasing in length depending upon how closely one measures its contours), so law can be 'mapped' from different perspectives and levels: 'there are many maps [of law], each of which draws attention to various features, scales, relationships, and values to the utter exclusion of others'.[97] Recognising this pluralism requires recognising that law, like the coastline, is fractal: it is 'an infinite line nested in a finite space'.[98] The unstructured 'madness' of irrationality is similarly held within the finite space of the Asylum, embedding infinite variation within the finite walls of the institution.

It is in this infinite world that Arkham becomes 'trapped', free from structure and order. Arkham faces his madness, he steps beyond the limits of rationality but fails to survive. His unreason is not controlled, his rational structure collapses; but in failing to find his way back to the sanctuary of reason Arkham discovers ultimate freedom. He is free from the strictures of rational logic, the limited shades of orthodox knowledge; the 'prison of sanity' does not limit his imagination or understanding. He remains lost in this other-world, outside law, outside order. In Arkham's failure to 'escape' this world, in his inability to return from madness to the structures of reason, we find the fear of what facing law's unconscious might mean: that order and structure, and meaning, are lost. He represents the terrible threat of irrationality: the fear that by opening up to the irrational we will lose all the certainty, order, understanding, and truth that conscious law relies upon to function – too high the price of freedom.

Indeed, it is this unstructured world that exists as law's unconscious, the threat it carries with it. This 'freedom' is locked away (in Arkham Asylum, in *Arkham Asylum*, in law's unconscious, outside the rational order), repressed and feared. As the parallel between Batman and Arkham suggests, in his fight against the chaos of disorder and madness, Batman carries the threat of his failure with him. The infinite space of madness, of disorder and analogue potential, is nested – repressed – within the physically finite form of the Dark Knight.

95 See Tranter (2012) on the 'analogue' spaces that remain excessive to the 'digital' structures of rational law.
96 See Manderson (2000), pp 180–183.
97 Manderson (2000), pp 177–179, quotation at p 178. I discuss maps as a metaphor for knowing in Chapter 6.
98 Manderson (2000), p 179. See also Sousanis (2015), p 44.

In such processes of repression it can be seen that law is already more than the rational consciousness it presents itself as being. Law is more than its logical pronouncements, more than its reasoned judgments and rational rules. It is also constituted of rich dimensions of symbolic power and aesthetic adornment, of meaning and sensory experience, of metaphor and art. Law's unconscious, traditionally kept repressed, outside the rational order of justice, still remains part of law. As Kieran Tranter's reading of the *Serenity* comics demonstrates (in a digital rather than psychoanalytical frame), even where the technology of binary, logical legality becomes a living totality, there will always be 'gaps' or analogue spaces that escape the totalising code of law.[99] The legal order can never fully capture the 'madness' of life; its unconscious 'demons' always remain.

Law's demons (the threat of disorder and loss of meaning, of the destructuring of life) are contained in the Arkham house. And this house, in its repressive function, becomes the house of reason – the house of law. Law gives structure to life, it is the house of reason in the lawyer's head – but this house is full of demons, of madness, of that which exceeds its structure, that which is not captured or contained in law's net. The house in the lawyer's head has a severed head inside it: a repressed terror of chaotic disorder, irresolvable harm, and unstructured life. Framed jurisprudentially, the severed head in the house becomes the lawyer's head – dismembered, removed, the capacity to structure and order gone with it. The decapitated figure of Harriet Arkham, staring out to us in death, beyond the visceral trauma she represents for Amadeus, symbolises the threat of the legal unconscious: the lawyer's head in the house of law, the threat of chaos underlying the rational order.

Remember madness

Ultimately, *Arkham Asylum*'s relationship to law's process of reification or antirrhesis – the attempted encoding of excessive life into a rational consciousness of legality and the concomitant denial of that excess, and of the encoding processes themselves – is one of remembrance. The repression of law's aesthetic dimensions can be framed as a 'forgetting', whereby conscious legality loses awareness of those elements outside its rational order. Whilst Foucault's *History of Madness* traces the broad 'forgetting' of madness as part of humanity as it becomes subsumed by reason across the Renaissance and beyond, Goodrich's *Oedipus Lex* traces the Renaissance shifts whereby law's previously acknowledged aesthetic dimensions were repressed to become the unconscious of modern law.[100] Through Batman's symbolic navigation of his own unconscious in *Arkham Asylum*, this 'forgetting' of humanity's madness, and of law's epistemological unconscious, is undone.

Batman's encounter with the threat of unreason crystallises in the form of Killer Croc, who is symbolic of the forces of chaos and irrationality, the atavistic lizard

99 Tranter (2012).
100 See Goodrich (1995).

brain of our evolutionary past,[101] the Old Dragon of Revelations: the demon of unreason, Satan himself.[102] Croc is the condensed form of all those others to Batman's rational justice and the ordered world he strives for and defends – a cosmic, world-destroying madness. In his fight against Croc, and in his broader fight against the forces of unreason that populate the Asylum of his unconscious, Batman is allied with the figure of St Michael, the warrior angel of Heaven, leading the charge against the armies of Satan and evil.[103] But this apocalyptic subduing of the forces of evil symbolised by St Michael is configured in *Arkham Asylum* not just as the triumph of goodness, of heaven over hell, but (as Amadeus's description of his statue explained above) of reason over the irrational.[104]

In this encounter, Batman not only faces the dragon of his own unconscious, but also of law's unconscious. As Satan, Croc represents everything that is other to rational order, and thus everything that is other to conscious legal knowledge: chaos, disorder, irrationality, the aesthetic, the sensory – that which exceeds the rational encoding of life: the lawyer's decapitated head in the house of law. Batman's encounter is mediated via St Michael's spear, which he removes from the statue and uses to defeat Croc: the spear of reason, a shaft of solid metal that at the climax connects Batman to his dragon, skewering them both together, self and other, reason and madness, Jesus and Satan, order and chaos, law and threat, knowledge and uncertainty – the *komos* at work in *Arkham Asylum*'s alchemical culmination. Indeed, the linking via the spear is a visceral emanation of the broader epistemological process that is happening throughout *Arkham Asylum*: the meeting of law with its denied dimensions, of reason with madness. In the subsequent snapping of that spear, such that Croc falls to his defeat and Batman survives,[105] both Batman and law emerge from the other side of this dark night having faced and survived their other. The Moon Card, like the *komos*, has done its work. As Morrison explains in his original script, 'Batman has embraced the unconscious. As in the case of [Amadeus] Arkham, Dragon and Man are now one'.[106] But by embracing the unconscious, both Batman and law are altered: in confronting its epistemological outside, in its remembering of cosmic madness, legal rationality reaches its limits, snaps, and emerges aware that those limits can be crossed, and of the epistemological grounding they represent. Where Amadeus falls into madness and is 'lost', unable to regrasp the handles of reason, the legality

101 Although not directly concerned with law's unconscious, Manderson shows how modern law is based on the emergence of a civilised order, produced through the repression or suppression of the 'wildness' of our evolutionary past. Myth and storytelling encodes civility in us, privatising 'wild' aspects of humanity such as emotionality, friendship, and passion, with public government accordingly emerging as rational. See Manderson (2003).

102 Morrison (2004), p 51.

103 See also Holweck (1911) for description of St Michael's various ecclesiastical offices, including that of the warrior angel who defeats Satan.

104 Morrison and McKean (2004), np.

105 See Morrison and McKean (2004), np.

106 Morrison (2004), p 63.

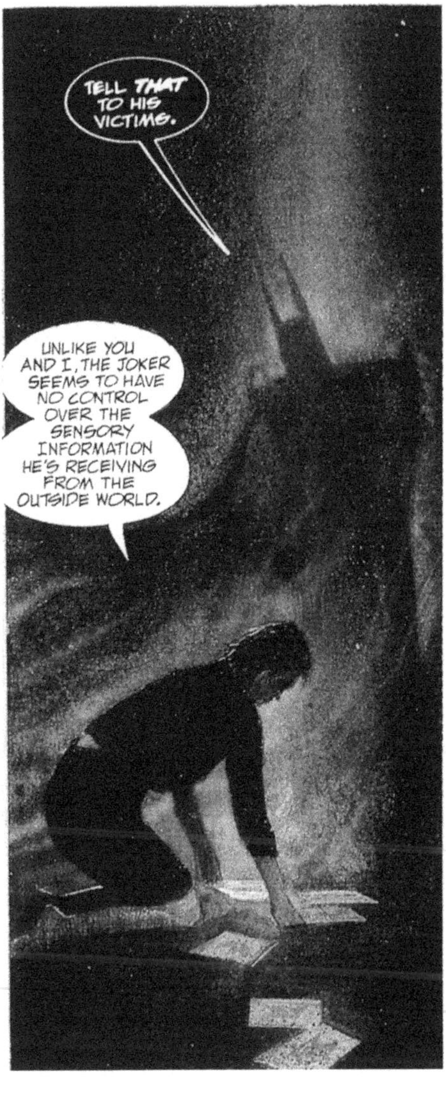

Figure 3.5 Morrison and McKean (2004), np. From Batman: *Arkham Asylum – A Serious House on Serious Earth* © DC Comics. Reproduced with permission.

represented by Batman emerges stronger and more sane in its acceptance of its own madness.

This embracing of their other is something that both Batman and law already do. Recall Batman's visual appearance in Figure 3.2, which is not one of stable certainty, but instead the uncertainty of flowing shadow, cape and cowl. In Figure 3.5 we see Batman in conversation with Dr Adams, one of Arkham Aslyum's therapists. They are discussing the Joker – psychotic killer, torturer of innocents, and Batman's nemesis – who is emblematic of all the violence, madness and disorder against which Batman fights. Adams, as a forensic psychologist, is outlining her rationalised assessment of the Joker:

> The Joker's a *special* case / … / we're not even sure if he can be properly defined as *insane* / … / we may actually be looking at some kind of super-sanity here. / A brilliant new modification of human perception / … / Unlike you and I, the Joker seems to have no control over the sensory information he's receiving from the world.[107]

As Foucault observed of prerenaissance madness, it was the insane who were privy to the secrets of the universe:

> These strange forms [of madness] belong from the outset to the great secret … the inaccessible, fearsome knowledge that the madman, in his innocent foolishness, already possesses. While men of reason and wisdom see only fragmentary figures that are all the more frightening for their incompleteness, the madman sees a whole, unbroken sphere.[108]

Madness was outside reason, a cosmic force of chaos and apocalypse that ultimately signalled death.[109] Adams's diagnosis suggests that Joker's foolishness may indeed be one that approaches a different order of truth, a total and unfiltered perception enabling a hyperknowing with which his mind cannot cope. But, *qua* diagnosis, we remain in the realm of the binary opposition – and thus mutual reliance – between reason and madness. Adams is wielding disciplinary reason in order to explain, and thus control, Joker's madness. True to Foucault's history, Adams's modern ratiocinations maintain madness as a distinctly rational category, quelling its power as a threatening force of otherness.

Adams's rationalisations are communicated via text, presented multimodally in Figure 3.5 against the swirling backdrop of the Asylum and of Batman. Adams is depicted with sharp clarity against her surroundings, the visual representation confirming the associations in the text: Adams, couched in the orthodox discipline of forensic psychology, is attempting to explain and control the world through the production of 'certain' rational knowledge and categories. In disjunction with this, Batman looms as a spectral and uncertain form, querying the extent to which Adams's explanations encounter the lived experience of crime: 'Tell *that* to his victims'. We can also see the divide between the phenomenal and the legislated, between the living experience of crime and victimhood and the attempts to capture and 'deal with' that experience through rational criminolegal structures. And it is the intricacies of the very form of comics-as-*komos* that articulate this, by

107 Morrison and McKean (2004), np. Emphases in original.
108 Foucault (2006), p 19.
109 Foucault (2006), pp 14–21.

playing reason, text, image and aesthetics off one another. Thus, in Figure 3.5, we can see Batman's aesthetic presentation as fluid and uncertain, a haunting otherness within the Asylum that threatens the rational order of Adams's logical deductions with the excessive phenomenal life they cannot contain.

Figure 3.5 also exemplifies the way Batman's substantive perpetuation of dominant ideals of criminal justice bleeds through his more expansive aesthetics. Batman appears here as a vision of spectral justice, challenging the rationalisations of dominant criminological knowledge – but by deploying the symbolic power of suffering victims, which invokes a key trope of white male criminal justice politics, and betrays the deep conservatism that shapes the particular brand of justice he deals out on the streets.[110] Indeed, like orthodox law and criminology, Batman seeks to order the world, to mediate the forces that threaten and thereby protect the innocent. Yet in Figure 3.5, he is cloaked in the rich uncertainty of existence that he, and, as Wender shows us, legal and criminological knowledge, seek to repress. Indeed, it is part of Batman's ironic composition that he is both rational detective, relying on forensics and ratiocentric deduction, and terrifying, mythic bat.[111] The disjuncture between these two elements initially seems to represent an irresolvable conflict, but there is a deep logic in Batman's constitution in terms of his phenomenal epistemology. Bruce Wayne, in presenting himself as the Dark Knight, takes that which is his opposite, that which is his other – the disorder and chaos of lawless madness, the unreason outside the ordered, knowable world – and cloaks himself in it. He uses that which terrifies him to make himself, in turn, terrible, as Dave McKean's presentation of the original logic behind Batman's genesis (included as an appendix to *Arkham Asylum*) makes clear (see Box 3.1).[112]

Batman thus locates himself on the boundary, mediating between juridical order and aesthetic disorder in the manner of the *komos*. The order Batman fights to bring about may be that of the rich, white male, but it is achieved by donning this 'cloak of otherness'. In doing so, Batman can be seen to undertake a form of edgework, seeking to encounter something beyond the limits of order. The basic premise of edgework can be understood as a means of experiencing, and thus discovering, something 'real', a kind of an authentic uncertainty beyond the confines of culture; edgeworkers 'discover "authentic" selves rooted in the objective

110 Beyond the conservative overtones of the hegemonic paradox noted above, note also that the very notion of the superhero may be connected with the violent desires of fascism: see Gavaler (2016).

111 See Giddens (2015b), pp 769–773.

112 This is taken from the appendix to *Arkham Asylum*, and reproduced here with similar typesetting to the original layout in an attempt to retain some of the aesthetics of McKean's presentation of Batman's psyche. See also the first telling of Batman's decision to become a bat:

> Criminals are a superstitious cowardly lot, so my disguise must be able to strike terror into their hearts. I must be a creature of the night, black, terrible ... a ... a ... A bat! That's it! It's an omen. I shall become a bat!
>
> *Detective Comics Vol 1 #33* (1939)

BATMAN:

CRIMINALS

CRIMINALS ARE A TERROR.

HEARTS OF THE NIGHT. I MUST DISGUISE MY. TERROR.

CRIMINALS ARE COWARDLY. A SUPERSTITIOUS TERRIBLE OMEN.
A COWARDLY LOT. MY DISGUISE MUST
STRIKE TERROR.

I MUST BE BLACK. TERRIBLE. CRIMINALS ARE.

CRIMINALS ARE A SUPERSTITIOUS COWARDLY LOT.
I MUST BE A CREATURE. I MUST BE A CREATURE OF THE NIGHT.

MOMMY'S DEAD.

DADDY'S DEAD.

BRUCIE'S DEAD.

I SHALL BECOME A BAT

uncertainty of their bodies' via the navigation of physical risk.[113] The physicality of the risks may be central,[114] but such risks can also be framed spiritually – as in extreme ritual practices, where physical risk becomes symbolic of destructive and chaotic forces beyond normal control that the practice mediates and domesticates[115] – and collaboratively – as in the context of sadomasochism, where the edges navigated, constituted in conjunction with another, also become emotional and psychological.[116] In the context of Batman's navigation of madness, it is the perceived characteristics of otherness that shape Batman's encounter with otherness and his attempts to quell it and bring it to order. There is thus something epistemological about his edgy activity: exploring the edge means navigating the limits of understanding and experiencing things that remain beyond definition, ineffable.[117] Indeed, Bruce Wayne perceives chaos and uncertainty as terrifying forces, so Batman becomes chaotic and uncertain; he cloaks himself in that which he is trying to control, in that which threatens him, adopting the mantle of irrational disorder as a defence against irrational disorder.

113 Lyng et al (2009), p 110.
114 Lyng (2004).
115 Bromley (2007).
116 Newmahr (2011).
117 See Lyng et al (2009), pp 108–109.

By mediating order and disorder – by embodying the *komos* – Batman makes excessive otherness present to conscious legality, but does so in a way that mediates it as he works towards his goal of justice. In Ultimate Fighting, for example, 'edgeworkers seek to find limits without transgressing them and to avoid crossing into the abyss of chaos where they are no longer in control',[118] and such activity can be linked to phenomenal participation in violent crime. Jack Katz explicates the logic behind 'being mean', observing how this is more than just an abstract choice for those who follow the 'ways of the badass': it is a way of accessing a rich world of interactions and transcending rationality.[119] Being violent and threatening and presenting yourself as imminently dangerous transgresses the 'edge' of rational order.

> They ['badasses'] understand precisely the nature of rationality and they position themselves carefully to manifest that their spirit, their meaning, is not limited by their need to make intelligible to others or even to themselves the purposive coherence or utilitarian sensibility of their action.[120]

Indeed, such presentations are 'a pristinely rational social logic for manifesting that one has transcended rationality'.[121] The epistemological ramifications of violent edgework can clearly be seen: navigating the edge in this way involves in an important sense navigating the edge of rational order. And in this navigation edgeworkers remain in control by taking charge of the chaos and disorder they explore. In the context of Ultimate Fighting, this is done by presenting oneself as violent and chaotic:

> the badass controls contingency – both his own and that of the other – by intentionally creating chaos … Such strategies draw on the very things they fear the most – uncertainty, unpredictability, and chaos.[122]

In order to keep chaos at bay (and thus stay on the edge, rather than over it), these kinds of edgeworkers no more or less than Batman take on the façade of that which they fear, cloaking themselves in the otherness of unpredictable, uncontrolled experience.

Just as the multimodal form of comics mediates between Adams's textual rationalisations of the Joker and the chaotic fluidity of the Asylum, in dressing himself up as a terrifying mythic bat-creature, Batman becomes a symbol of the *komos* that mediates between unreason and juristic order. Batman visually presents himself in the manner of his other in order to quell and control that other. This is,

118 Lyng et al (2009), p 113.
119 Katz (1988), pp 99–102.
120 Katz (1988), p 100.
121 Katz (1988), p 101.
122 Lyng et al (2009), p 117.

in many ways, the opposite of the reification that takes place in the criminal justice translation of 'life' into 'problems'. It is therefore a reminder of what criminal justice and criminology has forgotten or pushed aside: orthodox reason denies and hides that which is its other (the aesthetic, the image, the chaos of irrationality, the human origins of its pronouncements) in order to present itself as rationally stable, logical, and objective.[123] Batman cloaks himself in otherness in order to be stronger and more capable of facing that otherness; criminal law and justice, meanwhile, steep themselves in a dangerous and unstable denial, pushing aside the phenomenal, living dimensions of crime in favour of a clean, 'certain' knowledge – but a knowledge constantly under threat from that unconscious beyond. It is the edge of this 'certainty' that Batman's embodied *komos* navigates, with assistance from the comics-as-*komos* that articulates him, as he engages and absorbs aspects of the rich, sensual realm of aesthetic experience outside the rational order.

Batman uses his visual terror as a way of approaching his other, a way of striking fear into the heart of criminality; his own visual horror is a means of empowerment against the terrifying forces he battles. It is precisely through our senses – precisely as an aesthetic phenomenon – that Batman is encountered, and that he encounters criminality. Similarly, the rational structures of legal consciousness are also experienced and encountered aesthetically.[124] This signals a deep irony in the processes of reification and repression that law undertakes: it is not only that we experience rational law aesthetically, but that it is precisely these repressed dimensions that give law its power and meaning and that enable it to be recognised as powerful.[125] It is that which remains beyond the legal text – the conceptual and symbolic richness, the irreducible excess uncaptured by rationality – that represents the 'poetics repressed within institutional prose'.[126] Indeed, it is the aesthetic, and the visual in particular, that 'is reckoned as being the ultimate means of persuasion and conversion, of communication, knowledge and power'.[127] In law, this can be configured in terms of the tricks and presentations – metaphor, rhetoric,[128] body language, architecture,[129] dress,[130] and so forth – that law uses to display and articulate itself in its particular (rational) way,[131] but also the broad spectrum of cultural forms that are imbued with legality and that cultural legal studies revels in. Batman's mask, his whole flowing costume, is more than just a means of hiding his 'real' identity as Bruce Wayne, or even a way of masking his weak humanity in order to present himself as an endless symbol of justice: it is, like the unconscious

123 See Goodrich (1995), p 50; Manderson (2000), pp 160–161.
124 See Manderson (2000), pp 23–24.
125 Goodrich (1995), pp 30–32.
126 Goodrich (1995), p 30.
127 Goodrich (1995), p 56. As Goodrich observes, this is why there was such a forceful 'war of images' during the reformation.
128 Goodrich (1990), pp 111–148.
129 Haldar (1999); Mulcahy (2011).
130 McQueen (1999); Watt (2013).
131 See Goodrich (1995), p 187.

elements in law's presentation, precisely a deployment of the aesthetic as a means of approaching rational, ordered justice. It is a point of mediation, of *komos*, between the conscious and the unconscious. Batman ultimately retains his status of rationality, thus preserving the dominant legal order – but in a form that is more sensitive to its aesthetics and its unconscious dimensions.

Arkham Asylum's narrative thus takes a simple superhero premise (hero defeats evil and restores order) configured to take place within Gotham's Arkham Asylum (Batman defeats inmates and restores order), and turns it into a metaphor for Batman's general project (Batman defeats evil and achieves justice), whilst pushing it further into a symbolic catharsis for Batman's own personal struggles (Bruce Wayne faces his personal demons and emerges stronger). At the same time, the story – as *komos* – becomes symbolic of something much larger: of the mediation of order and disorder, of law's structural opposition to unreason and of the need to break down that opposition (law remembers its antirrhesis and emerges larger). The lawyer's head is severed, freeing law from the confines of reason and plunging it into a world of madness and dreams. *Arkham Asylum* is not just Batman fighting baddies, or Batman's journey into his own unconscious, but also law's remembering of the unreason outside, but that exists within and beneath, and *anima*tes, the conscious surface of its reified rational order.

Through his experience in the Asylum, Batman comes to understand that it is not only our conscious rational minds that make us what we are: we are also the products of the unknowable forces of unreason that flow through the unconscious. In this we retreat from the Foucaultian repression of madness as a counterpoint category of reason, returning instead to the kind of madness that flows outside and beyond rational disciplinarity. We see this in Figure 3.6, where Batman explains the lesson he has learnt whilst holding Dent's coin, that symbol of abstract, truly blind objectivity. And the same is true for law: it is not just the rational order of law that makes it what it is, but also those dimensions that are pushed aside through processes of antirrhesis, that law is reified away from, that lurk in its unconscious. By forgetting these aspects, ostensibly in order to protect its authority and thus make itself stronger, legal knowledge ironically becomes weaker and disconnected from the vast and complex human world it attempts to regulate. A mere house of cards, toppled by a draft or a wave of the hand. It concomitantly forgets its limits and fails to appreciate where its rational order ends, and that there may be legitimate legal meaning and justice to be found beyond its borders. And, importantly, that these dimensions may not necessarily be a threat, but rather a resource in the legal project.

It is the crossing of these borders that cultural legal studies undertakes, a movement into law's unconscious with an understanding and acceptance that law is always already more than its rational surface. In *Arkham Asylum*, Batman navigates these boundaries, between the rational order of law and the unreason that 'threatens' it via his encounter with his own unconscious madness. Through this encounter, he ultimately emerges stronger; he transgresses the rational order of law in his dark night of the soul and thereby exposes that order to its

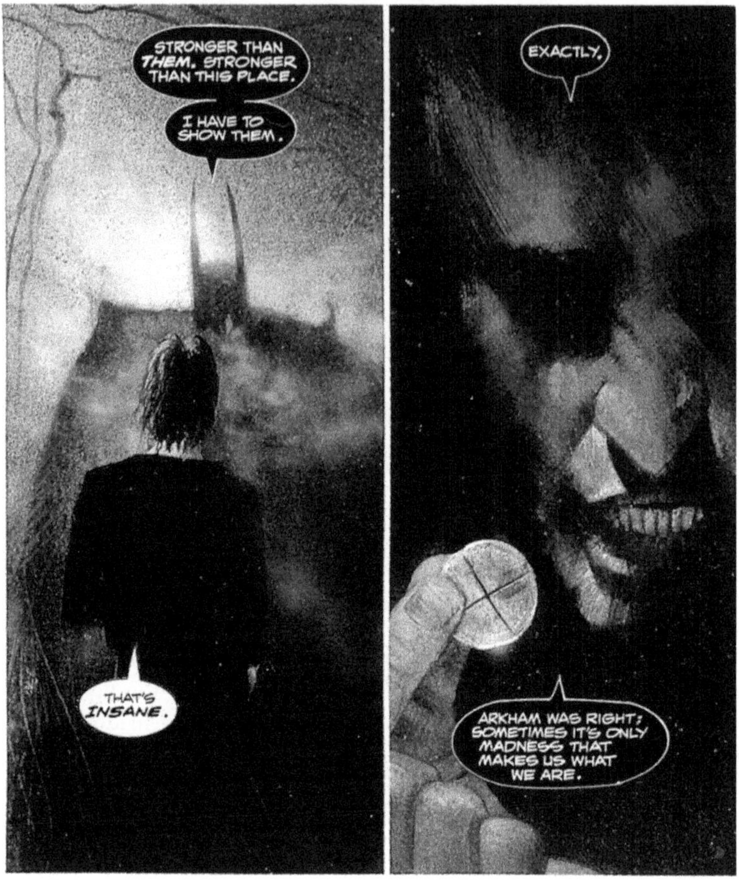

Figure 3.6 Morrison and McKean (2004), np. From *Batman: Arkham Asylum – A Serious House on Serious Earth* © DC Comics. Reproduced with permission.

(unconscious) outside, but in a way that does not descend into 'madness' and disorder. *Arkham Asylum* thus models a positive vision of a specifically cultural legal aesthetics: it recognises a whole world of law outside the reason of the lawyer's head. It is the navigation of law's limits, and the concomitant recognition that a whole world of legality exists beyond them. It is into this beyond, this infinite context outside conscious law, that we step in the next chapter.

References

Detective Comics Vol 1 #33 (1939) DC Comics.

Cary D Adkinson (2008) '*The Amazing Spider-Man* and the Evolution of the Comics Code: A Case Study in Cultural Criminology' 15 *Journal of Criminal Justice and Popular Culture* 241.

Maria Aristodemou (2000) *Law and Literature: Journeys from Her to Eternity*, Oxford University Press.
Maria Aristodemou (2014) *Law, Psychoanalysis, Society: Taking the Unconscious Seriously*, Routledge.
Michael Brody (1995) 'Batman: Psychic Trauma and Its Solution' 28 *Journal of Popular Culture* 171.
David G Bromley (2007) 'On Spiritual Edgework: The Logic of Extreme Ritual Performances' 46 *Journal for the Scientific Study of Religion* 287.
Jerome Bruner (2002) *Making Stories: Law, Literature, Life*, Harvard University Press.
Batman (1989) directed by Tim Burton, Warner Bros.
Chris Comerford (2015) 'The Hero We Need, Not the One We Deserve: Vigilantism and the State of Exception in *Batman Incorporated*' in T Giddens (ed) *Graphic Justice: Intersections of Comics and Law*, Routledge.
Don Crewe (2013) *Becoming Criminal: The Socio-Cultural Origins of Law, Transgression, and Deviance*, Palgrave.
Neal Curtis (2016) *Sovereignty and Superheroes*, Manchester University Press.
Joseph E Davis (2013) 'Social Science, Objectivity, and Moral Life' 50 *Society* 554.
Costas Douzinas and Lynda Nead (1999) 'Introduction' in C Douzinas and L Nead (eds) *Law and the Image: The Authority of Art and the Aesthetics of Law*, University of Chicago Press.
David Fagelson (2002) 'Justice as Integrity: Objectivity and Social Meaning in Legal Theory' 11 *Social and Legal Studies* 569.
Michel Foucault (2006) *History of Madness*, Routledge.
Chris Gavaler (2016) 'The Rise and Fall of Fascist Superpowers' 7 *Journal of Graphic Novels and Comics* 70.
Adam Gearey (2001) *Law and Aesthetics*, Hart.
Thomas Giddens (2015b) 'Natural Law and Vengeance: Jurisprudence on the Streets of Gotham' 28 *International Journal for the Semiotics of Law* 765.
Peter Goodrich (1990) *Languages of Law: From Logics of Memory to Nomadic Masks*, Weidenfeld and Nicolson.
Peter Goodrich (1995) *Oedipus Lex: Psychoanalysis, History, Law*, University of California Press.
Piyel Haldar (1999) 'The Function of the Ornament in Quintilian, Alberti, and Court Architecture' in C Douzinas and L Nead (eds) *Law and the Image: The Authority of Art and the Aesthetics of Law*, University of Chicago Press.
Frederick Holweck (1911) 'St Michael the Archangel' www.newadvent.org/cathen/10275b.htm
Jack Katz (1988) *Seductions of Crime: Moral and Sensual Attractions in Doing Evil*, Basic.
Stephen Lyng (2004) 'Crime, Edgework and Corporeal Transaction' 8 *Theoretical Criminology* 359.
Stephen Lyng et al (2009) 'Existentialism, Edgework, and the Contingent Body: Exploring the Criminological Implications of Ultimate Fighting' in R Lippens and D Crewe (eds) *Existentialist Criminology*, Routledge.
Desmond Manderson (2000) *Songs without Music: Aesthetic Dimensions of Law and Justice*, University of California Press.
Desmond Manderson (2003) 'From Hunger to Love: Myths of the Source, Interpretation, and Constitution of Law in Children's Literature' 15 *Law and Literature* 87.
Rob McQueen (1999) 'Of Wigs and Gowns: A Short History of Judicial Dress in Australia' 16 *Law Text Culture* 31.

Frank Miller et al (2002) *Batman: The Dark Knight Returns*, Titan Books.
A Moore and B Bolland (1988) *Batman: The Killing Joke*, Titan Books.
Alan Moore and Dave Gibbons (1986) *Watchmen*, Titan Books.
Grant Morrison (2004) 'Full Script and Notes' in *Arkham Asylum: A Serious House on Serious Earth*, Titan Books.
Grant Morrison and Dave McKean (2004) *Arkham Asylum: A Serious House on Serious Earth*, Titan Books.
Linda Mulcahy (2011) *Legal Architecture: Justice, Due Process and the Place of Law*, Routledge.
Ngaire Naffine (2009) *Law's Meaning of Life: Philosophy, Religion, Darwin and the Legal Person*, Hart.
Staci Newmahr (2011) 'Chaos, Order, and Collaboration: Toward a Feminist Conceptualization of Edgework' 40 *Journal of Contemporary Ethnography* 682.
Friedrich Nietzsche (1997b) *Daybreak: Thoughts on the Prejudices of Morality*, Cambridge University Press.
Batman Begins (2005) directed by Christopher Nolan, Warner Bros.
Timothy D Peters (2007) 'Unbalancing Justice: Overcoming the Limits of the Law in *Batman Begins*' 16 *Griffith Law Review* 247.
Timothy D Peters (2015) 'Beyond the Limits of the Law: A Christological Reading of Christopher Nolan's *The Dark Knight*' 24 *Griffith Law Review* 418.
Nickie D Phillips and Staci Strobl (2006) 'Cultural Criminology and Kryptonite: Apocalyptic and Retributive Constructions of Crime and Justice in Comic Books' 2 *Crime Media Culture* 304.
Nickie D Phillips and Staci Strobl (2013) *Comic Book Crime: Truth, Justice and the American Way*, New York University Press.
Dennis A Rendleman (2009) 'Two Faces of Criminal Prosecution: Harvey Dent, Mike Nifong, Craig Watkins' 9 *The Journal of the Institute of Justice and International Studies* 171.
Batman: Arkham Asylum (2009) developed by Rocksteady, Eidos Interactive.
Nikolas Rose (2001) 'The Politics of Life Itself' 18 *Theory, Culture and Society* 1.
Cassandra Sharp (2012) '"Riddle Me This…?" Would the World Need Superheroes If the Law Could Actually Deliver "Justice"?' 16 *Law Text Culture* 353.
Nick Sousanis (2015) *Unflattening*, Harvard University Press.
Kieran Tranter (2012) '"Come a Day There Won't Be Room for Naughty Men Like Us to Slip About at All": The Multi-Media Outlaws of *Serenity* and the Possibilities of Post-Literate Justice' 16 *Law Text Culture* 277.
Gary Watt (2013) *Dress, Law and Naked Truth: A Cultural Study of Fashion and Form*, Bloomsbury.
Jonathan M Wender (2008) *Policing and the Poetics of Everyday Life*, University of Illinois Press.
Alison Young (2005) *Judging the Image: Art, Value, Law*, Routledge.
Alison Young (2012) 'Criminal Images: The Affective Judgment of Graffiti and Street Art' 8 *Crime Media Culture* 297.
Alison Young (2014) *Street Art, Public City*, Routledge.

Chapter 4

Horrific jurisprudence

> Once upon a time, in some out of the way corner of that universe which is dispersed into numberless twinkling solar systems, there was a star upon which clever beasts invented knowing.[1]

Amidst the vastness of the cosmos, against the infinite backdrop of the indifferent universe, upon the fluctuating and shifting surface of an ancient satellite orbiting a gargantuan and ever-depleting ball of fire, within the flowing streams of human becoming and the interplay of swelling and ebbing forces of life, over the stresses, passions, desires, and pains of frail humans – law brings judgment. This is a vision of law without boundaries, of a legality roaming free in the madness and horror of the infinite universe. Within such a context, to judge – to interpret and apply the texts of law, to bring law to life – is to close down meaning, to end possibility and potential. To say, 'this is the answer' is to preclude all other possible answers, all other perspectives, meanings, and interpretations. To judge is to deny the infinite complexity of existence, and of the human living that takes place in its endless depths. To judge is to reduce, to destroy. To judge – is horrific.

The core trajectory of this chapter outlines a 'horrific jurisprudence' that is concerned with the response to the infinite context beyond the confines of rational-textual law. To navigate this, it is roughly split into two main sections. The first introduces, with HP Lovecraft and his recent comics reimagining by Alan Moore and Jacen Burrows, the horrific sublime invoked in an encounter with this infinite context and its framing as a 'Lovecraftian unconscious'. The second then shifts to examine the eruption of this unconscious in a juridical context, in the interplay between the comics characters of Judge Dredd and his colleague Judge Anderson. More specifically, the chapter begins by expounding the logic of Lovecraft's horror writing as a way of mediating that which exceeds or is beyond all forms of human knowledge before turning to Moore and Burrows's *Neonomicon* as a positive reconfiguration of Lovecraft's negative and fearful response to this beyond that also enables a cultural legal aesthetics that goes beyond the boundaries of conscious law. In the second half, Judges Dredd and Anderson are

1 Nietzsche (1990), p 888.

introduced, with Dredd symbolising a ghostless and doctrinal conscious legality that institutes life denying forms, whilst Anderson, in her fluid engagements with the supernatural, reflects an open and unending encounter with the uncertainty of existence. Ultimately, the structures and forms of conscious law are seen to 'blank out' the abyss beyond and outside knowing, thus closing down opportunities for expanding and engaging outside of the rational surface – an opening up facilitated by cultural legal aesthetics.

Call of the cultural-legal

The horrific sublime

> The most merciful thing in the world, I think, is the inability of the human mind to correlate all its contents. We live on a placid island of ignorance in the midst of black seas of infinity, and it was not meant that we should voyage far. The sciences, each straining in its own direction, have hitherto harmed us little; but some day the piecing together of dissociated knowledge will open up such terrifying vistas of reality, of our frightful position therein, that we shall either go mad from the revelation or flee from the light into the peace and safety of a new dark age.[2]

So begins what is arguably HP Lovecraft's most famous work, 'The Call of Cthulhu'.[3] Although just one work among many, *Cthulhu* is emblematic of Lovecraft's general conception of what he sees as the most profound horror of human existence: that 'one is a flea on the back of creation, wholly irrelevant, beneath the notice of the greater forces that populate the universe'.[4] Such a notion of vast and overwhelming powers that swamp the merely human is a clear invocation of the central trope of the sublime, which can be seen to navigate the limits of rational comprehension in the face of an awesome beyond. Lovecraft's work is particularly useful in considering this sublime limit in the context of the present work because it presents a context without boundaries; a context that, in legal terms, I contend is that of a cultural legal aesthetics. Evoking an endlessness amidst which conscious humanity exists, Lovecraftian horror encounters the sublime by revealing a world beyond our own that is so vast and unknowable, so dark and infinite and full of unhuman beings, that our everyday world pales into insignificance, at the whim of unknowable and indifferent forces. Humanity becomes nothing more than a 'flea' against the unending depths of the cosmos, the terrified response to which Lovecraft presents as negative and fearful. It is my work in this section to relate Lovecraft's negative trembling in the face of the infinite universe to the fearful response to the irrational threat that this beyond presents to conscious law, and to begin, in the following section, to counter this – through analysis of a reimagination of

2 Lovecraft (2011), p 61.
3 See Lovecraft (2011), pp 61–98.
4 Lowell (2004), p 49.

Lovecraft's work in Alan Moore and Jacen Burrow's *Neonomicon* – with the more welcoming embrace enabled by cultural legal aesthetics.

In Chapter 2, Dr Manhattan saw the infinitely vast system of the universe as something beautiful, against which humans are boring and predictable oscillations of matter; the Lovecraftian sublime maintains a similar view of humanity's insignificance but without destroying the meaning of this from the human perspective. Indeed, although Lovecraft is arguably antisubjective in the way he tells his stories,[5] encountering the full and frightful significance of our futile place in the universe is precisely the Lovecraftian project – an encounter that can never be made purely from the rational surface of knowledge, but requires an encounter with and beyond its boundaries. It is thus an encounter apt to bring a journey into the 'madness' beyond the limits of the rational text explored in the previous chapter. Indeed, Lovecraft's work can generally be seen to challenge rational modernity, seeking to move beyond the confines of reason:[6]

> The 'alterity' of the monsters and what they stand for is raised to an extreme degree by a systematic emphasis on its complete und [sic] utter incompatibility with anything known by means of the senses or reason, understandable by logic, or expressible in discursive language.[7]

Whereas in thinkers like Kant an encounter with the sublime can be a positive experience, Lovecraft's encounter with the beyond produces a negative and permeating horror, a terror and despair in the face of infinite, unhuman, and uncaring forces. Part of the way Lovecraft's horror operates is deeply textual – it is not just his penchant for infinite lurking beasts, but also his literary presentation that is important. Diegetically, Lovecraft often mediates or quells the erupting forces of the beyond through 'a careful negotiation of textual boundaries'.[8] But Timo Airaksinen argues that Lovecraft's formal articulation itself, via text, employs a style of 'unwriting' that disrupts literary norms. Lovecraft piles on adjective after adjective in the lead up to revealing his monstrosities, building expectation so that when they finally emerge they do not need to be described – they remain indescribed, and thus indescribable.[9] This technique makes way for a terrifying *something* that exceeds the textual order: Lovecraft's 'unwriting aims at somewhere which is beyond all narrative structure and possible worlds'.[10] This is reflected in Lovecraft's trope of assigning unpronounceable words and names to things beyond the human (e.g. 'Cthulhu', but also 'R'lyeh', 'fhtgan', and indeed a whole language

5 They are generally styled as objective reports, with little or no dialogue or characterisation. See Airaksinen (1999), pp 25–31, 100–102.
6 Airaksinen (1999), p 33.
7 Hanegraaff (2007), p 99.
8 Green (2013), p 254.
9 Airaksinen (1999), pp 91–93. On Lovecraft's technically 'bad' and overly descriptive writing style, see also Harman (2011), pp 46–47.
10 Airaksinen (1999), p 95.

built around inhuman speech-sounds[11]). Airaksinen suggests that this technique renders Lovecraft's works not text, but a 'scream'[12] that is without and beyond boundaries and limits.

But Lovecraft's movement into the 'beyond' is more than textual, as his approach to constructing his brand of horror story demonstrates: Lovecraft did not simply describe our familiar world populated with strange objects and beings, but worked to undermine and reimagine the ground of human existence. For Lovecraft, the banality of the everyday should be:

> undercut from within, by subverting the background conditions assumed by the existence [of the human world] ... There must be some deeper and more malevolent principle at work in our monsters that escapes all such [everyday] definition.[13]

In this way, Lovecraft uses allusion[14] and 'unwriting' to invoke the infinite context of human life that renders us insignificant in the cosmic order, and thereby also encounters the overwhelming terror of the sublime. However, Lovecraft's sublime differs significantly from the romantic sublime, such as that of Kant. Whereas the sublime for Kant was ultimately a positive experience, reinforcing the power of reason, Lovecraft's vision is one that trembles with fear in the face of the infinite – a response that links with the response of conscious law, but also leaves open the possibility of moving beyond the confines of the rational surface.

Kant distinguishes between the beautiful and the sublime: the beautiful, for Kant, is the perception of something that fits perfectly with our faculties of reason and our understanding of the empirical world; it represents those things that match our rational perception of the world, suggesting a link between beauty and order. The sublime, meanwhile, is associated with the experience of the might and infinity of nature – the night sky, storms, overhanging cliffs, raging seas – and the challenge such things pose to our ability to comprehend the world through rational concepts. The Kantian sublime exposes the limits of conceptual knowledge, and represents the threat of the unstructured chaos and irreducible infinity of the universe beyond its boundaries. In this, we can also see clearly the Lovecraftian project of facing the abyssal background of human existence. However, this aesthetic dimension of Kant's philosophy, as Jane Kneller argues, accepts a

11 Moore makes some extensive use of this language. For example: 'Shaggai, humuk Dho-hna, g'yll-gnaii yhh yr nhhhngr shoggoth, hrr yll'ngngr Nyarlathotep. Gh'll mhhg-gthaa tekeli-li y'golonac rrrthnaa'. See 'The Courtyard' in Moore and Burrows (2011), np.

12 Airaksinen (1999), p 95.

13 Harman (2011), p 22.

14 It is through allusion that Lovecraft can present the 'beyond' without reducing it or destroying its status as precisely 'beyond': Harman (2011), pp 237–240.

positive role for such an aesthetic encounter that embeds a sensory dimension into the otherwise reified structure of reason.[15] The Kantian sublime may be associated with the fracturing of the empirical world through the perception of its boundaries, but it also works by positing, through our faculty of reason, the existence of a supersensible realm 'beyond' that re-establishes the threatened order.[16] At its heart, the Kantian experience of the sublime is a discord, or conflict, between our rational understanding and our sensory experience, and the power of reason operates in this conflicting experience to restore order to our understanding of the world.

In experiencing the sublime we thus come up against the limits of what Kant calls our empirical imagination – our ability to synthesise the sensory world under concepts. Kant's system turns away from what is outside this conceptual understanding, what is outside the rational surface, by accepting the power of reason to order the world from beyond our experience – from the 'noumenal' realm that is beyond all possible human encounter – that remains 'veiled' outside the conceptual order. If we consider Christine Battersby's reconfiguration of the Kantian sublime, we can see this 'turning away' from the limits of conceptual understanding more clearly. In Kant's sublime, Battersby argues, it is not the existence of some veiled beyond that is exposed, but, rather, simply the limits of our ability to understand through rational forms:

> As apparently systematic knowledge systems get caught within their own illusions, Nietzsche suggests that a kind of false infinity arises as the circle of knowledge (which aims at completeness) conceals an 'infinite number of points' which could not possibly all be surveyed … [In facing the Kantian sublime] we confront merely that which has been excluded as the [rational] I positions itself as free, as a unity or as the 'master' of nature and the space-time which it imposes on the world.[17]

This Nietzschean reading exposes the chaos at work in relation to the Kantian sublime. The over-structured approach of Kant leads to unpredictable dynamic interaction as its 'illusions' (perspectival knowledge constructions) feed back into each other in 'a kind of false infinity' (like Arkham trapped in the 'maze of reason' in Chapter 3) that avoids going 'beyond the veil' of the empirical imagination; going beyond the veil is impossible for Kant. For Nietzsche, however, the sublime does not 'veil' a 'beyond', but rather, in approaching the boundaries and limitations of conceptual knowledge, the Kantian system turns away from the unstructured chaos of the universe outside rational knowledge and feeds back into itself. As Richard Sherwin notes, the sublime 'is that which remains inexpressible within that which is expressed'[18] – it is the world beyond Kant's rational system. This

15 See Kneller (1997).
16 See Kant (2000), pp 128–151.
17 Battersby (2007), pp 173–175.
18 Sherwin (2011), p 19.

formless 'beyond', for Nietzsche, is not seen as inaccessible, nor as a failure or an intractable problem for the business of knowing, but rather signals the turn to an epistemology that recognises the infinite possible encounters that can be had with the universe – of which reason is but one limited example.

In facing the sublime, we do not experience a veiling of a realm 'beyond', but rather we experience the limits of conceptual thought, of our ability to 'understand' the world. This experience, under Kant, is linked with emotions and feelings of awe: our world is shaken, and we experience internal conflict between our empirical imagination and the faculty of reason. Here Kant re-establishes the primacy and ordering ability of reason and the transcendental self. When we come up against something indefinitely vast, our ability to understand the world we experience through our senses fails us. As Battersby terms it, we 'sacrifice' our sensory experiences to the abstract power of reason, thus allowing reason to step in, as universal, and once again explain and order the world.[19]

Battersby's reading of the Kantian sublime notes that it is only those who are able to transcend fear, and thus experience the sublime 'successfully' (that is, in a way that allows reason to re-establish the order the world), that are able to become truly autonomous beings[20] – a status Lovecraft's terrified quaking in the face of Cthulhu and its kind arguably does not attain. As Janice Richardson observes, someone who is afraid cannot experience the sublime, and thus cannot develop full rational personhood.[21] The Kantian sublime experience covers up the looming abyss outside rational comprehension and re-establishes the faculty of reason as the power that can bring the world to order. And this is a movement that the Lovecraftian sublime does not achieve, instead surrendering to the infinite forces of the beyond that undermine and shatter the conscious human world. Whilst Kant's sublime reinforces the structural integrity of reason, facing Lovecraft's 'horrific sublime' leaves our conscious world shaken and unsteady.

In Chapter 2 it was argued that conscious law exists upon a rational surface, outside of which there is a chaotic realm of non-rational and non-linguistic indeterminacy. In Chapter 3 the threat posed by this irrational beyond was explored through a navigation of the boundaries between reason and madness. With Kant's sublime, the unstructured infinity that threatens from beyond the rational surface is held at bay as we approach the limits of conceptual understanding through the sacrifice of sensory experience to the supreme ordering power of reason,[22] masking that beyond in a way that acts to secure the hegemonic position of rationality in the ordering of the world, and thus to maintain the security of the rational surface as 'the' basis of knowledge. Kantian reason may thus be embedded in an aesthetic world of senses and feelings, but it maintains its strength through the denial of the experience of immanent insecurity of its borders in favour of the

19 Battersby (2007), pp 29–30.
20 Battersby (1995); Battersby (2007), p 60
21 Richardson (2007), pp 233–234.
22 See Battersby (2007), pp 28–34.

abstract ordering power of reason. It reifies itself, operating to cover up the insecurity and threat to the stability of the rational surface posed by the chaotic indeterminacy of the infinity beyond its borders; the threat to order is masked, covered up, or turned away from, as sensory experience is sacrificed to the primacy of rational explanation.

Lovecraft's presentation of the sublime as genuinely terrifying, however, undoes this reification, and accepts the futility of the human in the cosmic context of the endless beyond that cannot be denied. His horrific sublime thus exposes the motivations behind Kant's movement in terms of what is at stake in not suppressing the background abyss. And this Lovecraftian sublime has significant implications for legal knowing, as well as human knowing in general; by invoking a sense of endless terror beyond the confines of human understanding and experience, the profound limits of human knowledge are exposed. In addition to his method of 'unwriting', Lovecraft's descriptive details 'are so strange that they suggest another world … and thus imply something which is beyond, which cannot be told'.[23] Read as an epistemology, Lovecraft's horror thus implies that all the vast intricacies and compilations and evolutions of human understanding – of science, philosophy, and other attempts at knowledge-making, including law – are not only perspectival and necessarily incomplete, but are also insignificant, swamped by the infinity of the abyss that 'cannot be told', cannot be reduced to rational knowledge or text. We are revealed as tiny specks on a minuscule planet drifting amidst a never-ending and indescribable cosmos that is wholly indifferent to our existence, not to mention our petty concerns, beliefs, and moral quandaries.

Within this cosmic epistemology, law exists as an arguably futile attempt to codify and control insignificant human behaviour. Such conceptions suggest a meaninglessness that threatens the (textual) structures of law and the very ideas of morality and responsibility that law may be built upon, as well as the possibility of life itself having any meaning at all. As Miguel de Unamuno framed it, 'if some day all personal consciousness must come to an end on the earth … then to what end is this knowledge?'[24] But more than this, the idea of a wholly 'non-human' world beyond our own also implies the limits of human knowing, beyond which there is only threat:

> the non-human remains, by definition, a limit; it designates both that which we stand in relation to and that which remains forever inaccessible to us. This limit is the unknown, and the unknown … is often a source of fear or dread.[25]

It may or may not be the case that our petty human efforts upon this idly spinning planet amount to anything in the context of the wider universe. Melanie Williams faced this 'emptiness', and came out with an increased positivity about human

23 Airaksinen (1999), p 10.
24 Unamuno (1954), pp 30–31.
25 Thacker (2011), p 28.

knowledge against the abyssal cosmos: building human moral life against the empty, unending nothingness of space does not make that life meaningless, but pushes us to seek more profound meaning in our moral world-building: 'Adrift in the cosmos', she tells us, 'we must build in empty space … the greatest good that we can muster'.[26] Donna Haraway also rejects negative assumptions about the cosmic beyond, tackling directly the Lovecraftian vision of horror. She notes that Cthulhu, as a literary creation, is tied up with Lovecraft's own petty prejudices[27] – it is a 'misogynist racial-nightmare monster'[28] – whereas what she frames as the 'Chthulucene'[29] is not derived from Lovecraft, but from a rich vein of speculative, critical, and feminist thought 'that Lovecraft could not have imagined or embraced'.[30] Accordingly, Haraway's Chthulucene 'entangles myriad temporalities and spatialities and myriad intra-active entities-in-assemblages – including the more-than-human, other-than-human, inhuman, and human-as-humus'.[31] It is expansive, but not in a way that brings the terror of difference as it does for the prejudiced Lovecraft, nor the impulse to re-fortify the domain of reason as it does for the romantic Kant. For Haraway, the Chthulucene – that which lies beyond the Anthropocene that Lovecraft so clearly clung to in his fear of otherness[32] – is to be welcomed into the family, to be made kin.[33]

Ultimately, it is more in this positive vein that this book operates, a claim to which the expansive vision of cultural legal aesthetics as operating without epistemic boundaries attests. In part, a horrific jurisprudence is a jurisprudence that does not, and cannot, give certainty as the rational surface does – and it is in that lack of certainty that its horror for the structures of conscious law can be found. A Lovecraftian epistemology demonstrates clear limits to what we – and what law – can know, and also represents something of Lovecraft's own close-minded prejudice and fear of difference, his fear of the beyond as seen in his creation of the 'misogynist racial-nightmare monster' known as Cthulhu and that is emblematic of a radical otherness. This close-minded fear can also be found in the irrational threat felt to lurk outside the rational surface of conscious legality in Chapter 3, a threat that is irrational in both its technical constitution and in the more everyday sense of being unfounded or based on fearful assumptions.

26 Williams (2002), p 216.
27 Lovecraft's racism is well known; it is discussed, for example, at many points throughout Joshi (2001).
28 Haraway (2015), p 160.
29 Note the spelling difference. Although sharing etymology, 'Chthulucene' arguably links more directly with the Greek 'chthonic' than with Lovecraft's creation. 'Chthonic' relates to the underworld or the subterranean, and is thus eminently suitable for attempting to indicate a beyond that is below or beneath the notice of our conscious, waking world.
30 Haraway (2015), p 160.
31 Haraway (2015), p 160.
32 Kant, too, only permitted entry to rational personhood via the experience of the sublime to white European males: see, for example, Battersby (2007), pp 45–84.
33 See Haraway (2015), pp 161–162.

In this sense, a horrific jurisprudence is about stepping outside the rational order of law. Indeed, as Penny Crofts notes, horror, like the regulations of the criminal law, works to 'organise and express order and the transgression of that order'.[34] But by moving beyond the known order, a horrific jurisprudence becomes a jurisprudence of the ineffable and occult, of that beyond the limits of human knowing. Philosophical engagement with horror can approach 'a way of thinking the world as unthinkable, and the limits of our place within that world'.[35] As a way of recognising and perhaps overcoming some of those limits on an epistemological level, Lovecraft's work, despite his personal prejudices, can arguably be read in a way that seeks to expand human consciousness by revealing the 'terrible' expanse of the universe.[36] Working through the horror that such huge contexts bring for the close and intricate systems of human law, a horrific jurisprudence undermines law's rational edifice and expands its consciousness by placing it within its wider epistemological, cosmological, and supernatural contexts; it is law's encounter with the sublime. Whether these contexts are responded to positively or as a source of dread is precisely the point of this chapter, and indeed this volume as a whole. As a jurisprudence drawing on Lovecraft's horrific sublime, it is one that not only reveals something beyond law's considerable limits but also the fear and despair this implies for law's conscious processes.

In its concern with epistemology, a horrific jurisprudence is an aesthetic jurisprudence. In its removal of limits and unleashing of jurisprudence into the boundless universe, it is a jurisprudence that ostensibly brings dread and unease to the structures of conscious law. This is why it is a horrific jurisprudence rather than a jurisprudence of horror; in such a jurisprudence, the nature of law itself – as infinite – brings horror. In this way, Lovecraft connects with conscious law; Haraway, meanwhile, connects with the expansive vision of cultural legal aesthetics, of embracing the beyond as part of the legal family. Cultural legal aesthetics moves past or does not encounter such horror; it is a post- or never-was-horrific jurisprudence. As MacNeil makes clear, it is a *joyful* rather than a fearful jurisprudence. Moving towards this positive embrace, a horrific jurisprudence is one that is focused on drawing out and overcoming the negative responses to such a beyond that remain symptomatic of the conscious law within the confines of the rational surface.

New law of images

In order to flesh out this horrific jurisprudence through the medium of comics, we turn first to a recent representation of Lovecraft's mythos in Alan Moore and Jacen Burrows's *Neonomicon*,[37] in which Moore and Burrows present a

34 Crofts (2015), p 374.
35 Thacker (2011), p 80.
36 Green (2013), p 258.
37 Moore and Burrows (2011). See Appendix A for an overview and details of this work.

psychoanalytic reworking of Lovecraft's epistemology with significant legal overtones. 'Neonomicon' is a play on 'Necronomicon', a mystical book that appears often in Lovecraft's mythos. The title 'Neonomicon' itself can be translated from the Greek (*neo, nomos, eikon*) to mean the new law of images, and the visual presentation of the work – *qua* comics – reinforces the visual suggestions of this translation.[38] Where '*necro*nomicon' is associated with death, '*neo*nomicon' indicates a future of change; a movement from the dusty old powers of the past to the promise of new forces in the future. Moore and Burrows reconfigure the gargantuan beasts of Lovecraft's mythos, the so-called 'Great Old Ones' (such as Cthulhu), as being not infinitely ancient and lost in the history of the planet, but something that is also looming in our future; they exist outside time.[39] This vast atemporal unconscious thus becomes something that is not only repressed in our history – humans have forgotten or never knew the terrifying truth of the beings behind the surface of the universe – but something that will return in the future, and indeed something that interpenetrates all of time, always already *there* outside the limits of conscious existence. In a legal context – as a new law of images – this can be mapped onto the relationship between images and law: repressed in our history, possibly to return in our future via a visual turn in culture, but always already present as part of the unconscious of the legal institution.[40] The term 'neonomicon', then, implies that there is something *there*, of a different order to, and beyond, the conscious texts of law.

Beyond its title, one of the first things to note about *Neonomicon* in a legal context is its initial configuration of the Lovecraftian unconscious as something textual and linguistic – and therefore of obvious relevance to law as an institution built upon rational text. In 'The Courtyard' (the two issue mini-series that acts, and is included, as a preface to the full work of *Neonomicon*), an FBI agent we later come to know as Sax follows the trail of 'Aklo', which he believes to be a mysterious drug somehow linked with the violent murders he is investigating.

38 For lawyers and jurists, the '-nom-' in Necronomicon clearly invokes the Greek *nomos* – signalling the normative order of law. However, it may also be translatable as 'name' (from *onoma*). This alternative leads Moore to suggest the translation of 'neonomicon' as 'book of new names' – see Moore and Burrows (2011). However, the connection with *nomos* is overt when reading in a legal context, hence the translation to law. Indeed, 'law' is the preferred translation of Lovecraft himself, who translated Necronomicon as 'the image of the law of the dead'. See Mitchell (2001), pp 9–10. Accordingly, *Neonomicon* would translate as 'an image of the new law', or 'the new law of images'. Note that it has also been suggested that '-icon' is not necessarily related to *eikon*, but is merely a neutral suffix: Joshi (2008), pp 34–35. However, given the profoundly graphic presentation of *Neonomicon* it seems more appropriate to explore, rather than ignore, the possible connection with visuality that the *eikon* translation implies.

39 Atemporality is not an uncommon Moorean trope – note Dr Manhattan's ability to see all of time simultaneously in Chapter 2, and Moore's own philosophy of time in *The Mindscape of Alan Moore* (2003).

40 See, for example, Goodrich (1995); Goodrich and Hayaert (2015); Manderson (2018); Sherwin (2012); Wagner and Sherwin (2014).

Aklo, however, turns out to be something much more powerful and mind-altering than a mere chemical substance ('There's no drug with mind altering properties *halfway* as powerful'[41]) – it is a language. This language is the reader's first glimpse of the Lovecraftian unconscious: Aklo is the primordial structure that came before, and from which is descended, the conscious languages of humanity. It is the 'ur-syntax':

> the primal vocabulary giving form to those pre-conscious orderings wrung from a hot incoherence of stars, from our birthmuds pooled in the grand-mother lagoon; a stark, limited palette of earliest notions, / lost colours, / forgotten intensities.[42]

Already, then, we have encountered the notion of something old and primeval, some powerful force beyond and beneath the conscious world encountered in language – and thus available to the texts of conscious law. The Lovecraftian epistemology has considerable textual dimensions, as we saw above, but in Moore's hands this is developed significantly. Alan Moore is not only a writer, but a self-professed magician – although he would say they are one and the same: 'to cast a spell, as far as I understand it, is simply to spell'.[43] The linguistic art, like that of magic, is 'concerned with the creation and manipulation of worlds',[44] and words – particularly legal words – shape the world. Like Lovecraft, Moore tries to tame the vagaries and forces of the universe with text, by encoding it into the structures of language – a conscious project in no way dissimilar from that of the jurist. Presenting this textual elaboration in the visual context of the comics page, as seen in Figure 4.1, emphasises on a formal level the existence of something beyond conscious text.

In 'The Courtyard' we see the Lovecraftian dimensions of language: Sax, the agent of state law, encounters Aklo, the linguistic unconscious beneath the surface of his everyday and institutional language.[45] But, as a work of comics, this encounter is more profoundly embedded throughout the work, with that which exceeds linguistic representation at all points surrounding the presented text as in Figure 4.1. Diegetically, the particularities and cultural specificities of Sax's (legal) language are exposed; symbolically and formally, the history of law's textual reification, of its antirrhetic or repressive relationship with images and all things visual,[46] is encountered. Accordingly, the unconscious dimensions of the legal text are implicated from the outset of *Neonomicon* – embedded in the comics form,

41 Moore and Burrows (2011), np. Emphasis in original.
42 Moore and Burrows (2011), np.
43 Moore, quoted in Green (2013), p 257.
44 Green (2013), p 254.
45 Similarities can also be seen here with Wender's bureaucratic aesthetics in Chapter 3: conscious law encountering the living human world that it represses into the legal unconscious.
46 See Goodrich (1995).

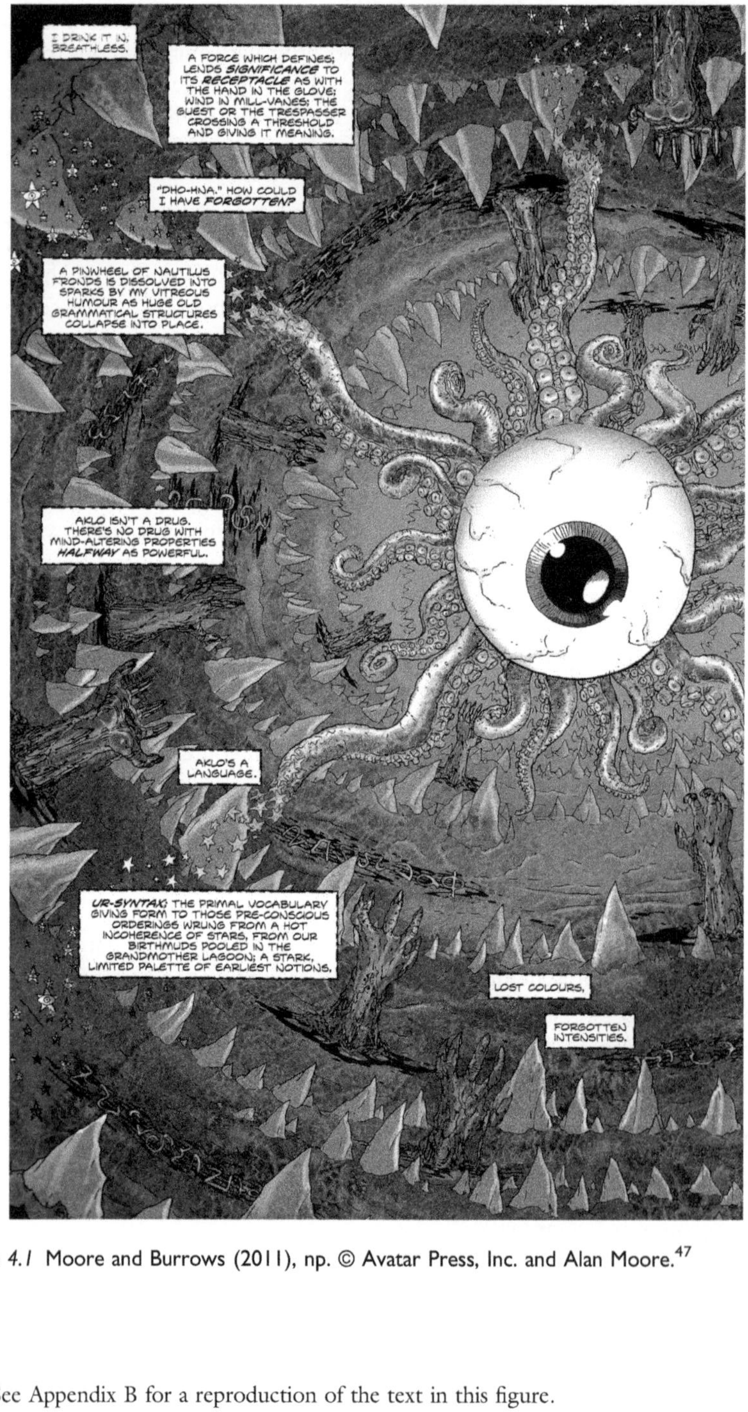

Figure 4.1 Moore and Burrows (2011), np. © Avatar Press, Inc. and Alan Moore.[47]

47 See Appendix B for a reproduction of the text in this figure.

but signalled by the diegetic context of Sax's encounter with Aklo. The detailed tentacular vistas and depictions of horror and dismemberment presented as additional images, in a 'Gallery' section after and outside the diegesis of the work, further present this excess visually, employing the physical form in its articulation: these images, inserted between the final diegetic boundary and the back cover of the bound volume, signify a background or outside filled with Lovecraftian horrors.

Across the narrative of *Neonomicon*, this linguistic unconscious is fleshed out as a fully fledged Lovecraftian unconscious. In particular, Moore and Burrows develop the dimension of sexual repression. Moore's interest in sexuality is evident elsewhere in his comics works,[48] but in *Neonomicon* Lovecraft's obsession with the universal otherness of tentacular horrors is suggested as a return of his repressed sexuality. Evidence relating to Lovecraft's own sexuality suggests that, although not completely asexual, he was not overly interested in sex. As his wife Sonia admitted after his death: 'he was far from unsexed ... [but his upbringing made] him squeamish and prudish about perfectly natural functions. The very mention of the word *sex* seemed to upset him'.[49] Although public discussion of sex with his friends made him uncomfortable,[50] it appears he had studied some techniques and understood his intimate duties;[51] his love-craft was not lacking, but was something that should remain very much hidden in the bedroom. As was indicated above, there is something of Lovecraft's own prejudices to be found in his creations, and in this vein Moore and Burrows play on some of the more hyperbolic suggestions around Lovecraft's (a)sexuality, with statements that he always remained clothed during intercourse and had barely a sexual bone in his body.[52] The evidence from Sonia Lovecraft suggests such claims are inaccurate, yet a conscious suppression of all things sexual from Lovecraft's public life – including his writing – remains evident.

In developing their reworked Lovecraftian unconscious, Moore and Burrows argue that, far from being expelled from his writings, Lovecraft's stories are inherently awash with sexuality. As one character eloquently puts it: 'You know? The monsters and all that? They're like a lot of cocks and pussies crawling round'.[53] This connection is made explicit (in more ways than one) in the diegetic use of orgies by a cult, infiltrated by the main FBI protagonist Brears and her partner (whose continuation of Sax's investigation makes up *Neonomicon*'s main

48 Most notably *Lost Girls*: see Moore and Gebbie (2006).

49 Everts (2012), np, quoting a recorded conversation with Sonia Lovecraft. Emphasis in original. It also appears that Lovecraft was a virgin prior to his marriage, and never initiated sexual relations himself. Sonia cites her husband's relationship with his mother, which included admonishments about his looks and a general Puritanical upbringing, as a significant factor in his repressive attitudes toward sexuality.

50 Everts (2012), np.

51 Everts (2012), np.

52 Moore and Burrows (2011), np.

53 Moore and Burrows (2011), np.

narrative), to attract a sea monster. The sea creature is attracted by the sexual 'orgone' energy, and subsequently joins in the action. The monsters and creatures in Moore and Burrows's vision of the Lovecraft mythos are thus far from asexual, and we even see Brears visiting the realm of the Great Old Ones whilst captive (the mysterious city R'yleh), drugged and unconscious and in the midst of being repeatedly raped by the aforementioned sea demon. As she nakedly wanders the ancient and decaying landscape, she senses her physiological reaction to the abuse of her earth-bound body.

In this, there are strong and overt sexual dimensions being developed to the Lovecraftian unconscious. The endless beings lurking outside the conscious universe, the cosmic forces beyond human knowledge, become tied up with Lovecraft's own repressed sexual desire, just as his presentation of this beyond as something fearful falls in line with his own racial prejudice. In this way, that which is outside the order of human knowing, the vast beyond of the infinite universe, becomes connected with our sexualities: the Lovecraftian beyond 'becomes associated with the depths of the mind associated both with inspiration and (sexual) neurosis'.[54] Indeed, in a seeming attempt to counter some of Lovecraft's misogyny, it is Brears's sexual reproductive capacity that gives rise to the new Lovecraftian order of the universe outside of time. The city of the Lovecraftian unconscious where Cthulhu waits to return, the place known as 'R'yleh', it turns out, is Brears's womb – directly indicative of sexual reproduction, and thus (as Moore and Burrows present it) of Lovecraft's own sexual repression. It is through her sexual abuse by the sea demon that Brears suffers her 'abject impregnation',[55] with the creature that grows within her set to become the first of the immense and unknowable Great Old Ones.[56] A woman thus becomes the source of the infinite powers of the universe. Whether this effectively counters misogyny or sexism is debatable, but in it we can see a movement beyond the terrified response of Lovecraft to the beyond.

Timo Airaksinen claims that there is no unconscious in Lovecraft's works; the 'lack of phallus' in his stories is due to his method of regressing and recapturing a child-like innocence, a pre-sexual state where, in Lovecraft's own biography, he was obsessed not with sex but with distant lands, imaginary monsters, and fantasies of exploration and discovery.[57] The asexuality of his texts, then, Airaksinen claims, is simply due to Lovecraft's lack of interest in such matters as a child, leading to them being ignored or misunderstood in adulthood:

> As his regression method dictates, his mood, images and emotions reach deep into the basic layers of the mind, yet fail to recognize some of its aspects for what they are, namely, bodily and sexual messages.[58]

54 Green (2013), p 269.
55 Green (2013), p 269.
56 Moore and Burrows (2011), np.
57 Airaksinen (1999), p 104. See, for more on Lovecraft's cultural immersion as a child, Joshi (2001), pp 8–39.
58 Airaksinen (1999), p 104.

But rather than signalling a lack of unconscious, this method reflects precisely a repression of sexuality in Lovecraft's creations; *Neonomicon* presents this sexuality as returning via the horrific creatures of the Lovecraftian otherness, ultimately mediated through Brears as something to be embraced. For Moore and Burrows, the phallus *is* present – as a tentacle. We can see this most clearly in Figure 4.2 and Figure 4.3. The sea demon eventually takes Brears underwater (Figure 4.2) and releases her back into the human world. As she emerges from beneath the waves in Figure 4.3, the reworking of the Lovecraftian unconscious is made overt, and the formal presentation of the page is employed in its articulation. The text that

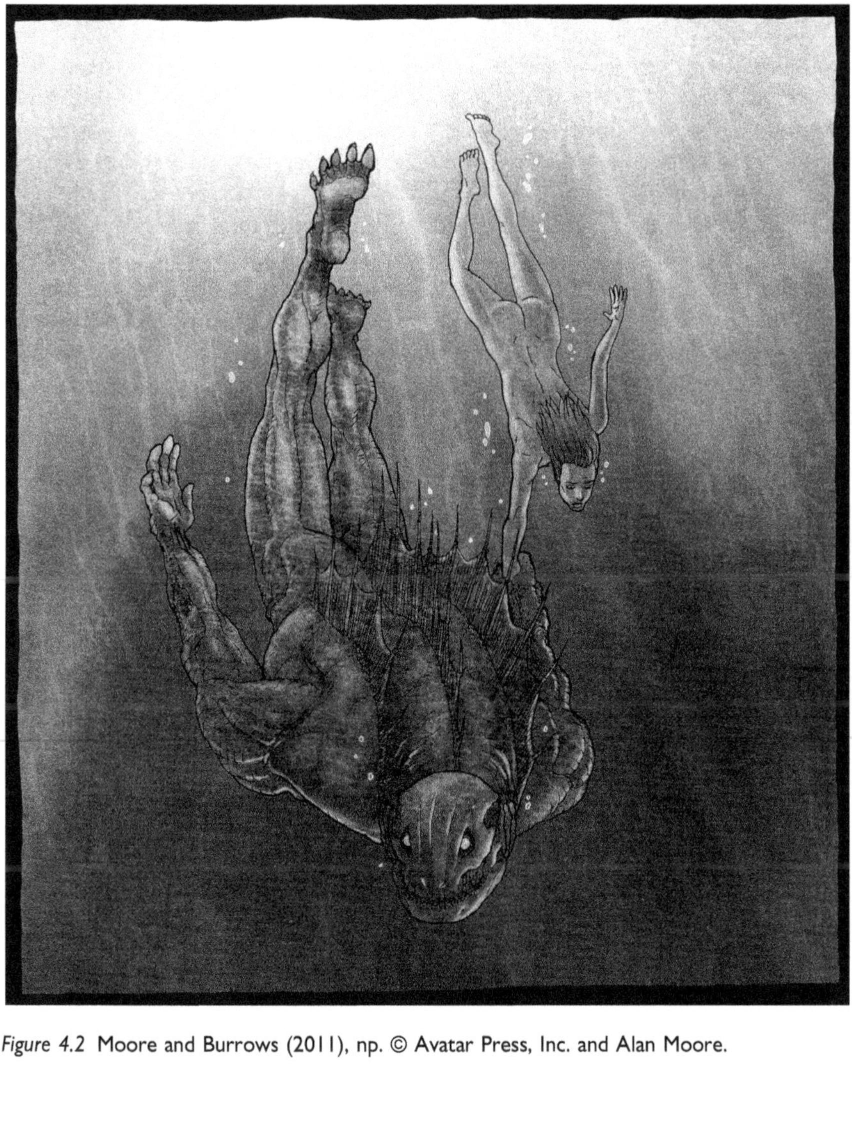

Figure 4.2 Moore and Burrows (2011), np. © Avatar Press, Inc. and Alan Moore.

traverses the images on this page tells of a dream that Brears is having in her delusional half-alive state following her imprisonment and abuse, a dream in which she is naked with Lovecraft himself who is responding in horror to not only her sexuality, but the monstrousness that emerges from her genitalia. Her clitoris becomes a penis, female genitalia becomes phallic; phallus becomes tentacle, sexuality becomes monstrous. Going beyond, and thereby countering, the textually focused assertions of Airaksinen that the 'scream' of Lovecraft's horror has no boundaries, and therefore cannot have an unconscious,[59] Lovecraft's tentacular fiends are configured in the multimodal *Neonomicon* as phallic, sexual beasts of a returning unconscious order – as a neonom*icon*, a potentially *visual* order, appearing on the page.

Where Airaksinen claims that Lovecraft's method is one of regression to a pre-sexual state, the images in Figure 4.2 and Figure 4.3 reinforce the sexualised reading. In Figure 4.2 we witness the naked Brears hand-in-hand with the radical otherness of the sea demon, solidifying the connection between her sexuality and the Lovecraftian unconscious and positioning it metaphorically 'beneath the surface' of conscious life. In Figure 4.3, Brears emerges from beneath the waves, from beneath the surface set up in Figure 4.2 – indeed, from beneath the multiple surfaces depicted above the final panel of the page, signalling perhaps how deeply repressed Moore and Burrows believe Lovecraft to have been, or how repressed the infinite beyond of the cosmos is in everyday waking life. In Figure 4.3, Brears emerges from the fluid and distorted realm beneath the visible surface of the sea, bringing her nudity, her experiences of violent sexuality, and her encounters with the otherness of the sea monster with her, and erupting through the water's surface with a guttural and pre-linguistic cry of 'PFFAHHH'.

As already noted, in *Neonomicon* the universal unconscious is reconfigured to be atemporal, outside the human realm and outside concepts of past, present, and future – it is always already there, lurking beyond or beneath our world, the endless pit of the cosmos. Moore and Burrows link the suggestion or eruption of this gargantuan beyond with human desire, with the depths of irrational urges and beliefs, of sexual yearnings, that inhabit us. Countering some of the presumed terror of Lovecraft's own work, *Neonomicon* suggests a communion with this beyond, finally claiming that desire lets us touch the beyond of this universal order. This communion is mediated through the experiences of Brears and her movement towards a motherly embrace of the Great Old Ones themselves, depicted within the *komos* of the comics medium – mediating waking life and the 'horrors' of the abyss. A repressive or negative response to this beyond is seen to lead to violence and horror, as is evident in the character of Sax: after encountering the protolanguage Aklo, Sax commits one of the horrific murders he is investigating. He eventually admits that sex is unpleasant to him: 'I mean, genitals, all

59 'Once the text becomes an unwritten scream, it may recognise no constraints whatsoever, no repression or shame': Airaksinen (1999), p 104.

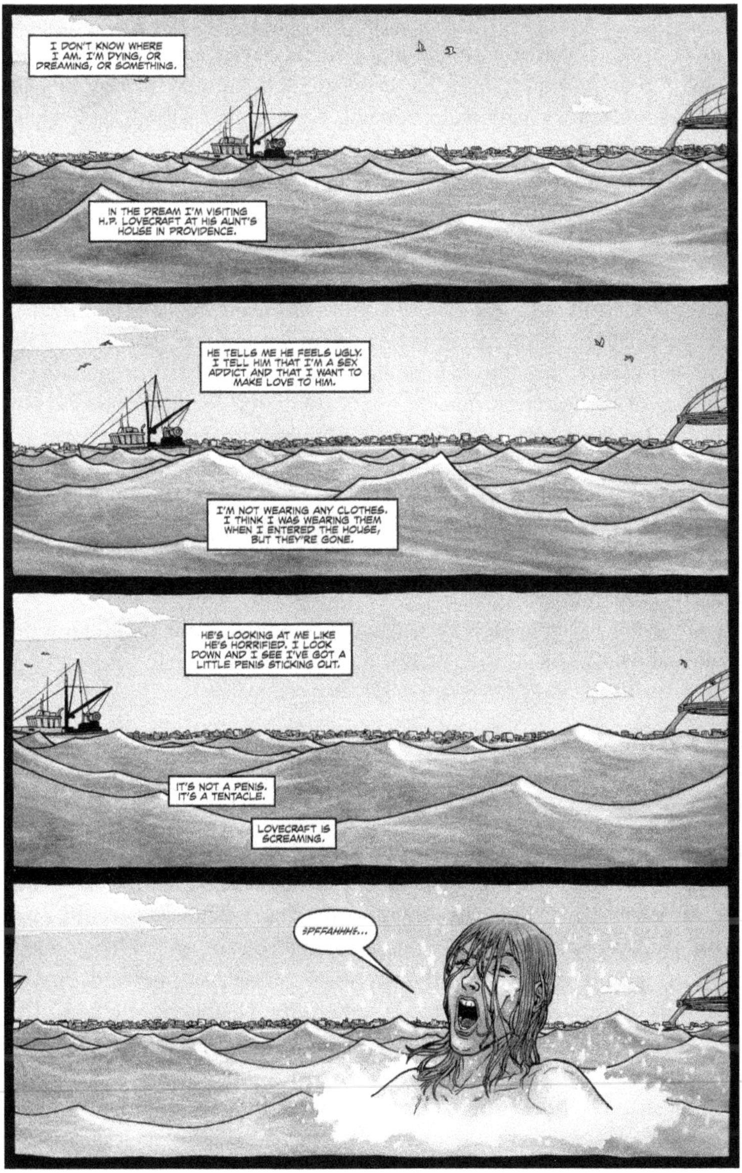

Figure 4.3 Moore and Burrows (2011), np. © Avatar Press, Inc. and Alan Moore.[60]

60 See Appendix B for a reproduction of the text in this figure.

that. It's all just ... horrible'.[61] The (hyperbolic) link with the sexual repression of Lovecraft is overt, and thus also the link with Haraway's view of Lovecraft's terrifying mythos as symptomatic of a close-minded bigotry: Lovecraft's personal idiosyncrasies infuse his creations, producing a vision that is both desexualised and terrified of otherness. Unlike Sax, Brears is a self-professed 'sex addict', a reveller in the sensory pleasures of the flesh; her sexuality is not repressed, and she is ultimately able to embrace the beyond, to accept her maternal role in the movement towards the new universal order.

As a work of comics, the reading of this embracing of the beyond as a 'new law of images' plays firmly into the role of comics as *komos*: *Neonomicon* mediates the conscious texts of law with an infinite Lovecraftian context, and is thus in part a horrific jurisprudence. In approaching the visual in its formal presentation, it is a jurisprudence of the mystery outside the text, of the ineffable beyond, of alternative modes for legal knowing. It encounters the visuality that exceeds text, the world beyond reason and outside human knowing. It is a jurisprudence sensitive to that which exceeds the conscious legal order, to the vast worlds beyond or beneath the traditional structuring of life into rational and linguistic codes. Working against the terror of the repressive, conscious lawyer, it is a jurisprudence that tries to undo the horror of the Lovecraftian unconscious and thereby begins to open up to the endless contexts of the Chthulucene, and the infinite potential of the cultural legal.

Judging in the abyss

The dread lawman

A leading example of conscious law in the comics medium is *Judge Dredd*.[62] Dredd signals judicial power and the juristic structuring of life into law, and, read in conjunction with his colleague Judge Anderson, he can be seen to operate in denial of a Lovecraftian unconscious.[63] Published in the UK comics series *2000AD* through the latter half of the twentieth century and beyond, *Judge Dredd* was created as a satirical response to the emerging Thatcherite politics of the late 1970s and early 1980s. In creating *Judge Dredd*, the writers and artists of *2000AD* were responding to the authoritarian approaches emerging in Anglo-American politics of justice,[64] and created Dredd as an over-powered judicial agent into whom are compressed all the elements of a justice system typically spread over multiple bodies and personnel (investigation, enforcement, arrest, trial, judgment, sentencing, and punishment). The rationale for such hyperpowered legal enforcers

61 Moore and Burrows (2011), np.
62 See Appendix A for an overview and details of this work.
63 See Giddens (2017).
64 See Wagner (2002). Wagner's own politics are opposed to Dredd's authoritarianism: 'I'd describe my politics as fairly left wing. Any kind of police brutality appalls [sic] me'. Wagner quoted in Keily (2012), np.

lies in the need to cope with the vast increases in criminality in the futuristic, sprawling, and densely populated urban environment of Mega-City One, which Dredd and his colleagues patrol.[65]

With his trademark statement of 'I am the law!', we see Dredd implementing hard line and draconian laws, enacting unforgiving judgments, and dishing out penal sentences for offences such as crossing the street or attempting suicide (and thus causing a public nuisance).[66] The original first issue of *Judge Dredd* saw Dredd sentencing and executing a citizen on the street for bank robbery and murder, before carting an onlooker off to jail for stepping off the pavement and questioning his judgment. Although this version was ultimately not used, Dredd retained his hard-line authoritarianism and this original incarnation is indicative of the satirical underpinnings of his production.[67] As Chris Lloyd tells us, highlighting that *Judge Dredd* can be read as a form of Rancière's 'critical art':[68] 'the comics house an inherent critique of the [violent] unchecked and yet legitimate police power wielded by [the state]'.[69]

Beyond this political questioning, what the satirical severity of Dredd highlights in a juristic sense is the way law, as an epistemological regime, produces judgment over the messiness of human reality. Mega-City One, the sprawling futuristic metropolis that Dredd patrols (also called the 'Big Meg'), is a vast and complex world; reminiscent of Young's 'legislated city' encountered in Chapter 3, it is Dredd and his colleagues at the Hall of Justice who offer legalistic order amidst the sprawling vagaries and madness of this complex future world. As Dredd himself tells us: 'Yeah … it's a mixed up world. That's why you've got laws … obey them'.[70] Moreover, a Judge 'can't afford to be *sorry* – he can only be *right*'.[71] The law must be certain, judgment must be final. It is this certain law that Dredd propounds, and that he applies to the streets of Mega-City One. It is this attempted production of certainty against the uncertainty of existence – which I will draw out below in conjunction with Judge Anderson – that connects Dredd to the Lovecraftian response to the infinite context of life, and thus to the concerns of a horrific jurisprudence.

In stark contrast to Dredd's strict rule-following attitude, his colleague Judge Anderson represents a more fluid vision of legality and judgment. Judge Anderson is a supporting character in *Judge Dredd* who gained her own spin-off series. She works in Mega-City One's 'Psi Division', and whilst Dredd predominantly hunts and judges criminals of various sorts, Anderson uses her psychic gifts to solve more Fortean cases. As an initial consideration of their jurisprudential relationship, consider the unlikely crossover where Batman ends up in Mega-City One and is

65 See Giddens (2017), p 389.
66 See, for example, Wagner et al (2005), np.
67 See 'The First Dredd' in Wagner et al (2005), np.
68 See Lloyd (2015), pp 206–208.
69 Lloyd (2015), p 208.
70 Wagner et al (2005), np.
71 Wagner et al (2005), np. Emphases in original.

arrested by Dredd. As a positive stickler for rules, Dredd is categorically opposed to Batman's activities as a vigilante – justice can only be enacted through technical law. From Dredd's perspective, the 'mask', 'costume', and 'weapons' can only represent a vigilante[72] – his own aesthetic presentation (his own judicial mask, costume, and weaponry) are unquestionable. Anderson, meanwhile, as a more 'intelligent' Judge, knows that justice does not come simply from the mechanical application of rules, but from judgment.[73] Depicted with a human face and flowing hair rather than the blank institutional mask of Dredd,[74] she recognises Batman's fight as one for justice, despite his technically illegitimate and non-institutional status.[75] Indeed, the explosion of Anderson's appearance in contrast to the staid institutional lines of Dredd signifies something of Anderson's more expansive vision of legality, which I discuss more directly in the following section.

Even more telling of Dredd's adherence to institutional text is what happens when Batman escapes and attacks Dredd. As can be seen in Figure 4.4, in his encounter with the world through the categories of law, Dredd can do nothing but add 'judge assault' to Batman's crimes. Figure 4.4 depicts the visceral, embodied violence of Batman punching Dredd in the face, and their subsequent struggles, with each hit adding time to Batman's sentence. Dredd's visceral, embodied experience of being pummelled by Batman is thus translated (via Wender's poetics) into the legal categories that Dredd not only lives to enforce, but simply lives – he is the law, after all. Figure 4.4's depiction – as *komos*, mediating embodied violence and legal categories as it does text and image – highlights the inadequacy of Dredd's legal speech to meaningfully reflect the experience depicted. The play of the plainly styled spoken text and more fluidly rendered diegetic sound-effects further opens up the distance between Dredd's embodied encounter and his abstract verbal enforcement. As the embodiment of law in all its institutional dimensions (police, courts, punishment, etc), Dredd does not encounter the living human or social world, but only the world of conscious law.

Dredd judges and enforces his judgments on the living streets of Mega-City One; his court is everywhere, not confined to a single room. The movement of the place of judgment out of the formal courtroom and onto the streets has profound ramifications. With Dredd we see the law brought to life, in multiple senses: Dredd applies and implements legal regulations in the context of flowing human life, judging and sentencing citizens in accordance with the rule of law; Dredd is

72 See 'Judgment on Gotham' in Wagner et al (2012), p 21.

73 Again, see 'Judgment on Gotham' in Wagner et al (2012), p 21. See also Manderson (2003) on judgment.

74 On the function of the uniform, as part of the way the legal institution 'masks' the human and thereby presents itself as endless and just, see Moran (2008), p 300; Moran (2009), pp 95–96. And, in relation to Dredd and Anderson, Giddens (2017), pp 395–396.

75 For more on Batman's complexities in terms of the legitimacy of state authority when faced with his vigilante activities, see Giddens (2015b).

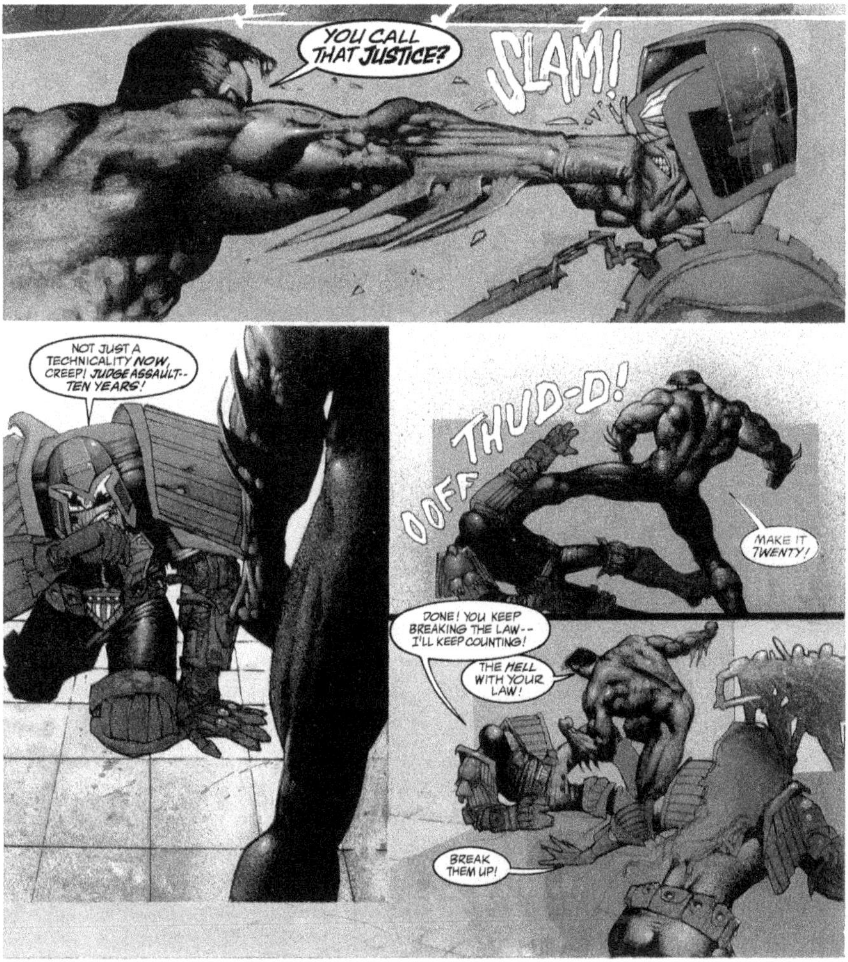

Figure 4.4 'Judgment on Gotham' in Wagner et al (2012), p 25. THE BATMAN/JUDGE DREDD COLLECTION © 2012 DC Comics and Rebellion A/S. All Rights Reserved. BATMAN and all related characters and elements © and ™ DC Comics. All Rights Reserved. Used with permission. Judge Dredd and all related characters, their distinctive likenesses and related elements featured in this publication are trademarks or registered trademarks of Rebellion A/S. 2000 AD is a registered trademark.

also the law made living, he is the animated embodiment of legal power and judgment. Dredd is the law, made living flesh. In bringing law to life in this way, in shifting judgment from courtroom to street – or in expanding the courtroom to encompass the world – law becomes totalised and the dream of conscious law comes true:

> [T]he simplified procedure and the effectiveness of execution [in Dredd's instant justice], endows the law with the kind of prowess that it wishes [or dreams] to accomplish in its regular course.[76]

And this is most significant in the relationship between the texts of law and its *in vivo* application in the courtroom: the court is a place where legality lives, where the texts and written categories of law are suspended to allow judgment to issue forth.[77] In court, it is not so much the text that matters,[78] but the performance of that text – its bringing to life via interpretation and application.

Making all the world a court pushes back the life that is outside or is not seen as technically significant to legal categories and adjudication. Despite practical and traditional priority being given to the textual performance of law, even the physical and architectural setting of the courtroom is embroiled in the judicial project of legal administration[79] – the world encountered in the court is infused with legal meaning, both conscious and unconscious. Unbounding this site turns the whole world into a judicial theatre, the pragmatic point of legal application, of decision, of adjudication. Dredd navigates Mega-City One with the eyes of the judge as the living application of text to fact, of rule to life, employing his environment and official tools[80] in his judicial project. Beyond embodying Wender's bureaucratic aesthetics,[81] this expanded court of life thus has no room for extra-legal, immaterial considerations. Life becomes instituted into the total order of conscious legality. Everything outside the juridical frame is repressed, destroyed, pushed back to the immeasurable and unreachable horizon created as the boundary of the court is expanded to infinity.

A similar suppression of life can be seen when Marianne Constable examines the way jurisprudence has tracked Nietzsche's history of the error of metaphysics. This Nietzschean error confused the 'real' and 'apparent' world. Culminating in sociological jurisprudence, which takes the empirical (apparent) world as the 'is' of law, Constable notes that legal sociology 'speaks the truths of positive law in the

76 Kozin (2014), p 931.

77 Judgment is always retrospective, always to some degree originary and separate from existing texts of law. As Manderson frames this Derridean point: 'interpretation is always a judgment on and after an act, and cannot be entirely pre-determined, [so] there is a sense in which the proper meaning of law is incapable of being understood in advance': Manderson (2003), p 107. The meaning of law's texts is thus suspended in court so that interpretation can be undertaken and applied.

78 Note the historical tendency to ignore the 'setting' in favour of the 'content' of judicial processes, even when examining courts: Bybee (2012), pp 1014–1015.

79 See Mulcahy (2011).

80 These include his 'Law-master' (a high-tech, computerised motorbike), and his 'Law-giver' pistol. This judicial sidearm literally emits violence and death, and is thus transparently symbolic of the multi-layered violence of law. On the various types of legal violence, giving an overview of Sarat and Kearnes's work, see, for example, Skinner (2009).

81 See Chapter 3.

languages of belief and appearance, the language of "legitimacy," "values," "norms," "distribution," and "policy" – from which "justice" and the "true" world disappear'.[82] The world becomes only that seen through the socio-legal lens, and there is nothing beyond. In Nietzsche's words, the real world is abolished as useless.[83] Dredd's experience of the world only through his judicial eyes similarly abolishes the world beyond that perspective, as did Dr Manhattan's adherence to the rational surface in Chapter 2. But part of Nietzsche's claim against metaphysics, his movement to recognise its error and overcome it, is that there are always multiple perspectives. As was indicated in Battersby's reading of the sublime, there is nothing beneath the surface, no 'beyond' or 'outside' – for Nietzsche, there is but more surface, infinitely complex and (re-)accessible as 'reality' from different perspectives.[84] And, according to Nietzsche, the jurist's penchant for textuality and textual interpretation does not encounter life – he or she simply repeats the past, reiterating and glossing around the texts of prior law, never going beyond the books: 'the jurist remains amongst the debris of the past, locked in the library'.[85] The lawyer's world is one constituted by legal texts, divorced from the 'real' premetaphysical world that has been destroyed, as Constable notes, through the historical development of rational knowledge.

Moreover, part of Nietzsche's problem with professional jurists as legal interpreters of texts is their intent to limit and restrain meaning, to close down interpretation rather than opening up its rich plurality.[86] As Peter Goodrich observes, lawyers generally are not willing to explore meaning by revelling in the possibilities and uncertainties of a text; rather they proceed by 'banishing ambiguity, by spending less rather than more time on the language of the text itself'.[87]

> Jurists tend to flee from indexicality or simple multiplicity of the text. They tend to take the short route, the rapid interpretation, … the literal reading. But it is hardly a reading at all … There are literal meanings, to be sure, but they are several and then one has to add the symbolic and the imagistic, the poetic, the cryptic, the chronic, and the chronological.[88]

Accordingly, in order to access greater meaning in a text and move beyond and outside the narrow 'epistemania' of the lawyer,[89] and perhaps approach the world that has been lost through rational abstraction, Goodrich proposes that we should read slower. Learning, gaining understanding, growing – these require the investment

82 Constable (1994), p 588.
83 See Constable (1994), p 552, citing Nietzsche's *Twilight of the Idols*.
84 See Battersby (2007); Nehamas (1985), pp 42–73. This is discussed in more detail in Chapter 5.
85 Goodrich (2005), p 186.
86 Goodrich (2005), p 191.
87 Goodrich (2005), p 192.
88 Goodrich (2005), p 197.
89 Goodrich (2005), p 188.

of time; reading for summary judgment, for outcomes or programmes for practice, eschews the investment of time and thus reduces the comprehension of meaning.[90]

As a site of *in vivo* legality, the courtroom is not the place for reading texts slowly – it is a site of application, of implementing the final or chosen interpretation in a specific case. It is not a site for reflection on possible meanings, for opening the text – it is ultimately a site for closing the text, for finally deciding meaning, for coming to a point. It is a site of praxis, where law acts as a living force, re-animating its otherwise dead manifestation or codification in texts through interpretation.[91] Slow reading can take place outside the court, but this outside is removed in Dredd's world; there is no place for it when the courtroom has no limit. But it is slow reading that truly brings texts to life in their full potential, Goodrich asserts – not the closed summaries and final, and therefore limited, readings of jurists.[92] While judicial interpretation can be seen as an eruption of a dimension of the legal unconscious, the symbolic order of justice animating the surface of dead letters,[93] the slow reader gains greater comprehension of law's unconscious by having:

> an appreciation of the existence that the text symbolizes, a perception of the images that it incorporates, and an understanding that the text models, inveighs, or institutes, a *modus operandi* or form of life.[94]

But there is an alienation at work in the legal text that goes beyond the closing down of meaning in judicial interpretation. As Pierre Legendre highlights, law institutes linguistic meaning, thereby guaranteeing the meanings of words and the range of legitimate interpretations available to the legal subject and binding the subject to the institution.[95] This meaning is separated from the subject as a sacred origin or source of truth, and also separates the subject from certain illegitimate meanings and taboos; the subject thus experiences him or herself as separated, divided, by the institutionalised text – a division that Legendre claims is only revealed via the insights of psychoanalysis:

> Psychoanalysis [of law] makes it possible for us to grasp … that the subject entering language is met by the institution of separation, a separation from things, from beings and from self by his words.[96]

90 Goodrich (2005), pp 195–196.
91 Goodrich (1995), p 31. Even in 'trial courts' where the focus may be on deciding facts rather than discussing the texts and principles of law, there is still an affirmation of the legal text – perhaps more so in such settings, since the text is not interrogated or 'read slowly', but is closed to a single meaning and applied to given questions of fact. Indeed, even the notion of a 'fact' is a product of the closure of the question 'what is a fact?'.
92 Goodrich (2005), p 197.
93 Goodrich (1995), pp 31–32.
94 Goodrich (2005), p 198.
95 Legendre (1998).
96 Legendre (1998), p 181. See also, on identity as divided and mediated by the mirror of the legal institution, Legendre (1997).

This means that the legal subject, the subject of text, 'is met by a limit, as the very condition of his symbolic life' in law[97] – the institutionalised legal text inherently alienates one from oneself, carving the legal subject away from the living human. At the same time, the social world becomes reduced to legal discourse: 'an assemblage of words, a textual order' arranged to address its subjects.[98]

This textual alienation, like the closing down of meaning, is exacerbated in Judge Dredd's totalised legal order of the unbounded court. Dredd does not read slowly; he has no place to read, no office or desk outside the courtroom – there is no outside when all the world's a court. He has no time to read, as he is constantly enacting the law in all its institutional guises (enforcement, sentencing, punishment, etc), endlessly applying the law to the world as he moves through the Big Meg. Even in the highly futuristic world of Mega-City One, populated by sophisticated technologies of teleportation, communication, surveillance, and data retrieval and storage – even here, the law is entom(b)ed within the pages of a book, the Judges' 'Book of Law'. But this text is pushed aside; space for written law, like that for its considered reading, is reduced as the theatre of application is expanded. The Book of Law still gives Dredd his ostensible authority – it is still text that institutes life in Mega-City One and separates subjects from themselves – but this book is not read, it is not 'walked, surveyed, and mapped',[99] it is not reflected upon and understood. The action of interpretation is replaced by the (more entertaining) action of street-level enforcement; the operations of justice, all combined and embodied in Dredd, become instant. Indeed, Dredd 'is not a thinking cop but an actor. Action defines and motivates his character as the primary, defining, and only characteristic'.[100] Perhaps more so than the institutional texts of western law in Legendre and the lawyerly readers against which Nietzsche lamented, the hyperbolic satire of the legal system in Mega-City One institutes 'life-denying forms'[101] – a ghostless totality of living legality; Dredd is an animation of law that ironically leaves no room for the openness of life, and also – like conscious law – represents a total denial of the infinite, unconscious context of human and judicial life.

Sleep of the jurist

In a short series of three episodes,[102] Judge Dredd is seen to briefly question his own judgment. He is uncharacteristically troubled by his shooting dead of an armed perpetrator where he could have shot to disarm or injure.[103] His mentor

97 Legendre (1998), p 183.
98 Legendre (1998), p 180.
99 Goodrich (2005), p 192.
100 Kozin (2014), p 927.
101 Goodrich (2005), p 188.
102 'Question of Judgement', 'Error in Judgement', and 'A Case for Treatment' in Wagner et al (2007).
103 'Question of Judgement' in Wagner et al (2007), np.

admonishes him for questioning his judicial training: 'Come on, Joe! We're talking about *basic procedure* here ... the *kill* shot is the *safe* shot'.[104] Dredd ends up in therapy to root out the cause of his problematic self-questioning, a reverie that undermines his efficiency as a Judge. His therapist, after extensive examination, diagnoses Dredd as a human:

> No matter how hard we try to control it, sooner or later the human being behind the mask always starts to come out. Even in a street-hard Judge like Dredd.[105]

The unconscious cause of Dredd's questioning of his own judgment is his humanity, which is repressed: as a genetic clone created specifically for Judge-ship it is bred out of him, and also drilled out in his institutional training through childhood and adolescence. The human is here presented literally as the unconscious of the judicial institution, excavated via the psychoanalytic examination of Dredd as the ideally dehumanised embodiment of law itself. In an uncharacteristic moment of reflection, Dredd admits that although he had never recovered from having feelings towards his clone-brother 'Rico' whom he had to kill,[106] it did not stop him doing his duty.[107] But to wallow in human sentimentalism is to undermine the judicial capacity for action, to destroy Dredd's efficiency as a practical law-bringer.[108] But whilst Dredd is emblematic of the wider legal system in Mega-City One, and represents the reduction of life when the courtroom's boundaries are removed, his colleague Judge Anderson signifies something quite different.[109]

Although a Judge, Anderson's world is not the strictly legal and thus devitalising one inhabited by Dredd. Anderson's, rather, is the eldritch world beyond the

104 'Question of Judgement' in Wagner et al (2007), np. Emphases in original.

105 'A Case for Treatment' in Wagner et al (2007), np.

106 Rico, although trained as a Judge like Dredd, believed himself above the law and committed offences for which Dredd had to sentence and punish him. See 'Return of Rico' in Wagner et al (2005), np.

107 'A Case for Treatment' in Wagner et al (2007), np.

108 However, although there is a persistent cultural script that states judges should be dispassionate, and that emotion undermines reason and leads to bias and uncertainty, exploration of law's unconscious shows that emotion is actually common throughout the judicial institution and arguably plays a positive role in decision-making processes:

> the traditional legal story casting emotion as stubbornly irrational is simply not true. Emotion's critical role in reflecting and enabling reason coexists with an ability to shape our experience and expression of it in accordance with a hierarchy of reasons.
>
> Maroney (2011a), p 649 (and generally)

See also Maroney (2012). Note, importantly, that this is still a process operating upon the primacy of reason – albeit reason working in conjunction with emotion. The emotional flatness of Dredd can thus be read as playing into a satirical critique of conservative visions of justice as necessarily dispassionate.

109 For a presentation of the tensions between Anderson and Dredd in the form of a judgment, made in an ultimately Lovecraftian context, see Giddens (2017). See Appendix A for an overview and details of Judge Anderson in general.

'everyday' and the 'normal', where she tackles sorcerers, demonic possessions, hauntings, parallel dimensions, telepathy, astral projection, and other psychic and paranormal phenomena – she enacts her judgments where the 'beyond' breaks through. While Dredd patrols the concrete streets of Mega-City One, Anderson navigates the uncertain world beyond, the Lovecraftian dimension behind or beneath the everyday world that is always lurking, threatening to erupt, and bring the despair of the infinite cosmos with it. An example of this terrible beyond can be seen in Figure 4.5, a complex, fluid and interpenetrating storm of horrors. Presented multimodally, and doing away with the frame of the panel, the comics form here highlights the way such a beyond breaks out of the closed boundaries of the multiframe and exceeds the boxed enclosure of the text.

The Lovecraftian challenge that Anderson's world brings to the legality of Dredd is overt – precisely a horrific jurisprudence. Their interactions are telling. While Dredd discounts the complexities of the world as something that is brushed aside when we turn to the rigour of enforced legal judgments ('that's why we have laws'), Anderson recognises the deep well of human life and cosmic uncertainty that exists outside the conscious categories of law:

> It isn't easy being a *psi*. / Every waking hour, your mind picking up everything the psi-band throws at you … black blasts of hate – barbs of poison greed – screams of distant suicides – / And always in the background, the pained static generated by the desperate, hopeless dreams of 400 million

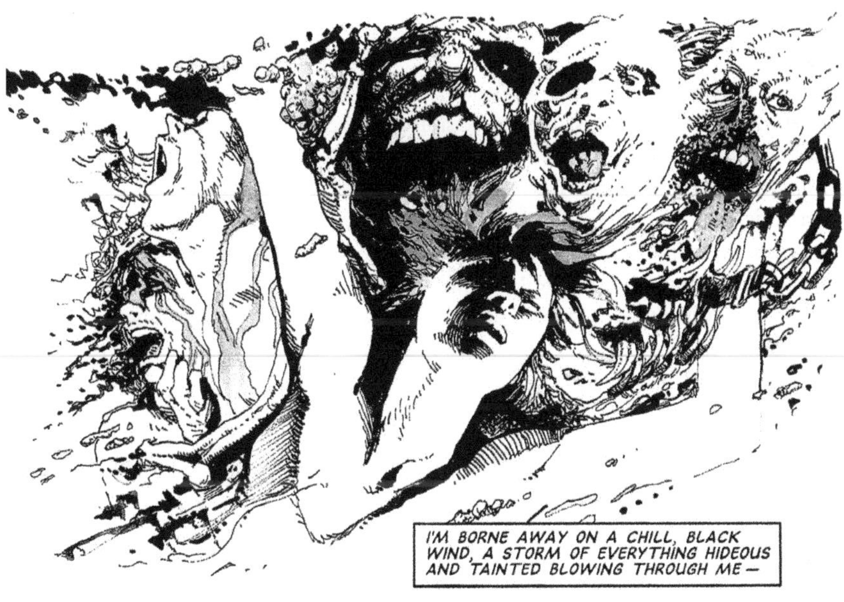

Figure 4.5 'Satan Part 1' in Grant et al (2013), np. Psi-Judge Anderson © 2017 Rebellion A/S. All rights reserved. Reproduced with permission of the copyright holder.

> unhappy people. / To save your own mind, you have to *blank out* every now and again.[110]

And 'blanking out' is precisely what Dredd does: he subdues the 'mixed up world' with the unyielding categories of law, enforcing them to the point of barbarism – to the point of death. Anderson, meanwhile, navigates and meaningfully engages with this uncertain world on a day-to-day basis. She does not repress her emotion as Dredd does,[111] and regularly transcends the physical, entering the minds of others, taking journeys of astral projection, communing with spirits and ghosts, and crossing dimensional boundaries. In doing so, Anderson is engaging not only with the world on the streets of Mega-City One, but at the same time with a hidden world – with the sublime beyond outside Dredd's conscious legality.

Although initially suggestive of the role of emotion in judicial processes,[112] her engagement without repression has a broader epistemic relevance; the hidden world she encounters, the supernatural beyond, can be understood as symbolic of the world-in-itself beyond the limits of our human knowledge. Sites of eldritch happenings and supernatural rupture represent the breaking through of the 'real' world into our structures of constructed knowledge, but in a way that retains the mystery of the world beyond. Like Batman's epistemological edgework, or Lovecraft's indirect depictions of horror, it is never fully revealed to us, it remains 'occulted', hidden – occluded.[113] Suggestive of this 'beyond', Figure 4.6 depicts the dark realm outside waking thought as it breaks through into our own via Anderson's psionic activity, the conscious forms of the world visibly disintegrating as the abyss opens up on the page, disintegrating the multiframe itself.

In this tension, we can also see the problems of praxis that law engenders: law must do something, it must make decisions in cases and provide answers. Dredd's terrible pragmatism effects such decisions, throwing lawbreakers into confinement and cleaning up the streets. But, as Anderson says, there is 'not a lot a telepath can do in times of disaster ... / except *suffer*'.[114] Dredd solves problems, Anderson suffers them – but in suffering, she understands and experiences the expansive depths of meaning beyond the 'ghostless' application of hastily read rules. Where Dredd seeks conclusion – judicial decision and sentence – Anderson has learned to

110 'Helios Part 2' in Grant et al (2009), np. Emphases in original.

111 The gendered dimensions of this (Dredd-man-unemotional; Anderson-woman-emotional) are of course overt, and with critical issues of their own beyond the scope of the present chapter. But see Giddens (2017), pp 395–400, for analysis of the visualisations of Anderson's sexual body, and its implications for the judicial institution in its rupturing of the façade of the costume.

112 For an account of potential emotional engagement and coping strategies for judges, see Maroney (2011b).

113 See Thacker (2011), pp 44–79.

114 'Triad Part 7' in Grant et al (2009), np. Emphasis in original.

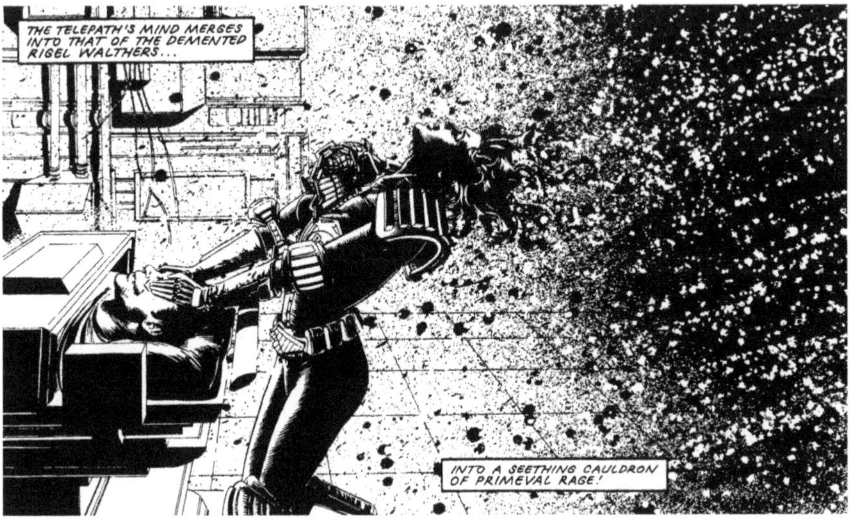

Figure 4.6 'Helios Part 4' in Grant et al (2009), np. Psi-Judge Anderson © 2017 Rebellion A/S. All rights reserved. Reproduced with permission of the copyright holder.

remain open to life's messy uncertainties: 'Who knows? Only thing I've learned in 20 years of psionics is – keep your options open'.[115]

This division between Anderson's openness and Dredd's closure can be seen in the 'Satan' storyline, where the connotations of Dredd's juristic attitude manifests itself in his becoming literally frozen in the face of evil – he is encased in ice by the Devil himself.[116] While Dredd's law is unable to meaningfully encounter Satan (symbolic of everything unlawful, evil, and outside the rational order – the dragon of unreason, as we saw in Chapter 3) and becomes static and unresponsive, Anderson is fluid and dynamic, open to discourse and understanding, and thereby plays the Devil at his own game and tricks him into admitting responsibility for his own evil. The Devil had previously held that he had no free will, that it was God who created him the way he was; but his admission of responsibility for the vast evils he has wrought upon the universe drives the Devil mad, and destroys him. Beyond dualistic questions of free will and determinism, this example is a clear emanation of Anderson's ability to think and act outside the cold mechanisms of law and the quest for summary judgment, to respond to the world beyond the legal order, beyond the rational text. We can also see this in the story 'Contact',[117] where Anderson's psionic abilities enable her to commune with an alien species on the fringes of the solar system and sense their lack of malicious intent – they only want to trade with Earth. Dredd, meanwhile, tries to arrest all the aliens as they land their ship in Mega-City One. While the Judges are ready to judge and attack

115 'Beyond the Void Part One' in Grant et al (2009), np.
116 'Satan' in Grant et al (2013), np.
117 'Contact' in Grant et al (2009), np.

the aliens, take their advanced transport drive, and thereby 'open up the whole universe to Mega-City law'[118] and reduce the cosmos to legal order, Anderson intuits that 'we can't judge the whole universe by the standards of own rat-hole'[119] – there is more to the world than the Dreddian jurists of Mega City One allow.

This tension between cold law and rich psionic life can be seen in the tragedy of Anderson's colleague Judge Corey, who is a fellow psi and an empath. In an episode detailing her movement towards suicide, Corey spells out in her farewell letter to Anderson the pain and emotionality that regular Judges cannot see:

> I don't know why I'm writing this down. / It won't alter anything. It won't mask the pain, or wipe out the futility. It won't change my mind. / It won't keep me alive. / Judges don't think this way. Judges are cold, clinical machines ruled by Logic and Order and Law. But Psis … / Psis are different. Psis have a special gift. / And Empaths have the most special gift of all. / We *feel.* / … / The irony of being an Empath! We punish the perps … and we feel their pain. / A really special gift. / … / I'm hurting inside, deep down in my mind, in the secret places only the Psis know. / … / I can't do ugly things any more. That's not what special gifts are for.[120]

The lack of understanding of her need to 'write it down' is telling. During the above account, Corey communes with what is perhaps the last living Blue Whale on earth, a massive being that she empathically connects with and comes to experience the 'unspeakable sadness' of the non-human world. Amidst the ebbs and flows and shifting forces of the emotional world of the empath, against the backdrop of an endless cosmos without human life or concern – what use is putting things into words? Words won't 'mask the pain' – they won't 'blank out' the background Lovecraftian horror beyond the boundaries of the 'cold, clinical', 'logic and order' of law. Despite law's attempts to encode into rational language, to repress the infinite depths of the universe and render summary judgment, this horror remains.

Trembling with fear in the face of the beyond, Lovecraft's protagonist in 'The Call of Cthulhu' bemoans: 'I shall never sleep calmly again when I think of the horrors that lurk ceaselessly behind life'.[121] In a similar vein, Figure 4.7 depicts Judge Anderson failing to sleep beneath a swirling emanation of her nightmares – the monsters of the eldritch realm she navigates. This image bears some resemblance to Goya's 'The Sleep of Reason Produces Monsters' (Figure 4.8), a work that can be read in terms of the unconscious of reason as part of a

118 'Contact Part 2' in Grant et al (2009), np.
119 'Contact Part 3' in Grant et al (2009), np.
120 'Judge Corey: Leviathan's Farewell' in Grant et al (2009), np.
121 Lovecraft (2011), p 91.

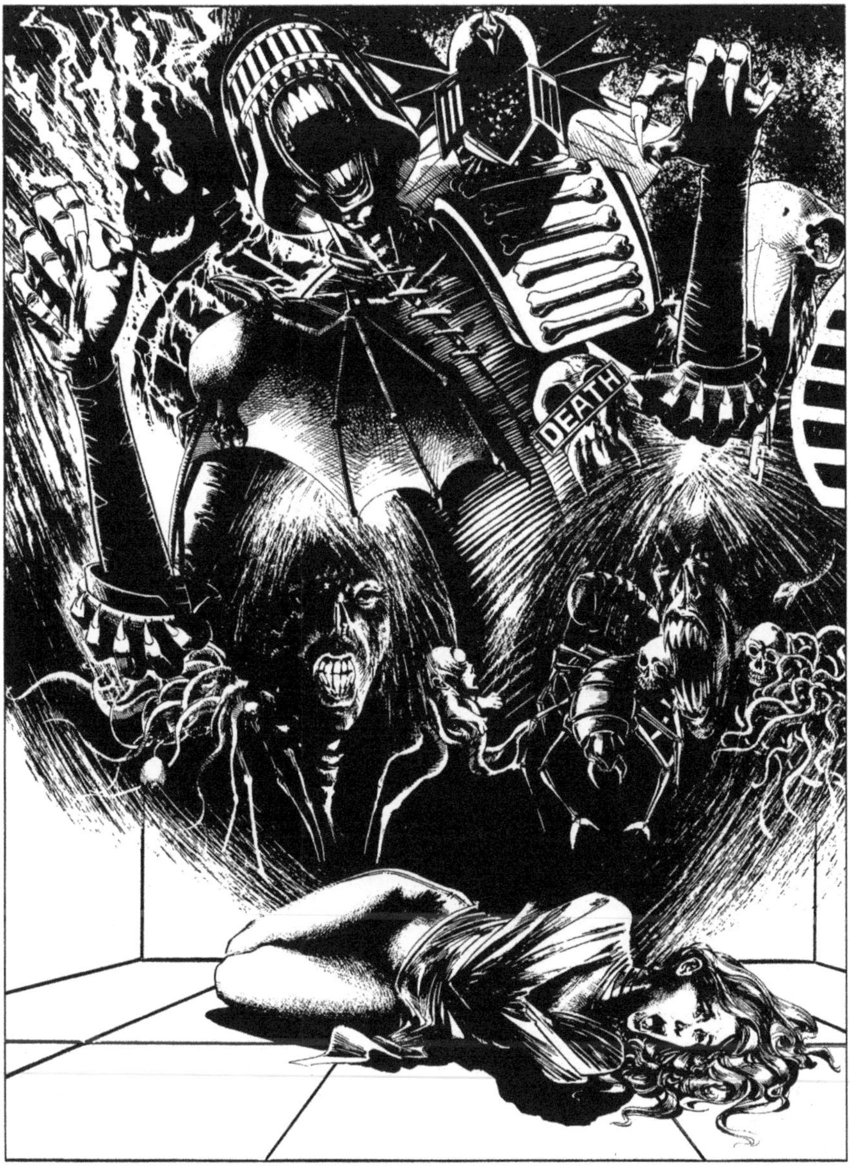

Figure 4.7 'Engram Part 7' in Wagner et al (2009), np. Psi-Judge Anderson © 2017 Rebellion A/S. All rights reserved. Reproduced with permission of the copyright holder.

horrific jurisprudence; thus we must first engage with Goya's image before approaching the image of Anderson. A leading interpretation of Goya's image, deriving from Goya's own notes and contemporary discourse on his work, is that we need to be awake in order to perceive (via reason) the 'monsters' of

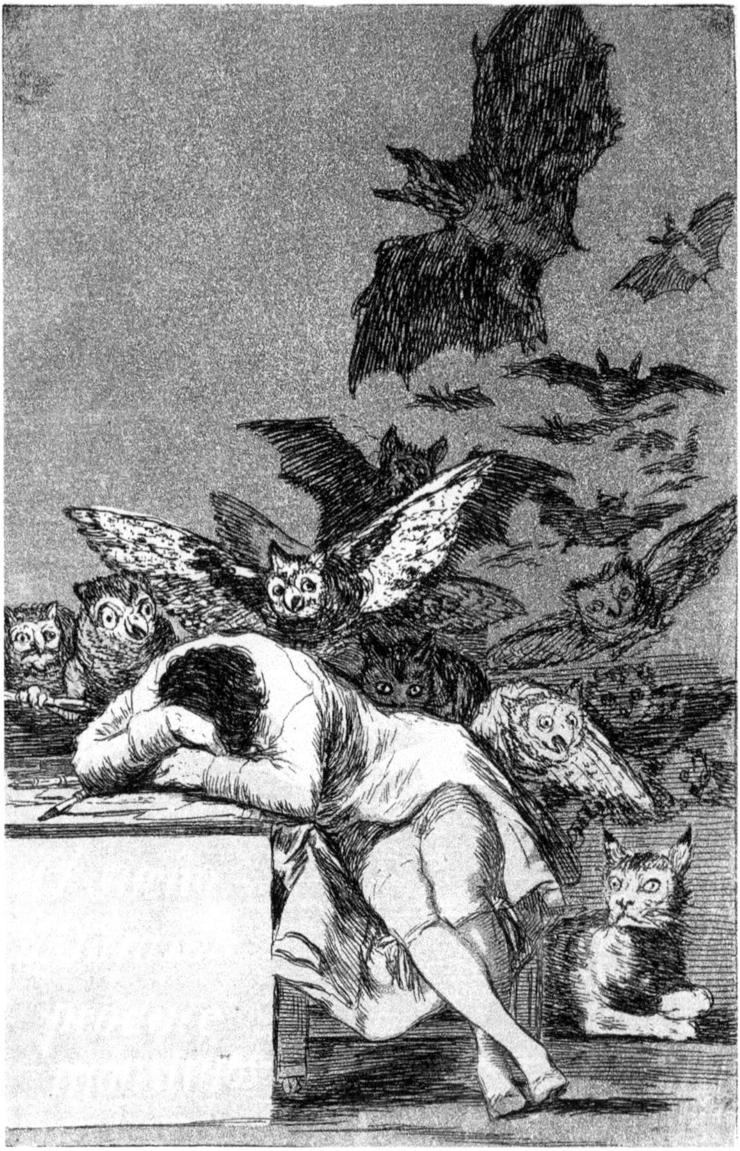

Figure 4.8 Francisco Goya (1799) *El Sueño de la Razón Produce Monstruos* [*The Sleep of Reason Produces Monsters*]. Image sourced via WikiCommons.

social harm, ignorance, and injustice.[122] Indeed, the image has generally been interpreted as either suggesting the need to remain vigilant, through reason, against bigotries and prejudice, or as representing the inevitability of these and

122 Bradshaw (2013), p 132; Nehamas (2001), p 37.

other all-too-human aspects of life[123] – both interpretations that do not engage with any possible psychoanalytical readings of the image.

Attempting to go beyond this division, Nehamas argues that what Goya's famous etching demonstrates is that 'reason is asleep when the imagination deserts it':[124] pure, cold, abstract rationality is at best half an understanding, and must be tempered by imagination, by the arts and humanities, in order to be fully human. Separately, 'reason and imagination produce monsters; together, they discern them, even if they cannot eradicate them'.[125] Nehamas then uses this brief interpretation to embark upon an extended discussion on the separation of reason and aesthetics that only engagement with the arts for their own sake can counter[126] – an engagement that fails to acknowledge the massive role that the aesthetic plays in the construction and experience of moral institutions such as law. Nehamas maintains the imagination very much as part of a rationalist approach to the world, ultimately ending up confusing the two: it is the 'combination of reason and imagination [in art] that makes us truly *rational* and therefore human'.[127] This inclusion of aesthetic dimensions as a conscious part of reason, coupled with the lack of recognition of the broader institutional relevance and unconscious presence of the aesthetic in public structures, betrays a vision that subsumes the aesthetic within the rational, a movement that overlooks the relationship between aesthetics as the broad context of sensory perception and living humanity within which rationality operates as a particular limited perspective, as we have seen above and in previous chapters. Like the general division in the image's interpretation noted above, it also betrays a focus that is unable to interpret the psychoanalytic dimensions of Goya's image – despite its obvious imaginary of the sleeping mind.

In line with Freud's approach in *The Interpretation of Dreams*,[128] a psychoanalytic reading of 'The Sleep of Reason' could be rendered thus: when reason sleeps, its unconscious reigns. This psychoanalytic interpretation has significant implications for the current project. The conscious, waking mind of rational thought deals in certainty, knowledge, progress – enlightenment. When that conscious mind falls into sleep, not only may it be unable to perceive or eradicate the injustices of the modern world, but its unconscious returns in the form of dreams. The possibility of translating *sueño* as 'dream' rather than 'sleep'[129] brings this Freudian reading to the fore. Reason's unconscious incorporates all those things that reason represses in order for it to prevail as a universal, ahistoric, and abstract form of objective discourse and knowledge. The dreams of reason, then, represent the return of this repressed 'other scene' of the rational order. All the uncertainty, all the unreason, irrationality, madness, horrors, fears, obscurities, and messiness of

123 See Asma (2009), p 151; Bradshaw (2013), p 133.
124 Nehamas (2001), p 38.
125 Nehamas (2001), p 41.
126 See, generally, Nehamas (2001).
127 Nehamas (2001), emphasis added.
128 See Freud (1997). We discuss this more fully in Chapter 6.
129 Bradshaw (2013), p 132.

life: the monsters – *the dragon* – of unreason. In Goya's image, we can see these monstrosities depicted in the animalistic beasts that swarm around the sleeping figure; they constitute a visual representation of the sleeper's dream; as it is reason that is sleeping, they are symbolic of that which is outside and repressed by the rational order. These can then be understood in a less psychoanalytic mode – as being those unjustifiable or irrational prejudices of modern society that reason must face and quell, as the inevitable 'dark, irrational and emotional forces' of human life,[130] or by expanding rationality to include artistic imagination – but in any case remain emanations of reason's unconscious.

Deeply invested in the structures of reason and rational text, the jurist, too, produces monsters in the throes of sleep. The monsters of the jurist's sleep are not only the monsters of unreason – the returning horror of uncertainty, of the life outside rational comprehension – but also the horror that is implied when law is brought to life in its completeness; the horror of a world with no legal outside, of a world that is nothing but law. The lawyer's dream, Goodrich suggests, is one of reason and justice – a dream of order to cover the melancholia associated with toiling within a system that is plural, overly complex, and without order. On this understanding, the legal unconscious becomes in part something that ties together the messy intricacies of the actual text into a unified and symbolic whole.[131] Such a 'hatred of disorder' can be seen within the development of the 'black letter' tradition of legal education in late Victorian England.[132] But the logical progression of this 'dream' of law, of the propagation of unified and instituted order, becomes terrible – the legal unconscious is not only filled with dreams, but also nightmares. Dredd himself can be seen as an emanation of the lawyers' dream of total order.[133] But when this dream becomes a judicial nightmare in the face of the horrific sublime in Anderson, it emerges as an uncanny and hyperbolic emanation of the desire to quell the fluidity and infinite ineffability of existence into logical categories, practical answers, and textual descriptors – to destroy life in favour of law.

This nightmare, this horror of rational law, is made manifest on the streets and amidst the psyches of Mega-City One with the emergence of Judge Death. Judge Death comes from a parallel dimension, where the power of law has been turned explicitly against life: without life there can be no lawbreaking, no crime, no illegality. Thus, anything that lives is judged and sentenced to death; the *anima* is completely repressed. In this, the nightmare of the totalised world of law, of the lawyer's vision taken seriously to its ghostless conclusion and brought to life in completeness, reveals a horrific dimension to judgment. As he describes himself, mapping the turn from the dream of benevolent and deific order of text to the horror this inevitably invokes:

130 Asma (2009), p 151.
131 Goodrich (1995), p 8.
132 See Sugarman (1991), notably p 47.
133 See Kozin (2014).

> In the beginning was the word. / I was that word. / I am everything. I am everywhere. I am always. / I am the way and the truth and the light – / And the dark. I am the dark! I am the monstrous. I am the abomination. I am the decayed. / I am *death*![134]

In Figure 4.7 we see Judge Anderson's nightmares manifesting above her prone figure. The sleeping jurist produces these horrors – with Judge Death taking centre stage, amidst other terrors, ghouls, and supernatural beasts. They are symbolic of the unconscious of the rational order, of the threat of unstructured and irreducible life beyond the text and categories of law, and the nightmare of denying their disorder. But Anderson, in her eldritch engagement, has her eyes open. Her nightmares erupt into her waking life (or she moves into her nightmares) as she navigates the supernatural world beyond the everyday surface of the Big Meg. Anderson, as a dynamic and open counter-point to Dredd's closing and repressive legality, can see the demons, can see the spectres of unreason that are produced as we build our particular rational structures and call them truth. Her eyes are open, she can see the horror of conscious law: its audacity and its limitations.

The sleep of the jurist thus encounters the abyss beyond legal consciousness, the cosmic uncertainty of the infinite world outside human knowledge. Judge Death and the horrors of which he is symbolic signal the return of this repressed outside in a reversed form: the uncertainties of existence return in the form of absolute and total certainty, but a certainty that takes the form of a spectre, of a fluid and insidious monster that transcends the conscious world as a demon. A ghost to haunt the ghostless machine. Judge Death is the juridical dream made total, but a twisted and uncanny emanation of it. He is satire built upon satire: where Dredd satirises the authoritarian justice policies of Thatcherism with his universalised, unreflective courtroom and hard-line, unfeeling judgments, Judge Death satirises Dredd as the judicial destroyer of life itself. But in this double satire, what is revealed is the process by which legal judgment necessarily closes down the endlessly unfolding potential of life and of meaning. The depiction of Death is significant in the way this closure is understood. Suggested in Figure 4.7, and evident also in Figure 4.9 where we see Anderson reacting to Death's presence, is the vision of Death's judgment as horrific – the horror of life being reduced, abstracted, its potential and openness destroyed in order to render summary judgment. As Legendre's institution of life suggests, to be the victim of judgment is to be alienated from your humanity and from the fluidity of life – to be separated from the self by words – to be reduced to a legal category, a pronouncement within the textual architecture of judgment.

What is also evident in Figure 4.9 is the imaginary nature of this horror. Judge Death is here depicted rendering judgment as part of a vision within Anderson's mind. The horror of this judgment, of Death's expelling of life from the legal order, is conceptual. It is an epistemological horror, and one that when set in the

134 'Beyond the Void Part One' in Grant et al (2009), np. Emphasis in original.

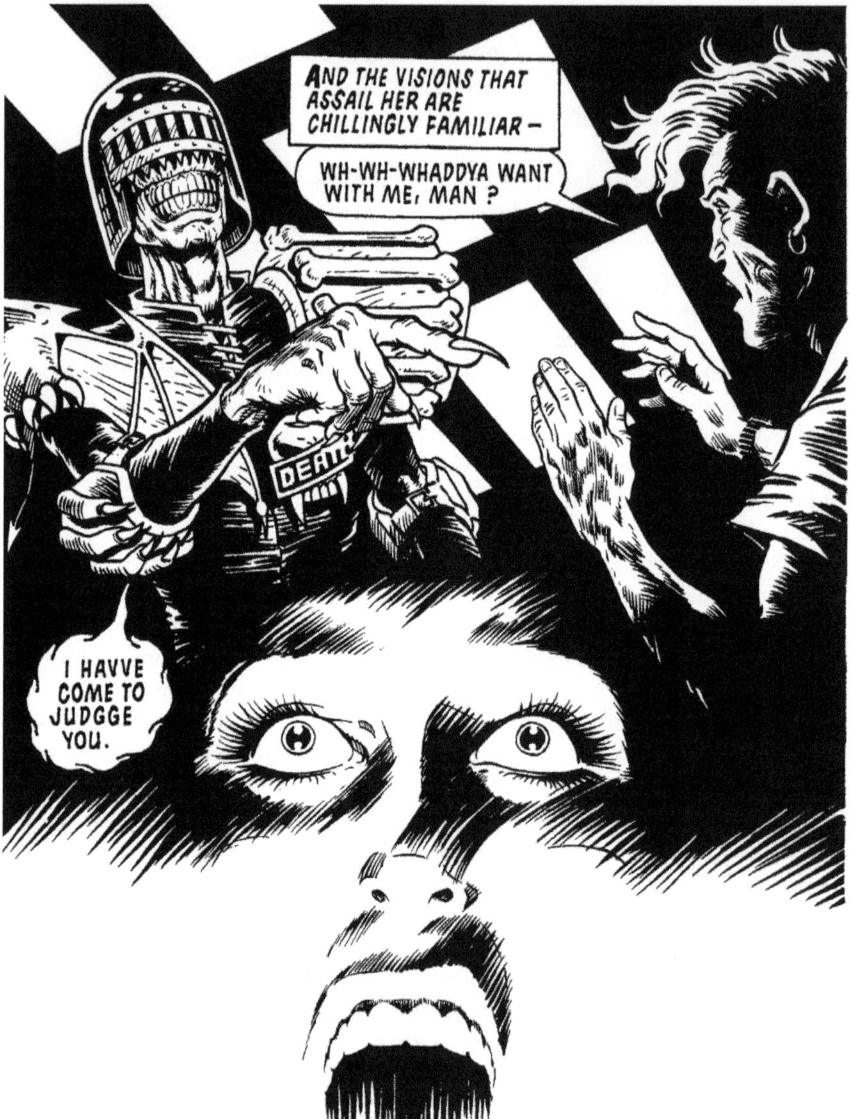

Figure 4.9 Wagner et al (2009), np. Psi-Judge Anderson © 2017 Rebellion A/S. All rights reserved. Reproduced with permission of the copyright holder.

wider context of a horrific jurisprudence becomes more dreadful. Amidst the vast cosmos, judgment gives an answer – *the* answer – enforced physically and instituted universally within the *nomos*. The horror of judgment may be conceptual, but its consequences become physical, psychological, social, and cultural. As we have seen, the text institutes a way of being, it constitutes life – as words of magic, as Alan Moore might say, it shapes the world – which is why we need to read slower to understand the text as best we can.[135] This is a process that, if it is to avoid closing down life, must ultimately be without end, must never get to the bottom of things, must remain open and defer any final judgment lest life be destroyed.

Such a commitment to openness and non-closure suggests a futility to the summary judgments of law that can never capture meaningful life or the infinity of existence. Indeed, what we have encountered across the bulk of this chapter is the idea of a world beyond human law, of a dimension of existence outside that encountered or available to the limited senses and understandings of humans, that legal texts and judgments suppress, that they 'blank out' or hide. Such a notion is central to a horrific jurisprudence that deals in the negative responses to the uncertainty and limitations of legal knowing – limitations that rational law denies in its reification. In Figure 4.10, Tom Kaczynski compresses the Lovecraftian unconscious and the human desire for its repression into a single-page comics work. Here we see the gradual expansion of awareness of our precarious and insignificant place in the planet's ecosystem, the natural processes of life, the tectonic time of geology, and finally the infinite cosmos.

From the very first panel, presented without borders, we are in an unbounded universe. The abyss breaks through when the blanketing effect of civilisation and technology pauses, and our terrible place in the universe becomes clear, before it is once again repressed by the small, close, comforting hum of a fan. In the final panel, this whole process is compressed into a single image: the infinite depths of cosmic blackness against which a neatly delineated 'whhhrrrrr', the crystallisation of the hum, enables the ignorant peace of sleep. The cosmic context may imply a meaninglessness in our attempts to know – a nothingness embedded within all knowledge, that ultimately our lives and attempts at understanding are futile and empty, destined to extinction and pointlessness. Against Corey's assertion that there is no point writing things down, and her subsequent abandonment to the abyss, it is precisely by knowing – by constructing concrete forms and epistemologies – that the cosmic abyss is 'blanked out', screened off, and we become safe once more. Thus, recalling Legendre's analysis of the subject as separated in its entry into language, the institutional texts of law can be seen as a barrier between us and the void, between us and the 'fantastic beyond of institutions':

> In this beyond, there is a logic that is not Aristotelian; in it, man confronts a category of nothingness, the void, negativity … the *speechless void*. To establish [legal] foundations is to erect a screen to protect us from the void. Upon this screen are inscribed all the historical and mythological stories of the world.[136]

135 See Goodrich (2005).
136 Legendre (1997), p 254. Emphasis in original.

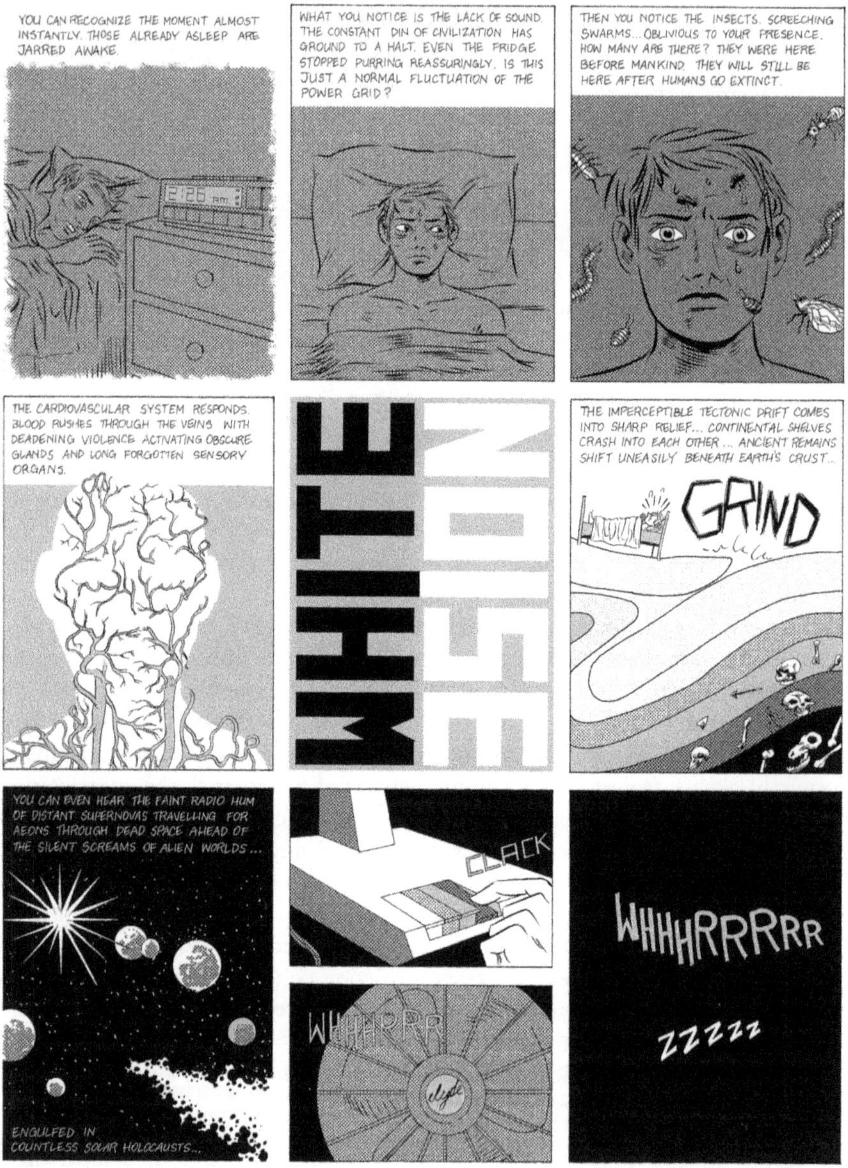

Figure 4.10 Tom Kaczynski 'White Noise' in Kaczynski (2012), p 45. © 2012 Tom Kaczynski. Reproduced with permission.[137]

137 See Appendix B for a reproduction of the text in this figure.

Or, in Kaczynski's terms, upon the void is inscribed the gentle hum of knowing, the hum that blanks out the abyss. But by presenting the safety of conscious forms via the peace of sleep, Kaczynski highlights that these forms are, of course, haunted by their dreams – as Anderson and Goya also remind us.[138]

The abyss implied by the existence of a universe beyond human influence and knowledge is not necessarily a void. The infinite context within which law operates is not an emptiness; the world beyond the limits of human thought, beyond rational comprehension, beyond human experience and interpretation (be it rational or otherwise) is not inherently nothing, not *nihil.* As the nature of Lovecraft's horror and Anderson's experiences of the abyss imply, it is full of beings and forces indifferent to us feeble humans. Where a 'void' can only ever be empty, an 'abyss' can be full. A void is a symptom of rational thought – a void opens up at the limit of thought, beyond which reason is unable to comprehend in its conscious, waking state. Hence Kant's desire to turn away from those limits in his experience of the sublime – in his rational system, there is nothing beyond its limits, only reason can order the world. Legalistically, as Legendre suggests, it is from the perspective of the rational texts of law that we cannot think this beyond – it is *speechless.* To deem this a void is to remain trapped inside the rational surface, to suppress the unconscious order and maintain that the universe can only be understood and codified through rational means – if it cannot, then it is nothing, it cannot be seen or encountered, it does not exist. To put it in terms of *Neonomicon*, it is to remain within the narrative text boxes of Figure 4.1 and not to recognise the multimodal expanse beyond their frames. To move beyond the limits of the rational surface, to explore the 'beyond' as Judge Anderson does, as a cultural legal aesthetics does, and as the multimodality of comics demands of its readers, necessitates a recognition that this beyond is not empty. An abyss opens up at the limits of rational text, but an abyss filled with unstructured sense, image, aesthetics, emotion, passion, desire, fear, madness – and infinite other ineffabilities repressed by the words *inter alia.* The texts and judgments of law are constructs built out of the material of that abyss, reduced, honed, codified, framed, and shaped into things amenable to the rational attitude. They are not built out of nothing.

Anderson understands that there is a whole world beyond the narrow confines of the hegemonic forms of conscious law, beyond the rational surface. Law can take other forms, can be encountered in the abyss in different ways. The world beyond is more than just the ecological planet or theological speculation that Thacker is concerned with in his exploration of horror.[139] Lovecraft's horrific sublime and the jurisprudence it brings about through Dredd and Anderson, and compressed in Kaczynski, do more than suggest there is a planet independent from us that has its own deep rhythms and perspectives, or that there is some vast, endless beyond. They also highlight the frailty and insignificance of the human

138 This haunting is the subject of the next chapter, Chapter 5.
139 See Thacker (2011), pp 105–123.

condition and the minutiae of conscious law: to glimpse the endless cascading depths of the cosmos is to witness the horror of law – that it cannot know, that it cannot bring objectivity, truth, certainty, moral solution in any meaningful way, at least not in its limited rational form. All it can do is protect us from the void, to 'blank it out' by affirming meaning and knowable forms – the hum of legality. But this horror is two-fold: even against the infinite abyss, law still renders judgment, still claims to bring certainty and absolute answers, enforced over an already cosmically frail human populace.

The horrific jurisprudence of this chapter suggests the need for a neonomicon – a new law of images and everything they imply. Such a law would respond to this beyond as a Chthulucene rather than populated with 'racial-nightmare monsters'. It would engage in a more dynamic and fluid way than the static doctrines of the necronomicon – the dead law of images: paralysed in fear by the atextual beyond like Lovecraft. A law that can only see rational text remains inanimate and unresponsive in the face of images, of emotion, aesthetics, and the fluid, endlessly interpretable universe beyond the traditional legal order. It remains in the text box, disengaged from the expanse of multimodality that surrounds it. For such a law, the beyond remains empty, unknowable, a nihilistic void – an irrational threat. By reconfiguring law's epistemology, by turning to cultural, aesthetic, and visual forms such as comics that, as *komos*, can mediate different orders of knowing and experience, and thereby critically examining the boundaries of the rational text that has shaped law's conscious capacities, we can realise the non-existence of such limits and expand the legal project without the necessary reduction to life-denying forms of reason and text.

References

Timo Airaksinen (1999) *The Philosophy of HP Lovecraft: The Route to Horror*, Peter Lang.

Stephen T Asma (2009) *On Monsters: An Unnatural History of Our Worst Fears*, Oxford University Press.

Christine Battersby (1995) 'Stages on Kant's Way: Aesthetics, Morality, and the Gendered Sublime' in PZ Brand and C Korsmeyer (eds) *Feminism and Tradition in Aesthetics*, Pennsylvania State University Press.

Christine Battersby (2007) *The Sublime, Terror, and Human Difference*, Routledge.

Michael Bradshaw (2013) '"The Sleep of Reason": *Swamp Thing* and the Intertextual Reader' in MJA Green (ed) *Alan Moore and the Gothic Tradition*, Manchester University Press.

Keith J Bybee (2012) 'Judging in Place: Architecture, Design, and the Operation of Courts' 37 *Law and Social Inquiry* 1014.

Marianne Constable (1994) 'Genealogy and Jurisprudence: Nietzsche, Nihilism, and the Social Scientification of Law' 19 *Law and Social Inquiry* 551.

Penny Crofts (2015) 'Monstrous Bodily Excess in *The Exorcist* as a Supplement to Law's Accounts of Culpability' 24 *Griffith Law Review* 372.

R Alain Everts (2012) 'Howard Phillips Lovecraft and Sex: Or the Sex Life of a Gentleman' www.hplovecraft.com/study/articles/hpl-sex.aspx

Sigmund Freud (1997) *The Interpretation of Dreams*, Wordsworth.

Thomas Giddens (2015b) 'Natural Law and Vengeance: Jurisprudence on the Streets of Gotham' 28 *International Journal for the Semiotics of Law* 765.

Thomas Giddens (2017) 'Anderson v Dredd [2137] Mega-City LR 1' 30 *International Journal for the Semiotics of Law* 389.

Peter Goodrich (1995) *Oedipus Lex: Psychoanalysis, History, Law*, University of California Press.

Peter Goodrich (2005) 'Slow Reading' in P Goodrich and M Valverde (eds) *Nietzsche and Legal Theory: Half-Written Laws*, Routledge.

Peter Goodrich and Valérie Hayaert (2015) *Genealogies of Legal Vision*, Routledge.

Alan Grant et al (2013) *Judge Anderson: The Psi Files Volume 03*, Rebellion.

Matthew JA Green (2013) 'A Darker Magic: Heterocosms and Bricolage in Moore's Recent Reworkings of Lovecraft' in MJA Green (ed) *Alan Moore and the Gothic Tradition*, Manchester University Press.

Wouter J Hanegraaff (2007) 'Fiction in the Desert of the Real: Lovecraft's Cthulhu Mythos' 7 *Aries* 85.

Donna Haraway (2015) 'Anthropocene, Capitalocene, Plantationocene, Chthulucene: Making Kin' 6 *Environmental Humanities* 159.

Graham Harman (2011) *Weird Realism: Lovecraft and Philosophy*, Zero Books.

ST Joshi (2001) *A Dreamer and a Visionary: HP Lovecraft in His Time*, Liverpool University Press.

ST Joshi (2008) *The Rise and Fall of the Cthulhu Mythos*, Mythos Books.

Immanuel Kant (2000) *Critique of the Power of Judgment*, Cambridge University Press.

Tom Kaczynski (2012) *Beta Testing the Apocalypse*, Fantagraphics.

Karl Keily (2012) 'John Wagner Discusses 35 Years of *Dredd*' www.comicbookresources.com/?page=article&id=40172

Jane Kneller (1997) 'The Aesthetic Dimension of Kantian Autonomy' in RM Schott (ed) *Feminist Interpretations of Immanuel Kant*, Pennsylvania State University Press.

Alexander V Kozin (2014) 'Judge Dredd: Dreaming of Instant Justice' in A Wagner and RK Sherwin (eds) *Law, Culture and Visual Studies*, Springer.

Pierre Legendre (1997) 'Introduction to the Theory of the Image: Narcissus and the Other in the Mirror' in P Goodrich (ed) *Law and the Unconscious: A Legendre Reader*, Macmillan.

Pierre Legendre (1998) 'The Other Dimension of Law' in P Goodrich and DG Carlson (eds) *Law and the Postmodern Mind*, University of Michigan Press.

Chris Lloyd (2015) 'Judge, Jury and Executioner: *Judge Dredd*, Jacques Derrida, Drones' in T Giddens (ed) *Graphic Justice: Intersections of Comics and Law*, Routledge.

HP Lovecraft (2011) 'The Call of Cthulhu' in *The Call of Cthulhu and Other Weird Tales*, Vintage.

Mark Lowell (2004) 'Lovecraft's Cthulhu Mythos' 63 *Explicator* 47.

Desmond Manderson (2003) 'From Hunger to Love: Myths of the Source, Interpretation, and Constitution of Law in Children's Literature' 15 *Law and Literature* 87.

Desmond Manderson (ed) (2018) *Law and the Visual: Representations, Technologies, and Critique*, Toronto University Press.

Terry A Maroney (2011a) 'The Persistent Cultural Script of Judicial Dispassion' 99 *California Law Review* 629.

Terry A Maroney (2011b) 'Emotional Regulation and Judicial Behaviour' 99 *California Law Review* 1485.

Terry A Maroney (2012) 'Angry Judges' 65 *Vanderbilt Law Review* 1207.
Charles P Mitchell (2001) *The Complete HP Lovecraft Filmography*, Greenwood.
Alan Moore and Jacen Burrows (2011) *Neonomicon*, Avatar.
Alan Moore and Melinda Gebbie (2006) *Lost Girls*, Top Shelf Productions.
Leslie J Moran (2008) 'Judicial Bodies as Sexual Bodies: A Tale of Two Portraits' 29 *The Australian Feminist Law Journal* 91.
Leslie J Moran (2009) 'Judging Pictures: A Case Study of Portraits of the Chief Justices, Supreme Court of New South Wales' 5 *International Journal of Law in Context* 295.
Linda Mulcahy (2011) *Legal Architecture: Justice, Due Process and the Place of Law*, Routledge.
Alexander Nehamas (1985) *Nietzsche: Life as Literature*, Harvard University Press.
Alexander Nehamas (2001) '"The Sleep of Reason Produces Monsters"' 74 *Representations* 37.
Friedrich Nietzsche (1990) 'On Truth and Lies in a Nonmoral Sense' in P Bizzell and B Herzberg (eds) *The Rhetorical Tradition: Readings from Classical Times to the Present*, Bedford Books.
Janice Richardson (2007) 'The Law and the Sublime: Rethinking the Self and Its Boundaries' 18 *Law and Critique* 229.
Richard K Sherwin (2011) *Visualizing Law in the Age of the Digital Baroque: Arabesques and Entanglements*, Routledge.
Richard K Sherwin (2012) 'Visual Jurisprudence' 57 *New York Law School Law Review* 11.
Stephen Skinner (2009) 'Stories of Pain and the Pursuit of Justice: Law, Violence, Experience and Jurisprudence' 5 *Law, Culture and the Humanities* 131.
David Sugarman (1991) '"A Hatred of Disorder": Legal Science, Liberalism and Imperialism' in P Fitzpatrick (ed) *Dangerous Supplements: Resistance and Renewal in Jurisprudence*, Duke University Press.
Eugene Thacker (2011) *In the Dust of This Planet: Horror of Philosophy Volume 1*, Zero Books.
The Mindscape of Alan Moore (2003) directed by Dez Vylenz, Shadowsnake Films.
Miguel de Unamuno (1954) *Tragic Sense of Life*, Dover.
Anne Wagner and Richard K Sherwin (2014) *Law, Culture and Visual Studies*, Springer.
John Wagner (2002) 'I Invented Judge Dredd' http://news.bbc.co.uk/1/hi/uk/1820832.stm
John Wagner et al (2005) *Judge Dredd: The Complete Case Files 01*, Rebellion.
John Wagner et al (2007) *Judge Dredd: The Complete Case Files 08*, Rebellion.
John Wagner et al (2009) *Judge Anderson: The Psi Files Volume 01*, Rebellion.
John Wagner et al (2012) *The Batman/Judge Dredd Collection*, DC Comics and Rebellion.
Melanie Williams (2002) *Empty Justice: One Hundred Years of Law, Literature, and Philosophy*, Routledge-Cavendish.

Chapter 5

On haunted masks

If I am getting ready to speak at length about ghosts, ... it is in the name of *justice.*[1]

The legal subject is located – caught, pressed – between two spectral fronts. The legal subject, the persona, is a mask that is worn in order to come before the law, to enable oneself to be seen and addressed by the law. And masks, as we shall see, are haunted by that which they are unable to display. But the mask of the legal subject is haunted not just by the human it cannot contain or display, but also by the legal authority that watches and constitutes it. The legal mask is thus the boundary, the limit, between the spectre behind the mask and the spectre that observes the mask – this is what I mean by it being pressed between two spectral fronts. It is a mask that is doubly haunted: by the presence of two absences, by the image of two invisibilities: that which the mask does not show, and that which the mask cannot see. But the spectre brings with it the possibility of alternative forms – the presence of an other that watches (and judges) implies alternative perspectives, other scenes of knowing (and judging), that are present only as absences within law's conscious order. These other scenes of legal knowing imply the possible undoing of law, its disintegration and return to a prestructural chaos of infinite potential. Beyond what was seen in the previous chapter, the real horror of law might be that to be judged by law is to be judged with a finality that contains the seed of its own undoing. But this infinite openness, embedded throughout the structures of law, means the radical re-imagination of law is immanently available.

Much of the work of Chapter 4 was to expose the ways in which conscious law closed down or repressed the infinite context of human knowing. The present chapter takes the next step: it aims to undo this closure and return to a kind of originary blankness or indeterminacy, from and within which all forms could emerge, thus opening up to infinite alternatives. The chapter is roughly split in two halves: the first examines the spectre that haunts from behind the mask, whilst the second focuses on the haunting of the legal subject as it faces the law itself. After reflecting on the limits of knowing within the abyss exposed in the previous

1 Derrida (1994), p xviii. Emphasis in original.

chapter, the present chapter begins by reflecting on the processes of masking the human in juridical contexts as encountered by the character of Rorschach in *Watchmen*. It then turns to consider the haunted quality of the mask of persona more generally – it remains haunted by that which it does not show – and thereby articulate the concept of the *masca lex*, the haunted mask of law. The second half of the chapter then turns to analyse the judicial spectre depicted in the graphic novel *Adamtine*, developing the conceptualisation of the spectre to highlight how the legal subject is haunted by the absent space of legal authority. The final section considers the epistemological connotations of law's spectrality, with the spectre always implying an other that watches, and thus other possible frames of knowing. Framed in *Adamtine* as the return of the blank space, the legal spectre thus brings the possibility of the undoing or dissolution of law, and thus of its infinite possible re-imaginings, one of which will be gestured towards in the final chapter.

Masca lex

Nostalgia

To be human is to be limited by one's mortality, by one's flesh; to 'know' as a human is thus also limited by flesh, by our senses and capacities. This is a key aspect of Nietzsche's perspectivism: knowing is always already from a particular limited perspective, it is never total, complete, objective – there is always some other perspective that can be taken. Even the most objective and rational knowledges 'have no other reality than that which they possess as knowledge in the minds of those who study and cultivate them'.[2] The world thus loses any true or *a priori* status, and becomes only a product of our perceptions and interpretations. As Nehamas wrote, examining Nietzschean perspectivism:

> The apparent world … is not a world that appears to be and is distinct from reality but simply the world *as* it appears to any being that needs to survive in it and that therefore must arrange it selectively for its own purposes.[3]

Nehamas then goes on to argue that, although multiple perspectives and interpretations are available, we can produce ones that are 'better' than others, in the sense that they are better at enabling us to utilise and survive in the world.[4] Thus, we do not 'know' the world, but rather value it in different ways in relation to our survival, and construct it accordingly.[5] Miguel de Unamuno also argues that the underlying purpose of knowledge, the impetus that instigated our primordial curiosity as humans, is survival: knowledge is initially necessary that we should

2 Unamuno (1954), pp 30–31.
3 Nehamas (1985), p 45. Emphasis in original.
4 See Nehamas (1985), pp 43–73.
5 Nehamas (1985), p 54.

live.[6] The pursuit of knowledge seemingly for its own sake is in fact permeated with this underlying impetus towards life, towards human survival: 'variations of science depend upon the variations of human needs'.[7] Although this may undermine any claims to rational objectivity, Unamuno sees it as a core redeeming essence to even the most rationalised of positivist constructions of scientific reality (what we might here call a 'ghostless' reality).[8] Indeed, for Unamuno the human behind the thought should be excavated and celebrated. He criticises the 'professionals of thought' who repress and suppress their living humanity – body, soul, blood, life – and merely think:[9]

> Philosophy is a product of the humanity of each philosopher, and each philosopher is a [wo/]man of flesh and bone ... [who] philosophizes not with reason only, but with the will, with the feelings, with the flesh and with the bones, and with the whole soul and the whole body. It is the [wo/]man that philosophizes.[10]

Indeed, 'the philosopher is a [wo/]man before [s/]he is a philosopher'.[11] And in this recognition of the humanity of knowing, the perspectival limits of thought are encountered. It is these limits that bring a profound tragedy to life for Unamuno:

> The visible universe ... becomes all too narrow for me. It is like a cramped cell, against the bars of which my soul beats its wings in vain. Its lack of air stifles me. More, more, and always more! I want to be myself, and yet without ceasing to be myself to be others as well, to merge myself into the totality of things visible and invisible, to extend myself into the illimitable of space and to prolong myself into the infinite of time.[12]

There are strong echoes here of the universal network depicted in *The Ghost in the Shell* in Chapter 2. But whilst for Shirow we are always already intricately interconnected with the vast flowing uncertainties of the universe, Unamuno was acutely aware of the limits of his body and thus his bodily experiences. In the posthuman context that *Ghost* operates, this existential anguish is shared by Brother Cavil in the re-imagined TV series *Battlestar Galactica*. Cavil is a member of a race of hyperadvanced machines who were created to mimic human characteristics, and thus he can only experience the world through the 'ridiculous gelatinous orbs' in his skull – 'eyes designed to perceive only a tiny fraction of the EM spectrum' – and through 'ears designed only to hear vibrations in the air', and

6 Unamuno (1954), pp 22–23.
7 Unamuno (1954), p 23.
8 Unamuno (1954), p 23.
9 Unamuno (1954), p 14.
10 Unamuno (1954), p 28.
11 Unamuno (1954), p 29.
12 Unamuno (1954), pp 38–39.

through the limited touching of his 'prehensile paws'; Cavil finds he is unable to express himself properly because he has to 'conceptualise complex ideas in this stupid, limiting spoken language'.[13] To know is to know within the local system of the human[14] – the prison of flesh.

In this sense, law can be seen to be haunted by the embodied origins of legal knowing, origins that are repressed in order to enable law's rational independence and objectivity. As we noted in Chapter 1, for example, 'justice' may be something that we feel – it is emotional, passionate, and experiential, not just a ghostless intellectual exercise.[15] From this perspective, it is the aesthetic – our emotional sense of injustice and harm – that inspires the creation of 'just' social and philosophical systems – it is the human that jurisprudentialises, as Unamuno might have put it. Similarly, even the abstract rational system of Kant can be seen to derive from the cultural and historical context in which he lived,[16] hence the Kantian model of affectless autonomy is predicated not upon *a priori* truths, but on the masculine imperatives of Kant's own ineffable, flesh-and-blood life.[17]

In Chapter 5 of *Watchmen* (already introduced in Chapter 2), we witness Rorschach – one of the range of 'masked vigilantes' that populate the work's narrative – putting on his superhero costume in a vacant alleyway.[18] In this event, themes of justice and the tensions between rational abstraction and the human dimensions of knowledge can be drawn out. As he narrates his change of costume: 'Putting them on [his hero costume], I abandoned my disguise and became myself, free from fear or weakness or lust. / My coat, my shoes, my spotless gloves'.[19] Rorschach claims that in wearing his hero costume he is free from 'fear or weakness or lust' – it hides a limited, subjective humanity in the robes of one who purports to bring justice. But in the visual dimensions of the panel containing this text, behind the stained and filthy depiction of Rorschach's 'spotless gloves',[20] can be discerned an advert for a perfume. This perfume, called Nostalgia, is associated with emotional memories and feelings of desire in its advertising[21] and

13 See Horder-Payton (2009).

14 Kapica uses this limitation to argue for a move away from an anthropocentric humanism. As he observes, 'Cavil … exposes the limitations of the human, limitations which a humanist perspective neglects to address because it can only operate from a paradigm that places itself at the centre': Kapica (2014), p 630.

15 Douzinas and Gearey (2005), pp 28–32.

16 This perhaps explains, although does not justify, Kant's deeply problematic exclusion of non-male, non-European others from moral personhood. See Rumsey (1997). See also Battersby (2007).

17 Rumsey (1997), p 126.

18 See Moore and Gibbons (1986), Ch 5 p 18.

19 Moore and Gibbons (1986), Ch 5 p 18.

20 The discord between Rorschach describing his gloves as 'spotless' and the visual image of them as dirty raises awareness to the juxtaposition between text and image, and also highlights the symbolic dimensions of his costume as 'pure' and unencumbered by the 'dirt' of embodied contingency.

21 Note that the Nostalgia adverts run throughout *Watchmen*, but see especially the additional pages at the end of Ch 10.

employs the tag line 'Oh, how the ghost of you clings…'. A nostalgic scent, like a shadow or a photograph, implies the trace of something since departed. The advertisement's poetic phrase, embedded in the visual dimension of Rorschach's enrobing, and with its connotations of loss, sexual intimacy, and desire, suggests that an excessive, sensual humanity 'clings' to Rorschach's attempts at disinterested rationality. Thus, as Rorschach dons his costume and claims to enter a 'rational' order of justice, free from feelings and desires – a moral disaffection we might link to that of Kant – we glimpse instead the haunted nature of rationality, revealing the 'human feeling' Unamuno saw as underlying all knowledge.[22]

Beyond its multimodal copresence of text and image, *Watchmen* thus encounters something of the limits of rational knowing – of the division between rational knowledge and aesthetic sensuality; between the abstract and the living – but does so in a way that explicitly connects with the judicial institution, as can be seen more clearly in Rorschach's choice of costume. Whilst getting changed in the alleyway, Rorschach holds up his mask, describing how his costume covers up his traditionally 'true' identity (Walter Kovacs), making him unknowable – he abandons his disguise as Kovacs to become his real self, Rorschach. As a costumed hero, Rorschach takes his name from the shifting black and white shapes that make up his mask. The Rorschach ink-blot is a tool used in clinical psychology, whereby the blotchy images inspire fantasy and projection in the subject that a practitioner can then interpret, and thus gain some insight into the subject's mental state.[23] In a juridical context, it has been suggested that the police uniform can be seen as a type of Rorschach blot: it inspires fantasy and projection in people who encounter it, and in this way it conveys various associated meanings and enables officers to communicate their authority without resorting to the techniques of 'normal' conversation.[24] More generally, the business suit can be seen to efface the embodied human, making the individual more uniform, and thus enabling more 'rational' engagement in business and government.[25] Whilst wearing his costume, Kovacs becomes Rorschach: his weak humanity is suppressed in

22 See Unamuno (1954), pp 36–37:

> Can there exist pure knowledge without feeling, without that species of materiality which feeling lends to it? Do we not perhaps feel thought, and do we not feel ourselves in the act of knowing and willing? … Underlying even the so-called problem of knowledge there is simply this human feeling.

23 Although there have been findings to suggest links between certain test responses and a variety of psychoses (such as schizophrenia, psychopathy, and post-traumatic stress disorder), there is now much debate over the usefulness and validity of the Rorschach test: see, for example, Hunsley and Giulio (2001); Weiner (2000); Wood et al (2000). Dr Long also uses this tool to analyse Rorschach: see generally Moore and Gibbons (1986), Ch 6.

24 See Shon (2003).

25 See Collier (1998), pp 45–46. Collier notes that the historic lack of a similarly disembodying costume in female attire may be seen as a barrier to women's access to commerical and public life.

favour of his heroic persona, just as the judge – like the police officer and businessman – becomes an institutional rather than a human figure upon donning judicial robes.

In the panel where he holds up his ink-blot mask, Rorschach narrates this image by simply stating: 'My face'.[26] The visual associations and the juxtaposition of text and image in this panel complicate the identity-play of Rorschach's shift in costume. Whilst it is without his mask that nobody knows who 'Rorschach' is, the visual depiction of the mask highlights its abstract ink-blot nature, so it is actually when Rorschach puts on his mask that he loses his human face and becomes unidentifiable. By masking his fleshly self, his human face, with the visual indeterminacy of the Rorschach, Kovacs frees himself from his contingent, embodied life. He becomes abstract and unidentifiable; his limited humanity – the prison of his flesh – is hidden beneath a shifting and spectral costume capable of infinite interpretations. The Rorschach mask presents him as everyone and no one, everything and nothing: a chaos of shapes that can mean anything, a facelessness that masks his human face. In his costume, in his very visuality, Rorschach is spectral – the absent presence of humanity.

In his analysis of selected judicial portraiture of the New South Wales Supreme Court,[27] Leslie J Moran notes that the image of the judge does not simply represent the idiosyncrasies and individual physical traits of the judge under depiction. Perhaps more importantly, and within the aesthetic tradition of portraits of members of a society's political elite, it is the continuity of sovereign power, which transcends individual members, that shines through in the manner of Kantorowicz's famous 'two bodies' of sovereignty – one mortal, one eternal:

> Depictions of the judge, as the sovereign's representative, follow this tradition of portraying a double body; both natural and symbolic. Likeness and individuality in the judicial portrait are produced according to a rigorous aesthetic language associated with the values and virtues of the judicial institution … The subject is made in the image of an exemplar: the embodiment of the ideal.[28]

In the judicial image, the embodied individual recedes in favour of the embodiment of the institution, of the sovereign power of the state instituted by law. But this presentation of the institutional body over the individual can be seen not only in the static image, but also in the appearance of the judge in the courtroom itself. The enrobed judge, no less than the costumed hero, appears as a shrouded body – a somatic masking of flesh with justice. The human figure as instantiation of law. But the figure is human and non-human, both mortal and endless, alive and dead, subject and agent. The robed judge, the costumed police officer, becomes an invisible image – the absent presence of humanity. The costume operates to mask

26 Moore and Gibbons (1986), Ch 5 p 18.
27 Moran (2009).
28 Moran (2009), p 300.

the human shape it can never completely hide or show. As we saw with the humanity of Judge Dredd in the previous chapter, humanity always breaks through the mask. The institutional face is also a human face, the subject sees the judge looking upon it with judicial as well as human eyes – those 'gelatinous orbs' in the judicial skull. As Rorschach exposes, the costume – the robes of judicial office – operate to efface the weakness and individuality of the human body that wears it. The human becomes 'free from fear and weakness and lust', becoming a conduit for eternal justice. The mortal body becomes endless, continuous with the history of the common law as the mouthpiece of sovereign decree.

Behind the mask

This juridical division of bodies shares conceptual ground with the structuring and epistemology of the legal person. As we encountered in Chapter 2, the conceptualisation of the legal person is a limited tool or apparatus by which law comes to recognise – to know – the living human as a legal subject. Indeed, particular rules of law can be seen as masks that humans wear in order to approach the law,[29] and law in general can be seen as a mask that thereby gains political utility as a tool applicable across social life.[30] But more critically, the tradition of the mask in the politics of personhood serves as both a divide and mediation between supposedly 'natural' flesh and 'conceptual' persons:

> The mask or 'persona' … comes to emblematise a juridical relation in mediating between an abstract, political metaphor of organisation on the one hand, and a notion of nature and the natural person on the other – thus enabling the former on the basis of the latter.[31]

Already we can see the implication of the persona as limited: as a mask that does not completely show or capture the 'reality' of the face that wears it. And as a mask, as Goodrich makes clear, the apparatus of personhood is an image – it is what makes something visible within the theatre of the *nomos*, able to be seen and thus governed.[32] It may thus be suggested that if we are to develop structures of legal personhood that reflect the 'reality' of the individual, we need to remove the mask in order to access the living human behind it.[33] But instead of seeking the 'natural person' in this way, Connal Parsley reads Agamben as collapsing the separation between the natural person and the mask of persona by seeking to perfect, rather than remove, the mask. People thus become only their images, only their masks; the mask is not a representation of some deeper 'life' but is precisely

29 See Noonan (1976).
30 See Weyrauch (1978).
31 Parsley (2010), p 15.
32 See Goodrich (2012).
33 Noonan claims that to 'remove masks is to distinguish between them and the persons' they are presumed to conceal: Parsley (2010), p 20, quoting Noonan (1976).

an image of the person.[34] For Parsely, Agamben 'work[s] towards the *perfection* of the mask technic, so that any underlying natural substance may no longer be separated from the mask or political *imago*'.[35] In this way, what would otherwise be a limited tool becomes truth, but a truth that can be manipulated and developed towards ethico-political ends. Indeed, this collapsing of mask with wearer – leaving no 'real' wearer to be found beneath – opens up critical relations to be examined between different kinds of mask, notably between the broader juridical mask of moral-political personhood and the technical masking in law.[36]

This collapsing of mask and wearer shares similarities with the Nietzschean sublime that we briefly encountered in the previous chapter, and can thus be expanded as an epistemology. Nietzsche's metaphysics models reality as an infinitely complex surface that is far richer and more complex than reason can capture:[37] it is something in which one can become 'absorbed, buried, and immersed' once we move 'outside' the limits of rationality,[38] and transcends the dialectic of surface and depth.[39] As Battersby terms it, the surface of reality is 'folded' with multiple perspectives, rendering it 'neither simply a plane nor a façade', nor able to be comprehended in its entirety;[40] our knowledge and experience of this surface is always limited by our perspective of it[41] – by our fleshly encounters as well as the frames we attempt to capture it within. To put it in other terms, there is nothing under the mask, no deeper truth, no 'natural' and 'unmediated' reality of the human that we can access, since all encounters are necessarily perspectival, invoking their own frames (and multiframes) – their own masks.

Pushing this idea further, and in light of the human limits of knowing outlined above, it can be conceived that all conscious forms are metaphors for the unstructured universe outside the rational order, and vice versa.[42] There is no knowable 'essence' (no unbounded truth, no possibility of removing all masks or eliminating all frames), but only that which we encounter through representations that remain metaphors for reality, never reality itself.[43] Language and rationality are single examples of the different avenues of knowing that could be travelled; legality and the mask of persona – like all knowledge – thus become metaphors for the inaccessible and unstructured universe. As Wender highlighted in Chapter 3, there is a metaphorisation that takes place in the translation from lived experience

34 Parsley (2010).
35 Parsley (2010), p 31. Emphasis in original.
36 Parsley (2010), pp 31–34.
37 See also Berrios and Ridley (2005), p 99.
38 See Nietzsche (1997a), p 66.
39 For a discussion on Nietzsche's understanding of the sublime in *The Birth of Tragedy* as a genealogy of his later reconfiguration of surface/depth, see Battersby (2007), pp 157–176.
40 Battersby (2007), p 182.
41 This metaphysics can be read in *Watchmen*: see Giddens (2012), pp 106–108.
42 Kofman (1993), p 25.
43 Kofman (1993), p 14.

to the structures of bureaucracy. Indeed, the infinite variety of the complex surface of life is repressed by the general metaphors of knowing:

> Every concept arises through the equation of unequal things … we obtain the concept, as we do the form, by overlooking what is individual and actual; whereas nature is acquainted with no forms and no concepts, and likewise with no species, but only with an X which remains inaccessible and indefinable for us.[44]

The Nietzschean sublime involves the recall of these forgotten differences,[45] the recognition of the infinite complexity of the surface, which shatters the general categories necessary for conceptual understanding. The 'masks' of knowing are always threatened by the destructive return of the totality they cannot contain, as well as the other masks that undermine their claims to 'truth'.

Like the un/conscious structure of law, this immanent outside-of-knowing can be framed psychoanalytically: the conscious forms of knowledge are always created through the repression of an unconscious that is made up of the infinite totality they can never contain, as well as the other possible forms they could take. As Susan Stewart phrases it on a textual level, the 'lie of writing is … the displacement of another writing'.[46] This epistemic tension between conscious forms and their infinite unconscious is one of the general concerns that can be seen throughout *Watchmen*. The work employs a central motif that permeates its formal appearance from the cover of its first issue to its final panel: the image of a yellow smiley splashed with blood. As Gibbons himself says of this image, it shows 'the ultimate simplistic cartoon image splattered with real, messy blood'.[47] The abstract form of the emoticon-style smiley face was analysed in Chapter 2 as symbolising the ghostless knowledge symptomatic of the rational surface. The full motif, complete with blood splash, thus suggests the abstract person being disrupted by the 'flesh and blood' human; it suggests conceptual understanding – simplified, rational forms – being disrupted by the 'messy', chaotic, life-blood of the universe: the excess and threatened return of the endless intricacies and expanses beyond understanding.

This central motif of *Watchmen* thus symbolises the Nietzschean sublime, literally depicting the blood of a (once) living individual splattered across the abstract image of the person; the full-blooded infinity that haunts the 'happy' complacency of the rational surface. We can now also see the commonality with the hiding of the living human discussed with Rorschach: the conceptual structures of the mask of persona hide the excessive, living reality of the individual, just as the judicial mask seeks to hide the limited human on the bench. But in neither

44 Nietzsche (1990), p 891.
45 Battersby (2007), pp 188–189.
46 Stewart (1991), p 141.
47 Gibbons et al (2008), p 45.

case is this hiding complete: a trace of the 'reality' behind the mask always remains. In a similar vein, Parsley observes that in the face of the persona can be detected 'the spectre of nature, hiding behind the mask of *nomos*'.[48] And if we take this 'spectre' seriously, it can be said that all the 'other masks' that can be situated in a broad multiframe of personhood following the collapse of mask and wearer (nature, biology, the infinite possible alternatives in Nietzsche's sublime) now come to haunt the mask of the legal subject. In short, the rational surface is not ghostless – but haunted.

We can expand on the spectral quality of the mask of the legal subject through further engagement with *Watchmen*. Rorschach is well-known for his strong sense of retributive justice,[49] but there are references throughout *Watchmen* to Rorschach's specifically haunting nature: another masked vigilante admits Rorschach gives her 'the creeps',[50] and sounds 'frightening';[51] Rorschach stares eerily at the forensic psychologist analysing him,[52] to the point where the reaction to a particularly horrific statement moves against the narrative flow, following the line of Rorschach's stare;[53] Rorschach leaps unexpectedly out of a fridge;[54] later, in the same location, the re-intruding Rorschach leaves a note in the refrigerator reading 'behind you' (the searcher turns to discover Rorschach waiting patiently for him in the darkness);[55] there is Rorschach's disembodied voice, inexorable violence, and patient stalking of a convict through the dark and shifting atmosphere of a prison riot;[56] and, perhaps most telling, a detective gets shivers when he unknowingly passes Walter Kovacs (Rorschach's unmasked alter-ego – his absent presence, his spectre) in the street.[57] Even Rorschach's closest friend is uncomfortable having him in his home.[58]

Rorschach thus haunts the diegetic world of *Watchmen*. And there is something excessive about this haunting, something that cannot be captured. Midway through the narrative, Rorschach is arrested and incarcerated.[59] He is processed and categorised, stripped of his identity (his costume, his personal effects, his 'face'[60]) and reduced to a mere criminal. Although focused on the capital punishment context, Manderson has shown that the living, embodied individual is hidden and suppressed – masked – in order to display only the legitimate object of penal justice: the (purely) criminal other. As he observes:[61]

48 Parsley (2010), p 26.
49 See, for example, Held (2009); Petty (2015).
50 Moore and Gibbons (1986), Ch 9 p 15.
51 Moore and Gibbons (1986), Ch 6 p 8. Emphasis removed.
52 Moore and Gibbons (1986), Ch 6 p 2.
53 Moore and Gibbons (1986), Ch 6 p 17.
54 See Moore and Gibbons (1986), Ch 2 p 20.
55 Moore and Gibbons (1986), Ch 5 pp 2–3.
56 Moore and Gibbons (1986), Ch 8 pp 17–20.
57 Moore and Gibbons (1986), Ch 1 p 4.
58 Moore and Gibbons (1986), Ch 1 pp 11–13.
59 See Moore and Gibbons (1986), Chs 5–6.
60 See Moore and Gibbons (1986), Ch 5 p 28.
61 See generally Manderson (2000), pp 95–128.

> The body and the emotions of the condemned man must be restrained. Otherwise he may turn out to be more human than we want … [and thus break down the] barriers of isolation and objectification which the system has so carefully manufactured.[62]

Sherwin notes that we see the criminal other as an imaginary figure that haunts us as a fearful repression of urges that we can never completely destroy; it is a part of humanity we push outside.[63] Invoking something of the Nietzschean sublime, Hutchings suggests that the individuality of any actual person will always exceed the category of 'criminal'; the criminal thus remains a concept that is insubstantial, a phantom that cannot be 'pinned down', that is never fully present.[64] Reflecting this, Rorschach cannot be secured outside the civilised order as merely criminal – any attempts to reduce him to something other, to deny all the human aspects of his being in favour of the mask of 'criminal', do not succeed as he breaks free from, and thus remains excessive to, both the conceptual and actual prison within which law tries to encase him.[65] He continues to haunt.

But *Watchmen*'s spectral dimensions extend beyond the spooky and uncontainable presence of Rorschach: the work is haunted by an image of spectral humanity. This image is the shadow – the trace, the memory – of two absent lovers embracing. As Rorschach himself notes of the appearance of this shadowy couple as graffiti on a doorway: 'Didn't like it. Makes doorway look haunted'.[66] These shadowy figures, captured in graffiti on various walls across *Watchmen*'s New York City, recur at multiple points throughout the panels of the work.[67] And there are visual links between these lovers and the shadows cast by other embracing couples: Rorschach's prostitute mother and her client;[68] the psychologist Dr Long and his wife;[69] and vigilantes Drieberg and Juspeczyk as they try to make love,[70] and again as they console each other towards the troubling end of the narrative.[71] Dr Long also observes the visual resemblance between this graffiti image and the physical trace left behind by those caught in the atomic blast at

62 Manderson (2000), p 124. Note also Madiera (2014), pp 849–871, where semiotic processes of execution are argued to render the condemned invisible so that 'justice' becomes visible.
63 Sherwin (2000), pp 184–185.
64 See Hutchings (2001).
65 Note the unsettling influence he has on Dr Long: Moore and Gibbons (1986), Ch 6, especially pp 26–28. Note also the violence that he instils within the prison: Moore and Gibbons (1986), Ch 6 pp 14–17. Finally, note his actual escape from prison: Moore and Gibbons (1986), Ch 8 pp 18–21.
66 Moore and Gibbons (1986), Ch 5 p 11.
67 See Moore and Gibbons (1986), Ch 5 pp 11, 18, 23, Ch 6 pp 16, 27, Ch 8 p 3, Ch 10 p 22, Ch 11 pp 6, 9, 24, 27, Ch 12 pp 5, 7.
68 Moore and Gibbons (1986), Ch 6 pp 3, 4.
69 Moore and Gibbons (1986), Ch 6 p 9.
70 Moore and Gibbons (1986), Ch 7 p 15.
71 Moore and Gibbons (1986), Ch 12 p 22.

Hiroshima.[72] These 'Hiroshima lovers', as Long calls them, are thus 'braided'[73] throughout the multiframe of *Watchmen*. They are deployed in such a way that they become – as spectral traces – a complex nexus of humanity: they are loaded with the 'dirty' lust of the sex trade, the tenderness and passion of lovemaking, the symbiosis of weakness and reassurance of a consoling embrace, memories of human tragedy, the fear of loss, and powerlessness in the face of immanent death.

With this haunting trace of humanity, we can begin to elaborate the conceptual contours of the spectre more fully. Indeed, a shadow perfectly exemplifies the spectre, being both an absence (it is categorically not that which casts the shadow) and a presence (it is something there to be perceived, as well as always implying the existence of that which casts the shadow). Like the absent presence of Rorschach without his costume, these shadows are quintessentially spectral. This notion of the spectre as an absent presence can be found in Derrida. At the outset of *Specters of Marx*, Derrida observes:

> the specter is a paradoxical incorporation … neither soul nor body, and both one and the other. For it is flesh and phenomenality that give to the spirit its spectral apparition … [but there] is something disappeared, departed in the apparition itself.[74]

The flesh and blood individual gives presence to the spirit, the *anima*, but the spirit remains absent, 'disappeared' from the fleshly appearance itself. Like the mask of persona that mediates spirit and flesh in its impossible unity, showing as it hides its absent 'beneath'; like Walter Kovacs who appears only ever as a disappeared Rorschach (and vice versa). Indeed, the rupturing of the seemingly simple division between absence and presence is a significant element in the work of the spectre:

> If there is something like spectrality, there are reasons to doubt this reassuring order of presents and, especially, the border between the present, the actual or present reality of the present, and everything that can be opposed to it: absence, non-presence.[75]

In its absent presence, the spectre transcends binary divisions, and thus becomes the 'shadowy third' of *différance*; it is the 'paradigmatic deconstructive gesture'.[76]

72 Moore and Gibbons (1986), Ch 6 pp 16, 27.
73 Braiding is the notion of a series of panels or images that appear within, but as a *series* exist beyond or outside, the narrative sequence of comics panels, emerging as part of the broader network of interrelations that make up a comics work. See Groensteen (2007), pp 145–147. See also Chapter 1 on the atemporal dimensions of the comics page.
74 Derrida (1994), p 5.
75 Derrida (1994), p 48.
76 Weinstock (2013), p 63.

Indeed, as Derrida himself noted, it is via the logic of spectrality that deconstruction is able to find its home in the heart of philosophy.[77] *Watchmen*'s braided shadow of embracing lovers (like all shadows) is thus a trace: an image of that which is absent, the presence of an invisibility. Moreover, the notion of haunting, like the mask of persona, is something visual. As Derrida describes it:

> The specter is first and foremost something visible. It is of the visible, but of the invisible visible, it is the visibility of a body which is not present in flesh and blood. It resists the intuition to which it presents itself, it is not tangible ... [As a spectre] something becomes almost visible which is visible only insofar as it is not visible as flesh and blood.[78]

The spectre is visible, but is embedded with its own invisibility; it is simultaneously seen and unseen, visible and invisible, present and absent. The spectre is an invisible image. To be haunted, then, is to see the invisible image, to witness the absent presence or the presence of absence. And it is precisely the absence of the 'flesh and blood' human – the radically unique, inaccessible, or non-existent 'true reality' of the individual – that is made present by the mask of persona.

As we have already noted, like the spectre, the limited quality of the persona is also visual. Indeed, it 'relies upon the *image of* a "flesh and blood" natural life (potentially "without law") which underlies and animates it'.[79] In this sense, the fleshly individual becomes the *anima* – the ineffable 'something' of the human – that breathes life into the abstract structure of the person. And the trace of this *anima* haunts: when we encounter the costumed agents of the state, just as when the persona seeks to make visible the ineffable human, we encounter limited forms haunted by what remains outside their limits. Indeed, this spectral quality is already inherent in the very concept of the mask, as something that hides as it shows the human face. The mask is the absent presence of the face, the invisible image of humanity. Indeed, the very term 'mask' is etymologically linked with the Latin *masca*, meaning both mask and spectre.[80] The notion that there is nothing beneath the mask means the mask is representative of nothing, it is presence with no 'beneath', it is literally the presence of absence; both mask and spectre – the *masca* of knowing. And as *masca*, the mask is always already haunted, always already an invisible image of that which cannot be seen.

The masking of the living human in concepts of personhood is an overt example of the more general epistemic masking of the universe that takes place in the multifaceted business of knowing: the metaphoric equation of unequal things that constructs the vast multiframe of knowabilities. Framed jurisprudentially, we can now articulate what we might call the haunted mask of law: the *masca lex* (with

77 Derrida and Stiegler (2013), p 39.
78 Derrida and Stiegler (2013), p 38.
79 Parsley (2010), p 20. Emphasis in original.
80 Chambers Dictionary of Etymology.

the Latin here being significant in the dual meaning of 'mask' and 'spectre' as described above). The term *masca lex* signifies the structures of legal knowing that seek to represent what cannot be known in its entirety, and that always remains a mediated, framed, and particular representation – always mask and never 'beyond'. At the same time, it represents the haunting of this mask of legal knowing by that which it does not contain or show – by the legal unconscious.

This haunting can be articulated as a 'spectral sublime', as highlighted in *Watchmen* when the character Dan Drieberg awakes from a dream of himself and fellow costumed crime fighter Laurie Juspeczyk embracing and being taken apart by an atomic explosion.[81] This reference to nuclear death evokes *Watchmen*'s diegetic backdrop of looming nuclear war between the USA and Russia. The page depicting Dreiberg's actions after waking from his dream[82] is constructed in an equally spaced three-by-three, nine-panel grid, with nearly all the panels populated with softly lit (if slightly lurid) depictions of Drieberg waking up next to Laurie on his couch, gently kissing her sleeping hand, and carefully clambering over Laurie so as not to disturb her. But amidst these figures of gentle and considerate love, in the very central panel of the page, between the two panels showing Dan kissing Laurie's hand, sit two figures of massive nuclear destruction, repeating the images from Drieberg's dream. The page thus locates images of nuclear destruction in the central space of the comics grid, surrounded by various images of Drieberg beside a peacefully sleeping Juspeczyk; read atemporally, cataclysmic fear is nestled within the intimate spaces of life. As images recalled from a nightmare,[83] this depiction also represents the return of the unconscious to Drieberg's waking mind,[84] the returning threat of being taken apart, being undone, by a nuclear blast.

As Dan and Laurie are destroyed in Drieberg's dream, they are kissing: their bodies silhouetted against the bright white of the nuclear explosion, embracing as they are taken apart by the explosion. The two figures embedded within the images of nuclear destruction, again embedded amidst the intimate spaces of life as Drieberg recalls them after waking, are thus heavily reminiscent – visually, conceptually – of the 'Hiroshima lovers', thus forming part of that braided frame of *Watchmen*. The figures are entwined and freighted with spectral connotations: as shadows, as remnants and traces, as absent presences. There is a strong temporal quality to Derrida's spectre, which – as a *revenant* – always '*begins by coming back*'.[85] Indeed, Derrida frames the present moment not as an absolute 'now', distinct from past and future, but as the spectre of what has passed and what is to come. There is no such thing as 'purely real time': the 'absolutely real present is already memory, anticipation, in other words, a play of traces' – of spectres.[86]

81 See Moore and Gibbons (1986), Ch 7 pp 16–17.
82 Moore and Gibbons (1986), Ch 7 p 17.
83 See Moore and Gibbons (1986), Ch 7 p 16.
84 We discuss some of the epistemological implications of dreams and the unconscious in the next chapter.
85 Derrida (1994), p 11. Emphasis in original.
86 Derrida and Stiegler (2013), p 47.

> The present is what passes, the present comes to pass [*se passe*], it lingers in this transitory passage (*Weile*), in the coming-and-going, *between* what *goes* and what *comes*, in the middle of what leaves and what arrives, at the articulation between what absents itself and what presents itself.[87]

This is part of the juristic sense of spectrality, that it evokes both the traumas of the past as well as the healings of the future:[88] justice must always occur in this spectral space, the here-now that is both connected to and 'out of joint' from the flow of time, lest it does not attend to the particularities and radical alterity of the other:[89] the 'necessary disjointure, the de-totalizing condition of justice'.[90] An imperative, too, must always appear as an absence – as some potential future.[91] The spectre, then, is thus always at play – in the flow of time, in the project of justice.

As Drieberg kisses Laurie's hand, the spectre of atomic destruction appears as a *revenant* – it begins by coming back from Drieberg's nightmare, erupting into his intimate life as the absent presence of both past and future. This eruption of unconscious peril, then, is a haunting: Drieberg's life is haunted by that which threatens it – immanently, at all times – just as *Watchmen* is haunted by the looming spectre of nuclear war and the shadowy figures themselves. The formal presentation of Drieberg's recall of the nightmare thereby signifies the spectral presence of the threat of destruction within the waking mind, the invisible image of the undoing of the world within conscious thought. In terms of Niezsche's sublime, it is the constant threat of the return of the infinite, irreducible complexities of the surface that would destroy the multiframe of knowing. It thus becomes a spectral sublime: the splatter of blood across all knowledge. But for Derrida, this possibility of undoing, as something spectral, also brings with it the possibility of justice. For although it is a space that can also bring forth 'evil', as it is a space of potential, we must enter the open, haunting, 'out-of-joint' if we are to approach the radical alterity of the other.[92] Accordingly, it is to the inherent possibility of dissolution that the spectral quality of law brings, via the haunting of the subject by law, that the chapter now turns.

Invisible images

The watcher that judges

The legal subject is caught between two spectral fronts: it is haunted by the living humanity that created it and that its rational structures seek to quell and

87 Derrida (1994), p 29. Emphases in original.
88 Derrida (1994), p xviii.
89 Derrida (1994), pp 32–34.
90 Derrida (1994), p 33.
91 Derrida (1994), p 39.
92 Derrida (1994), p 34.

categorise; it is also haunted by the legal authority that constitutes it as a watcher that judges. The first half of this chapter has sought to expound the first dimension of this reciprocal haunting (the haunted quality of the *masca lex*), and discussion now turns to draw out the second via an encounter with the judicial spectre that haunts the legal subject in *Adamtine*,[93] the intimate ghost story from creator Hannah Berry.

As we have already noted, with Derrida the spectre is a liminal figure, present as an image of absence. Navigating such liminality, *Adamtine* is a haunting, spectralised work, infused with a seething and building terror and a persistent concern for justice. Switching between multiple interconnected narratives, it weaves a tapestry of events and lives surrounding the notorious acquittal of an alleged serial kidnapper (and supposed killer) known as Rodney Moon. Amidst national public outcry, Moon was released after a jury failed to convict him. Moon claimed during his trial that it was a nameless 'bogeyman' that committed the crimes, with Moon merely handing written notes to the various victims (his handwriting did not match the notes found). The public were not appeased by Moon's acquittal, and neither were the families of the victims. Moon was eventually murdered by family members of one of the victims, and across the layered narrative of *Adamtine* we bear witness as the above history is revealed in flashbacks during the bogeyman's return, years later. This return plays out in a stranded train carriage, at night, in the middle of nowhere – a horror story on British public transport.

Across the narrative, the bogeyman passes judgment over four train passengers who were all connected to Moon's original case. We learn early on that the nameless 'bogeyman' is out for judgment: the notes left behind at each historic disappearance recount 'moments of bad judgement by the victims, told in cold, detailed third-person accounts'.[94] And as each of the present-day train passengers is inexorably devoured by spectral darkness, they receive a written note seen only by the 'victim', presumably detailing their poor judgment in relation to Moon's case. In this sense, then, *Adamtine* is a tale of the return of some repressed or forgotten aspect of the past to bring the present to account – the ghost of the characters' historical misdeeds returning to judge them.

The spectral judge of *Adamtine* thus begins by coming back. But for Derrida, as already indicated, the spectre is more than just the return of a *revenant* or ghost. This can be seen in the fact the spectre is 'first and foremost something visible',[95] but a visibility that involves a complex play of invisibility: it is that which is present but unseen or liminal in its (dis)appearance. Such liminal or unseeable visibility can be detected upon careful inspection of Figure 5.1, wherein is depicted not only the poorly lit figures of two train passengers making their way along pitch dark railway tracks, but something else too. Amidst the pure blackness of the backdrop, in the top right quadrant of the page, can be discerned a subtle and

93 Berry (2012). See Appendix A for an overview and details of this work.
94 Berry (2012), np.
95 Derrida and Stiegler (2013), p 38.

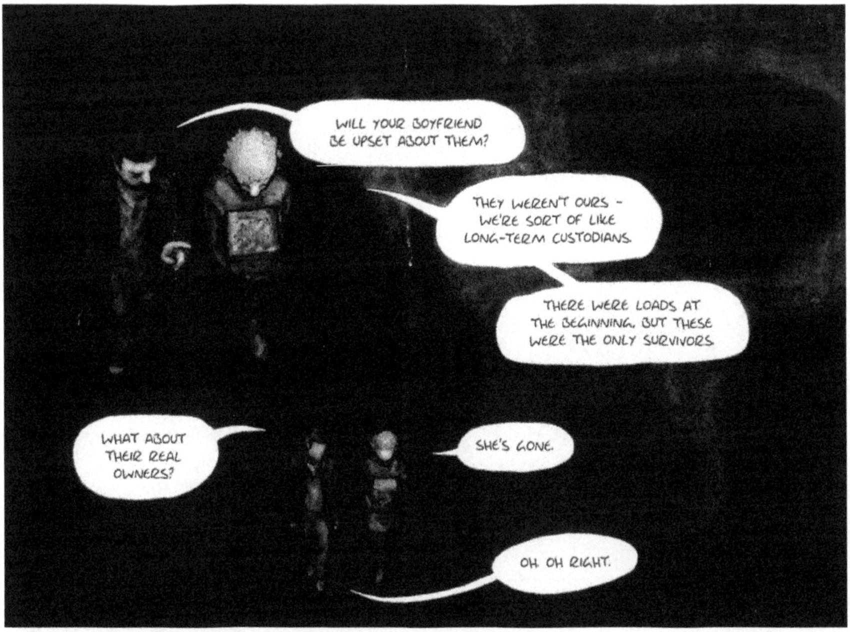

Figure 5.1 Berry (2012), np. From *Adamtine* by Hannah Berry. Published by Jonathan Cape. Reprinted by permission of The Random House Group Limited. © 2012.

looming face, an almost-invisible figuration of empty eye sockets and gaping mouth. This presentation is not just a face, but as something almost (in)visible, something liminal in its appearance, it is quintessentially something spectral.

Semi-visible depictions such as this occur at various points throughout *Adamtine*, (dis)appearing in the backgrounds of pages (see, for example, Figure 5.2). These silently screaming faces, these invisible images, typically occur outside the diegetic grid of the comics page, haunting the borders. The border or frame of an image – in this context, the border of the comics page – can be seen as itself spectral. The frame is seen, but is outside what 'should' be seen: the frame is 'a visible invisibility … to be perceived, but not noticed'.[96] To frame thus always involves the spectre, and locating her liminal images within the border-regions of the page means they intrinsically haunt Berry's central figures. This edgy location also signals something of their otherness – the spectre is present in the diegesis only as an absence, as something depicted outside the diegetic order – something other.

In Figure 5.1 the spectre is not strictly outside the grid; the background of the page is pure black, and the panels here are so dark that the boundaries of the page's grid breaks down and the spectral presence can permeate the diegetic space,

96 Crawley (2015), p 195.

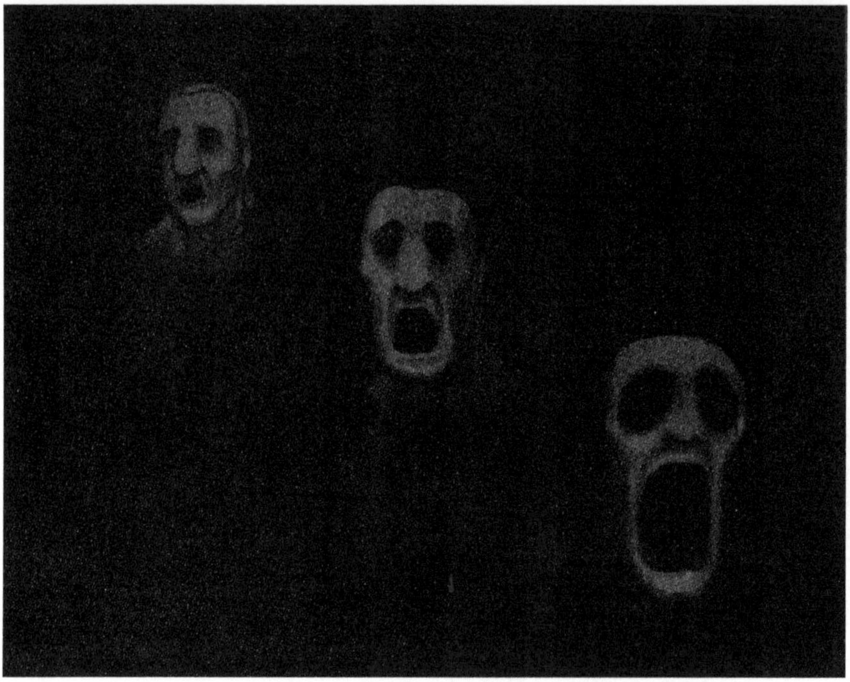

Figure 5.2 Berry (2012), np. From *Adamtine* by Hannah Berry. Published by Jonathan Cape. Reprinted by permission of The Random House Group Limited. © 2012.

bringing its liminal visibility with it. The inside thus becomes haunted with the outside, with the spectral beyond. But even in Figure 5.1 the spectre is not wholly present – it fills the upper right corner, but remains liminal and at the same time obscured by the mundane conversation of the characters, the idle words deployed to keep their fear at bay – the hum of discourse, hiding the (in)visible presence of the haunting.

We may be able to see the spectre, but it remains an image of something that we cannot see – it is '*nothing* visible'.[97] And this haunting has some potentially upsetting connotations. Turning again to Derrida, the 'spectre' as such, as something linked up with concerns of visibility, is also something that sees, that watches us even though we may not be able to see it in its fullness. It gazes: the spectre 'is not simply this visible invisible that I can see, it is someone who watches or concerns me without any possible reciprocity',[98] a phenomenon Derrida calls the visor effect. The presence of a ghost implies that we are being seen, gazed upon, watched, in*spect*ed. Derrida makes an explicit connection between this other that

97 Derrida (1994), p 5. Emphasis in original.
98 Derrida and Stiegler (2013), p 41.

watches, implied by the spectre, and the law: 'we do not see the one who sees us, and who makes the law, who delivers the injunction'.[99] We are watched, he comments, 'as if by the law':

> we are 'before the law', without any possible symmetry, without reciprocity, insofar as the other is watching only us, concerns only us, we who are observing it (in the same way that one observes and respects the law) without even being able to meet its gaze.[100]

As we have already seen, for Derrida the spectre is deeply connected with justice: it is only through the spectral present, where the other's alterity can be encountered, that justice can be achieved. In the visor effect, however, the entanglement of Derrida's spectrality with legality takes on a more haunting quality: the spectre in this sense comes to represent a juristic haunting of the legal subject, just as *Adamtine*'s bogeyman haunts the victims of its judgment.

There are many ways in which individuals may be haunted in a juristic context. Christine Battersby, for example, explains how Emily Dickinson's poem 'One need not be a chamber – to be haunted' rejects the singular and stable 'I' associated with traditional concepts of Kantian moral autonomy premised upon the rational mastery of the universe.

> On the contrary, in this poem otherness is internalised and is within the embodied mind … the one contains within itself the bodies and ghosts of the others that haunt it.[101]

Battersby is concerned with our phenomenal interrelations with others, here arguing with Dickinson that we become a plural self, 'haunted' by the innumerable relational links with those around us and in our past that cannot be severed – in a manner similar to the universal network, as discussed in Chapter 2. Ultimately she connects this with the Nietzschean sublime, such that the otherness to the rational 'I' becomes a sublime dimension of ourselves, always ready to disrupt the masculine presumption that 'I' can order the world by wielding reason.[102] David Gurnham also notes the spectral presence of the other within our selves – represented by the reflected image of Narcissus which vanishes as he tries to touch it – that he claims can push us to consider the specificity of the other when tackling ethical problems.[103] Furthermore, just as in the naming of Rodney *Moon* we see the face that reflects light in the darkness – the dark mirror of waking humanity – Richard Sherwin explains the construction of the criminal as the 'deviant other' of

99 Derrida (1994), p 7.
100 Derrida and Stiegler (2013), p 40.
101 Battersby (2007), p 113.
102 See Battersby (2007).
103 See Gurnham (2004).

civilised society in terms of our desire to repress that which we fear within ourselves, as was noted above; we arguably project the possibility of 'irrational' violence erupting from within outwards onto 'the other', denigrating it as 'criminal', and thus (appearing to) control it.[104]

On a cultural level, we are also haunted by the 'afterlife of criminal evidence': by the prosecutorial archive of law, as posthumous courtroom and trial artefacts that circulate into the aesthetic economies of found art. Katherine Biber highlights that this cultural circulation of deceased archival evidence raises important questions about sensitivity in its use, as much of it may be humiliating or damaging, despite being ostensibly 'public' as part of judicial processes.[105] Indeed, this afterlife of criminal evidence instantly signals a *revenance*, a return of the past – but not necessarily one in need of rectification, as justice has already officially been done. Rather, it represents the return of trauma, of the record of trauma and of its juridico-cultural processing. These evidential items are no longer 'alive' within the machinery of justice, no longer active and salient, but remain present within the system and wider culture, marking the trace of the law's effects on the human world it regulates. As it transgresses the boundaries of the archive, this cultural haunting of law moves outside the official order into aesthetic culture,[106] but retains its aura of bureaucracy. It becomes the invisible image of law beyond juridical boundaries. And in the preponderance of visual images – records of what was seen by the agents of law, the absent presence of their gaze – the watching presence of law-as-spectre is suggested.

But the watching presence of law-as-spectre operates most profoundly on the level of the constitution of the legal subject. The self may be haunted by its other(s), culture may be haunted by law's ghostly afterlife, but the haunting of the legal subject itself is of a different order. On one level, the fact that conscious law is deeply invested in its textual form arguably produces a certain spectrality: written texts can be seen to be haunting in the way they can present something 'other' within or beyond the text, but that remains absent as the mere printed figures that make up words on paper[107] (or pixels on screen). The textuality of law, then, already introduces a spectral quality to the legal subject, as something articulated in texts and as the subject of texts; here we are encountering the dimension of the *masca lex* described above: the mask of the subject and its spectral excess. But *Adamtine* depicts a haunting of the subject by the text itself, and a text that brings judgment. Recall that the notes given to each victim detail their bad judgment and misdeeds 'in cold, detailed third-person accounts' – a description that could also be made of the facts in many judicial case reports. These 'bad' activities are rendered into written notes – into text – linking the project of *Adamtine*'s spectre

104 See Sherwin (2000), pp 172–185.
105 See Biber (2013).
106 Attending to this movement can enrich understandings of the nature and (ethical) use of evidence: Biber (2013).
107 See Wolfreys (2013), pp 72–73.

again with that of the jurist, whilst at the same time suggesting, in the inexplicable appearance of these notes as the bogeyman claims its victims, that the law can see the subject without being seen, and thence that judgment is immanent.

Legendre's psychoanalytic jurisprudence can be helpful in developing this spectralised vision of law's asymmetrical visuality. Legendre, as discussed in Chapter 4, shows how the subject of law is separated or divided from themselves as they become instituted by the legal text. This separation is also from the source of law as a sacred space that guarantees truth (*qua* interpretive legitimacy), and thence justice. The 'other dimension' of law,[108] as Legendre terms it, can thus be strongly configured as something spectral. It is something other to the legal subject, something that is 'outside' the order of legitimate subjecthood, but that is present to the subject insofar as they are aware of and addressed by the law – insofar as they are bound to the institution. It is the one who sees us and who makes the law, but that we cannot see. As Berry's spectral bogeyman approaches its victims, as it moves to claim judgment and dissolve them into blankness, we witness this haunting of the subject by law. The spectre is other, it is present to its victims as an absence – as a watcher that cannot be seen, as a space of judicial authority that we are 'before' but cannot enter. As Derrida says, without reciprocity. The law haunts its institutionalised subject, present as an otherness that remains inaccessible and thus absent.

There is an overt panopticism in the immanent, watching presence of the judicial spectre in *Adamtine*. Berry's spectral judge observes, watches – in*spects* – its subjects with a seemingly omniscient gaze, produces written judgments, and enacts sentences. The logic of the panopticon, whereby subjects are not aware whether or not they are being watched but at any point could be, suggests that we regulate our behaviour as if we are being watched; within the panopticon, we feel watched even if we are not.[109] And as we have already discussed, we are watched by the masked bodies of judicial agents – the spectres of humanity framed by the institution. But *Adamtine* indicates that this 'watching' goes beyond the embodied encounters with law; the subject is always haunted not just by the invisible image embedded in the judge or the police officer (which one may be able to hide from or avoid), but by the law itself. The legal institution encodes conduct and relations in a multiframe, constructing regulations in minute and ever-increasing detail; the fact a police officer or judicial agent may not actually be watching our every move does not undermine the conceptual presence of law within our experience. The legal subject, although not necessarily watched in a literal sense, is always operating under, and in relation to, law's codes. As legal subjects we always exist in the context of legal regulations, whether we are aware of it or not. Even where the law may be absent in terms of physical surveillance, the inaccessible

108 See Legendre (1998).

109 See Madiera (2014), pp 851–854. See also Foucault (1977). And, significantly, on the connections between Derrida's and Foucault's reliance on asymmetrical visuality (the visor effect vs panopticism) in the context of biopolitics, see Lloyd (2016).

space of law's authority, of its otherness to us as subjects, remains present to us as a panoptic spectre – always already framing us as legitimate/illegitimate, our conduct as permitted/forbidden, acceptable/taboo. In this sense, it can be said that the legal subject remains haunted by the law, which is always already present to it as an absent space of authority. Law is always with us, but always separate so that it remains able to watch, to judge, to bind us to the institution as the arbiter of truth and justice. The legal subject is not only haunted by that which the mask of persona cannot contain, but also by the spectre of law it remains before – by the watcher that judges.

Other scenes of judgment

The epistemological connotations of the law's dual haunting – the spectral fronts that surround the legal subject – are profound. They relate to the inherence within law of its own undoing or disintegration: insofar as law is spectral, it contains its own dissolution, its return to a primordial chaos or originary blankness. To undo the world, to return knowledge to the primal, unstructured abyss from which it was wrought, can be a disturbing if not a melancholic venture. As Miguel de Unamuno invites us:

> Retire, reader, into yourself and imagine a slow dissolution of yourself – the light dimming about you – all things becoming dumb and soundless, enveloping you in silence – the objects that you handle crumbling away between your hands – the ground slipping from under your feet – your very memory vanishing as if in a swoon – everything melting away from you into nothingness and you yourself also melting away – the very consciousness of nothingness, merely as the phantom harbourage of a shadow, not even remaining to you.[110]

Even the spectral 'consciousness of nothingness' – the presence within thought of its own absence – is here destroyed and undone. In Unamuno's imaginary reverie we are taken back to a space of pure emptiness, of the empty void. The world and self are undone, and nothing remains, perhaps not even spectres. But this 'nothingness', as I have already suggested in the previous chapter, is not empty. As Lovecraft would have it, the abyss is filled with tentacular horrors; Haraway, our extended family;[111] and Manderson, a generative chaos.[112] It is the unstructured abyss from which knowledge is wrought.

In *Adamtine*, Berry navigates this 'undoing' of the world and renders it juristic. For it is the spectral judge, the invisible image of the bogeyman, that undoes the world of its victims through the process of judgment. In judging its subjects,

110 Unamuno (1954), p 42.
111 Haraway (2015).
112 Manderson (2000), pp 180–183.

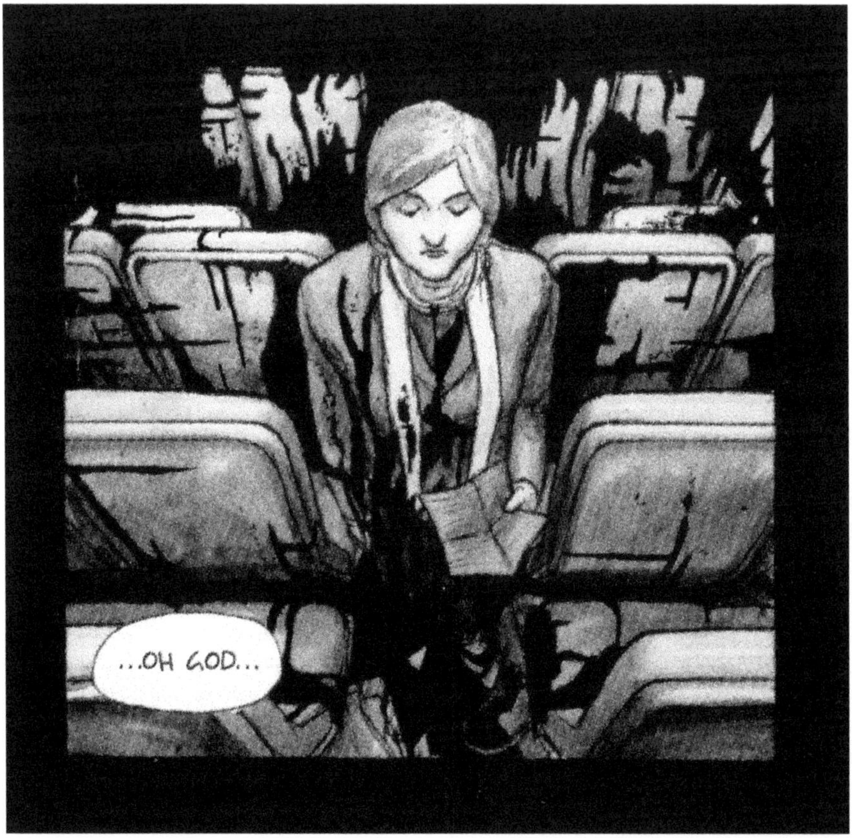

Figure 5.3 Berry (2012), np. From *Adamtine* by Hannah Berry. Published by Jonathan Cape. Reprinted by permission of The Random House Group Limited. © 2012.[113]

Berry's watcher defigures them and returns them to a nothingness that is anything but empty. It can be seen that Berry employs the formal dimensions of her medium in the epistemological work of her watcher that judges. As each of the train passengers succumb to the spectre, there is a visual intrusion and devouring of the diegetic figure by pure blackness. Each time this occurs, the background of the page itself is black, thus this devouring becomes a bleeding into the image by its outside. The page background itself erupts into the image – an intrusion into the figure by the form. This can be seen, for example, in Figure 5.3: the blankness of the dark space outside the image, of the spectral border-frame, seeps into and erupts through the diegetic figuration, claiming its victim and returning it to nothingness – an empty, blank space absent of anything visible (one of these

113 The spoken words in this Figure, ' ...oh God ...', are an expression of horror from a fellow passenger as they witness this judicial defiguration.

disintegrative moments also adorns the cover of this book). In Unamuno's terms, as we read we witness the figure 'crumbling away between our hands'.

Although ostensibly empty, the blank spaces in comics – and in Berry in particular – are not necessarily without meaning; indeed, more generally the 'empty space is never simply empty'.[114] In his brief analysis of blank comics panels, Pont argues that 'blankness encapsulates the anxiety of deletion and reacts against the proliferation of visual stimuli that characterizes modern life'.[115] Despite the potential an empty space might imply,[116] blankness, he claims, signals loss. The eruption of the blank page into the figure challenges our perception of the visual,[117] allowing 'the viewer to gaze at the medium itself'.[118] This blankness is not simply emptiness – it is material and potential. In terms of haunting, Pont claims 'it suggests a spectral quality, since the white panel represents the return of the untouched page as it resurfaces, therefore making it a *revenant* blank'.[119] Blankness is thus the return of what Baudelaire called the 'forgotten canvas';[120] it is the *revenant* of the primordial blankness of the medium, the ghost of the empty page before artistic figuration.[121] The invasion of Berry's diegetic images with the blank materiality of the page can be seen in this sense to begin by coming back: it appears first as a return of the medium itself, reclaiming the figures and returning them to the potential of the prefigural space of the unmarked page. It is both a return, and a loss – a return of the form, and a concomitant loss of diegetic figure.

Adamtine's spectre, previously located outside the diegetic space, invades the narrative world as it devours and returns Berry's figures to the blank page upon which they were illustrated (the name of the work also signals this return to origins on a cultural level, with its reference to Adam, the first human created in the Western Christian mythos). Of importance to the linguistic context of law, this undoing of Berry's diegetic world can also be seen in the spectral speech bubbles emitted from the train's telecommunications system: typically verbal spaces filled with the chaos of static and occasional snippets of text – bubbles visually filled with the generative possibilities of unstructured, prelinguistic chaos (see Figure 5.4).

But the blankness to which Berry's figures are returned is not as blank as it could be – if it were the pure white of the unadulterated page, that Pont discusses, this would arguably be 'more blank' than the purely black page, which is not so much devoid as completely full – of ink, of colour, of presence.[122] This blackness

114 Goodrich (1999), p 94.
115 Pont (2012), p 254.
116 See, for example, Goodrich (1999).
117 Pont (2012), p 262.
118 Pont (2012), p 264.
119 Pont (2012), p 262.
120 See Baudelaire (2015), p 51.
121 Note Goodrich (1999), who discusses the *tabula nuda* of the blank canvas in an art historical context. For Goodrich, the blank spaces he examines represent the space *in potentia* of sovereign power and as-yet-unwritten law. I discuss whether this empty legal space need be filled be text or image in the next chapter.
122 Pont (2012), p 263.

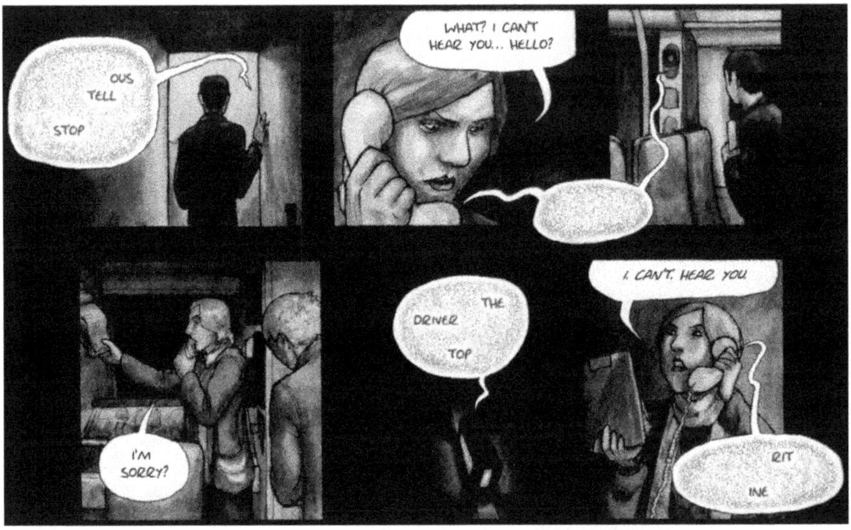

Figure 5.4 Berry (2012), np. From *Adamtine* by Hannah Berry. Published by Jonathan Cape. Reprinted by permission of The Random House Group Limited. © 2012.

thus becomes a form of absent presence, signifying both nothingness and complete saturation. Indeed, Pont argues that even spaces of pure white paper are both full and empty:[123] just as a space free from any content lacks perspective, and is thus both flat and of infinite depth, white spaces also oscillate between figure and form and in this oscillation anxieties over visual perception and loss are encountered.

> [For] it is in those moments in which the image is either all-subject or all-space that our preconceptions regarding the visual are shaken. The blank panel is a constant reminder of the balance between image and surface that the medium demands … leaving it at the threshold of visibility. It constitutes a noticeable fissure in the structural integrity of the form, representing, rehearsing and even heralding loss.[124]

123 A note on the shifting nature of the comics form. Electronic comics are becoming increasingly significant, with many readers encountering graphic narratives via digital platforms (for examination of the impact for comics theory, see, for example, Goodbrey (2013)). In this context, the 'empty page' arguably becomes black rather than white – a powered-down screen is not white. The white space becomes full – of light. But within the context of reading, it remains the white space that arguably signals the 'blank page' within the digital comics environment that seeks to emulate the printed form, just as when using a word processor it is a 'blank' white page that we fill with text as we type. The powered-down screen is not showing anything – not even blankness, and certainly not the comics form, whether blank or otherwise.

124 Pont (2012), p 270.

This tension in comics' blank spaces renders those spaces spectral. More overtly with the black space in Berry that consciously invades the diegesis and is replete with ink on the printed page, in the encounter with emptiness the figural space of the page is returned to a pregnant nothingness, a saturated emptiness, both full and empty, brimming with infinite potential. It is a quintessentially spectral space, both open and closed, present and absent, an invisible image of the materiality and potential of the comics form and the blank page. Blankness thus signals much more than loss – infinitely more; it is the recognition of infinite possibility, the potentiality of creation and change, but one that first requires an undoing. In Berry it is the legal spectre that brings this undoing, it is the watcher that judges that dissolves the worlds of its subjects, returning them to the originary abyss. The implication is that law's spectrality – the haunting watcher that judges – brings with it the seed of this undoing.

The invisible image of the spectre is not just any image, but is profoundly an image of otherness, of something external to the current order – the presence of something absent and thus something other, beyond, outside. Peter Hutchings, for example, observes associations between the spectral and processes of othering, not only of the criminal spectre mentioned above with which he is primarily concerned,[125] but also in relation to madness, women, and the genius. Hutchings notes that madness falls outside traditional understandings of human volition, which 'presumes an ordered, purposive subject as opposed to the peculiar, random order of violence'[126] or a beast-like animality.[127] Women also resisted definition within the rational categories of Enlightenment thought,[128] as did the exceptionally creative and intellectually powerful 'genius' – a term etymologically associated with creation and the magical *jinn* or 'genie', 'a spirit for a nonspiritual age'.[129] Hutchings connects these forms that are present within Enlightenment rationality only as absences in understanding (as spectres), and that serve to destabilise rational categories – ghosts in the ghostless machine.

Indeed, like *Adamtine*'s 'nameless' bogeyman, the Derridean spectre is 'unspeakable', and engagement with it seeks to 'encounter what is strange, unheard, other' without reducing it to rational knowledge; it is 'not a puzzle to be solved' but invokes 'structural openness' and possibility, and 'pushes at the boundaries of language and thought'.[130]

> Conversing with spectres is not undertaken in the expectation that they will reveal some secret, shameful or otherwise. Rather, it may open us up to the experience of secrecy as such: an essential unknowing which underlies and may undermine what we think we know … [Derrida's spectre represents] a

125 See Hutchings (2001).
126 Hutchings (2001), p 58.
127 Hutchings (2001), p 62.
128 Hutchings (2001), p 88.
129 Hutchings (2001), p 167.
130 Davis (2013), p 58.

productive opening of meaning rather than a determinate content to be uncovered.

The spectre, then, invokes the more general limits of knowing, which is itself haunted. In its absent presence within the structures of knowledge, the spectre represents that which is unknown, presented as an object of knowledge. Hutchings's criminal spectre, for example, is identified by its unidentifiable nature, its unknowability producing its criminality and thence its absent presence within rational knowledge – neither fully understood nor fully understandable beyond being 'other' to the rational order.[131] As in *Adamtine*, the spectre lurks outside the order of the grid that it is present within, and present only as something outside, remaining only ever a presence of absence. Even as it enters the diegesis, the spectre is at best liminally visible, but more often it appears as the spectral blankness of the saturated void of the black page. It seems we can know the spectre, but it remains immaterial and cannot be fully captured or reduced to rational codes; it is that which lies beyond, behind, or outside the mask, the inaccessible made present by the mask, and that which the mask cannot show. Just as it is an invisible image, an absent presence, it is also the knowledge of non-knowledge, the *masca* – the haunted mask of knowing – the named unnameable:

> Names, conventionally applied, fix the limits of an identity. Yet this 'strange name' – *spectre* – names nothing as such, and nothing which can be named as such, while also naming something which is neither something nor nothing; it names nothing which is neither nothing nor not nothing. The idea of the spectre, spectrality itself, escapes even as its apparitional instance arrives from some other place, as a figure of otherness which traverses and blurs any neat analytical distinction.[132]

The spectre is the haunting of knowledge by its outside, by that which cannot be known and cannot be named – that beyond human knowledge and understanding, outside the structures of reason, of text, and thus of law. As we have seen, the spectre is also a watcher – in a juristic context, the watcher that judges. And this 'other' gaze – of the spectre, and of spectral legality – implies an 'other scene' of knowing:

> What I call the gaze here, the gaze of the other, is not simply another machine for the perception of images. It is another world, another source of phenomenality, another degree zero of appearing.[133]

Tied up with the spectre is more than just the invisible image of the ineffable world, but the suggestion that there are other perspectives to which the world

131 See Hutchings (2001), pp 174–175.
132 Wolfreys (2013), p 71.
133 Derrida and Stiegler (2013), p 42.

appears – that is, from which the world can be accessed, lived, encountered – seen – and reduced, judged. The spectral quality of the page frame is implicated in this process in *Adamtine*. Timothy D Peters argues, with Shklovsky, that the goal of an image 'is to impede or slow perception so that the focus is not on the directness of the image as representation, but on the presentation of the representation itself'.[134] To frame is to draw attention to the frame, not the representation: to invoke reflection on the framing of things. By drawing attention to its own framing – through the depiction of spectral faces outside the grid, by invading the diegesis with the page border at key judicial moments – *Adamtine* effects something similar, couched in expressly spectral terms. Namely, that there are 'other scenes' of knowing – other frames – that always haunt conscious (legal) knowledge. The vast complexity of human knowing, the many alternate and competing masks of conceptualisation and epistemological structuring, thus become a multiframe: a varied and varying multiplicity of different forms of presentation.

And this implies an ethics, an injunction to expand our knowledge and encounter alternative frames if we are to approach 'truth' or enact justice based upon 'reality' rather than delusion. In one sense, ghosts signify an error – they are a return of a repressed other scene of perception, an other knowledge within the infinite possible forms of the epistemic multiframe that has been forgotten or overlooked. In this sense, ghosts are needed if we are to move towards the attainment of justice and the 'correct' answer. It is necessary to be haunted, for – as Weinstock reduces it – 'How can we get it right if we do not know that we have [previously] gotten it wrong?'[135] Along similar lines, recalling Constable's examination of Nietzsche's history of the error of metaphysics in Chapter 4 (whereby the apparent world comes to be mistaken for the 'real' as the real world is destroyed or forgotten within the increasing complexity of rational knowledge), it is necessary for the trace or spectre of the 'real' to erupt inside the 'apparent' if we are to even start to recognise this error.

But the idea of there being an imperative to be haunted makes little sense, as it would be an imperative paradoxically built upon something unknowable that only the haunting it requires would make invisibly apparent, and thus able to ground the imperative. Indeed, the haunting of knowledge is of a different order than such (il)logical imperatives: it is an inherent part of knowing that our structures involve the spectres of their other, of their outside and possible reconfigurations. To know is to be haunted. In Legendre's terms, the screen that protects us from the 'speechless void', upon which law and all other myths and stories are inscribed – upon which the fluctuating multiframe of knowing is formed – retains a trace of the void's 'fantastic beyond'.[136] Each epistemic frame may be haunted by other possible frames, but the multiframe itself remains haunted by the infinite

134 Peters (2015), p 264.
135 Weinstock (2013), p 64.
136 See Legendre (1997).

chaos, the pre-epistemic blankness, before and outside all forms. It is precisely this generalised spectrality that Luckhurst takes issue with, noting for example Derrida's claim that spectrality is embedded at the origin of all concepts.[137] For Luckhurst, if all of modernity is haunted then any value in the concept of the spectre is destroyed; by being everywhere, it is nowhere.[138] But being everywhere and nowhere – both absent and present – is precisely what spectres do. And this spectral presence across knowing, signalled juristically by the return of the blank space in *Adamtine*, also signals the potential for a retreat from knowledge, a movement to a field of openness, of unfigured space – and thence to new possibilities, to other frames – to other scenes of knowing.

Law is deeply infused with spectrality, in the pressing of the legal subject between its spectral fronts: the presence of irreducible life remains absent behind the mask of persona, and the absent space of authority that constitutes the mask of the subject remains present as a watcher that judges. The first of these spectral fronts signifies an epistemology that exposes the presence of Nietzsche's sublime within all structures of knowledge, an atemporal haunting of general categories by that which is not known and not knowable within the present order – a spectral sublime. The second of these spectral fronts brings with it the implication of other scenes of knowing: the absent presence of alternative perspectives implying that knowledge is always already haunted, always already perspectival and built upon the repression of its outside, and thus can be disintegrated, undone, and reconstituted. The rational certainty of law is no exception, and remains haunted by its own undoing, its dissolution.

Law is thus a haunted mask – a *masca lex*: it masks the fullness of the universe whilst repressing other scenes of knowing that remain as spectral presences, invisible images of alternative orders that thus imply the unravelling of the present order. Perhaps the true horror of law is not that it is limited in the infinite context of the abyss, as the previous chapter indicated, but that it judges with a certainty that contains the seeds of its own unravelling, a certainty produced through the institution of masks that are haunted by the spectres of infinite other possible masks, via a multiframe haunted by the infinite other frames it excludes as well as the endless chaos that cannot be known. As legal subjects, the very presence of the watcher that judges – of the institution that holds us to account with its summary judgments and ultimate interpretations – implies the infinite potential of alternative visions of justice. The truth of judgment contains untruth; the certainty of justice contains doubt and alternative possibilities of what might constitute law, justice, knowledge, the world.

More generally, the epistemological unconscious of the abyss always already haunts all structures of knowledge – rational, textual, visual, aesthetic, or otherwise. We can expand the vision of law by opening it up to the visual and aesthetic, by rupturing and venturing beyond the limits of the text and the rational surface

137 See Derrida (1994), p 202.
138 See Luckhurst (2013), pp 83–84.

and thereby encounter other 'frames' within the vast multiframe of knowing. But even such a gesture invokes its own spectres, its own repressions and its own unconscious – and thus unknown or unknowable – dimensions. The infinitely complex, folded surface of life cannot be reduced in its entirety to human understanding or experience, there is always an other scene of knowing, an other frame, as well as a background ineffability – that haunts. But conceived as a multiframe, knowledge itself can be defined as a form of comics, and as a *komos* that mediates between the chaos of the universe and knowable forms. And hence the comics medium, in its modelling of the multiple frames of knowing – its traversing of text, image, reason, aesthetics, and so on – may be able to provide a (multi)mode of knowing that potentially remains in touch with the abyss that haunts.

References

Christine Battersby (2007) *The Sublime, Terror, and Human Difference*, Routledge.

Charles Baudelaire (2015) *The Flowers of Evil / Les Fleurs du Mal*, Digireads.

Ruben Berrios and Aaron Ridley (2005) 'Nietzsche' in B Gaut and DM Lopes (eds) *The Routledge Companion to Aesthetics*, Routledge.

Hannah Berry (2012) *Adamtine*, Jonathan Cape.

Katherine Biber (2013) 'In Crime's Archive: The Afterlife of Criminal Evidence' 53 *British Journal of Criminology* 6.

Richard Collier (1998) *Masculinities, Crime, and Criminology*, Sage.

Karen Crawley (2015) 'The Critical Force of Irony: Reframing Photographs in Cultural Legal Studies' in C Sharp and M Leiboff (eds) *Cultural Legal Studies: Law's Popular Cultures and the Metamorphosis of Law*, Routledge.

Colin Davis (2013) 'État Présent: Hauntology, Spectres and Phantoms' in M del Pilar Blanco and E Peeren (eds) *The Spectralities Reader: Ghosts and Haunting in Contemporary Cultural Theory*, Bloomsbury.

Jacques Derrida (1994) *Specters of Marx: The State of the Debt, the Work of Mourning, and the New International*, Routledge.

Jacques Derrida and Bernard Stiegler (2013) 'Spectrographies' in M del Pilar Blanco and E Peeren (eds) *The Spectralities Reader: Ghosts and Haunting in Contemporary Cultural Theory*, Bloomsbury.

Costas Douzinas and Adam Gearey (2005) *Critical Jurisprudence: The Political Philosophy of Justice*, Hart.

Michel Foucault (1977) *Discipline and Punish: The Birth of the Prison*, Penguin.

Dave Gibbons et al (2008) *Watching the Watchmen*, Titan Books.

Thomas Giddens (2012) 'Comics, Law, and Aesthetics: Towards the Use of Graphic Fiction in Legal Studies' 6 *Law and Humanities* 85.

Daniel M Goodbrey (2013) 'Digital Comics – New Tools and Tropes' 4 *Studies in Comics* 1.

Peter Goodrich (1999) 'The Iconography of Nothing: Blank Spaces and the Representation of Law in *Edward VI and the Pope*' in C Douzinas and L Nead (eds) *Law and the Image: The Authority of Art and the Aesthetics of Law*, University of Chicago Press.

Peter Goodrich (2012) 'The Theatre of Emblems: On the Optical Apparatus and the Investiture of Persons' 8 *Law, Culture and the Humanities* 47.

Thierry Groensteen (2007) *The System of Comics*, University Press of Mississippi.

David Gurnham (2004) 'The Otherness of the Dead: The Fates of Antigone, Narcissus, and the Sly Fox, and the Search for Justice' 16 *Law and Literature* 327.

Donna Haraway (2015) 'Anthropocene, Capitalocene, Plantationocene, Chthulucene: Making Kin' 6 *Environmental Humanities* 159.

Jacob M Held (2009) 'Can We Steer This Rudderless World? Kant, Rorschach, Retributivism, and Honor' in MD White (ed) *Watchmen and Philosophy: A Rorschach Test*, John Wiley.

Gwyneth Horder-Payton (director) (2009) 'No Exit' *Battlestar Galactica* Season 4 Episode 17, David Icke Productions.

John Hunsley and Gina di Giulio (2001) 'Norms, Norming, and Clinical Assessment' 8 *Clinical Psychology: Science and Practice* 378.

Peter J Hutchings (2001) *The Criminal Spectre in Law, Literature, and Aesthetics: Incriminating Subjects*, Routledge.

Steven S Kapica (2014) '"I Don't Feel Like a Copy": Posthuman Legal Personhood and *Caprica*' 23 *Griffith Law Review* 612.

Sarah Kofman (1993) *Nietzsche and Metaphor*, Athlone.

Pierre Legendre (1997) 'Introduction to the Theory of the Image: Narcissus and the Other in the Mirror' in P Goodrich (ed) *Law and the Unconscious: A Legendre Reader*, Macmillan.

Pierre Legendre (1998) 'The Other Dimension of Law' in P Goodrich and DG Carlson (eds) *Law and the Postmodern Mind*, University of Michigan Press.

Chris Lloyd (2016) 'Deconstruction and Bio-Politics: Asymmetrical Visuality, Spacing, Power' in S Marusek (ed) *Synesthetic Legalities: Sensory Dimensions of Law and Jurisprudence*, Routledge.

Roger Luckhurst (2013) 'From the Contemporary London Gothic and the Limits of the "Spectral Turn"' in M del Pilar Blanco and E Peeren (eds) *The Spectralities Reader: Ghosts and Haunting in Contemporary Cultural Theory*, Bloomsbury.

Jody L Madiera (2014) 'The Visibly Offensive Offender: A Semiotic Phenomenology of an Execution' in A Wagner and RK Sherwin (eds) *Law, Culture and Visual Studies*, Springer.

Desmond Manderson (2000) *Songs without Music: Aesthetic Dimensions of Law and Justice*, University of California Press.

Alan Moore and Dave Gibbons (1986) *Watchmen*, Titan Books.

Leslie J Moran (2009) 'Judging Pictures: A Case Study of Portraits of the Chief Justices, Supreme Court of New South Wales' 5 *International Journal of Law in Context* 295.

Alexander Nehamas (1985) *Nietzsche: Life as Literature*, Harvard University Press.

Friedrich Nietzsche (1990) 'On Truth and Lies in a Nonmoral Sense' in P Bizzell and B Herzberg (eds) *The Rhetorical Tradition: Readings from Classical Times to the Present*, Bedford Books.

Friedrich Nietzsche (1997a) *On the Genealogy of Morality*, Cambridge University Press.

John T Noonan (1976) *Persons and Masks of the Law: Cardozo, Holmes, Jefferson, and Wythe as Makers of the Masks*, Farrar, Strauss, and Giroux.

Connal Parsley (2010) 'The Mask and Agamben: The Transitional Juridical Technics of Legal Relation' 14 *Law Text Culture* 12.

Timothy D Peters (2015) 'Reading the Law Made Strange: Cultural Legal Studies, Theology and Speculative Fiction' in C Sharp and M Leiboff (eds) *Cultural Legal Studies: Law's Popular Cultures and the Metamorphosis of Law*, Routledge.

James Petty (2015) 'Violent Lives, Ending Violently? Justice, Ideology and Spectatorship in *Watchmen*' in T Giddens (ed) *Graphic Justice: Intersections of Comics and Law*, Routledge.

Xavier M del Pont (2012) 'Confronting Whiteness: Blankness, Loss and Visual Disintegration in Graphic Narratives' 3 *Studies in Comics* 2.

Jean P Rumsey (1997) 'Re-Visions of Agency in Kant's Moral Theory' in RM Schott (ed) *Feminist Interpretations of Immanuel Kant*, Pennsylvania State University Press.

Richard K Sherwin (2000) *When Law Goes Pop: The Vanishing Line between Law and Popular Culture*, University of Chicago Press.

Phillip Shon (2003) 'Rorschach-in-Action: Some Further Observations on the Semiotic Summons in Police-Citizen Encounters' 16 *International Journal for the Semiotics of Law* 101.

Susan Stewart (1991) *Crimes of Writing: Problems in the Containment of Representation*, Oxford University Press.

Miguel de Unamuno (1954) *Tragic Sense of Life*, Dover.

Irving B Weiner (2000) 'Using the Rorschach Properly in Practice and Research' 56 *Journal of Clinical Psychology* 435.

Jeffrey Andrew Weinstock (2013) 'From Introduction: The Spectral Turn' in M del Pilar Blanco and E Peeren (eds) *The Spectralities Reader: Ghosts and Haunting in Contemporary Cultural Theory*, Bloomsbury.

Walter O Weyrauch (1978) 'Law as Mask: Legal Ritual and Relevance' 66 *California Law Review* 4.

Julian Wolfreys (2013) 'Preface: On Textual Haunting' in M del Pilar Blanco and E Peeren (eds) *The Spectralities Reader: Ghosts and Haunting in Contemporary Cultural Theory*, Bloomsbury.

James M Wood et al (2000) 'The Rorschach Test in Clinical Diagnosis: A Critical Review, with a Backward Look at Garfield (1947)' 56 *Journal of Clinical Psychology* 395.

Chapter 6

Redrawing the law

> Pictures want equal rights with language, not to be turned into language … to be seen as complex individuals occupying multiple subject positions and identities … What pictures want, then, is not to be interpreted, decoded, worshipped, smashed, exposed, or demystified by their beholders, or to enthral their beholders. They may not even want to be granted subjectivity or personhood by well-meaning commentators who think that humanness is the greatest compliment they could pay to pictures. The desire of pictures may be inhuman and nonhuman, better modelled by figures of animals, machines, or cyborgs, or even by more basic images … What pictures want in the last instance, then, is simply to be asked what they want, with the understanding that the answer may well be, nothing at all.[1]

1 Mitchell (2005), pp 47–48.

We have begun with a blank page. The 'forgotten canvas' has been recalled: a *revenant*, it begins by coming back, the eruption of materiality that shatters conceptual elaboration. The world has been undone, the figurations of law and knowing have been disintegrated and unravelled through the bringing-to-consciousness of the juridical spectre. Blankness is all that remains. Was all that remained. Now we have these words; the hum of discourse to fill the blank space of the page. The haunted quality of the multiframe of knowing brought such a defiguration, and returned us to a pre-structural, pre-epistemic blankness of both nothingness and infinity, both empty and full of all possible forms. This 'originary blankness' was both precisely as simple as the preceding unmarked page, and precisely as complex; it is both nothing and everything, unstructured, unknowable, and teeming with potential – the chaos of a universe we can never capture. So much we witnessed in the previous chapter, and it is from such a spectral and indefinable expanse that we begin this final chapter. The blank page above was not itself the void or abyss before and outside epistemic structures, it was not literally the ineffable, complex surface of the Nietzschean sublime, but it remains symbolic – metonymic, even – of this infinitely rich backdrop to all forms. The blank page 'behind' or surrounding, delimiting, the figures of this text is the absent presence of the abyss, the spectre over which the textual figuration of knowing elaborates its form and from which it can never escape. But why should these figures be those of language, words, text? My failure here is surely that I have not gone 'beyond' the textual form of conscious law – not truly. I have reduced and translated into text; surrounded limited multimodal examples with words in an attempt to indicate the expansive potential of a cultural legal aesthetics to challenge the rational texts of law. But then, all forms remain haunted. Our final gesture, before this current string of figures dissipates into the abstraction of the index, is thus towards a multimodal law: a law that, because of its epistemic complexity, is more sensitive to its spectrality, to its derivation from saturated blankness.

We begin with a coming back: the retelling of the preceding chapters through engagement with Isabel Greenberg's *The Encyclopedia of Early Earth*, which articulates a critical cartography that we can read as a metaphor for the epistemic processes of perspectival abstraction and haunting encountered hitherto. The chapter first traces the connections between maps as a technology of jurisdiction that institutes a demand not to 'go beyond', whilst at the same time being a limited form of knowing. It then turns to further interrogate *Early Earth* to reveal Greenberg's concern with the power of myth to order the world, thus encountering something of what is at stake in moving between epistemic modalities: the undoing of the order of the universe, as well as the complex jurisdictional assertions that share the same ordering function. The second half of the chapter shifts away from Greenberg to encounter directly the multimodal epistemology of comics and the possibility of a multimodal law. It begins by considering the way the interactions of words and images in the comics medium can be seen to reflect high-stakes ideological tensions over the presentation of knowledge, before shifting to the unconscious infinity embedded in our encounter with images – an infinite ineffability that is thus also embedded in the visual dimension of text, and thus the form of law, opening up to possibilities of re-imagining law as multimodal.

Drawing the world

Jurisdiction, mapping, knowing

When making sense of the world, when encoding reality into knowable forms, it is from blankness that we proceed; any inscription is necessarily preceded by the endless space that remains as a trace – a ghost amidst all knowing. Berry showed how this non-figuration haunts the structures of knowing with the potential to undo and defigure the world and the law; we saw the disintegration of the conscious world, the blankness in the comics form being employed to signal the return to the originary chaotic abyss before knowing, the blank space absent knowable forms. Now that we have undone the world, now we have returned to the infinite markings of the clean slate – the page left blank – we are in a position to reflect upon what law should fill this 'blankness' with, how it should inscribe and thereby institute the world. Although questions over the filling of blankness apply to all forms within the multiframe of knowing, law's formation is of particular importance as it has become a privileged source of truth in modernity.[2]

One of the most notable things about the comics medium is that, although not necessarily a definitional quality, the blank page upon which any comics work is created can be potentially filled with both text and image, with multiple modes of presentation. As we saw in Chapter 1, this multimodality is a key feature of much of the leading theorisation of the comics medium in general. Indeed, the empty pre-comics space need not be written, but can also be drawn or occupied by a host of other graphic figurations. But what of the pre-legal blankness? What marks should we make upon the empty space that may be occupied by law? Peter Goodrich argues that the law fills the blank space of potential with text, with linguistic forms that attempt to structure and manage social life,[3] with the blank panel remaining that which 'both precedes and exceeds language, a law that is beyond memory and beyond the power of inscription'.[4] Goodrich ultimately focuses on the transfer of sovereign power in *Edward VI and the Pope*, and the symbolic clearing of the visual image it represents in order to make way for the knowable texts of law.[5] In doing so, and as we also noted in the previous chapter, he necessarily highlights that blank spaces in paintings are more than unfinished or

2 See Hunt and Wickham (1994), pp 41–42; de Sousa Santos (1987), p 286.
3 See Goodrich (1999).
4 Goodrich (1999), p 113.
5 '*Edward VI and the Pope* represents a massive transfer of jurisdiction, a transmission that took place by means of a movement or reformation from image to imageless writing, from the ghostly power of the Church to the bare letters of law': Goodrich (1999), p 99.

merely empty spaces, but in many cases represent the potential of that which might fill them: the world that may be discovered, and 'the power and mastery of those who will discover, map, colonize and claim' the unknown world.[6]

For Goodrich, this cartographic metaphor can be seen in the *Self-Portrait* of Sir Nathaniel Bacon, where the painting's blank space is clearly embedded amidst a context of cartographical exploration and discovery,[7] and connections with the authority of those who do the discovering can be seen in *Elizabeth I when Princess*, where the blank pages of an open book denote the as-yet-unwritten laws of the future queen's reign.[8] The blank space, then, becomes the space on our maps that is not yet drawn: 'a new world that awaits discovery and charting'.[9] And the potential of the comics-space to be filled with multiple modes of presentation challenges, on both a practical and an epistemic level, the traditional filling of legal spaces with text: the world as constituted in law can also be consciously mapped in more multimodal ways. The use of the term 'mapped' here is not without significance, as Goodrich's cartographic metaphors indicate. Maps, like comics, are both visual and textual, employing multiple layers and levels of signification to articulate a vision of the landscape, of the world and our relation to it. As Boaventura de Sousa Santos argues, 'the relations law entertains with social reality are much similar to those between maps and spatial reality'.[10] But maps are not only a metaphor for legality – one worth taking literally[11] – but also for the processes of knowing more generally, in their tracing of the socio-physical landscape into a gridded structure that retains only a trace of the 'true' landscape it seeks to capture. Indeed, the only truly accurate maps are those on 1:1 scale – that is, the physical world itself,[12] if we can access such a thing – and any chosen scale necessarily eschews other possible presentations of the world, reminiscent of the multiframe of knowing: 'Each scale reveals a phenomenon and distorts or hides others'.[13] Accordingly, reading maps as comics, or reading comics cartographically, can help recapitulate much of the complex epistemological discussion undertaken in the previous chapters, before we move in the second half of the chapter to engage more directly with legal multimodality and the multiframe of knowing.

The analysis of maps presented in comics might be of particular usefulness, as within the bounds of comics there are not only the visual, textual, and rational elements consciously found in the technical presentations of maps,[14] but also more

6 Goodrich (1999), p 91.
7 See Goodrich (1999), pp 90–91.
8 Goodrich (1999), pp 91–94.
9 Goodrich (1999), p 90.
10 de Sousa Santos (1987), p 282.
11 de Sousa Santos (1987), pp 282, 286.
12 See Manderson (2000), p 178.
13 de Sousa Santos (1987), p 284.
14 Note that maps also involve iconic and conventional symbols, akin to the semiotic codes and practices of comics outlined in Chapter 1: see de Sousa Santos (1987), pp 285–286.

aesthetic forces that can enable and play with critical epistemic interactions made available by the multimodality of the comics multiframe. To that end, it is to Isabel Greenberg's *The Encyclopedia of Early Earth*,[15] a comics work deeply concerned with exploring and mapping the world through the aesthetic play of comics, that I first turn. The core premise of *Early Earth* is to follow the rhapsodic journey of a man known as the Storyteller as he traverses the mythic 'Early Earth' from North to South Pole in search of a lost piece of his soul, encountering many new and undiscovered realms and peoples along the way. With this peripatesis we already have a movement between worlds, between the realms of Early Earth, that can be read as metaphorical of the multimodal transitions that reading the comics medium demands, and that open us up to the plurality of knowing. Greenberg's work – concerned as it is with the formation of knowledge through myths, narratives, and maps, and presented in multimodal comics form – foregrounds the processes that take us from the abyss through to conscious structures. Accordingly, the basic trajectory I follow in this section is from abyss, to myth, to map (and thus law). Or, rather, I trace this backwards, recapitulating the journey of the previous four chapters (from ghostless machine to spectral abyss): map, via myth, to abyssal blankness. The starting point for unpacking Greenberg's critical cartography, then, is her cartographic presentation of the sovereign state of Migdal Bavel (a fictional state in Early Earth encountered by the Storyteller), reproduced in Figure 6.1.

There is a striking similarity between Greenberg's depiction of Migdal Bavel and the seventeenth century emblem of British jurisdiction found in John Selden's *Titles of Honour* (in Figure 6.2). Both images depict a building or buildings upon an island surrounded by the waters of the sea. Both show the seat of government in the depiction of the chief city[16] of each land. Selden's emblem depicts an island, surrounded by the wavy lines of the sea, indicating also the written lines of law, of authority and jurisdiction, upon which sits the castle of Britannia, complete with turrets;[17] Migdal Bavel is similarly encircled by battlements, a depiction of authority and administration (it is the seat of the royal power of Migdal Bavel's sovereign, the Sun King). As statements or declarations of sovereign authority, these images are 'vexillological as much as … representational', and thus employ resources of communication used in the heraldic construction of flags, most notably the placing in the upper left quadrant that which takes precedence within the image.[18] But where in this prominent space of Selden's emblem there is a book, signalling 'government under the dominion of the order and precedence' of the texts of law,[19] Greenberg's panel places a blank space. Indeed, this blank space is the seeming emptiness beyond the curved horizon that proceeds across the

15 Greenberg (2013). See Appendix A for an overview and details of this work.
16 See Goodrich (2018), p 58.
17 Goodrich (2018), p 59.
18 See Goodrich (2018), p 59.
19 Goodrich (2018), p 59.

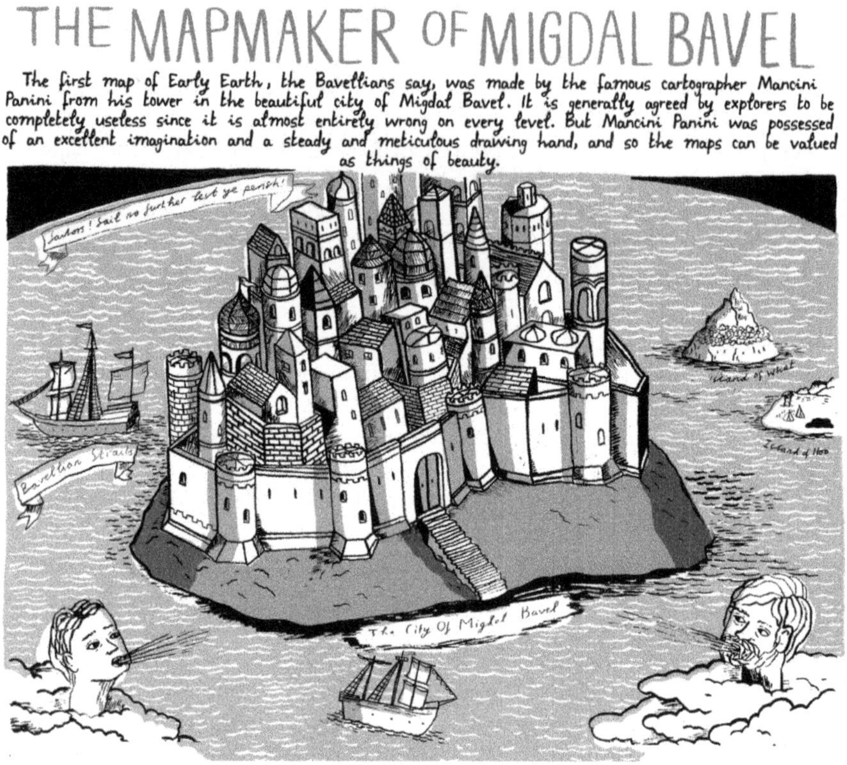

Figure 6.1 Greenberg (2013), np. © Isabel Greenberg. Reproduced with permission.[20]

whole top of the image, signalling the limit of the world. In the primary position, this curved boundary is also accompanied by a scroll, a written statement, a block of text – speaking semiotically, a *lexia*, indicative of a block of *law* – imperiously declaring: 'Sail no further lest ye perish!' This dominant quarter of the image *qua* declaration thus permeates the whole panel with its textual and legal interdiction against travelling beyond. Greenberg's image, akin to Selden's emblem, is a declaration of the sovereign state of the Bavellian empire as ruled (and, as we shall see, mapped) from Migdal Bavel, and states: this is the whole world, there is nothing beyond.[21]

As a declaration, Greenberg's cartographic image can also be seen as an announcement of jurisdiction. The interdiction not to venture beyond the limit of the map maintains the boundary of the world upon which the state of Migdal

20 See Appendix B for a reproduction of the text in this figure.

21 In some ways, this can be read in relation to the sovereign's function of delineating jurisdictional boundaries: it is the seat of power at Migdal Bavel that determines the extent of the Bavellian Empire. On this spatial dimension of sovereignty, as read through Dr Doom in Marvel's *Civil War*, see Curtis (2017).

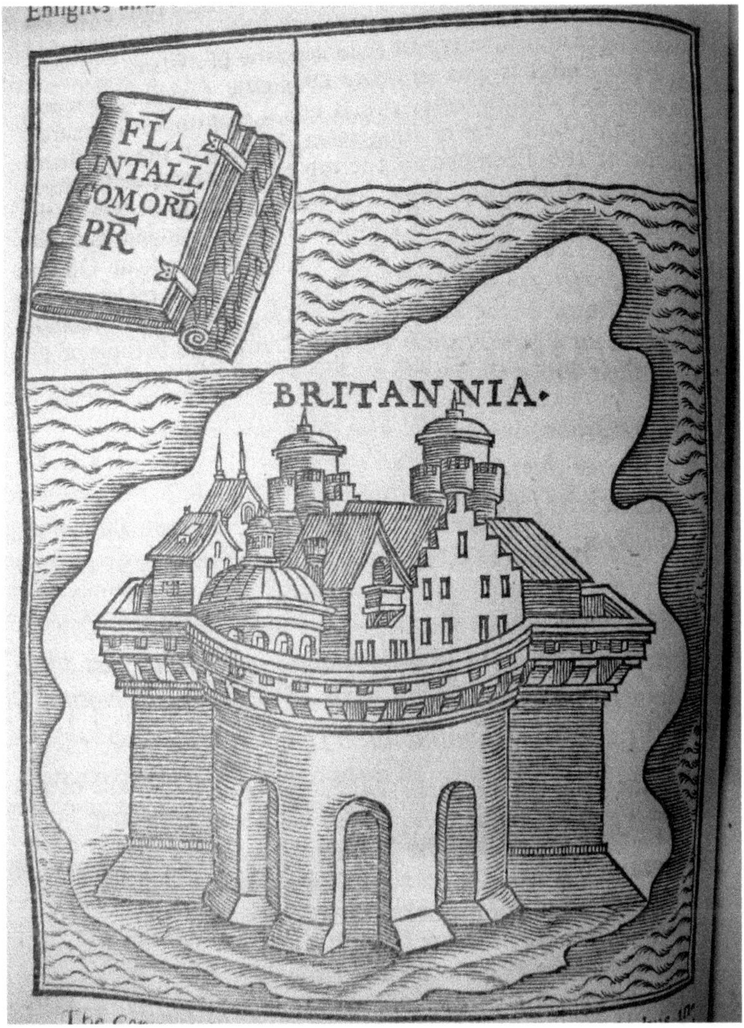

Figure 6.2 From Selden (1631) *Titles of Honour*, p 324. Reproduced with permission (Peter Goodrich).

Bavel rests. Sticking with Goodrich, the visive or visual nature of law's power can be seen to be bound up with its institutional display and the recognition of its jurisdiction:

> In that jurisdiction precedes law, in that it marks the point of entry into the juridical sphere and speech, it has to be visible in advance of utterance ... apprehended prior to any discursive intervention in the name of legality ... [Law] is framed not as speech alone but rather and advisedly by reference to

> writs and letters. This is not just so as to distinguish jurisdiction from mere speech, from the lightness of informal oral encounter, but rather so as to note the liminal space and transitional role of questions of jurisdiction. Writing here comes before speech … The law both comes in the form of and is in essence a writ, a writing, an emblematic sign.[22]

The question of jurisdiction is thus the liminal space through which we gain entry to the law; it is the boundary region where law first appears and announces itself. This announcement, according to Goodrich, is primarily textual (the writ, the summons), but generally takes an emblematic form,[23] as Selden's emblem indicates, and as we can see in the declarative dimensions of Greenberg's depiction of Migdal Bavel. Here, the mapping of the state portrays the limits of its juridical, sovereign order;[24] the multimodal display of territory, architecture, and text become part of the technology of Migdal Bavel's visive arrival – that is, its jurisdiction.

Public authority, Dorsett and McVeigh observe, can be understood as akin to 'an assemblage of jurisdictional devices and practices';[25] jurisdiction is concerned with 'the conduct of authority through technical means'.[26] As such, although typically associated on one level with physical territory, and as their analysis of the jurisdictional practices surrounding the East India Company reveal,[27] there is no necessary territorial element involved in jurisdiction: 'incidents of government are ordered through a range of statuses, rather than primarily through territory'.[28] Despite this, the significance of law's relationship with the land – and in particular in the context of mapping and cartography – remains important. As they note elsewhere:

> Mapping creates and makes lawful relations visible … As a technology of jurisdiction, mapping plays a part in the creation and representation of the visual form of authority. It helps with the crafting and representation of legal place by representing territory (and in other ways, persons and events) … [It] evidences the movement of a jurisdiction and a law – across land, between humans and between events.[29]

22 Goodrich (2008), p 214.
23 Goodrich (2008), p 217, notes other 'visive' displays of jurisdictional entry:

> The colour purple, as our armorialists note, but also the crests and coats of armour, the devises and blazons, the vestments and mitres, the orbs, sceptres and rods of office, the portraits and tones, the buildings and portals, trophies and scrolls, rites and ceremonies, the kiss of peace or the words 'oyez, oyez, all rise', are just so many passports [to the] court or realm.

24 Note that there is some complexity involved in separating out jurisdiction and sovereignty: see Dorsett and McVeigh (2014), pp 571–574.
25 Dorsett and McVeigh (2014), p 574.
26 Dorsett and McVeigh (2014), p 586.
27 See Dorsett and McVeigh (2014), pp 574–578.
28 Dorsett and McVeigh (2014), p 578.
29 Dorsett and McVeigh (2012), p 63.

Indeed, as Olivia Barr observes of roads: they 'are not stable entities that seemingly bypass legal spaces, but rather dynamic spatial practices that are an activity – or more aptly a technology – of jurisdiction that produce legal spaces'.[30] Roads, like the maps that trace them, are technologies of jurisdiction.[31]

Tracking the jurisdictional import of roads to the office of the surveyor, Barr demonstrates the integral place of both the construction of roads and the practice of cartographical surveying itself as techniques of jurisdiction in the building of empire.[32] Dorsett and McVeigh highlight the epistemological importance of maps for state-craft, particularly in the context of colonialism where mapping the world enabled Europeans to stake a claim on lands they had never actually seen.[33] Even in contemporary disputes over land use between states and indigenous populations, the 'power of the map' to offer legal recognition of ownership is not insignificant.[34] Maps are also able to be utilised in different ways, as practices of counter-mapping indicate, since 'different sets of maps are able to represent different hierarchies of social aspects of land and thereby are able to mobilize political and social power in specific ways'.[35] Despite this, the use of maps can arguably cause the entry of indigenous people into the neoliberal order of capitalism, by instilling property rights via the highly rational practices of scientific mapmaking.[36] Indeed, and maintaining an epistemic focus, mainstream cartographic practices and techniques can generally be seen as heavily indebted to the positive sciences: as Brown and Knopp explain in their experiences of producing a map using mainstream cartographic techniques and software with the aim of representing the complex identity politics of queer histories in Seattle:

> Given that the map project was guided by a queer epistemology and ontology, the project's constitutive politics necessarily reflected a process of negotiation and compromise with almost life-like forms of positivism, realism, pragmatism, and Cartesian rationality that insinuated themselves into the algorithms, hardware, and ongoing interpretation of our map production.[37]

Brown and Knopp conclude that the multiple epistemologies at play in their project were ultimately productive, enabling the limits of hegemonic methods and approaches to cartographic knowing to be appreciated and alternative modes of mapping to be explored,[38] thus encountering something of the wider multi-frame of knowledge. But this close adherence to Cartesian rationality – to the

30 Barr (2015), p 201.
31 See, generally, Dorsett and McVeigh (2012), pp 54–80.
32 See Barr (2015).
33 Dorsett and McVeigh (2012), p 63.
34 Wainwright and Bryan (2009), pp 153–154.
35 Fraley (2010), p 422.
36 See Wainwright and Bryan (2009).
37 Brown and Knopp (2008), p 48.
38 See Brown and Knopp (2008), especially pp 54–56.

'ghostless machine' of the rational surface, to put it in the terms of Chapter 2 – highlights an ongoing issue in mapmaking, and one that reflects the broader issues of epistemic limits with which the current book engages. It may be that maps enable the governance and claiming of lands never seen, but the land itself is arguably never actually seen by those who create maps in any case. As Barr indicates in her analysis of the cartographical practice of triangulation, whereby distances between points on the Earth are calculated in Euclidean space using trigonometry:

> There is an abstraction ... from the texture of the earth; an abstraction of common law from the land ... the smooth inferential projection of knowledge between known points, authorizing knowledge of the unknown on the basis of the little that is known.[39]

And this detached perspective is characteristic of the state's practices of seeing more generally: 'within the project of vision, the state practices a strong tendency toward a Cartesian perspective, one that highlights objectivity, scientificity, and detachment'.[40] The bird's eye view implied by maps – and similarly aerial photographs no less than full-body security scanners, as Braverman argues – connects to the prioritising of certain aspects for state scrutiny at the expense of others (the local, the human, the relational).[41] de Sousa Santos highlights the way different levels of mapping – local, national, global – produce different forms of legal system and understanding, with smaller scale world systems reducing the detail of social life.[42] Indeed, the production of maps can be seen to be as much influenced by the power relationships at play in their development, including concerns over the elements to be made visible, as by the physical world itself – if not more so.[43] Jumping back to our starting point: the jurisdictional assertion of Figure 6.1 is thus built on an abstraction; it is a statement made at a remove from the land of the Bavellian Empire itself, tied up with concerns of power and the limits of knowing.

When the Storyteller reaches the Bavellian Empire, and in particular its capital Migdal Bavel, we encounter not only the assertive image in Figure 6.1, but Mancini Panini, the Mapmaker of Migdal Bavel himself. Greenberg's depiction of Panini's maps are, from the outset, satirical in their overt recognition of their complete inaccuracy by any scientific standard (note the caption in Figure 6.1). Reflective of the colonial use of maps, as well as the deeper lack of encounter with the land that Barr explains in the context of triangulation, Mancini Panini is agoraphobic and cannot even leave his tower: he only ever maps land that he has never trodden. His method is one of vision, through his telescope (reminiscent of the aerial photographs that omit so much human detail for Braverman[44]), and

39 Barr (2015), p 211.
40 Braverman (2010), p 186.
41 See Braverman (2010).
42 See de Sousa Santos (1987), pp 287–291. See also Manderson (2000), pp 178–179.
43 See, for example, Crampton (2001).
44 See Braverman (2010).

vicarious knowledge, through his 'genius monkeys'. Panini has three trained monkeys, and he equips them with bags of sand, each with a tiny hole so that, upon their return, he can calculate (triangulate) the distances they have travelled and thus determine the dimensions of the world. But via this method he cannot appreciate the texture and intricacies, nor directions, of the monkeys' journeys. Literal attempts at mapping in *Early Earth* accordingly highlight the abstraction of mapping processes satirised in Panini, as visual comparison between Figure 6.3 and Figure 6.4 demonstrates.

In Figure 6.3 is depicted a map of part of Early Earth, specifically the regions of Britanitarka and the Bavellian Empire, and the expanse of sea between them. True to Greenberg's style, even this formal map is playful, embellished with fingerposts, a sailing ship, splashing waves, and sea monsters. As an aesthetic figuration of a map, the technical grid – usually a complete and necessary structure that gives a map its scale and thus its link to the physical world it masks as it seeks to make present – is incomplete, ruptured wherever land or Greenberg's playful objects are depicted. Thus Greenberg also foregrounds the constructed nature of the map, as representing or indicating something outside its own gridded order.

There is a second depiction of this stretch of sea, of which we are invited by the physical form of *Early Earth* to engage in a comparative analysis. Figure 6.3 takes up half the verso page, while Figure 6.4 takes up three quarters of the recto; the structure and layout of these copresent pages thus encourages us to compare the two images that face each other across the spine of the bound volume – the very physical form of the work, the geographic space of the page,[45] participating in its articulation. Already present in the more formal map of Figure 6.3 is the suggestion that perhaps it does not, and cannot, contain what it claims to depict. In Figure 6.4 this limitation is made explicit as a swirling mass of waves and the fluid horror of the living world erupts across the page – the Nietzschean sublime at work. Where the sea is a linear, two-dimensional block of shading in Figure 6.3, it is an interlaced mass of lines and swells in Figure 6.4. The occasional and playful wave shown in Figure 6.3, indicative of that which is not depicted, becomes an evocative mess of lines, chasing each other across the page. The closeness of many of these lines creates something of a shimmer effect in the gaze;[46] the image in Figure 6.4 is thus one of movement, a subtly crawling space populated by regions of human safety (islands, boats, the mainland) and that which threatens it (the figural lines of monsters and the relentless ocean). The waters of Figure 6.4 are far from the clean, abstracted certainty of the map in Figure 6.3, highlighted further by the absence of the containing, calming certainty of the grid lines.

The world of Panini's maps is thus deeply mediated, both in their encounter with the physical world they seek to represent and in their presentation through the medium of the map. The world encountered for the Mapmaker is only that

45 See Dittmer (2010).
46 For more on this 'shimmer' phenomenon, as deployed in *Black Hole*, see Mlodrag (2013), pp 201–203.

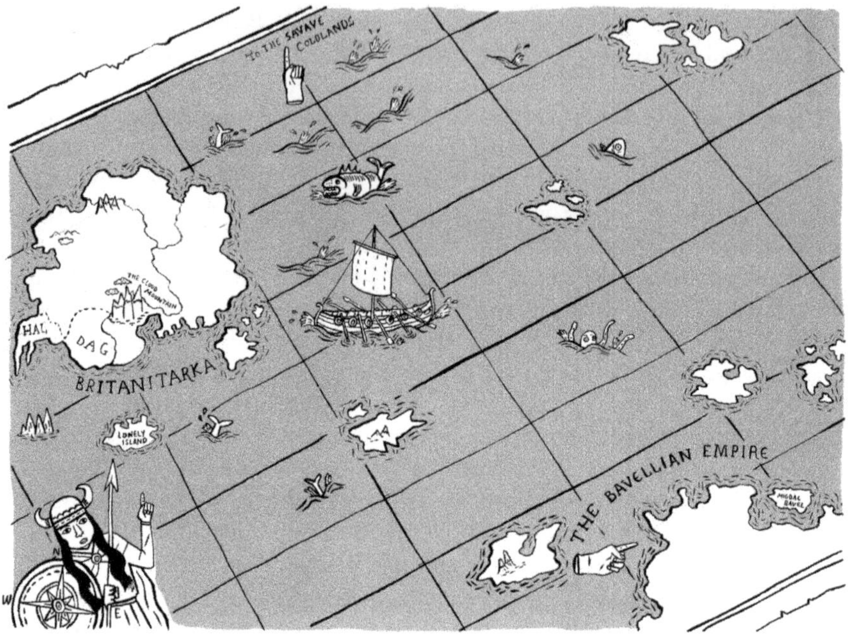

Figure 6.3 Greenberg (2013), np. © Isabel Greenberg. Reproduced with permission.

which can be experienced through his particular mechanisms of knowing, and within the prison of his human flesh. But despite this, and despite depictions of the mischievous genius monkeys having a nice time on the beach rather than exploring, the Mapmaker has complete trust in his monkeys and believes the world he creates in his maps to be completely true: 'He had trained them himself and believed them to be one hundred per cent reliable'.[47] Indeed, as the Mapmaker himself says: 'I trained them myself, you know. They are 100 per cent reliable'.[48] But, as Crampton observes, the 'map is not objectively "above" or "beyond" that which is represented; nor can one track back from the representation to some ultimate object, knowledge or mind'.[49] Maps are products of multiple decisional processes and intricate interactions of power, ideology, and interest,[50] including the interaction between the object of the map and those who encounter it in reading processes.[51] Building on the playful abstraction between Figure 6.3 and Figure 6.4, Panini satirises the 'truth' of the map in his overtly

47 Greenberg (2013), np.
48 Greenberg (2013), np.
49 Crampton (2001), p 240.
50 See, for example, Braverman (2010); Crampton (2001); Fraley (2010); Kitchin and Dodge (2007); Wainwright and Bryan (2009).
51 Kitchin and Dodge (2007).

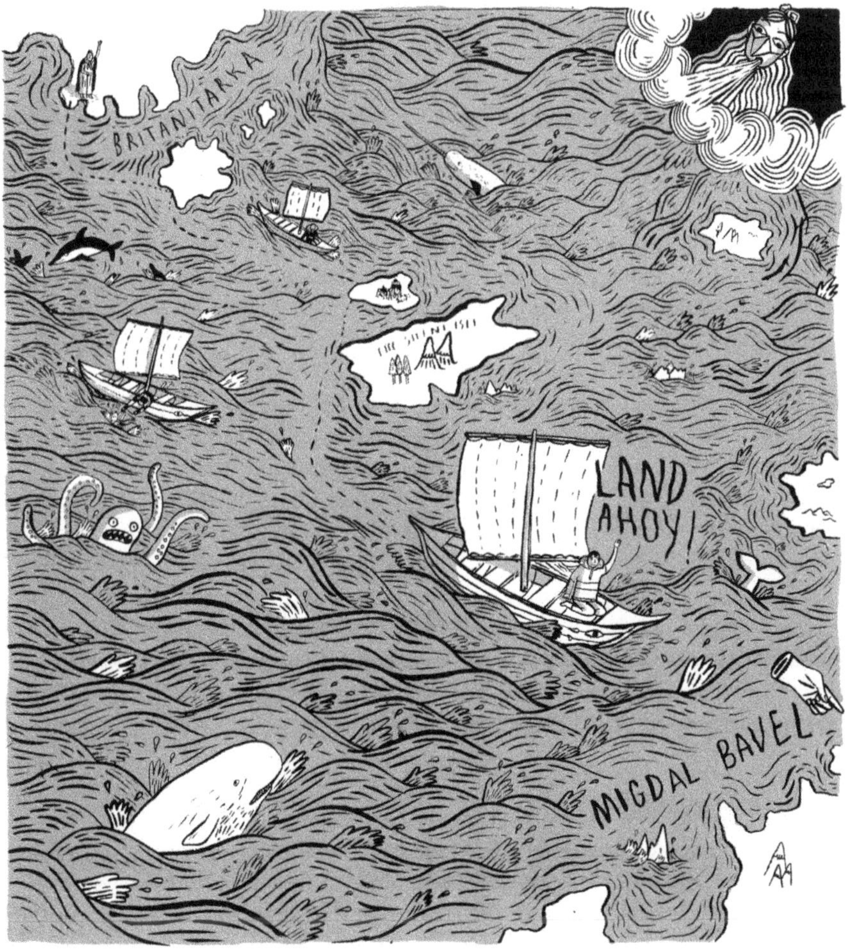

Figure 6.4 Greenberg (2013), np. © Isabel Greenberg. Reproduced with permission.

subjective and inaccurate telescope-monkey method: there is nothing beyond what he can see through his telescope, nothing beyond the distances he calculates his genius monkeys to have travelled, nothing beyond what they collect and return to him. The world of the map is reified into the physical truth of the world – 100% accurate. There is nothing 'out there' that is not on the map, and there is nothing beyond the edge of the map.

Greenberg's presentation of the Mapmaker highlights this reified truth status of maps, particularly in their intricate relationship with state power and jurisdiction, as Panini's official office of Mapmaker to the Sun King of Migdal Bavel indicates. Indeed, as well as reflecting power relations and subjective epistemic processes, maps 'are able to masquerade as scientific, neutral devices',[52] meaning they are able to propagate dominant ideologies under the guise of simple fact and thereby hide embedded power relations in plain view.[53] Such processes, as de Sousa Santos observes in his literal reading of the metaphor of cartography-as-law, underpin understandings of legality:

> Scale, projection and symbolisation are not neutral procedures. The choices made within each of them promote the expression of certain types of interests and disputes and suppress that of others. The autonomy of law as a specific way of representing, distorting, and imagining reality derives from [the] operation of these procedures.[54]

In a literal sense, then, maps claim to be a true and unmediated representation of the world, but fail to capture the immense complexity of the Earth's surface whilst at the same time function as technologies of jurisdiction and underpin ideas of legality. Perhaps, then, they are the perfect metaphor for the perspectivism of Nietzsche's metaphysics in relation to the infinite complexities of the surface of life in the context of legal knowing. But against these perspectival limits, Greenberg's critical cartography suggests that the official truth of the map is vehemently protected: it should not be challenged for fear of destroying the world itself. Thus, Panini's maps – as in Figure 6.1, as well as Figure 6.6 below – are embedded with various codes aimed at hindering or deterring any sort of movement beyond the limits of the map: sail no further lest ye perish!

Of maps and monsters

In Chapter 2 we encountered Dr Manhattan's ghostless 'rational surface' that repressed the complex universe into knowable forms. This surface was visually represented by the smiley face on the surface of Mars, the chance formation of the Martian landscape smoothed and formed into the abstract mask of the person. Tellingly, beyond this smooth surface Dr Manhattan referred to the complex geography as 'chaotic terrain'.[55] In Nietzsche's sublime, it is precisely this ineffable complexity of the world's surface, this unencounterable detail, that ruptures the smoothing of the world into abstract concepts, or indeed legal categories and lines on maps. Indeed, as we noted in Chapter 3, the line of the coast is never an accurate depiction of the 'real' coast: because one can always measure in more detail, the coast is of infinite length and thus categorically unmeasurable.[56] In this way, maps are a microcosm of knowing, as well as being part of the wider

52 Fraley (2010), pp 421–422.
53 See Braverman (2010).
54 de Sousa Santos (1987), p 297.
55 See Moore and Gibbons (1986), Ch 9 p 14.
56 See Manderson (2000), pp 177–178; Sousanis (2015), p 44.

multiframe of knowledge: they remain haunted by the ghost of that which they cannot or do not depict (the 'folds within folds'[57] of complex reality; the infinite other possible cartographies, those other scenes of mapping). As Greenberg's placement of the blank space in Figure 6.1 indicates, the presentation of Migdal Bavel is not just separated from the land, but from the originary blankness out of which it is formed and which it masks as a *masca cartographica*. Greenberg's critical cartography is not ignorant of these epistemic issues, as we can see in her wider engagement with the mythic – not just cartographic – ordering of the world.

As well as a work in critical cartography, Greenberg's *Early Earth* is imbued with a mythological richness and a deft wit: it is a rhapsodic articulation and reconfiguration of mythic human history told with humour and charm. Along his epic journey, the Storyteller from Nord – the fictional realm located at Early Earth's North Pole – encounters many lands and peoples, filling the *terra incognita* beyond the edge of the Nord map as he traverses multiple worlds and communal orders, as well as bringing with him that which is 'beyond the map' of the civilisations he encounters. Such a movement is reminiscent of the formal shifts that are demanded in the reading of the multimodal comics medium – between words, images, graphic layouts, image sequences, metonymic symbols, and so on, as well as between elements of the multiframe – and in his nomadic perspective, the Storyteller invokes the wider opening up to the haunted multiframe of knowing. It is of note that this man is known as the Storyteller; as he travels these new and undiscovered lands, he tells stories of his experiences, codifying the world in oral narrative as *Early Earth* itself codifies it in multimodality. And it is stories, as theorists from Robert Cover to Jerome Bruner have argued, that constitute the normative order[58] and help us make sense of and manage the complexities of life.[59] Recognition of this power and function of narrative runs deep in *Early Earth*, as can be seen in its concern with the mythic structures of the world, and in particular with its concern with origins – a concern that correlates with the filling of blankness.

There are three different versions of the origins of the universe presented in *Early Earth*. The all-powerful creator of *Early Earth* is a deific being known as Bird Man. Bird Man has two children, known as the Ravens. The first origin is not detailed: the people of Nord believe that 'the Universe was created and exists in the mind's eye of the Eagle God Bird Man. Night occurs when the Eagle blinks. The long Nordic winter is when he sleeps'.[60] The second version is encountered when the Storyteller gets to Britanitarka, one of the realms he visits on his journey to the South Pole. Here we witness a simple story of the originary blankness, as seen in Figure 6.5. As this figure depicts, there is a spectral blankness of infinite

57 Sousanis (2015), p 44.
58 Cover (1983).
59 Bruner (2002).
60 Greenberg (2013), np.

form and potential from which erupts a chaos of monsters and demons. In this version, these monsters are quelled by Bird Man and the Ravens. The third version is from the Bible of Bird Man, the sacred book of the Bavellian Empire. Again, the originary blankness is presented as a spectralised black space, and within this void, an egg inexplicably appears from which hatches Bird Man, who then proceeds to imagine things into existence.[61]

There are features that are common to these interconnecting myths, perhaps the most significant of which is the role of Bird Man as the central node of the universe as known by the different communities of Early Earth. The second and third origins are perhaps the most useful in this regard, as in both we see Bird Man as the force through which the originary blankness is masked or subdued into a formal structure of mythic reality: the universe becomes that which is ordered by Bird Man. In the Britanitarkan myth, Bird Man also subdues the chaos of monsters that emerges from the abyss, again bringing order to existence. The universe, under Bird Man, is also seen as something that if not imaginary itself is certainly derived from the imagination. Bird Man imagines things into existence. Indeed, we witness Bird Man, at some later point in the universe's history, playing a game with his two children The Ravens to see who can create the best world. Although it is Kiddo, his daughter, who creates humans and the complex world that would eventually become Early Earth (in her hair), Bird Man himself creates a world in the black space of his pupil, in his mind's eye.

This persistent engagement with the question of origins, and of the creation of the universe through the imaginary processes that give order to the ineffable potential of the originary abyss, gives a new poignancy to the interdiction of Figure 6.1. The instruction not to go beyond the boundary of the world – not to venture into the blank abyss – develops high stakes. For to make such a move is to undo the long and complex processes of mythmaking and worldmaking that have structured knowing out of the now-forgotten canvas, out of the monster-filled chaos of the abyss. More juristically, it is to undo the mythmaking of law – that is, the technologies of jurisdiction that have created the space for law to become articulated as something reified.[62] To bring forth acknowledgment of the originary blank space, the spectre of saturated chaos, as we saw in Chapter 5, is to bring forth the unravelling of law, and of knowing more generally. It is a move that defigures the map, that undoes its lines and points, that dissolves roads and

61 This does not necessarily undermine the notion that monsters also came from the void and were subsequently quelled by Bird Man, as in the Britanitarkan vision, if one were seeking a coherence between these various myths.

62 Manderson outlines the mythic dimensions of law and our entry into them as we become civilised beings: see Manderson (2003). As he notes:

> [Myth] provides us with a frame of reference that allows us to draw recognizable patterns of meaning from the jumbled world around us. It is a means of orientation in the world, and ... constitute[s] our relationships, to ourselves, to others, and to institutions.
> Manderson (2003), p 90

See also Fitzpatrick (1992).

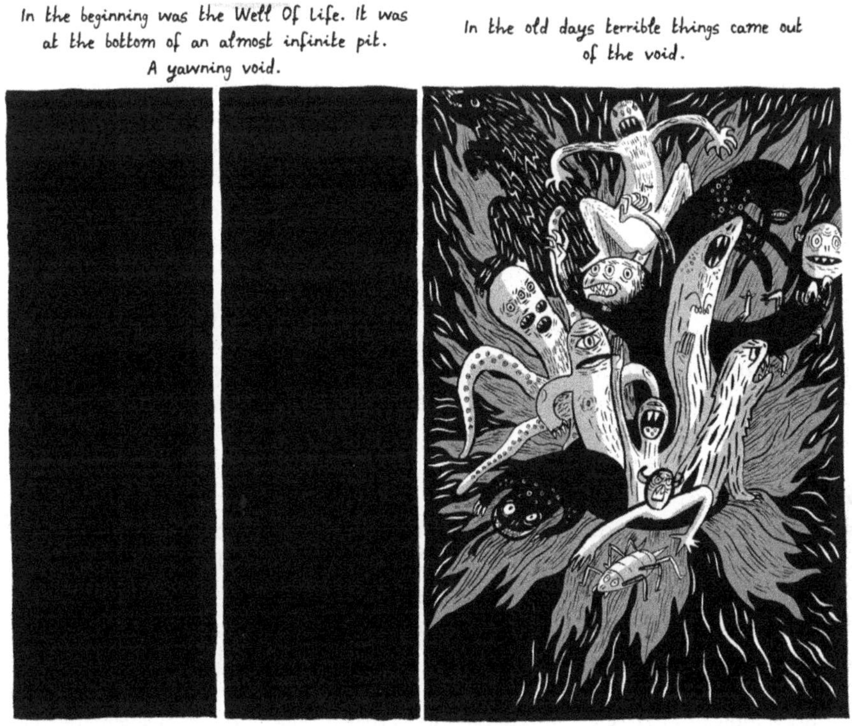

Figure 6.5 Greenberg (2013), np. © Isabel Greenberg. Reproduced with permission.[63]

cartographies and declarative appearances. For a ghostless machine that is grounded in its own denial of origins, such an interdiction is deeply significant; outside is irrational threat, the horror of infinity, and a rupturing complexity that cannot be quelled. But this move is precisely the one that cultural legal studies makes at its inception, and understanding the epistemological implications of this 'going beyond' is what a cultural legal *aesthetics* is all about. Greenberg's work suggests that the comics form – in its multimodality, in the peripatetic journey of the Storyteller between communal orders – can help us navigate such an unnerving removal of boundaries. In this, in its movement from map to myth to abyss, it is a microcosm of the preceding chapters of the current volume.

The demand not to go beyond embedded in Figure 6.1 is also encoded in another of Greenberg's maps, as seen in the first panel of Figure 6.6. This warning is not only reflected in the moving lines of the 'wild and unpassable' sea, but also in the uncertainty implied by the islands of 'Hoo', 'Wat', and 'Wen', the overt threat of dragons (repeated and linked with the blank beyond in the third panel, reminiscent of abyssal monsters and the dragon of unreason), and the 'Sea of

63 See Appendix B for a reproduction of the text in this figure.

Nowhere', a literal no-place at the edge of the map. In light of the spectral insights of the previous chapter, this demand that we should not venture into the blankness beyond can be read as a denial not just of moving outside the current order, but of the haunting of that order that could signal its disintegration. To go beyond the edge of the world is not just to move into an alternate space, but to disintegrate the world itself and to enable access to the originary blankness upon which the alternative forms of the epistemic multiframe can be inscribed. To move between orders, as the multimodality of comics demands, is to undermine their solidity and claims as true representations of reality; it is to open the epistemological cracks and see the haunting of the mask – the multiframe of plurivocal masks – of knowing. Accordingly, in the declarative image of Figure 6.1, as a juridical cartography depicted in comics form, we glimpse beyond the horizon of Migdal Bavel to the abyss within and from which the world was created, the infinite potential of spectral chaos.

In Figure 6.6 *Early Earth* works to problematise the closed world of Migdal Bavel and the epistemological blinkering it implies. When the Storyteller arrives from Nord from beyond the edge of the world in the final panel, he represents a deeply critical challenge to the very knowledge upon which Bavellian government and law is built. The Storyteller is a physical manifestation of what exceeds the map; a walking, talking, animated symbol of Panini's limits and perspectivism against his claims to objective truth, in his depiction literally emerging from the blank space beyond the edge of world. The critical vision of Mancini Panini's mapmaking methods indicates that such an interdiction as that of Figure 6.1 is problematic. The world that it says we should not question or reconfigure is not whole and complete, but is based upon a particular mechanism of knowing that cannot access the full reality of the universe, as symbolised by the unreliability of the genius monkeys. Legal knowledge maps – *knows* – the world, and legal maps are but one of many sets of possible configurations amidst the complex and haunted multiframe of knowing. This 'mapping' undertaken by law as it encounters and codifies human life fills the originary blankness upon which law is written, extending lines and symbols over the uncharted surface – and literally over the blank pages of law reports and journal articles – as it constitutes the world through text. As these continents and archipelagos emerge, something is lost. There are genius monkeys in the system. Indeed, the very form in which Greenberg presents Migdal Bavel – that of comics – in its multimodality suggests precisely a 'going beyond' on both a formal and an epistemological level, and a concomitant engagement with the multiple forms of text and image that can seek to recapture, or at least signal, this loss.

The Mapmaker of Migdal Bavel's ultimate defence against the disruptive claims of the Storyteller (that he comes from beyond the map) are tied up with the legal order: he eventually makes the Storyteller sign a written statement that he is lying, and that Panini's maps are true, before forcing him out of the country, repressing him back beyond the edge of the map.[64] Here the law becomes the tool of its

64 Greenberg (2013), np.

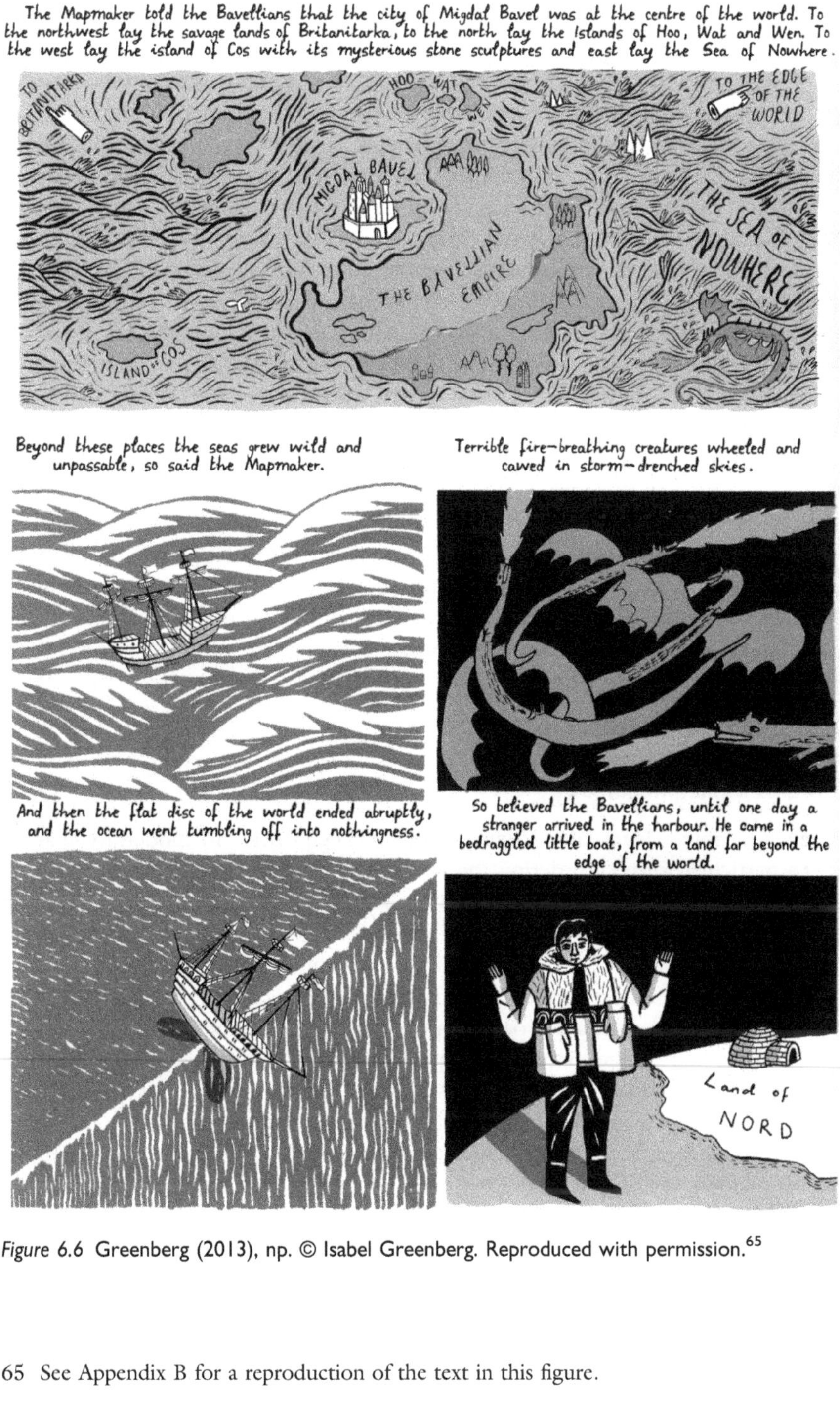

Figure 6.6 Greenberg (2013), np. © Isabel Greenberg. Reproduced with permission.[65]

65 See Appendix B for a reproduction of the text in this figure.

own affirmation: symbolic of the wholly internal system of black letter doctrine, it is only the law itself that can justify and explain the law. By embedding this well-worn critique within the multimodal field of the comics form, within a wider context of the interrogation of epistemic origins and the figuration of knowledge through critical cartography, Greenberg's work raises new challenges and opportunities for the form of legal discourse. Most notably, the complex and uncertain negotiation between text and image that is characteristic of many comics. As we have seen across this book, comics require us to move outside the boundary of any single map; to read the multimodal multiframe of any comics work, we have to traverse text and image, as well as the numerous appearances and absences, frames and borders, figures and non-figures, conscious forms and unconscious absences, that make up the work. Such a navigation opens us up to the multiframe of knowing itself. Reading comics is thus of high stakes: it requires the navigation not just of the boundary between reason and madness, between closure and openness, between absence and presence, but ultimately feeds right into the heart of questions over not only the appearance of knowledge – that is, of aesthetics – but of epistemic structures and disciplines in general. The multiframe of comics invokes the multiframe of knowing. And opening to this broad complexity, as we have seen that reading comics does, changes the form of law to render it more aware of its place within the economy of the epistemic multiframe. It is to this shift in the form of law that the final section now turns.

The haunted multiframe

Towards a multimodal law

As already noted, legal knowledge takes a privileged place in modernity. Law is also a particular form of ordering the world that produces concrete effects in the shaping of human life, delineating membership of the *nomos* as well as acceptable behaviours and relations with others. Understanding law – its form and function, as well as its epistemological grounding and limits – thus has profound significance. And so, whilst comics may enable a modelling and an engagement with plurivocal knowledges more broadly via the notion of the multiframe, it is to specifically legal knowledge that the remainder of this volume is dedicated – but this, of course, is a discussion that will necessarily also engage with comics' wider epistemological value, as well as its specific value in understanding law.

The aim here is to 're-form' law as multimodal, to re-imagine its appearance. Rather than delimiting a 'ghostless' conscious form and a rich unconscious of cultural legality, my argument has sought to remove such boundaries in order to assert that law has no limits, and thus let the richness and insight of cultural legal studies abound across legal realms. Such an expansion has been effected in previous chapters, from the ghostless machine of reason, via madness, the infinity of the cosmos, and the haunting sublime, to the conscious play of law's jurisdictional appearance against the pre-epistemic blankness. But we have nevertheless encountered limits to the formation of knowledge: blankness always haunts, it cannot be eradicated; there is always an unconscious. To make this journey meaningful – to give it a practical point, as a lawyer might desire – it is necessary that we begin to think through what a law without boundaries might look like, what form it might take. And it is my assertion, in line with the engagement with comics-as-*komos* that brought us here, that this re-imagined law should be multimodal. The basic justification is that multimodality, in its necessary shifting between orders and frames, remains 'in touch' with the unconscious inherent to all conscious forms. This has been indicated at a number of points already, but here we shall more fully elaborate this idea, through direct engagement with comics theory, in a legal context.

Encountering multimodality in comics has profound implications for understanding the multiple forms present in wider understanding and discourse. Although the relationship between text and image is not the only tension at play in comics – as the debates over its definition encountered in Chapter 1 indicated – the interaction of text and image remains largely emblematic of comics' multimodality. The specific relationships between text and image are thus of value in understanding the legal, as well as wider, significance of comics' multimodal appearance. The classic comics-practitioner analyses of Will Eisner and Scott McCloud argue for a shared origin and history of words and images that breaks down the boundary between the two when they come to operate together in the comics form[66] and arguably allows the medium to become a new form of communication (rather than a hybrid of pre-existing forms).[67] But conflations of word and image risk robbing understanding of the rich juxtapositions and tensions that the distinctions between text and image provide.[68] Moreover, not only are there potentially infinite ways that words and images can interact in comics,[69] conflating word and image in any context overlooks the differential conventions and ideologies that have arisen and developed around them.

On this point, WJT Mitchell's classic work *Iconology* excavates the cultural differences that are always present between forms of knowledge, with these differences constituting local systems of signs and symbols that come to reflect the value

66 Eisner (2008), pp 7–8; McCloud (1993), p 145.
67 See Giddens (2012), pp 89–91.
68 See, for example, Hatfield (2005), pp 33–67, who argues that the comics page is a field of tensions, not of unity, and meaning is produced through the reader's navigation of these tensions. Hannah Miodrag, through analysis of *Krazy Kat* and the works of Lynda Barry and Posy Simmonds, also demonstrates that comics can employ profoundly intricate literary devices and linguistic play that are lost through analyses that prioritise the image, or equalise image with text: see Miodrag (2013), pp 17–79. See also Giddens (2012), pp 93–95.
69 Such inability to completely stratify text-image in debates over the form's definition has led to reliance on such things as 'family resemblances' – see Varnum and Gibbons (2001) – and 'common sense' definitions along the lines of 'I know a comic when I see one' – see, for example, Harvey (2005). See also the debate on comics' definition in Chapter 1.

structures of a culture in relation to central philosophical and epistemic concerns,[70] including such profound questions as 'body and soul, world and mind, nature and culture'.[71] For example, certain kinds of images (photographs or 'realistic' paintings, for instance) are understood to be in some way transparent representations of empirical reality. In such empiricist notions, knowledge derives from a 'real', objective world via imagistic representation; true images represent the truth of reality, and philosophical ideas, expressed textually as verbal images, derive ultimately from actual images of the world (with such 'empirical' images then being in tension with the romantic structures of idealism, such as Kant's sublime).[72] Yet even the 'truest' images of the world (such as those held in photographs, or projected onto the retinas in our eyes) are products of mediating, mechanical systems that produce images in a particular way.[73] Like the hegemonic form of the map or of conscious law, the differential values attributed to various forms of knowing may reflect power relations as much as (or more than) 'reality':[74]

> The inverted images, whether in the eye or the camera obscura, are inverted, not by a simply physical mechanism of light, but by a 'historical life process', and they can be rectified only by a reconstruction of that process – that is, by a recounting of the material history of production and exchange that gives rise to them.[75]

By reconnecting images – particularly reified or abstracted images – to the history of their production, their status as 'a simple datum presented to the senses' can be radically challenged.[76] The same may be true of law, which 'functions by eliding its historical and material conditions of production and reception'.[77] The relationships between words and images, then, are not just technical pedantries or something to be glossed over in favour of a formal 'unity'. Mitchell's point is that they tap directly into questions over the articulation and reading of meaning, reflecting wider structures of value in the presentation of knowledge. Because of their textual-visual multimodality, such inquiry in the reading of comics thus necessarily unpacks the ideological baggage attached to law's hegemonic modes of knowing through rational texts.

It is the freeing-up from the detritus of the 'war-torn border between image and text'[78] that enables the ideological dimensions of text and image to be

70 Mitchell (1986).
71 Mitchell (1986), p 49.
72 Mitchell (1986), pp 23–25.
73 See Mitchell (1986), p 37.
74 See Mitchell (1986), pp 160–208.
75 Mitchell (1986), p 175.
76 Mitchell (1986), p 175.
77 Stewart (1991), p 19.
78 Mitchell (1986), p 154.

explored. But this suspension of the vying between text and image is not something that should be calm and settled; it should not be understood as:

> a matter for peaceful settlement under the terms of some all-embracing theory of signs, but as a struggle that carries the fundamental contradictions of our culture into the heart of theoretical discourse itself.[79]

In comics studies, this translates to the acceptance of ongoing and irresolvable tensions between words and images in the medium that opens up analysis to rich dimensions of meaning beyond the confines of any single necessary structure, and that reflect wider cultural conflicts. Indeed, the ideological battles engendered by and caught up in the debates over the relationships between text and image do not disappear just because we accept that words and pictures have a complex or irresolvable relationship. Rather, Mitchell's point is that we should understand, but ultimately move beyond, the 'surface' disputes: we should get over the formalities and recognise that different kinds of images, as well as language, 'are no more natural, automatic, or necessary than any other' form of representation.[80] Indeed, as Nick Sousanis observes, there are multiple alternative forms of knowledge;[81] thus, we do not need to abandon or unify textual and imagistic forms in order to access the world, but instead must recognise that they are each already informed by the world:[82] they are ways of knowing. And for Sousanis, opening up to multiple perspectives at once, as the multimodal form of comics enables, brings about deeper and renewed understanding.[83]

Importantly for understanding the place of comics in relation to law and public life, both words and images play their part in social reality and are not reducible to one another: 'Vision is as important as language in mediating social relations, and it is not reducible to language, to the "sign", or to discourse'.[84] Comics, as a medium, can thus be seen to circulate within and engage the high stakes of the ideological value attached to epistemic forms. Put into this wider socio-political context, its particular formal make-up, its multimodal multiframe, can be understood as a form of apparatus, or 'device'.[85] In applying it to comics, Harguindey summarises the apparatus as 'a network (*réseau*) of linguistic (speeches, laws, philosophical propositions) and non-linguistic elements (institutions, architectural installations) with a strategic role in power relations'.[86] He thereby invokes comics' multimodality in terms of the tensions between linguistic and non-linguistic elements, and moves further to expand the semiotic engagements with

79 Mitchell (1986), p 44.
80 Mitchell (1986), p 45.
81 See, for example, Sousanis (2015), pp 40, 136–137
82 Mitchell (1986), p 46.
83 Sousanis (2015).
84 Mitchell (2005), p 47.
85 Harguindey (2015).
86 Harguindey (2015), p 67.

form (as found, for example, in Groensteen's *dispositif spatio-topique*[87]) by linking them into the wider Foucaultian notion of apparatus. Accordingly:

> each device [apparatus] catalyzes a social, economic, and cultural circuit between production and consumption practices. Each device is a product of different agents (authors, publishers, distributors, retailers) whose nature and specific weight varies in determining it physically. Each device offers, although not predisposes, a different model of consumption, receptive practice and, ultimately, a community of readers with their own habits, values, and expectations.[88]

In light of Agamben's broad reading of the apparatus – that it is 'precisely … a set of strategies of the relations of forces supporting, and supported by, certain types of knowledge'[89] that enables activities of governance[90] – comics takes on the features of the wider ideological battleground unpacked by Mitchell as well as the tensions at play in the 'official' knowledge of government and law. The way we read the multimodality of comics can open a window onto cultural struggles over the wider production and presentation of knowledge, as well as the value placed on the form(s) of knowledge that are suitable for the important task of articulating lawful relations: in short, reading comics questions the form of law. In their multimodality, as well as their constitution of readerships, comics are a site where the form of knowledge is fought over, where the possible modes of epistemic being are engaged and played with, and the precarity of any singular form of knowing is made overt. It is in the epistemic peripatesis required by this multimodality that the multiframe of knowing – and its unconscious – becomes apparent. Thus, if we are to imagine a form of law that remains 'in touch' with its own position within the epistemic multiframe as well as the broader unconscious outside all knowing, a multimodal form is required.

But we need clarity on what we now mean by law's unconscious. We have removed the boundaries of conscious law to discover that there is always an unconscious to all forms of knowing – legal, cultural legal, aesthetic, scientific, and so on – in the form of the pre-epistemic blankness. If we consider all encounters with the chaotic infinity of the universe as a multiframe then we can identify two dimensions to the epistemological unconscious: first, the unconscious that is populated by all the infinite possible other frames and perspectives, what we might call 'other scenes' of knowing – the other frames of the multiframe; second, the deeper unconscious that is made up of the blankness of the pre-epistemic universe without the structures of the multiframe. The ghostless machine of conscious law represses the unconscious 'other frames' that cultural legal studies and other

87 See Groensteen (2007). I also discuss Groensteen's work in Chapter 1.
88 Harguindey (2015), p 69.
89 Agamben (2009), p 2.
90 Agamben (2009), p 11.

interdisciplinary legal works seek to engage and elaborate. By re-imagining law as multimodal, the relationships between different perspectives in the wider ecosystem of the multiframe can be acknowledged, opened, and engaged.

Once we shift our imaginary, it can clearly be seen that law is already multimodal. It involves written texts, for sure, but also oration and speech.[91] Courtrooms are filled with actors with defined roles, engaging in an embodied context within a physical – architectural,[92] spatial[93] – setting. Various legal actors wear costumes and specific forms of dress.[94] Lawyers regularly engage in visual presentations: to clients, to juries.[95] Indeed, cultural legal studies – in its particular focus on material culture – is precisely an engagement with law in its multimodal complexity. It is scholarship that recognises law beyond the confines of consciousness, in multiple frames of knowing that can be seen as clearly part of the broad multiframe of law. To the dimensions of the legal multiframe identified in Chapter 1 – the various framings of rules, sections, doctrines, and so on – we can clearly add these 'external' frames, expanding law – as a multiframe – in a way that removes any clear boundaries of traditional doctrinal consciousness. As a multiframe, as Sousanis describes it, we can see each 'frame' of legal understanding in relation, with 'multiple layers ... conveyed in unison', each with a 'distinct identity, while contributing to the whole', ultimately coming together 'in mutually affecting relationships'.[96]

And this legal multiframe is multimodal. But the multimodality of law can be identified even within the closed conscious arena of old-school doctrinal law, where the text is all there is and meaning must be derived from a purely 'internal' perspective. Of course, the interpretation and application of these texts (by lawyers, by judges) already goes beyond the text in ways that are embodied, theatrical, social, visual, and so on – as just noted, law is multimodal. But my point is that, even repressing those embodied, living dimensions of the institution revealed by cultural legal studies, the cold, doctrinal texts of law are themselves multimodal. In short, this is because as artefacts of language, doctrinal texts must still be encountered in a sensory context (i.e. reading).[97] Staying true to my claim that

91 See, for example, Parker (2015).
92 See, for example, Mulcahy (2011).
93 See, for example, Philippopoulos-Mihalopoulos (2014).
94 See, for example, Watt (2013).
95 See, for example, Sherwin (2000).
96 Sousanis (2015), p 65.
97 Critics amongst you may be thinking that such an embodied act of reading already goes beyond the pure doctrinal claim of law-as-text, thus undermining my claim to be demonstrating law's multimodality within a doctrinal frame. However, in many ways the difficulty or artificiality in discussing a law that is 'purely' text, in the abstract, shows how deeply ingrained in law multimodality is, as well as the problems of delineating any boundaries for conscious law: once we open up to the act of reading – as surely we must if we are to 'read' the doctrines of law at all – why not associated activities such as judging, advocating, and so on, and all the many aesthetic trappings they entail? The point here is rather to stay within a broadly doctrinal tradition of textual representation

it is through engagement with comics – as multimodal multiframes – that we can re-imagine law, in order to explain the multimodality of even 'plain text' it is to the relationships between comics and language that I turn.

As we have already seen, the tensions at play in comics are of high stakes in terms of querying the form of law. The argument over whether comics can be a language play precisely into this tension, arguably stemming from word-image tensions.

> The image is syntactically and semantically dense in that no mark may be isolated as a unique, distinctive character (like a letter of an alphabet) … Its meaning depends rather on its relations with all the other marks in a dense, continuous field … A differentiated symbolic system [such as linguistic text], by contrast, is not dense and continuous, but works by gaps and continuities.[98]

Understanding written language involves the decoding of discrete units or signs via the shared communal or cultural resources learnt by the reader; but the field of the image is continuous, with any particular mark or line only gaining meaning from its wider visual, cultural, and reading context. Hannah Miodrag accordingly argues for a fundamental structural difference between words and images in comics, such that they cannot occupy a single system of signification:[99] like the cyborg, comics resist a unitary structure. In the same vein, Barbara Postema states that 'the smallest elements of images have no set meanings, and the way these elements are combined or even repeated are not governed by rules like grammar'.[100] But Miodrag's point is that even these 'smallest elements' can never be identified as part of a general system of comics: the continuity of the visual field prevents any foundational or 'minimal unit' of signification from ever being found.[101]

It is possible to take issue with this distinctly structuralist perspective on the nature of language taken by analysts such as Miodrag and Postema. Neil Cohn, for example, highlights the fact that structuralist notions of linguistics have abated in the field of cognitive linguistics[102] – there are other frames of language beyond structuralism.[103] But despite scientific work such as Cohn's, and many comics scholars claiming to have determined foundational sets of common symbols,[104] there remains nothing in the image that is a transcendental 'minimal unit' of

and analysis that would see the wider contexts and appearances of law as outside what law is understood to be, and show that even this is multimodal.

98 Mitchell (1986), p 67, reading Nelson Goodman.

99 See Miodrag (2013).

100 Postema (2013), p xvi.

101 See Miodrag (2013), pp 221–245.

102 See Cohn (2014), p 59.

103 But ironically, whilst Cohn's work is valuable, it is generally quite problematic in its insistence on being the only 'true' way to understand reading, and the reading of comics in particular. See, for example, his quite vociferous arguments against any 'other frames' of linguistics and comics reading beyond his cognitive-scientific approach in Cohn (2014). And, for a sustained example of his work generally, see Cohn (2013).

104 See Miodrag (2013), pp 169–174.

meaning, as for example a word or letter might be in written language systems. Images are not made up of foundational and identifiable objective elements or relationships that transcend particular uses.[105] Put less structurally, there is no necessary meaning or mode of comprehension inherent to any particular image. Following this insight further, Miodrag expands the concept of the multiframe, arguing that comics are sets of 'infinitely nested' units, always co-present together on the surfaces of its (once blank) pages, with different levels of symbolic meaning to be picked out and examined – pages, panels, parts of images, particular sequences or series of panels, texts, and so on – with no limiting 'minimal' frame.[106] Hence the particularities of any expression of the comics form can be framed in potentially infinite ways, and such particularities signal the infinite complexities of the comics 'system' that cannot possibly be surveyed or exemplified in totality, and their return that ruptures the conceptualisation of the medium – an example of the Nietzschean sublime.

But this lack of necessary structure is also true of text: considered as something encountered through our senses, it becomes clear that the doctrinal texts of law are never encountered in an abstract form. As a phenomenon of communicating meaning, language is always mediated in some way, be it as a physical sound wave or as a visual depiction of the symbols of letters arranged into words and sentences.

> The eye is in speech since there is no articulated language without the exteriorization of a 'visible', but it is there because an exteriority exists which is at least gesticulatory, 'visible', deep within discourse, which is its expression.[107]

The textual expression of law – like its jurisdictional arrival – is visual. Although it is possible to conceive of a structure of language that has discrete foundational units or conventional systems of operation, the actual experience of encountering those units requires the decryption of visual or aural information – information that is, by its sensory nature, continuous rather than discrete, analogue rather than digital, aesthetic rather than purely rational, and thus exceeds any kind of comprehensive structuring or capture, remaining in some sense 'beyond'. Indeed, as we saw of comics in general in Chapter 3, there is a phenomenal or sensory dimension to the comics page that exceeds all structures.

105 David Mazzucchelli's *Asterios Polyp* is the example Miodrag uses to expound this point, as a comic that is fecund in its capacity for developing its own *ad hoc* system of symbolic units for articulation: see Miodrag (2013), pp 169–196. As Postema phrases it, 'comics [can] signal their own reading processes, creating and instructing new ways of signification as necessary': Postema (2013), p 116, and see generally pp 116–123. Neil Cohn also admits that visual language can construct its own 'minimal units', rather than having to rely on conventionalised ones: Cohn (2013), pp 21–22.
106 See Miodrag (2013), pp 221–245.
107 Lyotard (2010), p 8.

Although similar arguments could be made regarding spoken words,[108] what is important for seeing law as multimodal – even in its most closed doctrinal form – is the visual depiction of text. The elements of textual language can always be broken down into smaller constituent parts: the lines and dots that make up the text you are currently reading have no inherent meaning, but are dependent upon their visual context no less than their cultural setting and conventional associations to gain meaning. This is precisely the way in which the infinite variety of lines, colour, and markings that constitute an image have no inherent or unitary meaning, because text is visual in its presentation – it is already an image. Lyotard examines the experience of encountering written language, highlighting the instinctual or culturally ingrained way that readers suppress the physical-visual form of text:

> Reading is hearing, not seeing. The eye merely scans the written signals. The reader does not even capture the distinctive graphic units: she or he does not see the misprints. Rather, the reader selects the significative units … The reader does not see what she or he reads, striving instead to hear the meaning of what the absent speaker – the author of the text – 'meant to say'.[109]

To pay attention to the form of law, then, is to be distracted from its structure(s) of signification, the general systems of linguistic communication that law rests on. This involves the exertion of effort to overcome the cultural and educational conditioning that teaches us to ignore form when reading.[110] The lines that construct the letters of this written text only become 'line' at the point they break out of or elude the structures and grammatical formalities of linguistic comprehension.[111] Lyotard thus suggests that the visuality of the page brings with it more than just an alternative mode of meaning-making, but a realm of figuration beyond any distinctly linguistic or grammatical structure. As the texts of doctrine, law always exceeds its own structures insofar as it is encountered in a continuous, sensory context: that is, invariably. Upon recognising this inherent visuality of text, as encounter with the multimodal form of comics demands, on one level the Nietzschean sublime is invoked and the general structures of language are shattered. Put multimodally, by forcing us to move between different orders of knowing, different modes of communicating, comics exposes these multiple conventions and conceptual structures – that is, these multiple normative orders of knowledge – to the repressed other scenes of knowing that haunt. Just as the

108 The argument related to linguistic sound-forms might go along the following lines: the analogue nature of sound means that any particular aural element has no inherent meaning outside of its wider context as part of a spoken word and/or as part of linguistic communication.

109 Lyotard (2010), p 211.

110 Lyotard (2010), p 212. And note again the way legal training focuses on doctrinal reading at the expense of creativity and imagination discussed in Chapter 1: see Webster (2013).

111 Lyotard (2010), pp 212–214.

emergence of the Storyteller from beyond the boundary brings a radical threat to the authority of Panini's maps, this movement reveals the precarity of single forms as neutral or natural expressions of 'truth'.

In this movement between orders, and the concomitant exposure of the precarity of those orders, what is ultimately encountered is the saturated chaos of the universe. The comics medium is not just a meeting ground for text and image, nor just reason, aesthetics, layout, materiality, and so on. Rather, comics – as *komos* – can be seen to mediate between the disorder of the unstructured universe and the multiple structures of knowing. In imagining law as multimodal, the shifting between epistemic modes that perhaps seems so threatening to the conscious practicality of law (as we explored in Chapter 3) becomes part of how law operates, just as in reading comics we take part in the wider circuitry of knowing. In concomitantly bringing forth the deeper unconscious of the abyss, the function of the *komos* is also at play: mediating the chaos of infinity and the formation of epistemic frames that necessarily repress the beyond, screening it off. As *komos*, the multiframe thus opens up and allows high-stakes play with multiple forms of knowledge and modes of representation, ultimately mediating between order and disorder, knowing and chaos, conscious form and unconscious potential. It enables a law that is never unitary, never takes a single form, but is compound – cyborg – in its constitution as an interconnected and nested relation between multiple frames, existing in relation to the wider infinity of 'other frames' to which it is also connected. And behind or beyond it all, like the gaps surrounding the multiple frames on a comics page, like the *anima* amidst the universal network – the infinite, unknowable potential of the blank space.

Into the Dreaming

The multiframe has no minima; my claims regarding knowledge as a multiframe suggest that it also has no maxima. The multiframe can be extended outwards, linking and connecting with other frames, nested in the broader haunted multiframe of knowing: comics everywhere.[112] The idea of knowledge as a multiframe thus becomes more than a suggestion that the comics form can be understood as a metaphor for knowledge, but instead asserts the structure of the multiframe as something that extends to connect all forms knowledge as well as the frames on a comics page. In order to elaborate this much-expanded idea of the multiframe, which extends far beyond the traditional confines of a comics work (i.e. the printed volume), I turn to Neil Gaiman's *The Sandman*.[113]

112 As Ernesto Priego stated in the opening quotation of Chapter 1, once you start looking, 'comics appear everywhere': Priego (2014), np.

113 See Appendix A for an overview and details of this work.

The pivot and fulcrum around which the rhapsodic epic of *Sandman* revolves is the character of Dream. One of the Endless,[114] he has many names: Morpheus, Dream King, Lord Shaper, Sandman, Kai'Ckul, Onieros, the Prince of Stories – he is the Lord of Dreams, King of the realm of the Dreaming. This in itself is indicative of the multiple framings suggested by the multiframe of knowing. In the short stand-alone episode called 'The Castle', in which an unknown dreamer chances upon the Dream King's citadel home in the heart of the Dreaming, we see Morpheus reaching out to the viewer as he invites us to remain in the world of dreams: 'But you have seen very little, mortal dreamer. Would you like to stay longer?'[115] For the Dreaming is a place where there are many things to learn, and – as I will argue – there is always another frame to be opened.

As we are told by that other master of dreaming, Sigmund Freud, 'Dreams … are not meaningless';[116] they can be interpreted – moreover, can be interpreted as more than the mere somatic processing of random sensory data or as an insignificant fragment of the brain's activities.[117] The broad point of Freud's work in *The Interpretation of Dreams* is that dreams are an expression of (and for the analyst are thus are a way of accessing) aspects of the unconscious.[118] In its focus on the mythical figure of Dream, *Sandman* is thus from inception linked up with the unconscious. Following the psychoanalytical connection to dreams, it is Freud's notions of interpretation, expanded and elaborated via the work of Didi-Huberman and Lyotard, that will help us understand the connections between the frame(s) of *Sandman* and the infinite multiframe of knowing.

Sandman also connects explicitly to law. Dreams, Freud tells us, are wish fulfilments. As a work of comics, throughout *Sandman* text and image are co-present, inscribed in the same space; more than indicating the visuality of text, as we have already discussed, this co-presence also moves us toward desire. As Lyotard indicates:

> It is written in the same space as something else, in this case an image. Now the topical unity of writing and scene indicate that the text, having taken up a position on the same plane as the image, will submit to the strictures of that plane and betray the strictures of writing. By this simple placing of the inscription, we pass from linguistic space, that of *reading*, where one *hears*, to visual space, that of painting, where one *looks*. The eye no longer listens, it desires.[119]

114 *Sandman*'s Endless are personifications of a number foundational – and alliterative – human concepts: Destiny, Death, Dream, Destruction, Desire, Despair, and Delirium (who was once Delight).
115 'The Castle' in Gaiman et al (2012), np.
116 Freud (1997), p 147.
117 Freud (1997), pp 121–145.
118 Note his maxim: '*The interpretation of dreams is the royal road to a knowledge of the unconscious activities of the mind*': Freud (1997), p 604. Emphasis in original.
119 Lyotard (2010), pp 263–264. Emphases in original.

Freud draws out the ubiquitous presence of desire within dream-thoughts, linking it with the processes available to us in the childhood state to which we generally regress as we dream: direct associations between a need, a desire or wish, and the fulfilment of that wish, through the presentation as a dream of a sensory image we have associated with the satisfaction of our needs.[120] To dream is to fulfil a wish – to desire.[121] Lyotard thus suggests that the co-presence of text and image places us in the realm of dreams. In *Sandman*, Dream's function is to give shape to the chaos of the dreamstuff, suggesting that knowledge and form is what is desired. Dream thus represents the desire for order, for a knowable node of control over our inner uncertainties, our desires and instincts.[122] Moreover, Dream is associated with justice and judgment. To give a few examples: Dream sentences a man to madness for the imprisonment and repeated rape of one of the classical muses;[123] in his past, he had sentenced to Hell a lover who wronged him;[124] and, in the very first issue, in which Dream is captured and unable to fulfil his onieric functions, he sentences his captor to an eternal nightmare.[125] Indeed, as the Dream King he is the sovereign ruler of the Dreaming, and is bound by various rules and agreements with other beings. He thus represents a desire for justice. But, in his function as the Lord Shaper, he mediates between formation and the chaos of the raw dreamstuff, indicating a justice that is caught in a tension between kingly order and onieric disorder: a *komos* that mediates between order and chaos, formation and potential. *Sandman*, with co-present text and image, is thus precisely a dream of justice.

The structuring of dreams indicated by the work of Dream – his fulfilment of the desire for order and justice – connects further with Freud's work. A key distinction Freud lays out is that between the manifest content of a dream, and its

120 See Freud (1997), pp 550–571, especially 564–567.

121 Although, as siblings, Dream and Desire rarely see eye-to-eye, *Sandman* makes it clear that the order of appearance of the Endless at the outset of the universe places Dream ahead of Desire: beings were dreaming before they were desiring, thus indicating that one cannot have a wish that needs fulfilment without being able to dream. That is, one cannot desire without dreaming.

122 Freud himself hints at a further, deeper level of meaning in dreams that stems back from the subjective dream-thoughts (very often derived from childhood) into a collective and innate psychic structure of humanity:

> dreaming is on the whole an example of regression into the dreamer's earliest condition, a revival of his childhood, of the instinctual impulses which dominated it and the methods of expression which were then available to him ... a picture of the development of the human race, of which the individual's development is in fact an abbreviated recapitulation ... we may [thus] expect that the analysis of dreams will lead us to a knowledge of man's archaic heritage, of what is psychically innate in him.
>
> Freud (1997), p 550

123 See 'Calliope' in Gaiman et al (2010a).

124 See, notably, 'Episode 8' in Gaiman et al (2010b).

125 See the tellingly titled 'Sleep of the Just' in Gaiman et al (1991).

latent content that psychoanalytical interpretation can bring to awareness.[126] It is latent meaning that brings forth Freud's method of interpretation that goes 'beyond the surface' of what is immediately presented, tracing associations and resemblances that enable a 'deeper' or symbolic meaning to be encountered. For Freud, this is a route to the unconscious, but it requires an unpacking of the processes that produced the dream. Freud's concept of the 'dream-work' represents the structure of the mental processes of dreaming, and these are distinct from the dream content. The dream-work is the way latent dream thoughts are processed into manifest presentations in dreams: literally, the work done to produce the dream. Like Morpheus's creations in the Dreaming, the dream-work gives shape and structure to the raw materials of dreams.

The dream-work has particular processes for Freud, from which dream images are produced and that arguably account for many of the assumptions of illogicality and randomness with respect to the sleeping mind.[127] But dreams are not meaningless, representing instead a particular kind of mental activity, which Freud believed had real therapeutic benefit. And it is through the tracing back from manifest content to latent, unconscious thoughts, that this benefit becomes manifest. In our epistemological frame, the central point here is that dreams represent an order of understanding different from that of the waking mind; an order that permits movement beyond immediate forms, and thus – it is my claim – expands comics reading into a wider multiframe of knowing. As a dream of justice, Morpheus and the Dreaming over which he presides are, in a legal context, symbolic of this order of knowledge signified by dreams. Hence elements of conscious legal knowing might be unpacked and re-examined, thereby exposing repressed 'other scenes' of knowing. In this sense, *Sandman* indicates that cultural and interdisciplinary legal studies can be understood as a psychoanalysis of law, bringing the other scenes of law's unconscious to light. But it is my broader claim that the haunting epistemological unconscious brings with it the possibility of interpretation without end: a potentially bottomless process of re-framing that traverses the entire breadth of knowing. Thus, as part of this multiframe, law becomes boundless.

Freud himself, of course, was working out a clinical tool, to be employed in a utilitarian context towards a concrete therapeutic end – the diagnosis and treatment of his patients. But Freud's work has profound ramifications beyond this environment of analytical closure. Much of what is discussed in *The Interpretation of Dreams* is precisely the process of interpretation, of how or whether we are able to reach the 'true meaning' of a dream. Freud's work has thus been applied directly in discourses on our encounters with images and language. Georges Didi-Huberman warns that images are always more than simple analytical objects that

126 See Freud (1997), pp 160–188.

127 See Freud (1997), pp 296–363, noting in particular the way dream images can represent multiple different unconscious thoughts through the distortion produced by the censorship of the conscious mind – for example, displacement: Freud (1997), pp 322–326. On the function of censorship generally, see in particular Freud's chapter on 'Distortion in Dreams': Freud (1997), pp 159–185.

can be accessed and fully understood via rational empiricism; he claims there is something negative in the image that undermines its own certainty and challenges its ability to be fully understood or captured in interpretation.[128] In approaching the image we must account for this core of ineffability[129] by recognising the role that the unconscious plays within the image, and thus as part of our experience of the image. And what applies to images, of course, also applies to text as something mediated via a sensory visual encounter – highlighted by the comics form of *Sandman*, where an inscription alongside an image is 'a kind of non-writing ... to be seen, not read'.[130]

Didi-Huberman notes that the processes of Freud's dream-work also produce new forms: the dream-work is 'both formation *and* distortion'.[131] Indeed, the dream-work requires particular forms of representation,[132] and thus the figuration that takes place within dreams is not simple representation, but involves the reconfiguration of forms, a distortion constrained by the features of figuration available in dreams[133] – a shaping, as the title 'Lord Shaper' implies. Freud's statement that the dream-work 'does not think, calculate or judge at all'[134] thus highlights the fact the dream-work does not operate in the same way as waking thoughts or conscious law, but rather is the thing that enables the forms within dreams to take shape.[135] As Lyotard highlights, it is not the content of the dream that is its essence, but the enabling structure of the dream-work.[136] Moreover:

> when we look into the dream's ways of figuration, we understand better why it proves pointless to distinguish what belongs to language from what belongs to the visible: ... [the dream figure resists] pure and simple visibility of a 'figurative' representation.[137]

This indicates that the lacuna Didi-Huberman argues is embedded in the image also lingers in the form of text. As Lyotard phrases it, the text 'has something trembling trapped within it'.[138] Didi-Huberman presents this uncertainty within the figuration of the dream-work as a rend, claiming that it opens the dream figure – which is neither text nor image – to infinite digressions and asides, to the tumbling associations of the unconscious, expanding meaning beyond any closed or ultimate representation:[139] 'it triggers the infinite process of the tangent that is

128 Didi-Huberman (2005), pp 142–143.
129 Didi-Huberman (2005), pp 143–144.
130 Lyotard (2010), p 264.
131 Didi-Huberman (2005), p 155. Emphasis in original.
132 Freud (1997), p 354.
133 Didi-Huberman (2005), pp 153–154.
134 Freud (1997), p 351.
135 See Lyotard (2010), pp 234–235.
136 Lyotard (2010), p 234.
137 Didi-Huberman (2005), p 154.
138 Lyotard (2010), p 9.
139 Didi-Huberman (2005), p 154.

a fundamental characteristic of the very notion of [the Freudian] figure'.[140] Despite his clinical project, Freud himself explicitly understands this potential for infinite tracing of associations, and calls it 'the dream's navel, the spot where it reaches down into the unknown':

> The dream-thoughts to which we are led by interpretation cannot, from the nature of things, have any definite endings; they are bound to branch out in every direction in the intricate network of our world of thought.[141]

But there is, of course, a difference between the formation of knowledge and the formation of dreams. 'We see them [visual forms] with open eyes, but this may be what hinders us and makes us miss something in them'.[142] There is a tension at play between the content and the appearance of a visual form, a rend or 'scission' between its representational features and its appearance. And in this rend 'something is at work that I cannot grasp … because I am not dreaming'.[143] Recognising this divide, Didi-Huberman shows us that this inability to perceive the visual fully without closing one's eyes from wakefulness – from conscious orders of knowing – becomes the 'vanishing point' towards the 'oblivion' outside rational knowledge.[144] Moreover, this 'sleeping' dimension upsets our customary waking relation to visuality: it is an eruption of the unconscious, a psychoanalytic symptom.[145] This symptom, as an expression of the unconscious and not just the 'less visible' aspects of a form, is outside any position within consciousness and knowledge,[146] and thus means that full, codified (waking) knowledge is impossible.[147]

> [T]he opening to the symptom gives us access to something like an *unthinkable* that comes before our very eyes … The residue of a conflict the sum total of whose ins and outs we will never know, the return of a repressed whose every name we will never be able to decline with exactitude, at once formation and distortion … It is here that the fabric will have encountered the event of its rending.[148]

There is an oscillation between 'figuration' and 'disfiguration'; between our ability to see something, to 'grasp worlds' in it and pursue the infinite associations that lead to the vast epistemic multiframe, and its collapse[149] as the spectrality of the

140 Didi-Huberman (2005), p 154.
141 Freud (1997), p 528.
142 Didi-Huberman (2005), p 156.
143 Didi-Huberman (2005), p 156.
144 Didi-Huberman (2005), pp 157–158.
145 Didi-Huberman (2005), p 158.
146 Didi-Huberman (2005), pp 162–170.
147 Didi-Huberman (2005), pp 170–182.
148 Didi-Huberman (2005), p 182. Emphasis in original.
149 Didi-Huberman (2005), p 228.

Nietzschean sublime takes hold. We thus encounter 'an obstacle and its endless hollowing … as if facing something that conceals itself'.[150]

Legal texts, as visual forms, thus contain an unknowability that is in constant tension with our presumed ability to decipher them in their entirety. Written text makes present that which we cannot reach, the infinite possibility of meaning and association that sucks us down into the endless associations of the unconscious. It is thus spectral: the presence of visuality brings with it the absence of knowing, the absent presence of unknowability, the haunting ineffability that permeates all forms. The multiple formations of knowing – the epistemic multiframe – thus become embedded with the oscillations of the unconscious, between endless possible alternative frames and the unknowable chaos of infinity that lies beyond the multiframe. The rend of Freud's navel is the return of other scenes of knowing alongside this deeper ineffability of the blank space; the *revenance* of the infinite potential of the multiframe and of the pre-epistemic abyss, the dual infinity of what we might call the distinctly epistemological unconscious.

We thus begin to approach a reading of *Sandman* that demonstrates the lack of any maximum limit to the multiframe. Dream invariably speaks via his characteristic black speech bubbles, with his text figured in white. This blackness, understood as signalling the unstructured abyss before and outside knowledge, explicitly brings forth the spectre of the epistemological unconscious. All of Dream's speech is rendered in this way, and although all major characters in *Sandman* have their own distinctive typography linked with their nature,[151] Dream is the only one to explicitly speak from the abyss itself, to have his textual figures presented directly over the fantastic beyond in such an overt way that foregrounds the blankness it seeks to cover up. In this way, the appearance of Dream's speech is reminiscent of Legendre's protective screen,[152] as well as the hum of discourse with which we began (and continue) the textual presentation of this chapter, and indicates the wider masking of the beyond that can be seen in any figuration of text over a blank background – that is, *inter alia*, any statute, judgment, journal article, or legal theory monograph – as well as the general haunted mask of the epistemic multiframe.

To return to Dream's invitation to remain in the Dreaming in 'The Castle', mentioned above: in that encounter he states the following:

> But you have seen very little, mortal dreamer. Would you like to stay longer? / After all, there are a thousand thousand other sights to see here in the dreaming. And many things to learn …[153]

The longer we stay, the more we learn. The Dreaming, as Didi-Huberman's analysis tells us, is a world where meaning goes on forever, where the infinite potential

150 Didi-Huberman (2005), p 228.
151 On the way text's visuality can accent meaning in comics, see, for example, Postema (2013), pp 82, 84.
152 See Legendre (1998).
153 'The Castle' in Gaiman et al (2012), np.

of the blank space is continuously shaped and formed by the Dream King whose words appear directly over the abyss itself. The stuff of the universe can be endlessly shaped, knowledge is a tumbling cascade of creation, a multiframe endlessly wrought from the chaos of an existence we can never fully access or capture, restlessly repressing the epistemological unconscious in different ways to allow multiple conscious formations of knowing to appear. And comics, as a multimodal encounter that opens up to dreaming, invokes this broad epistemological mediation – this *komos*.

Any particular panel frame from *Sandman*, and the infinite nested frames within it (of text, image elements, colour, and so forth), is part of the frame of the page it sits within, as well as the frame of the story and wider volume of *Sandman* from which it is taken, including frames made up of atemporal and braided elements. But, in light of the preceding discussion, interpretation can go further – infinitely so. Thus, we can imagine a frame that includes all published issues of *Sandman*. Or one that also includes associated works, or all works written by Neil Gaiman, or all work by the same artist, or lettered by Todd Klein. The material frame of the work may also extend to the bound volume, to the material and cultural history of its publication, of comics publication more generally, of the history of the book; it might extend to its embodied reading, to the lived context of its reading, and the genealogy of the family of the person reading it, to the history of civilisation, and so on. As part of a wider tradition of comics reception, and the constitution of readerships as discussed above, a *Sandman* panel would take its place within a broad socio-cultural frame. Or, in reading *Sandman*, we might be undertaking certain cognitive processes, which would thus include it within the same frame as, for example, the work of Neil Cohn, or the frames of reading such as Miodrag's and Postema's. *Sandman* can also be framed as a dream of justice, and as indicating the profound ineffability that is embedded in the texts of law that are always mediated through their visual appearance. *Sandman* could equally be placed within a broad frame that traces the history of visual personifications of mythic concepts, or in a frame that also includes the psychoanalytic work of Sigmund Freud on dreams. Like many of these example frames, of course, the work of Freud can also occupy other frames that do not include any element of *Sandman*. Thus we can see how the multiframe has no maximum element: each of these frames are multiframes in themselves, nested with infinite other frames that overlap and intersect it, as well as being linked into the wider multiframe of yet more 'other frames' that can be pursued, without end.

Because interpretation is infinite it can always be re-framed, and thus the multiframe is also infinite. The multiframe is opened to a bottomless formation of endless expansion and reduction – an endless variation of scale, to return to our cartographic metaphor – that signifies the ultimate unknowability of the universe. Because this process is infinite, it encompasses both the endless 'other scenes' of the multiframe, but also the deeper unconscious of the unknowable blankness of the chaotic universe. To unpack an object of reading and encounter its rend, its opening to infinite potential, is to peer into Freud's navel, to gaze down into the irreducible complexity of the unconscious. Through analysis of classical legal emblems, Peter Goodrich presents this as an opening to the eternal, to the divine author of law,[154] but in terms of cultural legal aesthetics this movement becomes the transcendence of the boundaries of conscious law, the joyful expansion of juristics into the infinite world beyond the unitary frame of rational text. That is, to open legal discourse to an endless shifting amidst the complexity of the multi-frame, and to acknowledge the saturated blankness beyond all knowing.

It is not just the visuality of *Sandman*, or the manifest content of Dream himself, that brings forth the unconscious – but the co-presence of multiple forms together. In *Sandman* it becomes apparent that comics, perhaps more readily than images (if we can distinguish them), open up to this epistemological unconscious. In a multimodal law, the text becomes part of the visual field – more accurately, it is always already open to the visual field insofar as it appears visually (that is, invariably – even in doctrinal contexts). This opening to the visual field, as Lyotard's reference to desire indicates, is also an opening to the dream-work, to the unconscious, to the bottomless connections of the multiframe and its ineffable other. As Goodrich argues (taking film credits as his contemporary example, alongside the classical emblemata of law), it is the point text becomes image that it opens words to the infinite.[155] In comics, text is directly presented alongside image, discourse alongside figure – and reading involves traversing the two, shifting between epistemic orders as we also shift between localised elements of the multiframe. Goodrich's emblematic analysis focuses on the liminal point where the visuality of text becomes apparent, the threshold between word and image. Balancing the excess of the sensory image against the closure of the linguistic text in legalistic reading, he positions the image as a mediating point between the two: it 'mediates between discourse and figure, text and subject, word and action';[156] it is 'the mediator of word and sense through which the text opens to vision'.[157] Recognising the visuality of text, as a multimodal law does, opens even doctrinal legality to the dual infinity of the epistemological unconscious. The co-presence of multiple modes of presentation – that is, multimodality – links law into the infinite ecosystem of the multiframe, of alternative orders of knowing and its mediation of universal disorder as *komos*. Thus 'law, is never precisely how it appears'.[158] It is always *more* – and *always* more.

Dream's invitation to remain in the Dreaming invites us to fall forever, to plumb the bottomless depths of meaning, of the epistemological unconscious, not only in its linguistic content, nor merely in the inviting pose of Dream with hand outstretched as he states his question in 'The Castle',[159] nor even just in the fact the figure of Dream is a symbol of dreaming itself and its associated whirlpool to

154 See Goodrich (2018).
155 See Goodrich (2018).
156 Goodrich (2018), p 67.
157 Goodrich (2018), p 70.
158 Goodrich (2018), p 72.
159 See 'The Castle' in Gaiman et al (2012), np.

the unconscious – but in all of these, and moreover again in *Sandman*'s very formal construction, in its very presence as a multimodal medium that employs text and image within its many dimensions that we must traverse as readers. By meditating on this complex multimodal boundary, by employing and deploying various features and dimensions in unison and in tension, comics exposes rational text to the dual infinity of the epistemological unconscious, of the other to waking thought and the endless interconnected frames of knowing. Like law, the medium is always already more than its conceptualised structures or its constituent parts, as its parts are always already more than their perceptible surface, always integrated into an unending cascade of frames.

Law's texts are infused with the dreaming, haunted by the unconscious. They are part of the complex multiframe of law, but also the broader multiframe of knowing – interconnected, boundless. Comics are not just the combination of multiple forms and dimensions, but are also the effect of that combination – the opening of the cracks in the system, the seeing through the surface, the exposure of the fantastic beyond and the infinite abyss outside knowing, as well as the processes by which that beyond is mediated into the forms of the multiframe. And that beyond haunts the multiframe as that which it is not, as that which is repressed to enable its infinite distinct-yet-interconnected emergences and affirmations, but which appears whenever frames are traversed. Comics-as-*komos* navigates a zone between waking and dreaming, between reason and madness, knowing and chaos, closeness and infinity, thereby opening up the presentation and structure of knowledge to its absence. For law, comics are more than the practical suggestion that images have their place in legal relations and discourse, but that the very form of that discourse – of any discourse – masks an infinity it can only make present as an absence. And, as a mask, law's multiframe is necessarily haunted by that infinity, as it is by its endless alternative frames, with the spectre always bringing with it the potential for law's reformation.

References

Giorgio Agamben (2009) 'What Is an Apparatus?' in *What Is an Apparatus? And Other Essays*, Stanford University Press.

Olivia Barr (2015) 'A Jurisprudential Tale of a Road, an Office, and a Triangle' 27 *Law and Literature* 199.

Irus Braverman (2010) 'Hidden in Plain View: Legal Geography from a Visual Perspective' 7 *Law, Culture and the Humanities* 173.

Michael Brown and Larry Knopp (2008) 'Queering the Map: The Productive Tensions of Colliding Epistemologies' 98 *Annals of the Association of American Geographers* 40.

Jerome Bruner (2002) *Making Stories: Law, Literature, Life*, Harvard University Press.

Neil Cohn (2013) *The Visual Language of Comics: Introduction to the Structure and Cognition of Sequential Images*, Bloomsbury.

Neil Cohn (2014) 'Building a Better "Comic Theory": Shortcomings of Theoretical Research on Comics and How to Overcome Them' 5 *Studies in Comics* 57.

Robert M Cover (1983) 'Foreword: Nomos and Narrative' 97 *Harvard Law Review* 4.

Jeremy W Crampton (2001) 'Maps as Social Constructions: Power, Communication and Visualization' 25 *Progress in Human Geography* 235.
Neal Curtis (2017) 'The Law of Doom: Spaces of Sovereignty in Marvel's *Secret Wars*' 7 *The Comics Grid: Journal of Comics Scholarship* 9.
Georges Didi-Huberman (2005) *Confronting Images: Questioning the Ends of a Certain History of Art*, Pennsylvania State University Press.
Jason Dittmer (2010) 'Comic Book Visualities: A Methodological Manifesto on Geography, Montage and Narration' 35 *Transactions of the Institute of British Geographers* 222.
Shaunnagh Dorsett and Shaun McVeigh (2012) *Jurisdiction*, Routledge.
Shaunnagh Dorsett and Shaun McVeigh (2014) 'Jurisprudences of Jurisdiction: Matters of Public Authority' 23 *Griffith Law Review* 569.
Will Eisner (2008) *Comics and Sequential Art: Principles and Practices from the Legendary Cartoonist*, WW Norton.
Peter Fitzpatrick (1992) *The Mythology of Modern Law*, Routledge.
Jill M Fraley (2010) 'Images of Force: The Power of Maps in Community Development' 46 *Community Development Journal* 421.
Sigmund Freud (1997) *The Interpretation of Dreams*, Wordsworth.
Neil Gaiman et al (1991) *The Sandman: Preludes and Nocturnes*, Titan Books.
Neil Gaiman et al (2010a) *The Sandman: Dream Country*, DC Comics.
Neil Gaiman et al (2010b) *The Sandman: Season of Mists*, DC Comics.
Neil Gaiman et al (2012) *The Sandman: The Kindly Ones*, DC Comics.
Thomas Giddens (2012) 'Comics, Law, and Aesthetics: Towards the Use of Graphic Fiction in Legal Studies' 6 *Law and Humanities* 85.
Peter Goodrich (1999) 'The Iconography of Nothing: Blank Spaces and the Representation of Law in *Edward VI and the Pope*' in C Douzinas and L Nead (eds) *Law and the Image: The Authority of Art and the Aesthetics of Law*, University of Chicago Press.
Peter Goodrich (2008) 'Visive Powers: Colours, Trees and Genres of Jurisdiction' 2 *Law and Humanities* 213.
Peter Goodrich (2018) 'Faces and Frames of Government' in D Manderson (ed) *Law and the Visual: Representations, Technologies, and Critique*, Toronto University Press.
Isabel Greenberg (2013) *The Encyclopedia of Early Earth*, Jonathan Cape.
Thierry Groensteen (2007) *The System of Comics*, University Press of Mississippi.
Breixo Harguindey (2015) 'The Order of Comics: Dynamics of the Ninth Art's Devices' in J Cañero and E Claudio (eds) *On the Edge of the Panel: Essays in Comics Criticism*, Cambridge Scholars Publishing.
Robert C Harvey (2005) 'Describing and Discarding "Comics" as an Impotent Act of Philosophical Rigor' in J McLaughlin (ed) *Comics as Philosophy*, University Press of Mississippi.
Charles Hatfield (2005) *Alternative Comics: An Emerging Literature*, University Press of Mississippi.
Alan Hunt and Gary Wickham (1994) *Foucault and Law: Towards a Sociology of Law as Governance*, Pluto.
Rob Kitchin and Martin Dodge (2007) 'Rethinking Maps' 31 *Progress in Human Geography* 331.
Pierre Legendre (1998) 'The Other Dimension of Law' in P Goodrich and DG Carlson (eds) *Law and the Postmodern Mind*, University of Michigan Press.
Jean-François Lyotard (2010) *Discourse, Figure*, University of Minnesota Press.

Desmond Manderson (2000) *Songs without Music: Aesthetic Dimensions of Law and Justice*, University of California Press.
Desmond Manderson (2003) 'From Hunger to Love: Myths of the Source, Interpretation, and Constitution of Law in Children's Literature' 15 *Law and Literature* 87.
Scott McCloud (1993) *Understanding Comics: The Invisible Art*, HarperCollins.
Hannah Miodrag (2013) *Comics and Language: Reimagining Critical Discourse on the Form*, University Press of Mississippi.
WJT Mitchell (1986) *Iconology: Image, Text, Ideology*, University of Chicago Press.
WJT Mitchell (2005) 'What Do Pictures Want?' in *What Do Pictures Want? The Lives and Loves of Images*, Chicago University Press.
Alan Moore and Dave Gibbons (1986) *Watchmen*, Titan Books.
Linda Mulcahy (2011) *Legal Architecture: Justice, Due Process and the Place of Law*, Routledge.
James Parker (2015) *Acoustic Jurisprudence: Listening to the Trial of Simon Bikindi*, Oxford University Press.
Andreas Philippopoulos-Mihalopoulos (2014) *Spatial Justice: Body, Lawscape, Atmosphere*, Routledge.
Barbara Postema (2013) *Narrative Structure in Comics: Making Sense of Fragments*, Rochester Institute of Technology Press.
Ernesto Priego (2014) 'Popping Up: Cities and Comics as Common Place' in E Priego and DN Wright (eds) *The Multimodality of Comics in Everyday Life*, MediaCommons.
John Selden (1631) *Titles of Honor*, Stansby.
Richard K Sherwin (2000) *When Law Goes Pop: The Vanishing Line between Law and Popular Culture*, University of Chicago Press.
Boaventura de Sousa Santos (1987) 'Law: A Map of Misreading. Toward a Postmodern Conception of Law' 14 *Journal of Law and Society* 279.
Nick Sousanis (2015) *Unflattening*, Harvard University Press.
Susan Stewart (1991) *Crimes of Writing: Problems in the Containment of Representation*, Oxford University Press.
Robin Varnum and Christina T Gibbons (2001) 'Introduction' in R Varnum and CT Gibbons (eds) *The Language of Comics: Word and Image*, University Press of Mississippi.
Joel Wainwright and Joe Bryan (2009) 'Cartography, Territory, Property: Postcolonial Reflections on Indigenous Counter-Mapping in Nicaragua and Belize' 16 *Cultural Geographies* 153.
Gary Watt (2013) *Dress, Law and Naked Truth: A Cultural Study of Fashion and Form*, Bloomsbury.
Elaine Webster (2013) 'From Interpretive Imagination to Contingency in Law: An Argument for Moving Beyond Text' in Z Baríkowski et al (eds) *The Arts and the Legal Academy: Beyond Text in Legal Education*, Ashgate.

Appendix A

Details of comics discussed

This appendix contains short summaries of, and contextual information related to, the key comics works analysed and discussed across this book. Whilst I have sought to include relevant detail as needed in the main text, it is hoped the outlines in this appendix will be useful for those readers who may be unfamiliar with the works I discuss, giving them a more general – albeit brief – understanding of the works. Full citations, along with relevant analytical details, page references, narrative events, discussion, and formal considerations are provided in the main text; the descriptions here, meanwhile, are intentionally done with a broad brush, presenting narrative summaries and publication context for each work (I should also add that there are numerous spoilers in the narrative summaries below; consider yourself warned).

The Ghost in the Shell (Masamune Shirow)

The main protagonist of *The Ghost in the Shell* is Major Motoko Kusanagi. Kusanagi is a member of an elite police counter-terrorism squad known as Section 9. The narrative of *The Ghost in the Shell* follows Kusanagi, alongside her highly trained colleagues, as Section 9 investigate a number of incidents of 'ghost hacking' – the infiltration of individuals' minds made possible through the highly advanced technologies present in the world of *The Ghost in the Shell.* These technologies have produced highly advanced cybernetic beings, such as Kusanagi and her colleagues, made up of human brains and brainstems integrated into prosthetic bodies. But through their investigations, Section 9 discover that the mind behind the ghost hacking is actually an artificially intelligent being known as the Puppeteer, who was born of the sea of information. The Puppeteer was created by a secret government department, but broke free of his programming to become a living being. The narrative concludes with Kusanagi and the Puppeteer merging and taking up residence in, or integrating themselves into, a new prosthetic body.

As discussed in Chapter 2, Shirow's work raises many difficult questions around the nature of humanity and our relationship with advancing technology. Originally published in Japan by Kodansha in 1991 (it was translated into English and published by Dark Horse Comics in 1995), it is a foundational cultural text in relation to the cyberpunk genre, as well as human/machine and artificial life narratives more generally, having impact on a number of subsequent works, most notably *The Matrix* (1999). It also spawned two sequel manga works by Shirow: *The Ghost in the Shell 2: Man-Machine Interface* (2001) and *The Ghost in the Shell 1.5: Human Error Processor* (2003). In addition, it has been adapted into anime in the films *Ghost in the Shell* (1995) and *Ghost in the Shell 2: Innocence* (2004), and expanded upon in numerous television series. Most recently (2017) a Hollywood live-action adaption has been released. As noted in the main text, I do not engage with this expansive transmedia canon, focusing only on the original manga version of *The Ghost in the Shell.*

Watchmen (Alan Moore and Dave Gibbons)

Set against the backdrop of an alternate 1980s US on the brink of nuclear war, the world of *Watchmen* is one where 'masked vigilantes' or 'costumed adventurers' have become a social norm. Articulated as a work of gritty realism, these 'heroes' have sparked intense public backlash in relation to their seeming lack of legitimacy as forces of governance outside the state, eventually leading to their explicit banning under the fictional Keane Act. All this backlash has happened in the past of the main narrative of *Watchmen*, and is revealed through references and flashbacks. The main narrative instead focuses ostensibly on the investigation of the murder of a prominent hero, The Comedian, that may be part of a wider scheme to kill costumed adventurers. Across its intensely detailed and complex plot, the chequered history of many of the characters is revealed, alongside the social tensions surrounding the existence of 'superheroes' outlined above, with a deep and sustained questioning of the legitimacy of authority, of free will, of moral choice, identity, politics, violence, and the formation of knowledge itself. The culmination of the story reveals that it was one of the costumed adventurers own number who had murdered The Comedian, as part of a grand plan to bring about world peace. This plan, which the protagonists fail to stop, involves the staging of a fake alien attack in New York City, killing thousands, but bringing the world together against a larger, external threat. The work ends by suggesting the likely undoing of this peace through an unthinking public revelation of the plot that brought it about.

Originally published in 12 instalments by DC Comics between 1986 and 1987, *Watchmen* was collected as a 'graphic novel' in 1987 and has since received critical (*Time* placed it on their list of 100 best novels, for example) and commercial success, leading to a blockbuster adaptation in 2009. It has a very technical formal structure, with intricate and methodical variations to a regular three by three grid layout across the work. It embeds a story-within-a-story in the form of a horror pirate comic, being read by an incidental character, which is deployed at key moments to augment and allegorise aspects of the main narrative. With this story, and with the way the 'superheroes' or 'masked vigilantes' are treated by society in general, *Watchmen* also engages the problematic history of the comics medium around its legitimacy and free speech. Indeed, *Watchmen* is generally taken as a leading example of the number of works that appeared in the 1980s that helped to 'mature' the medium out of the assumed juvenility that had led to its censure in the 1950s. Layered with internal references, allegory, invocations of comics history, and a sustained critique of the superhero genre, it is widely regarded as a classic of the medium. Recently, it has given rise to a series of 'prequel' editions under the title *Before Watchmen* (2012), exploring the earlier history that forms much of the backdrop to the original narrative. Alan Moore, quite vociferous in his opinions about his own work and the unique formal values of the comics medium in general, has denounced both these 'prequel' comics and the cinematic adaptation. As I note in the main text, given the immense complexity and breadth of *Watchmen*, my analysis only focuses on a few specific issues and characters.[1]

Arkham Asylum (Grant Morrison and Dave McKean)

Arkham Asylum is the infamous mental health institution in Gotham City. Often dubbed a 'home for the criminally insane', it variously houses many of Batman's more eccentric enemies – notably Joker, Scarecrow, Two-Face, and so on. In the narrative of *Arkham Asylum*, originally published by DC Comics in 1989, the current inmates have run riot and taken over the asylum. After entering Arkham, Joker forces Batman to play a game of 'hide and seek', with Joker setting a one hour time limit before he sends the escaped inmates to hunt Batman down. Navigating the asylum, Batman encounters a number of the inmates he has put there – Clayface, Maxie Zeus, Scarecrow, Mad Hatter – eventually battling the bestial Killer Croc. Intertwined with Batman's narrative is that of Amadeus Arkham, the man who founded the Asylum. At many points, Arkham's narration is laid over the visualisation of Batman's story, and the dual narratives are deeply connected, with both Batman and Arkham sharing an encounter with madness. But where Amadeus Arkham ends up going mad, housed in his own institution, Batman accepts his repressed traumas, defeats Killer Croc, and emerges from the Asylum stronger. As the story reaches its climax, we learn that one of the staff members, Cavendish, has undertaken to continue Arkham's work, releasing the inmates in order to lure Batman to the asylum so Cavendish could stop him bringing more troubled souls to the institution. In the ensuing struggle, Cavendish is killed by a fellow staff member (Dr Adams). The story closes with Two-Face tossing his coin to decide if they should kill Batman or not, with the inmates letting Batman leave and telling him there will always be a place for him in Arkham.

1 For a more extended legal analysis, readers may wish to consult my PhD thesis, which focused exclusively on *Watchmen* for its substantive analysis, and forms the groundwork for some of the analyses in the present volume. See 'Comics, Crime, and the Moral Self: An Interdisciplinary Study in Criminal Identity' (University of Exeter 2011) https://ore.exeter.ac.uk/repository/handle/10036/3622

What makes *Arkham Asylum* stand out from other Batman stories is the richly symbolic and psychological approach taken to the storytelling. Morrison layers many symbolic aspects to the narrative, making connections between the Tarot, eastern mysticism, Christianity, Alastair Crowley, and psychoanalysis, amongst other things. Combined with Dave McKean's haunting and uneasy artwork, it makes for a comics work of troubling psychic impact, playing on associations between madness and mysticism and the world beyond reason in both its visual style and cultural reference points. It presents a version of the Dark Knight that is at odds with the strong and stable hero of most stories, interrogating the inner weaknesses and underlying trauma that feed his clearly eccentric behaviour of dressing up as a bat to fight crime. This theme – of Batman's madness – is one that other comics have also engaged with, most notably Alan Moore and Brian Boland's *The Killing Joke* (1988) published around the same time. *Arkham Asylum* has enjoyed continued acclaim, with a 15th Anniversary special edition – which included Morrison's original script – being published in 2004. There have been no direct translations of Morrison and McKean's work into other media, although the video game *Batman: Arkham Asylum* (2009) is loosely based on the story.

Neonomicon (Alan Moore and Jacen Burrows)

In 'The Courtyard', which is a short preface story to the main narrative of *Neonomicon* (and included in the same volume), an FBI agent we later come to know as Sax is investigating a series of gruesome murders, to which he believes a drug called 'Aklo' is connected. He tracks down a dealer, Carcosa, discovering that Aklo is an ancient unhuman language. After hearing some of this language, Sax commits murders in the style of those he is investigating. The main *Neonomicon* narrative then follows FBI agents Brears and Lamper as they investigate what they believe is a copycat killer. They follow Sax's old lead from his case file to try and track down Carcosa, who eludes capture. However, Brears and Lamper manage to trace some of Carcosa's belongings to a sex cult. Brears and Lamper attend an orgy undercover, discovering the cult use the orgies to attract monstrous sea creatures. The cult exposes them as FBI agents, killing Lamper and raping Brears. They then take Brears captive, locking her up with one of the sea creatures. This creature repeatedly rapes Brears for days on end, during which time Brears has visions of Carcosa in a mystical dimension and she learns about the reality of HP Lovecraft's Great Old Ones. The sea creature eventually works out that Brears is pregnant (it smells and tastes her urine), then takes her into the sea and releases her. Brears then takes the FBI back to the cult, only to discover the sea creature has killed them all; the creature is gunned down. The story closes with Brears visiting Sax, now able to understand the Aklo he speaks, and coming to realise she is pregnant with Cthulhu and that Lovecraft's fiction was actually a prophecy.

'The Courtyard' was originally published as a short prose story by Alan Moore (1994), but was adapted into comics by Moore and Burrows and published in two issues in 2003 by the small Avatar Press. *Neonomicon* was published in four issues across 2010, before being collected, along with 'The Courtyard', in the 2011 edition. The story connects explicitly with the work of HP Lovecraft, engaging not only Lovecraft's Cthulhu mythos as a genuine supernatural reality, but also Lovecraft himself – not just as a creator, but as a prophet of Cthulhu. The occasional prominent use of the language Aklo, which Lovecraft used for his unhuman beasts, and the mythic names and places that appear across *Neonomicon* – such as R'lyeh and Nyarlathotep – solidifies the connections. *Neonomicon*, then, is not just a retelling of the Lovecraft mythos, but situates Lovecraft himself as part of a 'real' mythos that he was able to communicate through his stories. Although not adapted across any other media, Moore and Burrows's work has been well received, and a continuation of *Neonomicon*'s re-imagined Lovecraftianism has recently been collected under the title *Providence* (2017).

Judge Dredd (John Wagner and others)

Created by John Wagner and Carlos Ezquerra, Judge Dredd is an authoritarian lawman in a dystopian future. He is a Street Judge, dishing out justice in the vast urban landscape of Mega-City One. In the world of Dredd, Mega-Cities – sprawling urban regions – emerged in North America across the twenty-first century, gaining devolved powers from the US government. Mega-City One is located along the East Coast of America, growing out of a merging of Washington DC and New York City. Other Mega-Cities sprung up across the globe. At the same time, the 'Judge' system came into being as a means of coping with the increase in crime and violence brought about by the densely populated Mega-Cities. This system instituted 'Judges' with powers of investigation, arrest, sentencing, and punishment – collapsing the traditional activities of the criminal justice system into a single person in order to expedite justice and remove the barriers inherent in a due process model. By 2070, the Judges had overthrown the government, with this new judiciary gaining extensive unchecked powers to manage the state. The *Judge Dredd* titles tell of Judge Joe Dredd's adventures policing the streets of Mega-City One in his hard-line fight against crime.

First published in 1977, in the comics magazine *2000AD* (published by Rebellion), *Judge Dredd* has been a longstanding title in the magazine, continuing to the present day. His narratives have developed into a dedicated publication series called the *Judge Dredd Megazine* (1990 onwards). As is discussed in the main text, Dredd was originally created as satire of the right-wing crime and justice policies of Margaret Thatcher and Ronald Reagan. This satirical aspect at times had to be made more explicit as many fans expressed a liking for Dredd's style of justice. *Judge Dredd* has proved immensely popular over the years, with two Hollywood movie adaptations being produced (*Judge Dredd* in 1995, starring Sylvester Stallone, in which Dredd controversially removes his helmet which he never does in the comics, and more recently *Dredd* in 2012), and various boardgames and video games, extensive merchandising, a series of audio plays, and numerous prose novels also being created. Due to this explosive canon, I only engage with a relatively small set of examples in my analysis, focusing on the central character of Dredd as a practical, hardline enforcer.

Judge Anderson (Alan Grant and others)

Inhabiting in the same diegetic universe as *Judge Dredd*, Judge Cassandra Anderson is also a Judge in Mega-City One, working in Psi Division. This division of the Judge system specialises in psychic and supernatural phenomena, with its officers generally having some sort of psychic ability – telekinesis, clairvoyance, telepathy, empathic abilities, and so on. Anderson is a telepath (she also has some skills in precognition). Psi Judges are often utilised by Street Judges such as Dredd in order to solicit information from unwilling suspects and the recently deceased. But in contrast to Dredd's authoritarianism and mechanical application of the law, Anderson's character is more fluid. She is critical of the problems with the over-strict Judge system and engages on a human level with her colleagues and fellow citizens.

Anderson first appeared, along with the monstrous Judge Death discussed in Chapter 4, in 1980 as a supporting character in the main Dredd series. Due to her popularity, she secured her own spin-off title, *Anderson: Psi-Division* (1988 onwards). There are strong gendered aspects to her development – least of all the 'strong' male Dredd and the 'soft' female Anderson – that are largely symptomatic of a wider sexism that can be identified in comics publishing generally. This primarily relates to the sexual objectification of female characters, generally resulting in skimpy and impractical superhero costumes, but also awkward and unrealistic body positioning and physiology. Anderson's visual presentation suffered the same effects of the male gaze, but often depended upon the artist involved. Arthur Ranson's work, for example, tended away from overt sexualisation in favour of genuine characterised depiction. In terms of her translation into other media, as a supporting character to Dredd she has quite naturally appeared in many of his adaptations, notably the 2012 *Dredd* film. There are also a number of novels based explicitly on Anderson. Again, as with Dredd, the expanse of Anderson's narrative life – albeit not quite as extensive as Dredd's – precludes a comprehensive engagement, and my analyses in the main text focus on key examples related to her engagement with the supernatural that is symbolic of the world beyond law.

'White Noise' (Tom Kaczynski)

'White Noise' is a one-page comic that is included in Tom Kaczynski's collection of his short comics stories, *Beta Testing the Apocalypse* (2013). Kazynski's work is distinct in its combination of precise, architectural visual style and theoretically informed narrative. The broad themes of *Beta Testing the Apocalypse* critically traverse globalisation, capitalism, human history, existentialism, utopia, and the alienation of technology. Kaczynski himself has been nominated for the prestigious Ignatz and Eisner comics awards, and runs the independent comics publisher Uncivilized Books. He trained as an architect, has been involved in graphic design projects for well-known brands, and currently teaches comics at Minneapolis College of Art and Design.

Adamtine (Hannah Berry)

Adamtine (2012) oscillates between past and present, telling the interconnected stories of four characters who all find themselves stranded on the last train home in the middle of nowhere. The four characters all have connections to an infamous missing persons case, in which a number of seemingly random people disappeared with nothing but small notes left behind. The suspect, Rodney Moon, claimed he did not do the disappearing – it was a nameless bogeyman. Following his acquittal (there was not enough evidence for the jury to convict), Moon was killed by the family members of one of the victims. The four characters stranded on the train consist of a justice-charity worker who refused Moon emigration assistance after his trial, a member of one of the victim's family, a newspaper editor, and someone who witnessed Moon's murder. *Adamtine*'s narrative alternates between the present-day story of the four passengers on the train and their respective narrative histories, telling each history in turn, with all four characters eventually being devoured on the train by the nameless bogeyman as their past misdeeds catch up with them.

Hannah Berry utilises the formal elements of the comics medium in distinct ways in articulating her narrative. The historical narratives are all presented on white pages, as is typical of most comics stories, whilst the night train sections are on black pages – evocative of the nocturnal setting, as well as permitting her formal play as the spooky bogeyman dissolves the passengers into blackness, as discussed in Chapter 5. The work is dotted with internal references to the four passengers and their respective culpabilities with respect to Moon's demise. Berry herself is an independent comics creator, with her other works including *Britten and Brülightly* (2008) and, most recently, *Livestock* (2017). All three of her works are published by Jonathan Cape in their line of 'graphic novels', and she is much more in the 'independent' tradition than the mainstream serialised publications mentioned above.

The Encyclopedia of Early Earth (Isabel Greenberg)

Another 'independent' work, Isabel Greenberg's *The Encyclopedia of Early Earth* (2013) is a rhapsodic wandering through human myth. It tells of the Storyteller's journey in search of a lost piece of his soul. The Storyteller was discovered as a child by three sisters in the land of Nord (located at the North Pole); they fought over him, and eventually got the local Medicine Man to split the child into three. The sisters went their separate ways, and the three children grew; eventually they rejoined into a single boy, and the sisters reconciled. However, it later transpired that the Medicine Man had lost a piece of the boy's soul during the separation process – and this piece was no longer in Nord. The boy leaves Nord in search of his soul, telling tales of his journey to the peoples and civilisations he encounters along the way. *Early Earth* details not just the Storyteller's exploits, but also the mythic background to life on Early Earth, including the gods who created it – Bird Man and his children – and who oversee the lives of humans. One of Bird Man's children, Kiddo, ends up interfering (against her father's commands) to help the Storyteller reach the lost piece of his soul, which is located at the South Pole. Once there, the Storyteller finds the piece of his soul in the care of a woman, and the two protagonists fall instantly in love. Bird Man, on discovering his daughter breaking his command, goes into a rage and inadvertently alters the magnetic fields around the two protagonists; as a result, they cannot come within one metre of each other. They grow old and die together, only ending up in each other's arms as their bodies are placed in their shared funeral boat.

Early Earth has been very well received, being nominated for two Eisner awards. Its style mimics traditional woodcuts, using a limited pallet of only three or four solid colours, reflecting something of the prehistoric nature of the world being depicted. Greenberg's work is shot through with wry humour and internal references, as well as a knowing charm. As an 'encyclopaedia', the work includes a number of appendices detailing additional myths, stories, histories, and other aspects of the world of Early Earth not encountered in the main narrative frames. Like *Adamtine*, it was published by Jonathan Cape in their line of 'graphic novels'. Greenberg has recently published *One Hundred Nights of Hero* (2017), which also takes place in Early Earth.

The Sandman (Neil Gaiman and others)

The Sandman was originally published by DC's Vertigo imprint, which specialises in titles for mature readers. It was published in 75 issues between 1988 and 1996. Written by Gaiman, with artwork by numerous artists, it focuses on the character of Dream, one of the Endless. The Endless are seven siblings, personifications representing foundational aspects of human existence: in order of their appearance at the beginning of time, they are Destiny, Death, Dream, Desire, Despair, Destruction, and Delight (who later became Delirium). The opening issue tells the story of Dream's summoning and capture by a mysterious cult who were attempting to trap, and thereby cheat, Death. Dream waits decades until his release, and in subsequent issues embarks upon a number of difficult journeys to reclaim the powerful artefacts into which he has put much of his power as the Dream King. Across the expanse of issues, narratives are woven around Dream and related characters, at times with Dream in only a background or cameo role, as his realm of the Dreaming and the wider mythic landscape is developed. Ultimately, Dream is forced to accept his own death, being destroyed and reforming himself in a new image.

Engaging philosophy, myth, literature, and intertextual references to other comics series (notably the British supernatural investigator *John Constantine)*, *Sandman* is an epic work of dark fantasy. It has enjoyed popular and critical success, with a large number of spinoff and follow-on comics and prose series developing out of it – some of which were written by Gaiman himself (although most were not). Although published in 75 individual issues, the original series was collected into 10 trade paperbacks that have recently been reissued (2010–2012), as well as being produced in DC's prestigious 'Absolute Edition' format (oversized hardback collectors editions with slipcases, published from 2006–2008), which is testament to the ongoing popularity of the series. Many of the issues in the main *Sandman* series play into the wider narrative progression of the series, with each collected edition roughly spanning an individual story arc, although many issues are standalone stories. Like other works mentioned above, the expanse of *Sandman* means comprehensive engagement is not possible in the scope of this book, with my analysis instead focusing on key relevant aspects.

Appendix B

Text from figures

Due to the physical print size, the text in a number of the figures presented in this volume may be unclear or difficult to read. The affected figures are 4.1, 4.3, 4.10, 6.1, 6.5, and 6.6. Accordingly, the text from these figures is reproduced below for clarity.

Text from Figure 4.1: Moore and Burrows (2011), np.

I drink it in, breathless. / A force which defines; lends *significance* to its *receptacle* as with the hand in the glove; wind in mill-vanes; the guest or the trespasser crossing a threshold and giving it meaning. / 'Dho-hna'. How could I have *forgotten*? / A pinwheel of nautilus fronds is dissolved into sparks by my vitreous humour as huge old grammatical structures collapse into place. / Aklo isn't a drug. There's no drug with mind-altering properties *halfway* as powerful. / Aklo's a language. / *Ur-syntax*; the primal vocabulary giving form to those pre-conscious orderings wrung from a hot incoherence of stars, from our birthmuds pooled in the grandmother lagoon; a stark, limited palette of earliest notions, / lost colours / forgotten intensities.

Text from Figure 4.3: Moore and Burrows (2011), np.

I don't know where I am. I'm dying, or dreaming, or something. / In the dream I'm visiting HP Lovecraft at his aunt's house in Providence. / He tells me he feels ugly. I tell him that I'm a sex addict and that I want to make love to him. / I'm not wearing any clothes. I think I was wearing them when I entered the house, but they're gone. / He's looking at me like he's horrified. I look down and see I've got a little penis sticking out. / It's not a penis. It's a tentacle. / Lovecraft is screaming. / BREARS: 'PFFAHHH…'

Text from Figure 4.10: Tom Kaczynski 'White Noise' in Kaczynski (2012), p 45.

You can recognise the moment almost instantly. Those already asleep are jarred awake. / What you notice is the lack of sound. The constant din of civilization has ground to a halt. Even the fridge stopped purring reassuringly. Is this just a normal fluctuation of the power grid? / Then you notice the insects. Screeching swarms… oblivious to your presence. How many are there? They were here before mankind. They will still be here after humans go extinct. / The cardiovascular system responds. Blood rushes through the veins with deadening violence activating obscure glands and long forgotten sensory organs. / The imperceptible tectonic drift comes into sharp relief… continental shelves crash into each other… ancient remains shift uneasily beneath the Earth's crust… / You can even hear the faint radio hum of distant supernovas travelling for aeons through dead space ahead of the silent screams of alien worlds… engulfed in countless solar holocausts…

Text from Figure 6.1: Greenberg (2013), np.

The first map of Early Earth, the Bavellians say, was made by the famous cartographer Mancini Panini from his tower in the beautiful city of Migdal Bavel. It is generally agreed by explorers to be completely useless since it is almost entirely wrong on every level. But Mancini Panini was possessed of an excellent imagination and a steady and meticulous drawing hand, and so the maps can be valued as things of beauty.

In-image captions (clockwise from top left): 'Sailors! Sail no further lest ye perish!'; 'Island of What'; 'Island of Hoo'; 'The City Of Migdal Bavel'; 'Bavellian Straits'.

Text from Figure 6.5: Greenberg (2013), np.

In the beginning was the Well Of Life. It was at the bottom of an almost infinite pit. A yawning void. / In the old days terrible things came out of the void.

Text from Figure 6.6: Greenberg (2013), np.

The Mapmaker told the Bavellians that the city of Migdal Bavel was at the centre of the world. To the northwest lay the savage lands of Britanitarka, to the north lay the Islands of Hoo, Wat and Wen. To the west lay the island of Cos with its mysterious stone sculptures and east lay the Sea of Nowhere. / Beyond these places the seas grew wild and unpassable, so said the Mapmaker. / Terrible fire-breathing creatures wheeled and cawed in storm-drenched skies. / And then the flat disc of the world ended abruptly, and the ocean when tumbling off into nothingness. / So believed the Bavellians, until one day a stranger arrived in the harbour. He came in a bedraggled little boat, from a land far beyond the edge of the world.

Index

For Product Safety Concerns and Information please contact our EU representative GPSR@taylorandfrancis.com
Taylor & Francis Verlag GmbH, Kaufingerstraße 24, 80331 München, Germany

www.ingramcontent.com/pod-product-compliance
Ingram Content Group UK Ltd.
Pitfield, Milton Keynes, MK11 3LW, UK
UKHW011003180926
475701UK00004B/536
* 9 7 8 0 3 6 7 4 0 4 4 7 5 *